A Social and Cultural Hist
Early Modern France

A magisterial new history of French society between the end of the middle
ages and the Revolution by one of the world's leading authorities on early
modern France. Using colorful examples and incorporating the latest
scholarship, William Beik conveys the distinctiveness of early modern
society and identifies the cultural practices that defined the lives of people
at all levels of society. Painting a vivid picture of the realities of everyday
life, he reveals how society functioned and how the different classes
interacted. In addition to chapters on nobles, peasants, city people, and
the court, the book sheds new light on the Catholic church, the army,
popular protest, the culture of violence, gendered relations, and sociability. This is a major new work that restores the *ancien régime* as a key
epoch in its own right and not simply as the prelude to the coming
Revolution.

WILLIAM BEIK is Emeritus Professor of History at Emory University,
Atlanta, Georgia. His previous publications include *Urban Protest in
Seventeenth-Century France: The Culture of Retribution* (1997) and
Louis XIV and Absolutism: A Study with Documents (2000).

A Social and Cultural
History of Early Modern
France

WILLIAM BEIK

CAMBRIDGE
UNIVERSITY PRESS

CAMBRIDGE
UNIVERSITY PRESS

University Printing House, Cambridge CB2 8BS, United Kingdom

Published in the United States of America by Cambridge University Press, New York

Cambridge University Press is part of the University of Cambridge.

It furthers the University's mission by disseminating knowledge in the pursuit of education, learning and research at the highest international levels of excellence.

www.cambridge.org
Information on this title: www.cambridge.org/9780521709569

First published 2009

A catalogue record for this publication is available from the British Library

Library of Congress Cataloguing in Publication data
  Beik, William, 1941–
  A social and cultural history of early modern France / William Beik.
    p.   cm.
  Includes bibliographical references and index.
  ISBN 978-0-521-88309-2
  1. France–Civilization–1328–1600.   2. France–Civilization–17th century.
  3. France–Civilization–18th century.   4. France–Social life and customs.
  5. Social classes–France–History.   6. Social structure–France–History.
  7. Social change–France–History.   I. Title.
  DC33.3.B45 2009
  944′.03–dc22   2008053627

ISBN 978-0-521-88309-2 Hardback
ISBN 978-0-521-70956-9 Paperback

For Carl Kauffman,
in loving memory of
Eric Kauffman

Contents

Illustrations

Tables

Preface

Constructing a social and cultural history of early modern France is a fascinating but intimidating project. It requires an exploration of every level of society and an understanding of each group's life experiences, fears, hopes, beliefs. It requires knowledge of their access to resources, their collective efforts, the disparity of their class positions. Attempting to attain these goals was a humbling experience for me. Instead of simply formulating and organizing the accumulated knowledge of many years of teaching and research, I found myself scrambling to fill enormous gaps in my knowledge. Contrary to my intention of mastering the monographic literature on each topic, I ended up having to cite certain key studies without acknowledging many others.

The concept of social history is vast and undefined. There is no such thing as a master narrative that puts all the parts in their places. A would-be commentator must decide which aspects to feature and how they are to be connected. The result will be one particular story out of the many possible stories that someone else could put together by making different choices and exclusions. In my case the primary goal has been to explain how the social system operated in the period of royal rule, while at the same time conveying an appreciation of the lives and experiences of the working majority. I have tried to explain clearly the workings of institutions and processes that will be unfamiliar to a modern reader. The "culture" in the title is meant in the anthropological sense of customary behavior, belief systems, and ritual practices. This culture complements and extends an understanding of the social. I do not mean "high" culture in the sense of the creative arts, literature, philosophy, and science. Those achievements are lightly covered or not at all.

My approach to social history is no more value-neutral than anyone else's. Certain choices have colored my account. First of all, I emphasize the "otherness" of early modern French society. This means stressing the ways it was distinctive, not the ways it was becoming modern. It means thinking of the society as a system, held together by power relationships, cultural habits, and economic forces. This approach, which might be called "structural, " is decidedly out of fashion. But unless we think, however tentatively, of each element as part of a larger system, there is no way to assess the relationship of the parts to the whole or to each other, and consequently no principle for the selection of which elements to study. Why explore literacy, women's roles, the lives of servants, or crop rotations, for example? Focusing on structure also means emphasizing long-term continuities, but without denying the importance of change. There is no need to adopt the extreme position of certain *Annalistes* who think in terms of a Braudelian *longue durée* or of *l'histoire immobile*. Change is everywhere, and progress needs to be explored, but that is not the primary goal here.

Second, this is not a book that emphasizes conflicting interpretations. My goal has been to offer one coherent, descriptive interpretation which readers can grasp and use. The best way to understand a society is to acquire one consistent view of it and then to criticize that view by exploring alternatives, rather than approaching each issue as a heated debate. I encourage readers to approach my book in this spirit. Many alternative views can be found in the lists of further reading after each chapter. The emphasis is on accessible books in English, but I have also included certain key monographs in French.

Third, I concentrate on the sixteenth and seventeenth centuries as the center of gravity of this distinctive society which spans the years from 1400 to 1789. Those two centuries saw at its height the classic France of powerful monarchy, elegant society, and dominant nobility. Each chapter explores a different aspect of that society and its evolution throughout the period. Some go back to medieval origins, others follow through into the eighteenth century, but the focus is always on the central sixteenth and seventeenth centuries.

Fourth, my focus is the extensive France of many provinces, not the king, the court, and the city of Paris. Many vital events did take place at the center, but Paris was not France, and it is important to remember that we are dealing with a large, diverse country filled with tens of thousands of active participants who were not easily swayed by anything that happened at court or in the capital.

Finally, I often highlight longer, descriptive examples, drawn in many cases from lesser-known monographs, in order to convey more concretely the distinctive nature of life in those times. These longer descriptions occupy the space that might have been devoted to discussion of the many regional variations that were so characteristic of French society. Readers will have to accept on faith that the examples given are fairly representative of common characteristics, despite the fact that there were a great many variations on these common themes.

Choices also imply omissions. Those familiar with my book on absolutism may be surprised to find that I do not directly discuss state institutions or the way the political system worked. Issues of power and state development are important, of course, but I have avoided the complicated and tedious task of explaining how the government operated. Readers will therefore need a certain familiarity with the political history of France, because I do not discuss the reigns of kings or provide any political narrative. The brief synopsis of early modern French history provided on pp. 367–71 may help with their orientation.

Other dimensions are also omitted. Aspects of economic history, such as patterns of trade, systems of manufacturing, or types of business enterprises, are only lightly covered. Colonies and naval activities are slighted. Cultural values, as defined above, on the other hand, provide a natural complement to social–historical questions by adding psychological factors such as identities, motivations, and behavior to the material factors provided by social history.

The chapters begin with basic social and economic arrangements involving nobles, peasants, and towns. They move on to the rise of the new judicial–financial class, the many dimensions of religious life, the impact of the royal army, the sociology of group solidarities and conflicts, traditional cultural practices, and the rise of new cultural influences. The last two chapters explore the aristocratic forces at court and, finally, the changing world of the eighteenth century.

This book would never have been finished without the calm and intellectual stimulation I enjoyed as Senior Fellow at Emory University's Fox Center for Humanistic Inquiry in 2005–6. I am deeply grateful for this privilege. I was also assisted in 1999 by a research grant from the University Research Committee of Emory. I want to thank Richard Fisher and Michael Watson at Cambridge Press for their longstanding editorial support.

But above all, I want to acknowledge my deeper obligation to all the friends, colleagues, and students who have provided inspiration and encouragement during the long academic career that produced this book. My thanks go out to the students of History 311 at Northern Illinois University and History 315 at Emory University; and to graduate students who became friends from both institutions, including Greg Andrews, Darryl Dee, Carolyn Eichner, Amy Enright, Viviana Grieco, Chris Guthrie, Colleen Guy, Jeff Houghtby, Brian Kaschak, Nancy Locklin, Michael Perri, Doug Powell, Steve Reinhardt, Mike Rogers, and Jay Smith. A project like this is sustained over the years by more than just scholarly influence. Friends and colleagues, new and old, have been supportive and inspirational in many different ways. These include Wally Adamson, Yves-Marie Bercé, the late Tom Blomquist, Sue Bowen and the late Ralph Bowen, Jim Collins, Natalie Davis, Robert Descimon, Jonathan Dewald, Jim Farr, Margot Finn, C. H. George, Janet and David Greene, Alain Guery, Al Hamscher, Mack Holt, David Hunt, Jitka Hurych, Stephen Kern, Sharon Kettering, Charles McCollester, Jamie Melton, Judith Miller, Otto and Corinne Olsen, David and Margaret Parker, Matt Payne, Larry Portis and Christiane Passevent, Richard Price, Jonathan Prude, Marcus Rediker, Paul Robinson, the late Nancy Roelker, the late Marvin Rosen, Jacques and Danielle Sennelier, Helen Shirley and the late Jim Shirley, Jerry Soliday, Sharon Strocchia, and the late Chuck Tilly. Finally, above them all, there is Millie, friend, partner, lover, critic, whose influence has been immeasurable. This book is dedicated to Carl Kauffman in loving memory of his brother, Eric Kauffman.

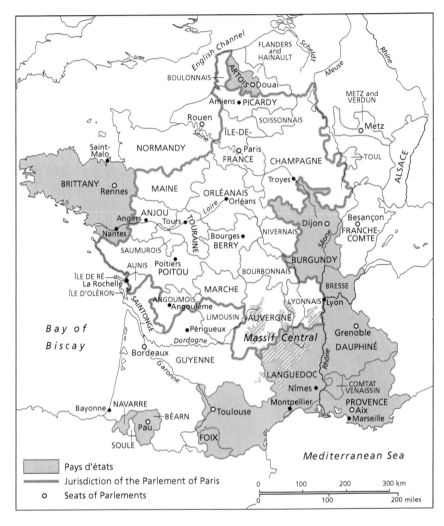

Map. Map of early modern France

Introduction: France and its population

Until the unification of Germany in the nineteenth century, France was the richest and most densely populated kingdom in Europe. It was also an attractive country, notable for the diversity of its regions and the creativity of its people. But despite its identity as the kingdom ruled over by the Merovingian, Carolingian, and Capetian kings, France never had a single geographical, cultural, or institutional center of gravity, and by the end of the middle ages it was already the product of a great many historical cross-currents. As we explore its rich history, we will constantly be reminded that there was no typical village, province, or customary practice, and that even its kings had to accommodate diverse power structures and varying levels of privileges as they attempted to unify all these parts into one centralized entity.

The creation of France

"France" only emerged as a political and cultural entity through centuries of interaction between a succession of rulers and a variety of peoples. Geographically, it can be defined as the territory over which the kings of France had long held suzerainty (feudal overlordship), and over which they gradually established sovereignty (ultimate political authority). Its jurisdictional limits had been set in the Treaty of Verdun in 843 when Charlemagne's grandsons divided up the Carolingian empire. They established a frontier following the Scheldt, Meuse, Saône, and Rhône rivers, which separated what became the Holy Roman Empire, to its east, from what became the kingdom of France, to its west. The Iberian peninsula, set off by the line of the Pyrenees mountains, was not included. This ancient boundary delimited "France" as an area of some 425,000 square kilometers where the king was recognized as overlord, but the various provinces contained within it were only gradually assimilated into the king's direct rule. This smaller medieval France was about three-fourths the size of modern France, and most of the last fourth was added during the years under consideration.

The years from 1400 to 1789 constitute a period that can loosely be labeled "early modern." By the mid thirteenth century, what we may call French "medieval" civilization had reached its full flowering. Paris was a center of European university life, the French Gothic style was being copied everywhere, and the reigns of Louis IX, Philip III, and Philip IV (1226 to 1314) were laying the groundwork for permanent governing institutions. In the next generations a succession of crises undermined these medieval certitudes. The Hundred Years War with England, waves of bubonic plague, demographic collapse, and the schism in the Catholic church created what historians often call a "general crisis." The year 1400 represented a nadir from which France began to recover. The "early modern" period can be considered to extend from this period of revival through the sixteenth and seventeenth centuries, when the monarchy reached its height of power and influence. The eighteenth century saw the final flowering of these achievements, but also experienced the changes leading to the Revolution. The year 1789 is a good place to end because the Revolution destroyed the institutions and social structures that had prevailed since the middle ages. Historians today emphasize that many early modern characteristics continued well into the nineteenth century. But the Revolution was nevertheless as major a turning-point as any in history.

During the period we are examining, royal authority gradually reached out across the ancient eastern frontier into Dauphiné (1349), Burgundy (1477), Provence (1481), Franche-Comté (1678), and later Alsace (1648 in part, all by 1681) and Lorraine (1766), with small additions on the northeastern border and the southern Pyrenees frontier as well.[1] In the west, Brittany was subjected to direct royal control between 1491 and 1532. By the late seventeenth century, France had grown to 460,000 square kilometers (178,000 square miles), or a territory about 66 percent the size of Texas and more than three and a half times the size of England. This area was inhabited by some sixteen to seventeen million persons in 1328, a number that collapsed down to as low as ten million in the 1440s after a century of plague and warfare, then gradually recovered, with intermittent fluctuations, to 19 million in 1600, 22 million in 1700 and 30 million by 1815.[2]

This territory, consisting of many provinces and multiple identities, was gradually coordinated into a rudimentary state by a long succession of monarchs. This consolidation process was not linear. Provinces were incorporated, lost, and regained in various ways. Starting with Hugh Capet, who came to the throne in 987, the French kings began extending their influence outwards from a tiny power base in the region around Paris (the Île de France). They concentrated first on managing the area which they controlled directly, and from which they drew revenues as direct lords; then on extending it by developing relations with the lords of the territories outside this sphere.

Sometimes they used their positions as feudal overlords to establish relationships with powerful figures such as the dukes of Burgundy or Brittany or the counts of Champagne. As overlords they could demand loyalty and service, and if it was not forthcoming, undertake military reprisals. Or they might arrange marriage alliances with these powerful families in the hope of ultimately drawing their patrimonies into the royal orbit. Recalling the sacred anointing they received at their coronation ceremonies, they could invoke a special relationship with God to intervene in the affairs of the church and build strong alliances with bishops, cathedral chapters, and religious houses, many of which were wealthy and influential in their own right. They might use their prestige as king and overlord to establish a system of judicial appeals, first in their own domain and later in the surrounding provinces. They might issue charters to towns in return for loyalty and tax revenues.

All these tactics established multilateral relationships with feudal rulers, churches, towns, and regions, rather than a single, uniform relationship between king and subjects. As time passed, the monarch strengthened his relationships with provinces and cities to the point where he was able to intervene more effectively in their affairs. Ultimately he began to legislate for the whole realm and build an administrative structure that would correspond to this theoretical aspiration.

The extension of royal power was not a one-way street. While the French kings were pulling together elements of a kingdom, other forces were pulling it apart. Regional lords rebelled; populations revolted; foreign kings invaded. During the Hundred Years War (1338–1453) the dukes of Burgundy, who stemmed from a younger branch of the French royal family, tried to establish their own independent kingdom in eastern France and the Low Countries by joining forces with the kings of England, who already ruled the whole of southwestern France (Aquitaine) and wanted to regain their hold on Normandy. By the 1420s France had been dismembered, leaving a Burgundian zone, an English zone, and a greatly reduced "France" controlled by Charles VII, who was derisively called the king of Bourges, because he did not even control the city of Paris. After this debacle, the monarchy had to reconquer and reinstate each province and town in turn, and win the loyalty of their inhabitants with new concessions of privileges and favors.

Thus the French kings had always enjoyed theoretical claims to preeminence, but in practice they had to make good their claims over and over again. Most French provinces and towns had been assimilated into the realm at least twice, first in the medieval period and then again in the Renaissance, and each time compromises were struck to conciliate their regional elites. Special tax exemptions were ratified, legal privileges were renewed, regional courts and local governments were allowed to continue to function under the auspices of the king. Many centuries of this sort of piecemeal construction had made France a very complex organism institutionally. Because the king's authority had been established through a variety of channels – military, administrative, legal, and ecclesiastical – his relationship with each region and town was slightly different.

Diversity of geography and culture

The difficulties faced by the crown were in part the result of France's geographical disunity. The mountainous "core" of the country, called the Massif Central, offered a formidable barrier to anyone trying to travel from north to south or east to west. This region, lying south of the Loire and extending like a backbone along the Rhône almost as far south as the Mediterranean coast, was a hilly obstacle consisting of rounded peaks and high plateaux cut by deep river gorges. Travelers from Paris had to go around this vast obstacle in order to reach the cities of the Midi, either by boating down the Saône and Rhône rivers toward Aix and Marseille, which was the preferred route, or by traveling overland through the hilly western country toward Bordeaux, via Tours, Orléans, and Poitiers. Once in the south, the traveler still had a long journey if he wanted to complete the circuit between Bordeaux and Marseille, or vice versa. A reasonably swift traveler could make it from Paris to Aix or Bordeaux in about ten days. The fastest messenger could make the trip in about half that time, but troops and merchandise moved much more slowly. Any deviation from these few well-traveled thoroughfares to penetrate France's many other outlying regions was likely to encounter bad roads and major delays.

The Massif Central itself was a variegated landscape of distinct valleys linked by narrow paths used by shepherds. Its rivers flowed outwards in three directions, connecting particular highlands with particular lowland valleys and creating a variety of distinct subregions rather than one unified area. To complicate matters, France's main river systems flowed outwards in different directions. The Seine linked Paris and Rouen to the English Channel; the Meuse led to Germany and the Rhineland; the Loire pointed toward the Bay of Biscay and the Atlantic world, as did the Garonne and the Dordogne; while the Rhône took you toward the Mediterranean coast, Italy, and the Levant. These were advantageous connections for trade, but they resulted in regional centers with distinct interests that were not always complementary.

To this geographical diversity must be added significant cultural diversity. Even today the landscape of France reminds us of the fundamental difference between the Mediterranean civilization of the Midi and the Germanic civilization of the north. South of a line extending roughly from La Rochelle to Lake Geneva, the change is visible to the traveler. The sun comes out, and olive trees, terraced vineyards, and distinctly tropical plants appear. The tiled roofs take on a flatter, Mediterranean look. The houses display heavy wooden shutters, protecting deeply set windows designed to keep out the dry heat of the southern sun. Life moves into the open air and becomes visibly more animated in streets and squares that might almost be Italian. North of the La Rochelle–Geneva line the roofs are steeply sloped, people are more taciturn, and sociability takes place in the interior of cafés and brasseries. In Rouen, or Rennes, the older streets look English; in Dijon and Châlons-sur-Marne, they look central European. In Toulouse they look Spanish.

These superficial impressions remind us of a fundamental distinction that was more pronounced in the centuries before rapid transit and the triumph of international styles of architecture. The southern half of France (the "Midi") had been deeply romanized, and its

Figure 1. Regional contrasts. Top left: a street in Rennes (Brittany) looks like Tudor England. Lower left: the Midi looks Mediterranean (Saint-Guilhem du Désert in Languedoc). Right: in Beaune (Burgundy), the sloped roofs and pastel colors (not visible here) are reminiscent of Prague or Vienna.

culture was closely allied to that of the Mediterranean world, whereas the northern half was more influenced by the Germanic settlements of the early middle ages. The south remained more urban, more influenced by Roman law, more skeptical of northern influences. Its striking religious monuments were mostly romanesque in style because they dated from the economic and cultural revival of the twelfth century. The north was more rural, more feudalized, more closely tied to the Carolingian and Capetian dynasties. Its style was the northern Gothic of the thirteenth-century cathedrals. The people of the north and south spoke different versions of French – the *langue d'oil* in the north, the *langue d'oc* in the south.

But cultural distinctions were far more complex than a simple north–south divide. France is a country where, even today, people speak in terms of particular *pays*, intangible smaller territorial units about the size of a county that express the distinctiveness of local cultural practices and geographical features.[3] There were hundreds of these unofficial *pays* with names like the Vexin, the Sologne, the Charollais, the Lauragais, the Beauce, the Vermandois. Usually the terms had no administrative meaning, but they conveyed a sense of continuity and place. This diversity of micro-regions was reinforced by regional differences in the layouts of villages. As Braudel notes, "there was the Provençal hill village, with its narrow streets to shield one from the sun and wind; the Lorraine village, with its adjoining houses lining the broad street that also serves as a farmyard; and the very different Breton village, scattered and dispersed, its houses isolated on their own farmland."[4] There were many other combinations of field patterns, village layouts, and building styles that gave a particular "look" to a particular district. It is even possible to draw a map showing the regional distribution of ten different types of roofing.[5] Such diversity was matched by the different styles of dress, the many customary law codes, and the many different weights and measures used in local marketplaces. Early modern people had a strong sense of place that rivaled their identification with larger entities like the province or the kingdom.

There was also a diversity of dialects and languages. In addition to the Basque, Breton, Flemish, and German spoken in parts of the periphery, there were at least thirty varieties of *patois* (dialects of French). Gascon was not the same as Languedocien or Provençal, though all belonged to the *langue d'oc* family, and there were hundreds of local variations, vocabularies, and accents. Classical French was the language of Paris, of the aristocracy and, since the sixteenth century, of official documents. Only a small percentage of the rural population understood it, even at the time of the French Revolution. The upper classes were usually bilingual, speaking French when at court and switching to the local dialect at home when addressing servants and subordinates.

Historically speaking, then, there was no one preordained territory, culture, or language on which to hang a concept of Frenchness. This was something that would have to be constructed over time through a combination of collective historical experience and conscious state-building. But there were common elements already in place. In 1400 most of the inhabitants of the territory in question already thought of themselves as subjects of the king of France, whose reputation in legend and historical memory was powerful. Most had at least indirect experience of the monarchy from periodic military conquests and liberations, knowledge of privileges granted or revoked, or exposure to royal justice or royal taxes. Most adhered to the Catholic faith and shared its values, however differently understood by different parties, and they knew that the king had a special relationship with God and the church. The people in the various regions also knew one another through long-standing patterns of trade and exchange, and through the seasonal migrations of laborers.

Population and long-term economic environment

One very broad way of organizing the whole period 1400 to 1789 is to clock the ups and downs of the size of the population and use it as a way of organizing the chronology. The changing ratio of people to resources made a significant difference in the social landscape. To establish population trends, demographers have laboriously reconstructed the structure of families recorded in parish registers, as to the duration of their marriages and the number of their surviving offspring.[6] Population change was essentially a function of the number of births minus the number of deaths. The limiting factor was the high death rate. Each local community was vulnerable to three kinds of periodic catastrophes: bouts of plague or epidemic disease; years when small grain harvests led to shortages of food; and passages of soldiers who not only pillaged villages and fields, but transmitted contagious diseases. The most consistent problems were grain shortages resulting from bad weather. These shortages punctuated people's lives. For example, in Lyon there were grain crises in 1481–3, 1504–5, 1529–31, 1543–6, 1565–8, 1571–4, 1585–7, 1590–3, 1595–7, 1602, 1611–12, 1625, 1652–3, 1659, 1674, 1676, 1681, 1687, 1693–4, 1709, 1714, 1718, 1730, 1740, 1757, 1766, 1783, and 1787.[7] That adds up to 45 bad years out of 318, or once every seven years, although the crises were not that evenly distributed in time, and their frequency diminished in the eighteenth century. Most communities also faced periodic bouts of plague until 1720, when the disease disappeared, probably because of better sanitation and quarantine procedures.

Given the precarious state of many peasant households, periodic crises like those in Lyon typically set off a series of interrelated collapses. Bad harvests led to high prices and low yields. People became undernourished. Their resistance to plague or other contagious diseases was lowered. Then there would be a wave of deaths, including many men and women of child-bearing age. Population would decline. Finally, there would be a period of recovery during which the survivors would remarry en masse and produce many new births. The population would rebound within a generation, but it would simply recover its former level by the time the next crisis hit. When many villages throughout a region, or across the whole country, experienced these crises at the same time, the result would be an economic slump and a decline of population. This kind of crisis was especially common between 1580 and 1660, when periodic plagues and cold weather, along with the pressures of the Thirty Years War, caused French population growth to slow down and possibly even to decline. Using the indicators of population and economic change as a way of defining historical periods has the advantage of focusing on the way the population experienced good and bad times. But this is not the only way to think about demographic fluctuations. There were differences in the way the cycles affected different regions. Over the long term, the French population grew at a fairly steady annual rate of 1.75 to 1.9 percent, rising to 3 percent in the later eighteenth century. In developmental terms this steady, then increasing, rate of growth is significant. But averaging annual long-term growth conceals the shorter-term fluctuations which so drastically affected peasant life.

This recurring sequence of subsistence crises meant that death rates would be high, and high death rates meant that families would have to produce numerous children to replace the dead. One study of infant mortality shows that for every hundred babies born in the seventeenth century, twenty-eight would die in the first year, eighteen more would die between age one and nine, and four more would die between years ten and nineteen. By age twenty, 50 percent of the children would be gone. Other studies show similar results.[8] Research shows that for the population to grow, each family on the average would have to produce enough children to replace the adults and the children who did not survive. Barring illegitimate births (which were apparently few) and birth control (which was generally unknown), the maximum number of babies produced by a couple was determined by the number of years of fertility the wife had between her marriage and the age of menopause. The population would stagnate or decline if each couple produced, on the average, four children. Five children would lead to some growth, and any more than five would cause a healthy expansion. The key to the number of possible children per couple was the age at marriage of the wife. Marriage at twenty-five or later reduced the possible number of children, which was reduced further by the high mortality rate of women twenty-five to forty years old who died giving birth.

Close analysis of reproduction on this micro-level leads us back to the big picture of demographic change. Population growth, or failure to grow, impacted on the way of life of the common people. Most of them were peasants farming small, inefficient plots with relatively low yield, given the primitive technology and traditional methods then employed. If the population expanded rapidly, that meant more mouths to feed from the same inefficient plots. Then plots would be subdivided, and less productive marginal fields would be plowed under and seeded. Prices of grains would rise, the lords or landowners who enjoyed surpluses from their estates which they could sell would be better off, and the poorer peasants would be worse off. If the population fell dramatically, there would be more good land to go around, rents and prices would be bid down, and the poorer elements of the population would be better fed, while nobles and landlords would be worse off.

A major turning-point in the history of the French population was the crisis of the fourteenth century, a generalized catastrophe between 1350 and 1450 that laid the groundwork for the social relationships of the next four hundred years. The long medieval rise in population reached its peak around 1300, and the French countryside began to be overcrowded.[9] The sign that this crowding was taking place was the rising number of lean years when the harvests were inadequate, leading to outbreaks of disease and, increasingly, to real famines such as those that broke out in 1310, 1315–17, and periodically thereafter. This emerging crisis was amplified by the dramatic sweep of the plague, or Black Death, through Europe. This repulsive disease was carried from the Crimea to Genoa and Marseilles, and from there to the rest of France in 1348. It resulted in the immediate death of between one-third and two-thirds of the population, depending on the area, and then became a recurring problem that reemerged every ten years or so. During the same period, the Hundred Years War devastated certain regions over and over again, multiplying the effect of the plague by causing further deaths, destroying or removing crops, and dislocating persons.

The impact of the problem is best evoked by citing specific examples. Based on calculations involving a number of rural parishes in the region of Caux in Normandy, Guy Bois was able to evaluate the magnitude of the change. If we assign the index number 100 to the population of these villages in the year 1314, we find that in 1347 the population had already declined slightly to 97, even before the plague. Then came the big plunge. In 1374 the population was only 43 percent of what it had been in 1314. By 1413 it had risen again to 65, indicating the beginning of a recovery. But then the area became a battlefield and suffered more bouts of plague between 1415 and 1422. By 1425 the index was down to 34. It recovered again, reaching 43 in 1434; then more catastrophes brought it down to a new low of 30 in 1460, 70 percent lower than in 1314! After the fighting had left the area by around 1450, things began to improve, this time for good. The index reached 50 in 1493, 55 in 1530 and 75 in 1545. But the population of 1314 had still not been regained.[10]

These figures tell us that the blow from the initial rounds of plague was indeed severe, but that, faced with a one-time catastrophe, rural communities were perfectly capable of recovering over time. The real disaster was the cumulative effect of periodic waves of plague followed by exposure to repeated military campaigns. The low point came not after the onslaught of the Black Death in 1348, but around 1460 as a consequence of repeated warfare. It took more than a hundred additional years to regain what had been lost.

This same prolonged crisis occurred to one degree or another in virtually every region. In Burgundy four villages in the castellany of Saint-Romain recorded 120 households in 1285, 36 in 1423, and 50 in 1460. Ouges, another community of 80 households in 1268, had only 50 in 1400, 13 in 1423, and 40 in 1470.[11] In Lunel, a farming town in Languedoc, the number of taxpayers went from 891, in 1295, to 569 in 1396, and 500 in 1460.[12] In eighty parishes around Paris the decline between 1328 and 1470 was at least two-thirds.[13]

Such a long-term crisis had serious permanent effects. With half of its people gone and those who remained subjected to a generation of dislocations and emergencies, the typical village was unable to cultivate all the fields that had been cleared in the crowded days of the early fourteenth century. Plots were abandoned, especially the most outlying and those with the poorest soil. Squatters occupied vacant lands. Lords were no longer able to enforce work services on their tenants. The owners of extensive estates, whether noble or ecclesiastical, had trouble finding takers for their leases. Even worse, revenues from dues that were levied as a percentage of crops harvested declined as the harvests declined. In the bailliage of Senlis north of Paris, which was particularly hard hit by the recurrent civil wars of the early fifteenth century, it was difficult for landlords to find out even what lands and dues they owned. The monks of Saint-Germer reported that before the wars they had enjoyed 3,500 arpents of forest at Coudray, but they could never recover more than 1,500 of them because "the church of Saint Germer had been totally uninhabited for a long period of time ... and the chateau, farm, and house at Coudray had been completely destroyed." Most of their woods and other rights had been sold or appropriated by their neighbors. The prior of Saint-Leu-d'Esserent reported that his seigneuries of Trossy and Saint-Maximin had been usurped and granted out to tenants by the seigneur of Laversine, and he could not recover them because his papers and titles had all been burned by the English. There was no one still living who could detail for him the nature of his claims.[14] This general crisis of the fourteenth century extending, broadly speaking, from 1350 to 1450, had laid the foundations for early modern French society by bringing about major adjustments in social arrangements. We can look at the subsequent phases more briefly.

The next demographic period, around 1450 to 1550, was a time of recovery. During these "happy years," which more or less coincided with the French Renaissance, lords scrambled to reconstitute their sources of revenue by reviving their claims to property and finding ways to get it leased out and producing income. Those peasants who were lucky enough to have survived found themselves with new options for renting or owning land on more favorable terms than before, since there were fewer of them and their services were in greater demand. Noble families, merchants, churches, and the monarchy all adjusted their methods to the new circumstances.

In the third period, from around 1550 to 1730, the land filled up again and there was increasing conflict over the distribution of existing resources. Having pushed the yield of the land to its maximum – always given the existing social and technological conditions – peasants and landlords began to engage in an implicit struggle over who would own the resources and who would receive the surpluses produced. The king, now fully recovered and preparing eagerly for international struggles in Europe, joined in. If he was to extract more of the kingdom's resources in taxes to support his enterprises it would have to be at the expense of landlords, peasants, or townspeople. As the crown extended its influence over all three, the towns fought to defend their independence, the nobles grouped themselves into defensive client networks which fought one another, and the leaders of those networks tried to gain control of the royal court, and thus the state.

During the final period, 1730 to 1789, rapid population growth again began to strain France's traditional resources, while competition from English and Dutch capitalism began to reveal the weaknesses of the French economy. Progress became an obsession with the philosophers of the Enlightenment, as the state and a few entrepreneurs tried to bring about agricultural and industrial change in practice, with disappointing results. Meanwhile colonial riches began to complicate the equation by introducing new channels of wealth and intensifying competition with the maritime powers.

It is useful to remember these broad phases – 1350–1450, decline; 1450–1550, expansion; 1550–1730, stagnation; 1730–1789, rapid growth – because the fortunes and strategies of all social groups were tied in one way or another to these conditions. Late medieval society had gone through a crisis of adjustment which led to a period of reconstruction and redistribution of resources. Once production had been restored, distribution became the issue, with king, nobles, and other groups competing over how the existing wealth and power would be distributed. Finally, new expansion and a broader European economy put strains on the old system, which led to the Revolution.

Delineating these phases does not imply that the shifting balance of resources and numbers of people was the causal factor in the rise and fall of the monarchy, or the economy, or of conflicts between social groups. On the contrary, this crude outline begs the question of the reasons for technological change, or the absence of it, the changes in social relations, or indeed the effect of all of these on population growth or decline. There is much more to the story, but these broad phases provide a valuable frame of reference for the discussion that follows. It is good to remember that the foundation of everything else was the production of food on the land by peasants and that the vast majority of the population consisted of poor villagers who received only a minimal share of this production.

Suggestions for further reading: general studies

Baumgartner, Frederic J., *France in the Sixteenth Century* (New York, 1995).

Braudel, Fernand, *The Identity of France*, trans. Siân Reynolds, 2 vols. (New York, 1988–90).

Briggs, Robin, *Early Modern France 1560–1715*, 2nd edn (Oxford, 1998).

Collins, James B., *The State in Early Modern France* (Cambridge, 1995).

Constant, Jean-Marie, *La Société française aux XVI, XVIIe et XVIIIe siècles* (Paris, 1994).

Doyle, William, *Old Regime France 1648–1788* (Oxford, 2001).

Goubert, Pierre, *The Course of French History*, trans. Maarten Ultee (New York, 1988).

Holt, Mack P., ed., *Renaissance and Reformation France 1500–1648* (Oxford, 2002).

Kettering, Sharon, *French Society 1589–1715* (London, 2001).

Parker, David, *Class and State in Ancien Régime France: The Road to Modernity* (New York, 1996).

Salmon, J. H. M., *Society in Crisis: France in the Sixteenth Century* (New York, 1975).

1 | Rural communities and seigneurial power

All of French society was fundamentally built upon the life and work of people in the countryside. Eighty to ninety percent of France's population lived there, and most of the wealth was produced there. Even in the city, nobles, merchants, craftsmen, and priests were all directly influenced by the rural world outside. Town dwellers regularly encountered hogs being herded to market through their streets and lived beside attics stuffed with valuable sacks of grain. Those who ventured even a few yards beyond the town walls were plunged immediately into a rustic world of cultivated fields and carefully tended vineyards, followed by long stretches of wasteland and forest. Merchants whose business it was to transport their goods from place to place had to face long journeys on mediocre roads through menacing forests, or endure trips along shallow waterways, dragging their barges with the assistance of pack animals and human porters. The king himself traveled from chateau to chateau along the same dusty roads used by everyone else. Great nobles had fancy houses and parks in the country. Merchants and traders imitated them by acquiring country real estate and assuming titles and feudal claims. Even artisans often boasted of owning a patch of land or some vines. Thus everyone knew the smell of manure, the sounds of chickens and geese, and the joy of a successful harvest. When the crops were in, the roads into towns were clogged with carts bringing in, duty-free, the produce from the estates of the urban elite to replenish their granaries, pantries, and winecellars. Most significantly, the wealth of all the elites – nobility, officer class, and clergy – was invested in land, the bulk of which consisted of rural estates producing agricultural revenues, and the king drew most of his tax revenues from the same source. Events like a bad harvest, a rise or fall in the level of rents, or the passage of destructive troops would be a matter of concern for all kinds of people, whether they lived in the countryside or not.

Most of France's population was made up of peasant farmers inhabiting some 30,000 villages. They lived clustered together for protection and mutual aid, traveling out to work the fields during the day and returning home each night. A village might consist of as few as twenty or as many as several hundred dwellings grouped around a central square, which would probably be next to a parish church and its cemetery. Nearby might be a larger manor house or a partly ruined castle, surrounded by the private fields and gardens of the lord who had once dominated the community, and indeed might still do so. Each peasant cottage had a place to keep animals and a vegetable garden. The village territory might also include meadows or swamp-lands, a stream with its fishing rights, woods where firewood, nuts, and berries could be collected, vineyards or orchards. Beyond the village the cultivated fields extended as far as it was practicable to walk in a day and be able to return home at night. The community was not walled like the city, but there might be markers separating the village proper from the cultivated fields. Beyond the farthest plantings stood forest, wasteland, or the fields of the next community.

Villages varied greatly in layout. Some were elongated, stretching along a main road from which each plot had been cleared many centuries earlier. Others were circular, grouped around a central focus such as a river, a hill or a castle. In the great plains of the north, the east and the center, the land was flat and devoted to large open (unfenced) fields of grain. These areas had few meadows, wastelands, or properties devoted to communal use; cattle were rare because there was no place to graze them. In the west a very different landscape consisted of smaller clusters of houses, or hamlets, surrounded by irregularly shaped fields, each one separated by ditches and lined with hedges or fruit trees. There was a greater variety of crops in these areas; cattle were frequent because there were many meadows for grazing. In the Midi, where it was hot and dry, a large portion of the land was devoted to scrub and open areas used for grazing sheep and goats, while olive groves and vineyards were squeezed in wherever possible. On the hillsides of Provence walled villages clung to the sides of mountains for protection from the Islamic invaders of old. There were many other variations.

It is difficult for us to imagine how close peasant life was to the soil and the elements. Plowing, sowing, and harvesting were backbreaking work, done mostly by hand, aided sometimes by plow animals. Life was a struggle to grow enough to feed families and meet obligations. Crop yields were relatively low, and the average villager did not own

Figure 2. Lord and village. The ruined chateau of Sévérac (Aveyron) literally dominates the village of Sévérac, nestled below. The lord's superior wealth and broader outside connections are evident in the remains of an elegant Renaissance wing and an intimidating classical portal through which villagers would have to pass to have dealings with the lord.

enough land to live comfortably on what it could produce. Resources that might seem secondary to us, such as the peas and cabbages grown in the garden, the right to pick apples and pears or to gather berries in the woods, or the revenue from raising chickens and pigs, were of central importance. Life was closely tied to the weather and the seasons. There was little protection from wind, rain, and hail, which could ruin essential crops if they came at the wrong time. The annual cycle of the seasons made a profound difference in everyday life. Winter meant that everyone had to live on stored food which might run out if the harvest had been poor. Spring meant that fresh produce from the garden would become available and plowing and planting could resume. At harvest time everyone in the village worked in the fields during every hour of daylight. Marriages were scheduled to avoid such peak seasons. In fifteenth-century Brittany a moderately prosperous farm (*tenue*) might contain:

a principal room with a fireplace, sometimes a bedroom and a shed. There was no upper floor except in the towns, but sometimes there was an attic with, perhaps already at this time, an exterior staircase. In this land of frequent rain and wind, the walls of cut stone were only broken by a few small windows and a narrow doorway. The roof was made of straw. Around the house in an open courtyard were the "courtil" [an enclosed cottage garden] the threshing floor, a manure heap, a stable. a pig-sty, a shed for sheep. Every house had its gardens... The tenue was connected to the outside world by lanes and byways. Beyond it lay the meadows, the fields, the moors.[1]

Such dwellings had few material comforts before the eighteenth century. Even a prosperous peasant concentrated on accumulating fields, tools, and crops, not articles of consumption. We get a glimpse of this sparseness in Le Roy Ladurie's listing of the meager possessions of peasants in seventeenth-century Languedoc, taken from inventories of what they owned at the time of their deaths:

Raymond Vallier, farmer from Montpellier, comes from a rural background of illiterate weavers; in 1598 he lives (and dies) in two rooms; the main room has two chests, a bench, a box, a dresser; in the room where Vallier sleeps is a straw mattress on a camp bed. Tools and sacks of grain are thrown haphazardly in with the furniture...
Antoine Galabert, farmer (died 1605), has certain signs of prosperity: he buys vineyards and olive groves, he hoards things (a gold ring, six silver

rings). But his furnishings are stingy: a chest and a bed in his main room, a bed without mattress and a box full of papers in the bedroom. Similar findings at the vinegrower Antoine Raynaud's (died 1607): a bit of property – a vineyard, six pickaxes, several rings of gold and silver – but an extremely limited interior: bed, table, box, chest... Guillaume Leques (died 1604), a farmer, owner of fifteen plots of land, possesses a mule and a barn filled with hay, plus two stools, a bed, a bench, a table. As for Etienne Bousquet (died 1613), he cultivates his land extensively (130 sheep, two plows, a pair of oxen) but his domestic comfort is limited to a table, a chest, two beds... These poorly furnished farmers rarely own a chair, a phenomenal luxury which I only encountered twice between 1610 and 1620.[2]

Wherever tax rolls or land surveys enable us to measure the distribution of property in a given village, they reveal dramatic disparities in wealth. For example, we can examine the situation in the Norman parish of Saint-Nicolas d'Aliermont at the beginning of our period.[3] The village population around 1390 was 132 households. It slumped to 72 in the aftermath of the wars of the fifteenth century, but rose again to 153 in 1527 in the midst of the French Renaissance. Within that population Saint-Nicolas displayed considerable polarization. It has been estimated that the minimum amount of land needed to support an average peasant family in a normal year was 5 or 6 hectares. If this was the case in Saint-Nicolas, then a substantial share of the population – about 40 percent – fell below that standard, (see Table 1.1), while six to twelve individuals (4 to 8 percent) owned the only large farms. But Saint-Nicolas was relatively fortunate because another 50–60 percent did have adequate resources. Other villages in other regions did much worse. Table 1.2 shows that in Coudray in 1680 in the Beauvaisis, 76 percent of the inhabitants had tiny, inadequate plots and 8 percent had adequate ones. A middle group of 16 percent had marginally adequate resources. In Le Bosc in Languedoc one quarter of the population had no land at all in 1670 and the situation was worse in 1732.[4] These are just examples, but they can be considered representative. Property distribution was better or worse depending on the region and the date, but it was always extremely polarized. Villagers usually owned their house and an attached garden, but their control over the arable fields was, for most, minimal, and it declined significantly between the sixteenth and the eighteenth century. We should think of a French village, not as a collection of self-sufficient farmers, but rather as a highly

Table 1.1 *Land ownership in Saint-Nicolas (Normandy)*

	Number of households					
	Late fourteenth century		1477		1527	
Area of Holding (in hectares)	No.	%	No.	%	No.	%
Under 1 ha						
(Under 3 acres)	10	8	5	7	18	12
1 to 3 ha (3–7 acres)	23	17	7	10	22	14
3 to 5 ha (7–12 acres)	20	15	16	22	24	16
Level of minimum subsistence for a family in a normal year						
5 to 10 ha (12–24 acres)	35	26.5	19	26	42	27
10 to 25 ha						
(24–62 acres)	38	29	23	32	35	23
More than 25 ha						
(More than 62 acres)	6	4.5	2	3	12	8
Total	132	100	72	100	153	100

Source: Paul Bois, *The Crisis of Feudalism*, 149–51.

Table 1.2 *Property assessments in Coudray-Saint-Germer (Beauvaisis) And Le Bosc (Languedoc)*

Coudray in 1680 (area in hectares)			Le Bosc in 1675 AND 1737 (value expressed in livres)				
Size of farm	No.	%	Value of farm	No. in 1670	%	No. in 1732	%
Less than 1 ha	52	42.00	No property	52	21	51	25.3
1–2 ha	43	34.00	Up to 1 L 10 s	112	45	67	33.00
3–7.9 ha	20	16.00	1 L 10 s to 4 L	57	23	46	23.00
8–14 ha	9	7.2	5 L to 14 L	28	11	37	18.3
30 ha	1	0.8	18 L	–	–	1	0.4
Total	125	100	Total	249	100	202	100

Note: L = livre; S = sol

Sources: Goubert, *Beauvais et le Beauvaisis*, 158; Le Roy Ladurie, *Paysans de Languedoc*, 784.

differentiated community in which most people had to find alternative ways of supplementing what they could grow on their own land, especially in the periodic years when crops were poor.

How did these people survive? The most obvious answer lies in rented land. Those large plots that appear at the bottom of the tables were often leased out by their owners, either whole or in small parcels, to villagers who needed additional land. In some areas villages collectively owned common lands which could be used by poor inhabitants to graze their animals, gather wood, catch fish in the stream, or trap small animals. Larger estates with more extensive fields would employ wage labor during peak moments such as the harvest. The larger estates also employed servants and farmhands, male and female. There were always some villagers who practiced artisanal skills: thatching roofs, trimming hedges, gathering wood, wet-nursing, village sorcery, carpentry, tile-making, equipment repair. Another option in some areas was domestic industry. If peasants could process flax, spin thread, weave cloth, or make nails or needles in their homes during slack moments, or if the women and children could do this more regularly, commodities might be produced which could be sold in local markets. And when this activity was organized by merchant suppliers from the city who imported raw materials, hired the villagers to process them, and then passed them on to urban artisans for finishing – a phenomenon sometimes called proto-industry – the peasants might find themselves dependent upon the world of manufacturing and long-distance trade. In some poorer regions the men of the village left on annual migrations to work in other places at haymaking, harvesting, grape-picking, or threshing.[5] To complicate the picture further, peasant ownership of arable land declined significantly from the sixteenth to the eighteenth century as outside investors bought up more and more of the best fields.

Let us look more closely at village property relations in the rich, prosperous agricultural region south of Paris in the mid sixteenth century. Jean Jacquart details the disposition of property in seven large seigneuries (lordships) totaling 6,069 hectares, or about 23.4 square miles.[6] These holdings were extremely fragmented. They contained 2,584 actual plots owned by private parties, 88 percent of which were very small. The vast majority (81 percent) of these small farms, those consisting of 2.5 hectares or less, were owned by local villagers and local parish societies. Eighty-two percent of the

Table 1.3 *Ownership of seven seigneuries in the Hurepoix (south of Paris)*

Categories	%
Local inhabitants	24.6
Persons from other villages	8.5
Rural communities (collective)	0.6
Total locally owned	33.7
Seigneurial demesnes (directly owned by the lord)	31.9
Parisian bourgeoisie	23.3
Local bourgeoisie	5.9
Ecclesiastical communities	0.6
Local churches	0.8
Nobility	3.1
Miscellaneous	0.6
Total held by outsiders	66.3
Grand total	100.0

Source: calculated from Jacquard, *La Crise rurale en Île-de-France 1550–1670*, 135–64.

seventeen largest plots were owned by persons from outside the community, and 22.2 percent of the total area was owned by out-siders. These included a large contingent of notables from Paris, a smattering of rich farmers or professional people in regional towns, some corporate bodies, and some of the local nobility. Thus, in this region close to Parisian influences, rich Parisians plus some locally based nobles owned about one-fifth of all the farmed tenures, and this fifth included most of the larger farms, whereas the four-fifths owned by the local peasantry consisted almost entirely of very small plots.

Actually the domination of the capital over the fertile land south of the city was more extensive than this because the seigneuries in question contained not only the lands permanently alienated to pri-vate parties – the ones we have been examining – but also lands where the lord retained direct control (seigneurial demesnes). If we count these lands as property controlled by outsiders, it turns out that only a third of the entire 6,069 hectares was held by local people and 66 percent was held by outside parties (Table 1.3). With two-thirds of the land being owned by corporate bodies and private dignitaries from

Paris, we must see the rural population as being heavily dependent on external owners for their survival. This meant that they either rented farms from the owners or worked for them as hired labor. Far from being isolated, the local peasants were deeply embedded in larger social structures. This phenomenon was especially powerful close to Paris, but similar ties existed in the vicinity of every French city, and deeper in the countryside the influence of city people was replaced by the influence of powerful noble lords. Peasant life was anything but isolated, or autonomous.

Origins of the village community

The inhabitants of most French villages took part in three overlapping kinds of communities: the parish, the seigneurie (lordship), and the village as an economic and political community. Each imposed particular constraints and provided opportunities for collective interaction. The parish was the local unit of the international Catholic church.

The origins of most villages can be traced back to the period of the ninth through the twelfth century during the disintegration of the Carolingian world and the emergence of feudal principalities. At that time there were two forces behind the gathering of the rural population into clustered units. One was the Catholic church's gradual development of a system of rural parishes, each of which provided a place of worship, a priest, and a cemetery around which the community could coalesce. The other was the organization of rural estates dominated by local lords, which we call seigneuries or manors. Historians are not very clear on which came first. Parishes seem to have the earlier origins, emerging from the ninth to the eleventh century, but they may not have been fully formed before the twelfth century. Seigneuries have origins dating back to the Carolingians and even earlier, but as economic units organized by the lord, or seigneur, they probably date from the eleventh through the fourteenth century. Seigneuries seem to have been a stronger force in the north, whereas parishes were more influential in the south, but everywhere the two units overlapped and intersected.

Both systems tied the peasants to larger forces in their society. The parish system linked the community of believers to the Catholic church, most immediately through the tithe, a percentage of the crops in the fields that was collected in the name of the church and delivered to some designated recipient. The seigneurial system was predicated on the premise that the lord had originally owned the land, which he had granted out to the villagers to cultivate in return for work services and payments designed to acknowledge his authority. In some cases villages had literally been created by lords, who organized the clearing of fields from forests and the distribution of plots. In others a powerful individual with military force behind him had simply imposed himself on villagers lacking the force to resist. A considerable part of the lord's identity was based on the idea of "ruling" his estates. He could serve as a channel through which his peasants could be linked to other nobles with whom the lord had feudal or political connections, and ultimately to the king. But of course such ties were a source of power for the lord which might or might not benefit his peasants. These two units, parish and seigneurie, coexisted, but they were not coterminous. Many parishes coincided with physical villages, but others encompassed several villages. Seigneuries were geographically more complex. Some lords literally ruled particular villages, but others owned rights in more than one community, and many communities had two or more lords.

Besides seigneuries and parishes, the third local unit was the village as a center of habitation and agricultural production. Its houses, gardens, pasture, and fields formed a primary economic unit in which large landowners and small tenants produced grain or other products for the market and exchanged goods and services. In some communities where wine was produced, it was possible for a family to subsist on a small vineyard. There were also rural artisans who made their living as blacksmiths, millers, carpenters, innkeepers, and many others. But for the majority, the principal resource was the growing of grain. The inhabitants, coordinated by their own assemblies and strongly influenced by their lord, managed the physical resources of the village: the fields with their crop rotations, the harvests, and the auxiliary resources like meadows, streams, and grazing rights. The resulting crops and livestock, which might be scarce or abundant in a given year, influenced prices and availability. Each village contributed to the larger agricultural system by putting a share of what had been produced on the market. Some of this came directly from peasant surpluses, and some came from dues paid to the lord or tithes paid to the church. In either case it would ultimately be sold in local or regional markets, affecting prices and supplies.

Villagers who lived together in a single physical community naturally formed a community with common interests as well as internal disagreements. They worked side by side and shared more or less the same fears of natural disasters or attacks by enemies. In the late middle ages most villages had developed their own system of collective governance. Sometimes an assembly of inhabitants was organized by the lord, who needed an organism representing the village to help coordinate the collection of dues and the organizing of work services. Sometimes the villagers banded together in opposition to their lord and bargained for better conditions. Village government, the fourth form of community, gradually emerged from both of these processes. Meanwhile parish organizations, such as religious confraternities and committees to repair the church or keep up the cemetery, also brought people together, providing further instances of cooperation in cases where the parish and the village coincided. In the course of the twelfth and thirteenth centuries the idea of the village community as a self-governing unit emerged from these experiences. Some communities extracted charters of rights from their lords and developed assemblies dominated by the richer and more influential peasants. In the four-teenth century, when the king or a provincial ruler began to demand taxes from the peasants, this village community became the unit responsible for assessing and collecting this new burden. Once the *taille* became permanent it was necessary for every local community to have an ongoing political existence, and this process strengthened the community of inhabitants at the expense of the lord's authority.

The lives of French peasants were rooted in the village, but they were not at all isolated. Through the seigneurie they had connections, admittedly inferior ones, to the higher world of the nobility; through their crops they were tied to a broader network of markets and exchange; through the village government they were in touch with the tax demands of the king; through the parish they caught glimpses of the world of the international church.

The seigneurie

The seigneurie was of fundamental importance as a way of structuring the relations between working peasants and a traditional class of overlords. Its hold on the countryside weakened significantly in the early modern period, but because it continued as a framework for personal and property relations, it is something that we must explore in detail. The physical seigneurie consisted of two parts: lands which the lord owned directly, called the *réserve* (also called the demesne or domain), plus lands which he had granted out permanently to other parties, called the *mouvance*. The *réserve* consisted of the lord's manor house or castle, surrounded by gardens and grounds, forests and other uncultivated areas, plus the lord's own fields which were sometimes part of the arable land of the village. The lord's fields might be cultivated through work services owed by the villagers, or (less usually) by means of hired labor, or he might rent them out to peasants. The *mouvance* consisted of plots (*censives*) over which the lord no longer held direct ownership because he or his predecessors had bestowed them hereditarily on other parties. What distinguished these *mouvance* lands was the fact that the lord retained certain legal rights over them, even though he did not "own" them in the sense of being able to dispose of them at will. Technically speaking, ownership was divided. The lord retained the *domaine direct* (ultimate jurisdiction), while the tenants held the *domaine utile* (right of use). Usually the lord's claims included the right to collect a small, fixed annual tribute (*cens*) which served to acknowledge the subordination of the tenant's land to the lord's seigneurie, and sometimes they included a heavier annual tax representing a share of the crop (*champart*). He might also claim a mutation fee when the property changed hands (*lods et ventes*), and enjoy the right to buy back the property rather than see it sold to a third party (*retrait féodal*). Property rights over the *censives* were, in effect, split between lord and tenant, but legally speaking they gradually evolved in the direction of private property. In the sixteenth century jurists still considered the lord (as the holder of the *domaine direct*) to be the real owner of the *censives*; in the seventeenth century they began treating the lord and the tenant as co-owners; by the eighteenth century the tenant (as the holder of *domaine utile*) was being considered the real owner, and the *domaine direct* was being treated as a "servitude" which was "a sign of superiority but not of [absolute private] property."[7] In addition to these property rights, the seigneurie also entailed judicial rights and political functions.

Thus a seigneurie was a collection of lands directly owned, plus rights over other lands, plus rights over persons living in a particular territory, all concentrated in the hands of a particular lord. When the seigneurie was created in the middle ages the seigneur had been the principal political and social influence over a given village or region. But during the early modern period a number of changes diluted this immediate, personal quality and exploded the unity of the system. In reality, seigneuries took many forms. The greatest were vast collections of properties and prerogatives spanning many communities; the smallest included just a few tenures in a single community. In either case, the one-on-one connection of lord to village was broken. Some lords owned many seigneuries in different provinces and did not reside in any of them. Moreover, the "lord" in question might be a woman – a widow or an heiress – or a minor child. Seigneuries could also be owned by church organizations, or any other collectivity, in which case the lord might be a bishop, the monks in a monastery, or the rectors of an urban poor house. In addition, the various rights and dues could become separated and fall into different hands, and the territory over which the rights were exercised could become fragmented through sales and family decisions. A single village might end up under several distinct lords, and two neighbors might pay their *cens* to the same party but be subject to different seigneurial courts.

To get a more concrete idea of the scope of this phenomenon, let us look at the entire system of seigneuries in one well-documented region in the earlier part of our period, the fifteenth-century Vannetais in Brittany.[8] In the 1400s the region around Vannes included sixty parishes and contained 370 seigneuries. These properties were held by about 200 different noble families, or about three or four per parish. The seigneuries differed greatly in size. There were four very extensive ones, namely the lands of the duke of Brittany and three other estates called Largouët, Rochefort, and Kaër. The duke, whose main property lay mostly in other parts of the province, controlled three castles and some other strategic locations. The three other seigneuries covered respectively 40,000, 30,000, and 5,000 hectares (155, 116, and 19 square miles), including both *réserve* and *mouvances*. There were also five large ecclesiastical seigneuries, owned by the bishop of Vannes (14,000 hectares), the cathedral chapter (mostly urban properties), and three abbeys (respectively 2,000, 600, and 500 hectares). There were fifteen other smaller lay seigneuries, plus 300 small "sieuries" of 24–36 hectares. These last were lordships without seigneurial courts.

The seigneurie of Largouët was spread over nineteen parishes which were loosely grouped into two distinct clusters. In many places whole parishes were included, but in others only part of the parish was in the seigneurie. Largouët's 40,000 hectares were divided between a *réserve* of 10,000 hectares and a *mouvance* of 30,000. Its *réserve* included about 100 rented tenures, nine grain mills, one fulling mill, one paper mill, and two stone quarries. In its *mouvance* were 600 peasant tenures and 120 manors held by lesser nobles who were dependants of the lord.[9] Rochefort covered sixteen parishes, five completely. In addition to 1,000 hectares of forest, its *domaine* included at least 400 farms distributed mostly among four separate parishes, plus eighteen mills. These large conglomerations required real administering. The various properties were divided into districts called *bailliages* or *prévôtés* or *châtellenies*, in each of which a seigneurial agent, the *prévôt féodé*, collected the revenues.

The ecclesiastical authorities had similar properties. The bishop of Vannes included in his *réserve* his episcopal palace, with courtroom and prison, several old houses, two country manors, four ovens, seven mills, meadows, and some tenures in six different parishes. His *mouvance* included one-fifth of all the houses in the city of Vannes, and most of three rural parishes. He also had extensive judicial influence. The cathedral chapter owned 28 percent of the houses in Vannes plus three villages. Their *mouvance* covered 300 households. The abbey of Prières controlled the immediate lands, vines, and salt flats in its vicinity and also rented out some forty plots. It had a mill, an oven, a forge, barns and granaries. The Chartreux monks owned 120 tenures, mills, and rabbit warrens in five parishes grouped around their abbey, plus scattered lands elsewhere; they had another 120 tenures in their *mouvance*. In addition, these great church foundations also received most of the tithe, a church tax which, though not technically seigneurial, amounted to the same thing, since it was a percentage levy on all agricultural production paid in kind to various parties who "owned" the revenues, some of whom were lay nobles or commoners.

The scope of the fifteen smaller-scale seigneurs in the Vannetais was much more local. These lords were more likely to live in manor houses than in castles, though the manor might incorporate remnants of an old medieval tower. Their *réserve* of some 300–400 hectares usually represented 80 percent of the estate and housed several dozen tenants. The 20 percent of *mouvance* would include a dozen or so tenants who paid the *cens*. These smaller-scale seigneurs were usually dependants of the great seigneurs. There were not very many of them, but most still had seigneurial courts with rights of high justice.

Finally, the 300 "sieurs" were distributed throughout the region. Although they had no justice rights, they were still prominent men in their communities, as evidenced by their manor houses surrounded by gardens and fields. Their *réserve* might include a central farm to feed the household, a mill, or some tenures, but often only some of these. It was usually relatively small. Only half of the sieuries had *mouvances*. Properties were often scattered in parishes quite far apart.

It is difficult to assess the effect of all these lordships on the peasantry, but clearly there was a decisive impact. Most fifteenth-century tenants knew who their lord was and what they owed to him. Once or twice in a lifetime, at times of transfer through inheritance, every tenant had to perform an oath of fidelity and do homage to his lord. A document was drawn up by a notary acknowledging all the obligations owed to the lord and promising loyalty, which was then sworn to before a court of law. The annual tribute payment (*cens*) was usually modest, but it was very concrete. It had to be paid in two to six installments on certain precise dates. Thus on the Bogemeno tenure in Plougoumellen, the lord of Largouët was owed a measure of wheat and 16 deniers (small coins) on January 1, a chicken, some work service, and a measure of oats on January 3, and then 6 deniers on August 29. Sometimes more exotic items were required such as a pair of gloves or some bird feathers.[10] These tributes had to be delivered on those particular days in person, and since each party had slightly different obligations, there was a constant coming and going throughout the year of peasants delivering coins, or sacks of grain, or poultry, to the lord's agents. Some tenures owed unremunerated work services (the *corvée*) to the lord. While the *corvée* was not a heavy burden, amounting to one or two days of work per year, it could be exasperating if it came at a time when work was pressing elsewhere or if it required the furnishing of tools, plows, or animals. Even more annoying was the collection of the tithe, which acknowledged the authority of the church. Like the *champart* it was collected right in the fields by agents who suspiciously monitored the harvest. If the lord was also the bishop, the distinction between the tithe and seigneurial payments was not always clear to the peasants.

About twenty lay and five ecclesiastical lords had seigneurial courts in the Vannetais, thirteen of which exercised high justice. This meant that they maintained gallows and prisons and employed a staff of judges and clerks who tried criminal, civil, and feudal cases involving their tenants, including capital crimes. Periodically, though not frequently, they carried out executions. Middle justice included the power to enforce the tenants' dues and obligations; to register legal documents and seal them with an official seal; to adjudicate wardship and inheritances cases, disinheritances, and succession questions concerning bastards. Low justice meant resolving petty disputes.

It is worth pausing for a moment to imagine the impact of these seigneurial courts which existed in great numbers all over France. They were the centers of political authority in rural areas, and they employed a variety of petty agents, many of whom divided their time between several different courts or came out a few days a month from a nearby town to hold the local audience. At Bobbley, in the Vannetais, which was a seat of high justice with a tiny district consisting of only three parts of parishes, the court was run by two judges, a receiver, five sergeants, nine notaries, and several forest guards. Weekly sessions held on busy market days handled lawsuits and other legal matters. Once or twice a year a general session was held on one of the village's major fair or festival days. This was the occasion for a public audience at which all the lord's tenants and vassals were expected to be present. General regulations were read aloud, the lord's customary rights were proclaimed and attested to by witnesses, the tenants acknowledged the roll listing their fees and obligations, the court's employees reported on activities during the year that had been contrary to the lord's interests, and persons who had acquired land during the year were required to declare it and pay any mutation fees owed. At Pont-Saint-Pierre, a court of high justice in Normandy, weekly sessions were also the occasion for discussion and promulgation of economic regulations such as the dates for harvesting and gleaning, the registration of the ordinances of higher royal courts, the naming of guardians for orphans, public acknowledgment by unmarried women that they were pregnant, swearing of the oaths of office of newly appointed seigneurial or guild officers, and all manner of property and inheritance disputes. Lesser courts handled many of these same items, down to petty crimes and issues concerning roads, bridges, and boundaries.[11]

It is easy to see that seigneurial courts provided a way for the lord to intervene in the affairs of the villagers, while reminding everyone periodically that he was "the law" in their community. In particular they played a central role in protecting the lord's property interests, and those of the rest of the villagers. Thus the importance of these courts in local life extended beyond the fees collected, which were often only a modest portion of the lord's revenue. In later centuries, seigneurial courts gradually lost ground to royal jurisdictions and were increasingly regulated by rules imposed by the crown. There is mixed evidence on their declining importance. Small courts often went into steep decline, but certain high seigneurial courts, and those in areas such as Burgundy where seigneurial power remained strong, continued to flourish. In Pont-Saint-Pierre the number of sessions held per year declined from forty-eight in 1581 to seventeen in the 1760s.

Returning to the fifteenth-century seigneurie as a unit of economic and social power, it had been revived after the late medieval crisis and was still very powerful. The greatest lords resided in the province and operated vast economic units that were almost like small states, collecting extensive revenues, and exercising considerable judicial authority. The ecclesiastical seigneuries were compact, well-managed collections of rights enhanced by the prestige of the church. And every community had local lords, whose influence as the most distinguished resident landowners gave them considerable clout with the villagers. Other provinces had comparable arrangements, although there were many variations.

In subsequent centuries seigneuries continued to play a significant role, but how well they fared depended on how clever their owners were at adapting their methods in the face of new conditions. For example, in the Vannetais, the great lords continued to think of their properties in a traditional, feudal manner as a birthright to be enjoyed. Faced with rising costs, they continued to liquidate their *réserve* lands by transforming them into *censives* and noble "fiefs," even when the lands in question were already profitably rented out. They also became increasingly dependent on windfall profits which they obtained by selling timber from the *réserve* and by operating mills which depended in part on monopoly power over milling rights. Since they started out with vast *réserves*, the lords' revenues held steady and even increased up to 1555, using these techniques. But then inflation and the liquidation of resources caught up with them. Gradually, the great lords disposed of most of their *réserves*, especially during two waves of *censive* creation from 1550 to 1590 and from 1620 to 1640. This seemingly archaic conversion of potentially profitable *réserve* lands into *mouvance* lands which they no longer controlled made perfect sense to these lords because they viewed their estates as simply a source of revenue and prestige. By "selling off" lands as *censives* they could enjoy an influx of immediate cash and guarantee themselves a future income from the obligatory *cens* payments, while retaining their lordly prerogatives over the lands in question. But this process tied the lords to perpetually fixed payments which would rapidly lose their value. It also transferred to the purchasers the ability to rent out the acquired land at newly competitive rates. By opting to employ traditional strategies resting on seigneurial authority rather than undertaking aggressive management of their arable estates, the great lords had missed a major opportunity which would come with population increase and rising demand for agricultural goods. In Brittany many great seigneurial families held on until the mid seventeenth century or later; then they went bankrupt. Their estates might continue after being bought up by *parlementaires* or wealthy merchants from Nantes.[12] Some great families, such as the Rohans, survived handsomely.

The lesser lords in the Vannetais did much better. Living closer to the land, and lacking the alternative resources of the great lords, they took advantage of the new conditions to round out their properties and acquire new ones, thanks to the disintegration of the *réserves* of the great. They also attempted to take over common lands that had previously been used collectively by the villages. The number of "sieurs" in the Vannetais rose from 300 in 1480 to 450 in 1536, and the number of seigneurial justices also multiplied, as lesser lords usurped judicial powers or obtained authorization from the crown to set up new courts. This process was made visible by the construction of new manor houses and an increased demand for the observance of seigneurial prerogatives. A local lord would construct an imposing residence on a central plot, plant trees and gardens, and surround the whole estate with a wall. He would then adopt a new title for himself, borrowed from the name of this "estate," and negotiate with the villagers or the crown for an exemption from degrading commoners' taxes. As rising demands provided new opportunities for profit, the more alert lesser seigneurs could now lease out middle-sized farms to enterprising farmers who would be pressured by increasing rents to improve their yields. The landlords could share handsomely in the profits by using adjustable, short-term leases or sharecropping arrangements.

For example, consider the farm at La Bergerie (Normandy) which was leased out by the comte de Tancarville from 1477 to 1502. This was a multi-purpose operation of 85 hectares, with 50 hectares of grain fields, an oil-yielding crop, horses, pigs, and flocks of sheep, plus apple and pear trees.[13] Leased out on a sharecropping basis, the farm was worked by a combination of family and hired labor. The tenant and his family did all the basic work: plowing, harrowing, manure-spreading, and tending to the cattle. They hired labor to perform the following special tasks: cutting the winter wheat with a sickle (done primarily by women), reaping the spring grains (barley, oats, peas, vetch), cutting the *rabette* (an oil-producing crop, seventy days' work for one man), threshing and winnowing the grain, weeding the grain (ten to fifteen days' work, done by both men and women), shearing the sheep (done in a day by thirty to forty women). One shepherd tended the sheep year-round.

All the farm's wool was sold in bulk to a single merchant from the city, and the grain was sold off to the highest bidder. When the harvest was poor and prices were rising, the grain was held off the market until late in the spring, and then sold off in small allotments to allow the price to continue to rise. Thus the lord and his tenant shared the proceeds of a viable operation while giving some employment to many of the poorer members of the community. This tenant received an estimated net income of at least 70 to 80 livres, which would put him in the top rank of local peasants. The lord received an equivalent amount. This example of the possibilities of market-oriented strategy in Normandy contrasts sharply with the practice of the seigneur of Largouët in Brittany, who at the same time was cashing in his grain whenever he needed money, even if prevailing prices were disadvantageous. Here is the difference between a traditional seigneurial outlook, focused on easily extracted revenues, and the more market-conscious approach of an ambitious tenant, backed up by an enterprising lord in a sharecropping agreement where the lord received half the proceeds.

Both Brittany and Normandy were regions where property was fairly widely distributed, and farms struck a balance between livestock and agricultural products. It was a different story in the Paris region, where, as we have seen, uniform fields of grain were already being concentrated into vast *réserves* owned by churchmen and nobles from the capital and rented out in blocks of 30–100 hectares to *fermiers* who were themselves major players with considerable resources.

These *fermiers*, who were expected to pay the traditional fees (*cens*, tithe to the church), many small tributes (capons, fattened pigs), a substantial entry fee, plus a heavy annual rent, were the emerging "coqs de village," the two or three rich peasant farmers in each village who began to stand out over the rest of their neighbors.

This phenomenon of rich *fermiers* leasing from urban notables was unique to the Paris region and to a few other areas where intensive culture in grain was possible because of the ability to sell large quantities in important urban markets. The *réserve* could only be rented out in the form of large productive farms if the opportunities for intensive profits were combined with the availability of tenants who were both enterprising and solvent and who were willing to pay the rents demanded. Such a system was advantageous for the lord in that it produced the highest level of income the market could bear without an extensive investment, and the relatively short leases made it possible to adjust the rent periodically in accordance with prevailing conditions.

In less favored regions lords still found it attractive to rent out the *réserve*, but they were more likely to do it in smaller plots using the system of *métayage* (sharecropping), in which the owner paid half the expenses of the farm and received in return half (or more) the produce. *Métayage* generally reflected the poverty of the tenants. Unlike the *fermiers* of the Paris region, these were peasants who did not have the resources to set up and run a farm on their own. From the point of view of the lord, the return was far better than any seigneurial payment – half the crop in kind every year! But there were disadvantages as well. Sharecropping required the lord to share in operating expenses, and it required close supervision to avoid cheating or deterioration of the facilities. This system prevailed in much of the Midi. A much studied example was in the Gâtine of Poitou, a region where, between 1450 and 1550, the local nobles recaptured most of the land from impoverished peasants and reorganized it into compact farms of 40–50 hectares, two-thirds of which consisted of pasture for troops of animals. These new, coherent farms (*métairies*), which balanced livestock raising and farming, were then rented out on very demanding terms to middling peasant farmers.

Thus all over France lords were faced with critical choices. They could sell off their *réserves* or use their traditional authority to try to extract revenues from them. Or they could hold onto their lands and rent them out profitably for the highest revenues possible, given prevailing economic conditions. Great lords like those in Brittany were losing control of their landed resources by overdependence on traditional payments, while many local nobles or their urban successors were displaying an aptitude for managing their properties more effectively. Even in the backward hills of Auvergne where traditional seigneurial revenues were still strong, at least one lesser noble, Nicolas de Salers, was busily tightening up the leases on his dairy farms between 1500 and 1520, while laboriously buying up bits of land to consolidate his petty arable holdings into more viable economic units.[14] Contrary to the stereotype of dissolute spendthrifts, the local nobility, or at least the most able of them, were taking the initiative in reorganizing local productive life around reinvented seigneurial *réserves*.

Was the seigneur, who by definition derived income from special powers of command and control, becoming simply a landlord, who made his money from careful economic management? The answer is not simple. Clearly those who owned the land were increasingly deriving their revenues from market-driven land rents. But the shift was gradual, taking place over three centuries. Seigneurial prerogatives continued to be highly valued both for their prestige and because they gave the lord added local power which gave him an economic edge over someone who was just a landowner. Some seigneurial dues continued to be powerful extraction mechanisms especially where heavy *champarts* or work services still existed, or where feudal property rights gave the holder advantages in the marketplace.

The trend for the lord's revenues to shift from "seigneurial" sources to "market-driven" components is perfectly clear. In the fifteenth-century Vannetais the great lords were deriving between a fifth and a half of all their revenues from seigneurial rights, including *cens* and other seigneurial fees, fees for justice, and feudal charges. If we include the proceeds from the *banalités*, including mills which were often quite lucrative, this figure rises to about three-fourths.[15] Perhaps the most telling figures of this type are those calculated by Jonathan Dewald for a single middle-range noble estate in Normandy, the barony of Pont-Saint-Pierre, over the entire early modern period. In this case seigneurie-based revenues declined continuously, from 92 percent of total revenue in 1399 to 11 percent in 1780. The most archaic seigneurial dues declined the most, but there was also a drop in market fees and judicial fees.

Figures from other provinces vary widely, depending on the date and the method of calculation used. Bastier found the "traditional" seigneurial share of revenue in forty-eight seigneuries of eighteenth-century Toulouse to average 18.8 percent. Forster found it to be 5 percent of the revenues of sixty-eight *parlementaire* families of Toulouse. Paul Bois estimates 10.8 percent in the eighteenth-century Haut-Maine. Goldsmith notes that in the backward Auvergne the traditional revenues came to a significant 33 percent, payable in kind, from the late middle ages all the way up to the Revolution. Aubin studied fifty-two examples in the region of Bordeaux in the eighteenth century, which varied widely and averaged out to 11.28 percent.[16] In the eighteenth-century pays de Caux, Normandy, Lemarchand counted 20–50 percent for the large estates, while smaller estates were under 20 percent. We might conclude conservatively that by the eighteenth century around 10 percent of the income of seigneurs derived from their seigneurial rights, and sometimes as much as 40–50 percent, and that the share was much higher in earlier periods.

Another way to measure the impact of seigneurial charges is to calculate their weight on the peasants who paid them. This is an even more treacherous enterprise because it requires an estimate of the farmer's total net revenue. Dewald concludes that seigneurial dues were a relatively heavy burden on the peasants up through the seventeenth century – heavier than royal taxation – but that subsequently inflation reduced them to insignificance.[17] Other studies report wildly different results. The seigneur took about 10 percent of the peasant's net revenue in the backward Auvergne and only 1–2 percent in the pays de Caux. Aubin's study of the Bordelais finds a range of rates and concludes that 6.5 percent might be a good overall figure.

The general consensus would be that the peasants' seigneurial payments were mildly burdensome in the earlier centuries and much less so by the eighteenth. But these figures do not include the tithe, which came to an additional 8–12 percent of the harvest and which was largely seigneurial in form. We must also remember that a payment of 1–5 percent could constitute a considerable burden for a peasant living on the edge of subsistence, even if it was proportionally rather small relative to the harvest. It could be especially onerous if it had to be paid in a certain form on a certain date, and such payments might loom large in the mind of the cultivator as a major aggravation.

In view of these figures it is important to remember that the seigneurie still provided an important framework for rural life well into the seventeenth and eighteenth centuries and that even in terms of seigneurial dues it remained significant in many places. Jacquart found as much in the Paris region, where in the mid seventeenth century seigneurs, many of them newcomers, were consolidating their *réserves* and simplifying their holdings, but also exercising fully their rights of justice and proudly demanding their symbols of authority.[18] In Goubert's seventeenth-century Beauvaisis, the 432 parishes contained 617 seigneuries, the most important of which were owned by ecclesiastical organizations and notables from Paris.[19] In certain provinces such as Burgundy and Auvergne, traditional seigneurial relationships were still very powerful and seigneurial obligations remained heavy.

A better way to assess the continuing importance of the seigneurie is to ask how functional it was in the eighteenth century, and whether this function had changed. Was it just a vestige of the past in certain provinces, or did it play a significant role even in areas not known for strong seigneurial institutions? A good test case is the area around Bordeaux, which has recently been studied by Gérard Aubin.

The seigneurie was very much alive in the eighteenth-century Bordelais. Property was still defined in terms of *réserves* and *mouvances*, and new *censives* were still being created, saddled with obligations which purchasers and grantors were careful to specify in tightly worded legal contracts. These included the *exporle*, which was a small registration fee due each time the lord or the tenant changed, and sometimes the *agrière*, a sizeable share of various crops, paid in kind. *Prélation* was the lord's right to acquire a property that was being placed on the market before any other buyer. It often required the tenant to give the lord prior notice of any impending sale and sometimes even required his approval. *Corvées* were light, but they existed, especially in backward areas. They were often defined very precisely as transport duties (once a year, supply oxen and carts to transport the lord's wine to Bordeaux) or work services (three days' work with teams and plows plus three days' manual labor).

The Bordelais had 120 seigneurial courts which still functioned actively. The lord could enforce royal ordinances, regulate the public health and cleanliness, monitor the state of roads and streets, and regulate weights and measures and the prices of essential commodities

such as bread and meat. He could collect fines for infractions, confiscate unclaimed property and property abandoned through disin-
heritance or bastardy, and capture animals that were damaging crops.
These extensive prerogatives, derived from a day when the lord really
was the predominant local figure, were most effective in rural areas
where there were no royal judges to challenge him. These courts
attracted a swarm of legal practitioners who made their living by
drawing up documents for clients and arguing cases. Seigneurs collected 361 tolls on the roads and streams of the *généralité*, although
this number was reduced to 155 after the royal reforms of 1770.

The honorific advantages of becoming a seigneur were still highly
valued. The purchaser might acquire a title, a special place in church,
or patronage over the appointment of local priests. He or she also had
exclusive rights to hunt in the forest and to raise rabbits without the
villagers being allowed to trap them even if they damaged crops and
gardens. In 1759 Jacquette de Gombault de Benauge, heiress of her
father the seigneur of Gombault, took possession of her seigneurie of
Montignac, Omet, and Escoussans:

Accompanied by her notary, witnesses, and the substitute prosecutor of the
seigneurial court, she proceeded to visit each of the three parishes in succession. In each she was received at the door of the church by the curate
who offered her holy water; she sat down in the armchair designated as the
seigneurial bench; then she rang the church bells three times to signify her
possession of high justice and her status of "landed and direct lady (lord),"
in the presence of the inhabitants who had gathered at the sound of the bell.
She then visited each of the hamlets of the parish and walked back and forth
as many times as she saw fit, declaring to the peasants "that she was taking
possession of the church and the parish."[20]

Thus the importance of the seigneur was still brought home to the
residents in no uncertain terms.

On the other hand, many seigneuries were increasingly losing this
personal quality, and the more traditional rights like the *corvée* were
falling into disuse except where they were economically advantageous. Although the swearing of homage for a noble fief was still
actually performed on occasion, the vassal's obligations were often
translated into monetary payments in the eighteenth century, and it
was considered permissible to swear homage by proxy. The distance
of the resulting relationships from their original feudal purposes

is suggested by the following document drawn up on October 10, 1754:

Anne Madeleine Dalesme, widow of Antoine d'Essenault, baron of Cadillac, and Marthe Armande d'Essenault, mother and daughter, baronesses of Castelnau, authorize Philippe Laporte, subdeacon from Bordeaux, to render homage on their behalf and in their names for the fief "des Sarsins" located in the parish of Porge en Buch, to Madame the duchess of Gramont, who is lady of the seigneurie of Lesparre from which the aforementioned fief stems, and to do this in conformity with the age-old forms of homage that have been rendered in the past by preceding seigneurs of the aforementioned fief, and the said agent is to carry out everything that is required and necessary.[21]

Here two female lords, mother and daughter, are appointing a priest from Bordeaux, who probably handled their other family affairs, to render feudal homage to another female lord who owns the seigneurie from which their fief was detached. The procedure has become a legal formality.

By the eighteenth century, all of the components of an estate were thought of as marketable assets, some valued for their prestige value, others for their economic usefulness. A news sheet in Bordeaux regularly published classified ads like the following:

For sale: fine property in Médoc with high, middle, and low justice over two parishes; the chateau is very beautiful; it commands considerable *réserves* with vines of the highest quality, nice meadows and other property; rents in grains and coin; some *agrières* and some rights over butchers, all of which is fully laid out in a register which will be made available; contact M. Lacoste, notary, in the place de Tourny.

Another ad offered a noble property in the parish of Saint-Vivien, "supplied with more than 800 *journaux* [a measure of acreage] of lands consisting of fiefs owing dues in grain and money, with *agrières*, all of which is deliverable to the house [of the lord]."[22]

As ownership of the various elements of a traditional seigneurie became fragmented, collecting dues and fees from widely scattered tenants could become a nightmare. Property changed hands, tenants fell into poverty, and many simply refused to pay or serve. Ownership could become extraordinarily complex. A house in Bordeaux was "in the fief of the Benedictine monks, except for five feet, nine inches of its width through its entire depth, which belong to the réserve of the Saint

Seurin Chapter."[23] Because of this difficulty, owners often farmed all their rights out as a block to an entrepreneur who paid an annual return for the right to collect all the revenues.

By the second half of the eighteenth century, the best-organized lords were consolidating their claims by abandoning or exchanging rights that brought in little or that were not worth the cost of collection. At the same time they were consciously acquiring and enforcing seigneurial claims that were potentially valuable, not just for revenue but for control. The eighteenth century saw a growing market for feudal lawyers capable of consolidating and enforcing the claims of seigneurs, and for agents capable of managing all the properties of a given lord. This was a tough position to fill. The wanted ads indicated the desirable traits:

Wanted, a man completely familiar with the cultivating and planting of properties, and with the successful cultivation and planting of vines and the making of wines. He must also have a thorough knowledge of feudal law, be fully prepared to maintain archives, keep the register up to date, and be capable of redoing it if necessary. His moral qualities must be irreproachable, and his loyalty to the interests of his master must be absolute.[24]

In the course of three centuries, the seigneurie had evolved from a personally ruled mini-state to an investment portfolio, although the personal element remained important.

Another change in the eighteenth century was the increasing number of interventions by the crown to regulate, if not eliminate, seigneurial abuses. Judicial lords were required to maintain certain standards of justice that were increasingly monitored and regulated by royal ordinances and that could be costly to maintain. These included the hiring of competent judges and the prosecution of criminal cases at the lord's expense. The same was true of tolls on roads and streams, which required the upkeep of passageways, bridges, and ferries. The right to confiscate abandoned property was tied by law to the obligation to support children abandoned within the lord's jurisdiction. These duties were not always carried out conscientiously by the owners, but they could result in expenses that wiped out other advantages.

Aubin also finds that in the Bordelais the seigneurie served paradoxically as a major tool for the reorganizing and rationalizing of the great vineyards that were about to establish the reputation of Bordeaux wines. The more alert lords, who were often the great *parlementaire* nobles from the city of Bordeaux, were carefully maintaining their seigneurial rights precisely because they provided tools for extending holdings and regrouping them into large, viable units. The right of *prélation* (repurchase) gave them the ability to acquire choice plots, while the right of *lods et ventes*, collected when the property was sold, enabled them to make money from the fluid land market in which lands frequently changed hands. Many lords followed the practice of letting a tenant's payments lapse for twenty-nine years and then demanding full back payments, thereby deliberately throwing the peasant into bankruptcy and forcing him to sell.[25] By 1789 most of the larger estates had been bought up by the *parlementaire* families whose investment launched the great wine vintages that still exist today, and most of the rest was owned by lesser royal officials, merchants, and artisans from the city. Thus, concludes Aubin, "capitalist profits developed through seigneurial means."[26]

The seigneurie had come a long way from the days of its reconstruction in the fifteenth century. From being a form of personal rule by a lord over his peasants, it was on the way to becoming nothing more than an advantageous form of property. Still, landed estates remained the primary ingredient in the fortunes of French elites. Land, now enhanced by market-oriented production, was still the basic form of wealth, and the seigneurial prerogatives attached to it were taken very seriously for reasons of both status and economic utility. Nobles still adopted family names derived from seigneurial estates and grounded their personal identity in their command over rural tenants. Wealthy commoners scrambled to acquire properties that would enhance their claims to nobility. Villagers were still dependent. They were less burdened proportionally by seigneurial obligations, but they had lost most of the land to urban investors, and they could still fall victim to the inequalities built into feudal property law. In the countryside the honorific rights of local lords seemed all the more humiliating in that they were increasingly divorced from any obvious utility to the village community. The seigneurie had declined as a traditional source of revenue for the lords without reducing its impact on the peasants, who were all the angrier at new oppressive uses of traditional rights.

Suggestions for further reading: seigneurs and tenants

There are few studies on this subject in English.

Bois, Guy, *The Crisis of Feudalism: Economy and Society in Eastern Normandy c. 1300–1550* (Cambridge, 1984).

Dewald, Jonathan, *Pont-St-Pierre 1398–1789: Lordship, Community, and Capitalism in Early Modern France* (Berkeley, CA, 1987).

Gallet, Jean, *Seigneurs et paysans en France 1600–1793* (Rennes, 1999).

Hufton, Olwen, "The Seigneur and the Rural Community in 18th Century France: The Seigneurial Reaction, a Reappraisal," *Transactions of the Royal Historical Society*, 5th series 19 (1979), 21–39.

Jacquart, Jean, *La Crise rurale en Île-de-France, 1550–1670* (Paris, 1974).

2 | Peasant life, agriculture, and social distribution

The landscape looked very different if you were a peasant. Instead of thinking about collecting rents and managing properties, the bulk of the population were concerned with basic matters of subsistence. They were preoccupied with the everyday problems of producing enough food to feed their families, meeting their tax obligations, raising their children to carry on after them, and obtaining salvation in the next life. In carrying out these goals they had very specific worries. Would the weather hold out, would the crops get ruined, would the animals fall sick? They were not alone in these concerns; in fact, to some extent these were the concerns of the whole society, as we saw in Chapter 1. But peasants faced them directly, every day.

The agricultural unit: fields, commons, and *prélèvements*

As we have seen, the seigneurie was one reality which influenced the peasants' options. Another was the system of customary farming practices by which they worked the land. Resources were scarce, and crop yields were variable. Pressed on one side by payments owed to superiors and on the other by low yields owing to primitive techniques, they relied principally on hard physical labor to make ends meet. Their work varied seasonally, with periods of relative idleness followed by times of intense activity, but there was always something to do:

SEPTEMBER. After the threshing of the grain, the peasants clear and rake sections of the moor [to grow temporary crops] and clean up parks and gardens. OCTOBER: Wash the grains that are to be sold, put salt in the salt holder for the pig that will be slaughtered, plow the land. NOVEMBER TO FEBRUARY: Cut the brush on the waste, chop wood, bundle and transport it; harvest millet, plant the wheat and the rye. FEBRUARY: Agricultural life revives. Clear the brush from the roads, plant peas, enclose meadows and woods to keep the animals from going into the fields. MARCH: Plant gardens. Clip the hedges, stake the peas, plant beans and cabbages. Rake the moor again, and do it also in April and May. APRIL: Major field work: hoe and weed the wheat and rye. MAY: Shear the sheep, turn over the grain that is in storage, stake the peas, start cutting thorns and brambles. JUNE: Weed the gardens and plant cabbages. Seigneurs require work services for the repair of mills. JULY: Start the harvest of peas, beans, around July 19 harvest the rye. AUGUST: Harvest the wheat, thresh the wheat and the rye, shell the peas and beans, haymaking.[1]

This summary of a Breton peasant's annual cycle of tasks captures the need to maximize every available resource and underscores the amount of sheer labor that was involved. But it only hints at the most essential aspect of peasant agriculture, which was the system of crop rotations. Since medieval times the French had based their subsistence primarily on the intensive cultivation of grains. This practice made sense as a way of feeding a relatively dense population because it provided more calories per acre than, say, growing vegetables or fodder to feed animals. The poor state of transport made it prohibitively expensive to move goods over long distances, so all over the country peasants devoted their primary energies to growing cereal crops for local consumption, regardless of whether this was the most efficient use of resources in their particular locality. Yields varied markedly from year to year and region to region, so much so that it is hard to generalize. The normal range was between four and six grains harvested for each grain planted, although a return of ten to one was not unknown, and even twenty to one was possible. Five to one was barely enough to feed a family and pay the rent, given the need to hold back seed to plant the following year.

Villagers also needed animals to help plow their fields and to supply leather, dairy foods, wool, fat, manure, and meat. The age-old solution to their maintenance was a set of customary procedures that worked to balance needs and resources. Large herds were out of the question, except for areas where there was grazing land unsuitable for plowing, because the animals would eat up resources needed to feed the humans. But if grains were repeatedly grown in the same field, the soil rapidly became depleted and the yield plummeted. So villagers knew they had to leave a given field fallow periodically. The standard pattern in much of northern France was the three-field system. All the cultivated land in the village was divided into three sections (*soles*). One section was planted in the late fall with a winter grain, usually rye, wheat, or a mixture of both. This germinated in the early spring

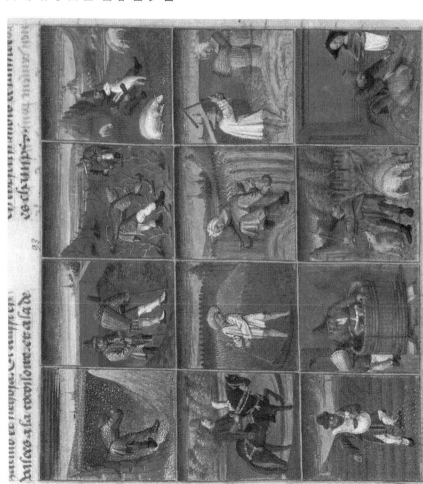

Figure 3 The seasons and their agricultural labors, an illuminated manuscript by the Master of the Geneva Boccaccio, around 1459–70. Reading left to right from top to bottom, peasants harvest grapes, prune the vines, shear the sheep, a noble with a falcon goes hunting, peasants harvest, bind, and winnow wheat, sow seed, crush grapes, feed pigs, and slaughter a pig.

and was harvested in midsummer. The next spring the same field would be planted with a spring crop such as oats, barley, peas or beans. This would be harvested in September and then the field would be left fallow for the entire following year. The other two sections followed the same rotation pattern, but in different years, so that in any given year one-third of the village fields were planted with winter wheat, one-third had a spring crop, and one-third lay fallow. That is where the animals came in. During the fallow periods and after the crops were harvested, the livestock of the village were allowed to graze in the fields on the stubble and weeds.

This method had the advantage of supporting some livestock while refreshing the soil. The fallow periods provided grazing and some manure and let the soil rest, but it meant that a third or more of the land lay idle at any given time, reducing the average yield of the whole system. In addition, the fact that the fields of the village were subdivided into a great many different holdings made necessary the system of "open fields," that is, fields without fences. If each plot had been fenced in, or if everyone had planted different crops which were harvested on different dates, it would have been impossible for animals to graze on the stubble or even for owners to pass conveniently from plot to plot. In the northern half of France the problem was all the more acute because each cultivated field was divided into long, narrow strips. The village arable would be divided into three large sectors for purposes of crop rotation, each sector made up of various fields, and each of the fields divided into many parallel strips separated only by a furrow. This practice, which dated from the distant past, may have been designed to enable the cultivator to plow long stretches without having to turn the plow around frequently, or it may have been a way of distributing the good and bad land more equitably among the villagers. In any event, each peasant needed to own strips in each of the three sections so that he was not left cropless when a given section was lying fallow.

The combination of three-field rotation, open fields, narrow strips, and obligatory grazing of animals on the fallow prevailed through much of the northern half of France, which was also the area best suited for the production of wheat. It meant that the villagers had to cooperate in planting and harvesting the same crops at the same time and in grazing their flocks of sheep, cows, or oxen together on their land. It also meant that there were constraints on private property.

Figure 4 The open fields. This detail from a land survey of the village of Ouges in Burgundy was commissioned by the lord in 1725. It illustrates the complexity of ownership. On the right is the edge of the village, with dark squares as houses, with roads leading off through the fields. The territory is divided into large sections or "contrées," each with a local name, no doubt for crop rotations ("les chenevières"). The long, narrow strips at the bottom of the map are cultivated fields owned by individuals, their owners indicated by numbers referring to entries in the survey. The irregular section at the top with dotted lines is probably a consolidated field owned by the lord or an outsider, whose dotted lines may indicate former strips. Just below it, the section labeled "Pasquier" is uncultivated pasture.

An individual peasant could not decide to plant a different crop or fence in his land for private use without incurring the wrath of the community.

The village system was further complicated in many areas by the existence of common lands: that is, lands not devoted to crops or houses but used collectively by the community. These were usually plots not suitable for planting because they were marshy or rocky, or they bordered streams or bogs. Sometimes there were common woods. Use of these areas was shared by the inhabitants according to elaborate customary procedures that dictated who might use them, for what purposes, under what conditions. For example, the cutting of firewood was often regulated so as to avoid denuding the woods of trees.

The use of the commons was always a source of controversy. The rules were usually not recorded in written documents, and it was sometimes difficult to distinguish the lord's seigneurial *réserve* from the lands enjoyed by the community. In fact, seigneurs often claimed the right to seize land not clearly owned by anyone else on the grounds that they were the original owners of the entire village, and conflicts of this sort could last for years, even generations.

This picture of the open-field village, as it is often laid out in textbooks, is deceptively simple. Much of France south of the Loire followed an open two-field system adapted to the lighter, drier soils of the Midi, in which half of the land lay fallow at any given time. Much of the middle of France, including Brittany, Normandy, and the Lyonnais, had plots that were on the average more modest in size and that were arranged in irregular shapes rather than long narrow strips. Some of these were enclosed by hedges or stone walls. Some of them followed irregular crop rotations which went through a more complex sequence of crops, after which the land was left fallow for several years. Many areas had fields outside the regular rotational system that were devoted to grapevines, olive trees, or specialized crops like flax (used to produce linen) or woad (used as a blue dye for textiles).

It would be confusing and tedious to review all the regional variations here. What most regions had in common was, first, the extreme fragmentation of land ownership; second, the rigors of a traditional, often mandatory, system of crop rotation; third, the existence of various community constraints on land use, notably the rules concerning the grazing of animals; and, fourth, the strong reliance on cereal crops with low but relatively reliable yields, even in areas where specialization would later occur.

The final element of this picture was what the French call *prélève-ment*, skimming off the share of the peasant's produce which went to the lord, the church, and the state. We have already seen that seigneurial dues could represent a sizeable portion of the crop and that this obligation often remained burdensome even though it was greatly reduced compared to earlier times. The church tithe was more serious. It was a tax of some 8–14 percent of most crops, levied in kind directly in the field. Villagers knew that very little of it stayed in the community to pay for local services, since much of it was siphoned off to church officials and even private owners. Finally there was the state land tax, or *taille*. Originating in the fourteenth century in the form of an emergency tax placed on hearths or households, and collected to fund a military venture by the king, it gradually became the backbone of the royal system of government and a major influence on France's economic development.

The royal *taille* was a tax which the king collected without consent after the 1440s. It was based on the value of landed property, and it fell largely on the rural peasantry, because through the years the more influential groups had negotiated better deals. The clergy were considered exempt because of their clerical status, and the nobility were excused on the increasingly improbable grounds that they gave their blood directly by serving the king in war. Townspeople theoretically paid the *taille*, but most of the more influential towns had been granted exemptions or special rates to ensure their loyalty. In very small country towns the bourgeois residents also paid a sizeable share.

To be sure, none of these groups – clergy, nobility, townspeople – was entirely free of taxes, since the monarchy had other ways of getting them to contribute, but they always paid on a different basis and often at a lower rate. Thus it was the rural peasants who supplied the bulk of the king's money. They offered the advantage of already being grouped in definable, taxable units, and their property was there for everyone to see. They were organized enough to undertake the necessary process of self-assessment and collection, but too isolated to mount much concerted opposition. It is true that because the country's wealth was largely agricultural, some sort of rural tax would have been inevitable. But it could be argued that such a tax should logically have included the clergy and the nobility, whose wealth was equally rural. Their exemption, and thus the exemption of many of the largest and richest plots in the countryside, was a fundamental reality that influenced the nature of French society decisively.[2]

The royal *taille* was a repartitioned tax, meaning that the king and his ministers decided first what total sum they wanted to receive and then divided it up among the various provinces according to formulas that were in many cases customary or out of date. This sum was then divided up among the provincial districts (called *généralités* for financial purposes), among their subdistricts (*élections*), and in turn among the villages of the subdistrict. The village would receive a mandate requiring it to assess all the eligible property owners in the village according to the value of their land, and name collectors who would be responsible for getting the money from each individual taxpayer, usually in three installments due on certain dates throughout the year. The village was collectively responsible for coming up with the total demanded. If some inhabitants could not or would not pay, their neighbors, or sometimes the richest taxpayers in the village, were required to come up with the difference. If the collector failed to turn in the required sum on the expected date, he was subject to a fine or imprisonment.

This system worked fairly well, but it had several important consequences. First, the king was provided with a reliable annual revenue without having to engage in much bargaining of a constitutional nature.[3] Second, the exemption of most of the "privileged" population meant that much of the country's wealth was undertaxed or tax-free, enhancing the advantages that noble lords and church foundations already enjoyed in the countryside and overburdening the rest. Avoidance of the *taille* was just another way in which seigneurs and church organizations had the upper hand in the countryside. Practice varied as to whether the owner or the tenant paid the *taille* on rented land, but in most cases it was the tenant. Third, the amount of the *taille* had no necessary relation to the peasant's ability to pay. The royal council started with a figure representing what the king needed for that year. This figure was not entirely arbitrary, of course, since it bore a relation to what had been charged in previous years and to perceptions of the king's advisors as to how much the country could bear. If the assessment went beyond the capacity of the population to pay, the result would be lagging returns, rural flight, and possibly resistance. But on every level of assessment – kingdom, *généralité*, *élection*, village – the repartition of the tax was based on customary assessments which were not necessarily proportionate to the ability of the unit in question to pay.[4] Thus the *taille* on a given locality bore very little relation to its actual revenues during the year in question. The process produced great inequalities that were only partially alleviated in the second half of our period.

The significance of these *prélèvements* by lord, church, and state was that most of the peasants were overburdened, relative to other groups, with taxes that had to be paid up front out of their meager resources. Like the customary practices discussed above, *prélèvements* reduced the peasants' ability to maneuver. Payments in kind reduced the size of the harvest and hit the best part of the crop. They also allowed seigneurs and church foundations to amass large stocks of grain and thereby influence the market. Payments in cash required the peasants to acquire currency by selling their best crops early in the year, which was not necessarily the optimal moment in terms of market prices. Furthermore, very few of the resources lost came back to the village in the form of services provided or investments in the land. Instead, these *prélèvements* were siphoned off to pay for the lifestyles of privileged nobles and churchmen, who usually lived elsewhere, and to fund the royal court, the king's military exploits, and the royal administration. Not only were these beneficiaries themselves exempt from the *taille*, but they received back much of what the peasants paid, in one form or another, and most of these resources left the countryside permanently. In a very real sense, the privileged groups could be said to be living off the work of the peasantry.

The extent of this *prélèvement* is almost impossible to calculate, given the many variables involved. Expert historians who have tried to estimate how much of a given peasant's production went for seigneurial payments, tithe, and *taille*, come up with many different results, depending on the time, place, and circumstances. In a famous example, Pierre Goubert calculated the budget of a relatively well-off *haricotier* in the Beauvais region in the 1680s, using conservative estimates.[5] He found that royal taxes would take about 20 percent of the farm's total production, the tithe 8 percent, local expenses for the church and the community would come to 4 percent, seed and various charges for milling, weighing, spoilage, and temporary labor would take 20 percent, and rent would take another 20 percent. This comes to 72 percent of the total production (including rent and assuming no significant seigneurial dues), leaving 28 percent for the farmer to feed his family and cover any other living expenses. At these rates, concludes Goubert, it would take $3\frac{1}{3}$ hectares of land in a good year to feed a family of six, and in a bad year 20 hectares, which was larger than most peasant plots.

Another conscientious estimate by Jean Jacquart posits a substantial farm of 120 arpents (40 hectares) in the Paris region during the relatively prosperous years around 1620.[6] The *fermier* rents good land and maintains a family of five, plus a farm hand, a female servant who tends the house and milks the cows, and a shepherd who watches the flocks. His two plows are pulled by a team of three or four horses. His entire operation revolves around the three distinct segments of his arable land, the *soles* of the three-field system. In the first *sole* he plants his basic crop, good winter wheat or a mixture of wheat and rye. In a good year he can expect to harvest 180 *setiers* of grain, in a bad year 60. After subtracting his costs of production, seed grain, and household consumption for the year, 103 *setiers* remain in a good year; in a bad year the farm would be ten *setiers* short of meeting expenses.

The second *sole* is more utilitarian. It produces oats, a more reliable crop which varies less from year to year and requires less manure and plowing. In a good year it produces 120 *setiers*, in a bad year 60. After saving seed, paying for threshing, and providing the horses' feed (the primary use for oats), there are 68 *setiers* left in a good year and 10 *setiers* in a bad year. The third *sole* will remain fallow. But it will support the grazing of 100 sheep. These will provide revenue through the sale of sixty lambs, a hundred fleeces, and twelve grown sheep, producing something like 240 livres of revenue which will be used to pay for the annual cost of the services of the carter, the shepherd, the female servant, the washers of the fleeces, the blacksmith, the saddler, and other petty expenses, leaving an estimated surplus of 20 livres.

To summarize, this substantial farm will produce a gross return of 103 arpents of wheat, 68 *setiers* of oats, and 20 livres in a good year; in a bad year it would have a deficit of 10 *setiers* of wheat while producing 10 *setiers* of oats and 20 livres in cash. If all the grain were translated into market prices, this gross return would become 1,074 livres in a good year and a deficit of 16 livres in a bad year. In a bad year the deficit is increased by the high price of the wheat that the farmer will presumably have to purchase to replace the deficit of 10 *setiers*. Jacquart then estimates the cost of the *prélèvements* to be 480 to 690 livres for rent to the landlord; 75 to 140 livres for the tithe; 24 livres for seigneurial dues and 150 livres for royal taxes. These charges against the gross return add up to between 729 and 1,000 livres annually. By these calculations, these charges absorb virtually all the surplus in a good year and cause a massive deficit in a bad year.

This estimate may be far too pessimistic. Modest peasants obviously did survive, and some even prospered. A formal balance sheet leaves out the many informal arrangements that existed for exchanging services instead of cash. Goubert and Jacquart completely ignored women's income, such as the sale of chickens, eggs, and dairy products. Global balance sheets omit wages earned by hiring out one's labor, from the cultivation of vineyards and orchards on the side, and from cutting wood. But this kind of calculation at least illustrates that the rural struggle with nature was intensified by the demands of the social system. The yield of the land was low because of its fragmentation into many dispersed tenures. Community constraints made improvements difficult. Even successful farmers were subject to the vast fluctuations in the size of their crops from year to year. In bad times farms were abandoned and whole communities took to the road or went to the city. Others defaulted on their debts and saw their lands taken over, and possibly rented back, by outsiders from the city. Heavy taxing of crops by privileged outsiders transferred surplus away from the land, diminishing resources that could have been used for reinvestment.

But within this general immobility there were a few pockets of dynamic change. At the top of the rural hierarchy, a few peasant families in a few favored localities managed to generate more sizeable revenues by producing for major urban markets. Jean-Marc Moriceau has provided a rich description of a hundred or so families from the region around Paris who exemplified this progressive kind of rural entrepreneur.[7] It is an open question how many like them existed anywhere else in France. These "great farmers" (*grands fermiers*) emerged in the fifteenth and sixteenth centuries and prospered between 1550 and 1640. They were aided by the tremendous demand for grain to feed Paris, by the capital's abundance of notables with money to lend, and by the region's relatively favorable laws concerning succession and disposition of property. Much of the richest farmland to the south and northeast of Paris was owned by urban dignitaries and corporations needing someone to manage their estates. These Parisians were sympathetic providers of capital and granted multiple-year leases to "grand farmer" tenants who were then able to produce good revenues which in turn made it possible to pay sizeable rents. The renters then acquired the teams of horses, plows, carts, wagons, flocks of sheep, and buildings needed to run a large successful farm. They intermarried and formed dynasties that passed down their farms from generation to generation.

These families were forever acquiring plots of land which they often rented rather than owned. They laboriously collected and exchanged fields, piecing together larger units, or renting out disparate plots to be farmed by local residents. But they were not consolidating them into large unified farms. Most of their properties were collections of medium- and small-sized units that continued to be cultivated in completely traditional ways, often by their previous owners. Success derived from the big farmers' scale of operations, the proximity of the Parisian market, and their control over the capital, tools, and means of transport to supply Parisian markets.

Their farms were centers of self-contained, individualistic enterprise and concentrations of resources that contrasted markedly with the collective constraints of the village. This center of operations was a compound consisting of a farmhouse and outbuildings surrounding a large courtyard, the whole protected by a high wall and entered by a gate broad enough to admit carts. The establishment might consist of a numerous family, various servants and farmhands, a shepherd, and hired help at harvest time. Everything was designed for utility, not comfort. The family lived on the ground floor, where there was also a kitchen, a dairy for the production of butter and cheese, a laundry, and a food pantry leading to a winecellar. Upstairs were storerooms for various grains, and rooms where children and servants slept. The enclosure might also include vegetable gardens and fruit trees. Around the courtyard were stables for horses, barns for bulls, cows and heifers, a kennel for dogs, sheds for pigs and sheep, and spaces to store carriages, carts, and other equipment. Unlike peasant dwellings, the humans and the animals were kept separate, except for stable boys who slept with the horses. Though hardly typical, these establishments are a good example of a dynamic sector within a largely traditional landscape.

The rural community

We will now return to the peasant villages which were, after all, the norm everywhere. The villagers had their own community and their own identity. A council of inhabitants had developed during the middle ages, largely in response to circumstances. This collectivity had various origins. The seigneur needed a group representing the community with which he could communicate, and that was the origin of some village councils. Many parishes organized religious confraternities to perform collective acts of piety and thereby gained experience in working together and collecting funds. Sometimes villagers got together to defend their interests against the lord or to distribute the burden of emergency levies laid on them by the seigneur or the crown. The uncertainties of the Hundred Years War encouraged these activities by highlighting the need for protection against marauding bands of soldiers and weakening the seigneur's hold over his tenants. By 1380 repeated calls for royal taxes had resulted in a concept of the village as a taxable territorial unit, and the king had ruled that village collectors should be chosen by the villagers themselves. The juridical status of the villages was never entirely clarified, but by the early modern period they were at least defined as tax-collection units, and in this sense the village clearly existed as an organization.

What was this community? In most cases it had no formal rules for admission. One possible definition would be that it included all resident landowners who were included on the tax rolls. However, that criterion fails to account for the resident poor or for servants living in the households of residents, who were usually accepted as belonging. People entered this community by birth or marriage. Excluded were those who came from somewhere else, such as itinerant beggars and migrant laborers. Great landlords who lived elsewhere and rented out their lands in the village were also considered outsiders even if they lived part of the year on an estate in the country. Thus the village community consisted essentially of those who lived and worked in it – those who had a place, who were known. It was perfectly clear to the villagers themselves who belonged and who did not, and the local sense of identity was very strong, as symbolized by the church tower and its bells, the patron saint, and the fervor expressed by the fierce contests between youth groups from neighboring communities. We will explore these cultural manifestations of community in Chapters 8 and 9.

There were many occasions when the village seemed to act with one voice. In 1768 in Dieme, after several meetings to consider the need for repairs to their church, the inhabitants divided themselves into four work teams each led by a captain, drew up lists of the work expected from each resident according to his abilities, and proceeded to tear down and rebuild part of the church, assisted by hired masons. "Everyone including the women and children worked at this zealously" and "there were no divisions, jealousies or disputes" as the whole community carried rocks and dug at the foundations. In 1649 when the royal tax collector arrived in the village of Saint-Just-la-Pendue to demand 2,352 livres of back taxes owed from 1647 from the local collector, Benoit de la Sommaye, the intruders were gradually surrounded by a growing crowd of angry residents led by the local priest and by Claude Rey, a prominent farmer, who growled, "By the death of the Lord you are all thieves, the *taille* has been paid." De la Sommaye, escorted by eight peasants carrying clubs, asserted that he had no money and that even if he had he would not hand it over; in fact "no one was paying in all of Forez or Beaujolais." When the authorities tried to arrest de la Sommaye, his wife cried out for help and the crowd chased the intruders out of the village, showering them with rocks as others rang the tocsin and people converged from all sides. Such incidents show the community joining together in a common purpose.[8]

At the same time the community was far from unified in any idyllic sense, for there were severe conflicts within it. Long-standing conflicts between families could turn into virtual vendettas, and quarrels over even small questions of property rights and inheritances could be fierce. The most obvious split was between the majority of inhabitants and the few rich peasants, notably the resident *fermier*. While he might belong to the community by birth and loyalty, he was also the man who lent his neighbors money, leased them his plow teams, hired them at harvest time, and foreclosed on their land. He was probably in league with the seigneur, passing along news about land transfers and village property relationships and handling the collection of unpopular dues and fees.

Every community had some sort of assembly of inhabitants which met a few times a year. There was also a *fabrique*, or parish committee, which met to deal with questions concerning the upkeep of the church and cemetery. If the parish and the village coincided, the two assemblies might be merged; if not, they might be rivals. The meetings were often held on Sunday after Mass, in the church itself or outside on its steps, in the cemetery, the public square, or the seigneur's court chamber. The general assembly was in a sense the village counterpart to the seigneur's court audiences. Although the lord might himself preside over the assembly, in some places elected syndics did so. The meeting was supposed to include all heads of household. Attendance usually fell far below this goal, except when there were decisions of critical importance. The leading landowners always dominated the discussion, and their names were listed separately in the minutes, whereas the rest of the village appeared only in a collective phrase such as "many other inhabitants." It is likely that the discussions were similarly restricted, though practice may have varied widely. This was one place where simple peasants may actually have had some voice.

These assemblies discussed matters such as the collection of taxes, assessments for local improvements, common rights, repairs to roads and ditches, maintenance of the church and provision of a presbytery to house the priest, and agricultural matters such as harvest dates, crop rotations, and problems with predators. They might hire a common shepherd or a forest guard. They also defended the community's interests against the seigneur, the local priest, the collector of the tithe, or neighboring communities. Syndics could be empowered to pursue a particular matter in the name of the collectivity, and it was not uncommon for rural communities to initiate lawsuits in defense of a wide variety of interests. When local schools became more common toward the end of the seventeenth century, it was the community's responsibility to hire the schoolmaster and to pay him. In all these matters we must imagine the few literate villagers, usually the curé, a few laborers, and possibly the seigneur, taking a leading role. There were few financial resources available, and communities invariably borrowed money or alienated their common lands when a major project was under way, leading to serious indebtedness, especially in time of war. In 1659 the king declared the communities to be legally minor in fiscal matters, meaning that they could not act on their own initiative. They were gradually placed under the tutelage of the royal intendant, whose approval was needed by the eighteenth century for even minor repairs.

But the intendant was far away and the villagers had to live with one another all the time. Their lives were built around a set of activities that were largely self-generated, in which they borrowed from, and built upon, a constantly evolving repertory of ways of dealing with one another and coping with the problems of life. Besides the cycle of the agricultural year, which engaged everyone directly in the critical enterprise of drawing value out of nature, they concerned themselves with family milestones like births, marriages, and deaths. They dealt with religious devotions of all sorts, trips to markets and fairs, raucous bouts of merrymaking, and somber moments of despair. Peasants were not chained to their village. There were annual cycles of migrant labor when men with certain skills would travel long distances to find work. Young men who joined the army disappeared for many years, returning crippled or changed to the point of not being recognized, as in the famous case of Martin Guerre.[9] Young women seeking work traveled to cities, where they joined neighbors and relatives who had already paved the way, to find employment as servants. There was also considerable migration of whole families from one region to another in search of better times.

Men, women, and families

Life in the village was organized around households. These took many forms. The normal pattern was a nuclear family consisting of parents and children. Often there were other persons living under the same roof, who might be servants, farmhands, grandparents, or a variety of cousins and other persons related by blood. There might also be several families living together, headed by two brothers, especially on remote farms needing more hands to maintain. These last arrangements, called *frérèches*, belonged mostly to an earlier era when the population was thinner.

We have already noted the tough demographic regime in which these people lived, with births barely exceeding deaths and population growth hindered by late marriage and by the early death of many women in childbirth.[10] High infant mortality meant that attitudes of parents toward children must have been somewhat ambivalent. Most historians no longer accept Philippe Ariès's claim that early modern parents did not recognize a distinct childhood phase of growth and showed little affection toward young children. On the contrary, there is plenty of evidence of grief at the loss of a little one. Still, parents' feelings toward living children must have been different when the odds of any particular child's survival to adulthood were fifty–fifty and everyone had personal experience with death. In addition, the frequent death of adults meant that remarriage was very common. One study from Anjou in the eighteenth century shows that of 181 widowers who remarried, 98 did so after less than eighteen months, and 26 did so after only six months. Other studies find half to three-fourths of widowers remarrying within a year of the wife's death.[11]

As a result of the high death rates and swift remarriages, mixed and broken families were very common. The lateness of marriage and the short average lifespan meant that households were less likely to include grandparents or older generations. On the other hand, children of different parents were likely to be thrown together with new steppar-ents, and orphaned children would often be sent to live with distant cousins. Under these conditions, families consisted of many mixtures of siblings, half-brothers and sisters, stepmothers or stepfathers, some-times all stemming from different marriages. Growing up under these conditions may not have provided the sense of security that comes with a permanent set of parents and grandparents, but it did mean that children grew up conscious of their inherited connections with other people in the community, and they learned early how to be sociable and make use of such contacts.

Peasants usually married within their own social milieu. Their betrothals took place at a relatively late age. In courtly circles, mar-riages of children at fifteen or even younger were sometimes arranged for high political purposes, but in the population at large men married on the average at twenty-eight or twenty-nine years old and women at twenty-five or twenty-six. A couple could not get married until they had the means to set up a separate household, and this took time, especially for the majority of poor people. Thus the couple's economic state was a prime factor in influencing the age at marriage. The bride and groom were usually neighbors. Studies show that among the peasantry 60 to 80 percent of couples found their mate in the same village, and most of the rest came from a village nearby. One reason for this was the church's rules of consanguinity which dictated that one could not marry one's cousins to the fourth degree, including godparents. When fol-lowed, these rules eliminated many of the local prospects and drove young men to neighboring communities in their search for brides.

Daughters were closely protected and courtship was difficult. Peasants expected the parents, and especially the father, to arrange the

Figure 5 A nocturnal *veillée* in the late seventeenth century portrayed by Jacques de Stella. In a rather prosperous-looking house (see the platters), the women are spinning and minding the children while the men drink (and smoke?). Note the petty game hanging from the roof.

marriages of their sons and daughters by negotiating legal documents that linked two families together advantageously. An older Catholic tradition recognized unions in which consenting adults simply exchanged vows with one another, but by the sixteenth century both church and crown were insisting that mutual consent was not enough. Publication of banns of marriage by a local priest were required to avoid elopements and ensure parental consent. However, authorities did recognize that it was desirable for the couple to be pleasing to one another, and marriage for affection was not unknown. Gradually, by the eighteenth century, affectionate relations between spouses and children became more acceptable.

Meanwhile young men continued to court and woo. They might catch a glimpse of eligible daughters at markets and festivals, or in church. The custom of neighborly gatherings in barns during cold winter nights also provided an occasion for boys and girls to look one another over. Women and girls would spin or sew, while the men told tales and the boys played games. In wintry Auvergne such gatherings could last all day:

Neighboring families assemble together spontaneously and choose for the purpose the biggest and warmest cowshed. In the morning after the soup, everyone hastens to join the group: they sit in a circle on benches, they chatter, they laugh, they complain about taxes and the tax collectors, they repeat the gossip that is circulating about the girls and young men, or they just sit and meditate. At five o'clock they part company to go and have their meal, then they return chatting for a while, and then each one returns to his own home to sleep.[12]

Rétif de la Bretonne describes the maneuvering of parents and youths over courting in the eighteenth-century countryside:

The boys look over the girl long before speaking to the parents, to see if she pleases them and they will please her. They lurk around her house, sometimes for months, before being able to speak to her. People from the region gossip, and the girl learns that a certain Pierrot or Jacquot is hanging around the house on account of her. One evening out of pure curiosity she invents a pretext to go out, such as having forgotten to close the chicken coop...The parents are not fooled. If they like the boy, they say nothing. If he does not please them, the mother or the father stands up, pushes the girl back into her chair and says, "Stay there, I'll go myself."[13]

Attitudes concerning the roles of men and women were firmly established. The authority of the father over wife and children was universally recognized. He was "king" of his household. The family owed him absolute obedience, and he even had the right to beat his wife, at least within acceptable community norms. "It is licit for the man to beat his wife, without bringing about death or dismemberment, when she refuses her husband anything," said the thirteenth-century customs of the Beauvaisis.[14] Surviving proverbs reveal chauvinist attitudes. "A woman who talks like a man and a hen that crows like a cock are not worth keeping." "Suffer not your wife for any reason, to put her foot on yours, for tomorrow the silly whore will want to put it on your head." "At all times dogs piss and women weep. Where woman is, silence is not."

The gendered division of labor was well established. Women were in charge of running the household and seeing to the animals in the immediate "courtyard." Men took care of the fields, the purchase of animals at markets, and commercial transactions signed in the cabaret. Men and women sat separately in church, were segregated at wedding banquets, and marched apart in processions. Men handled the money, but women were in charge of the linens, the pantry, the housecleaning materials. If the wife went outside the house at all, it was to feminine sites such as the well, the wash house, the ovens. An old Gascon proverb said it all, "Women in the house like the dogs, men in the street like the cats."[15]

On the other hand, peasant women worked to the point of exhaustion when there was plowing or harvesting to be done. As members of households that were often faced with scarcity, they were capable of joining in to help with almost any task. As a result, middle-class observers were still finding peasant women ugly and crude in the nineteenth century. In the Aveyron their condition "is arduous and wretched ... for them instead of being a time of happiness and freedom, marriage is often a harsher servitude." "Their parents treat them with a kind of barbarity and force them from the most tender age, to devote themselves entirely to heavy labour in the fields."[16] As we will see in Chapter 8, women were not at all subservient. They had the capacity to step in when the husband was away, and many of them knew it. They fought fiercely to defend the honor of husbands or children, and they often participated in riots.

Conclusion

Peasant life as we have observed it here gives the impression of long-standing continuity. The fields, the villages, the crops, the uncertainties were similar enough that a peasant from 1400 who was transported to his village in 1789 might have felt right at home. But beneath the similarities were subtle changes that were gradually transforming the rural landscape.

First was the change in the nature of the lords' control over the countryside from one based predominantly on coercive political power to one based on coercive legal and economic advantages. The lord's dues and powers of command were still important in 1789, but their impact was less. Put another way, the seigneurial system was on the way to becoming just a set of legal procedures.

Second was the shifting nature of the *prélèvement*, caused by the relative decline in seigneurial dues and the rapid rise of royal taxes.

The peasants were arguably just as burdened as before, but the necessity of paying their *tailles* in currency drew them into the marketplace to sell their produce, and their efforts now supported the king, the army, and the court more than the lifestyles of the peasants' immediate lords.

Third was the growing disparity in the ownership of rural property between a small elite of *coqs de village* and a growing mass of semi-landless owners of tiny plots. In many places the result was the consolidation of a few holdings and the fragmentation of the rest. At the same time, outsiders from nearby towns and cities were buying up rural properties and seigneurial rights. Meanwhile, the peasants saw their lands foreclosed by creditors, to the point where the majority of the rural population became renters rather than owners, and their holdings were reduced to many tiny farms. In the Île-de-France only a third of the population were owners in 1540, and this number declined to 21 percent in some places by the seventeenth century. In the Beauvaisis in 1717 the figure was 40 percent, and 20 percent near the towns. In the south it was similar. The peasantry survived en masse, but there were fewer prosperous owners and many more external landlords who were churchmen, professional people, and well-connected nobles, especially those from the growing ranks of royal officers. One result was that more and more of the village's production was carried off to the city. Another was the decline of the village community and its popular customs, although these did not disappear completely.

A fourth and final trend was the appearance of pockets of agricultural growth here and there in the French countryside. This subject is controversial and much debated by economic historians. Some argue that eighteenth-century France was not very different from eighteenth-century England, where an agricultural revolution of rising investment and increasing agrarian productivity was in full swing. We have noted the enterprising great farmers in the Paris region who developed larger-scale production for the Paris market. If we focus on such favored locations near major markets, and on places where land consolidation was advanced and progressive tenants were experimenting with scientific ways of increasing yields by modifying crop rotations, introducing new crops, and especially improving marketing and transporting techniques, it is possible to argue that productivity was rising. We will revisit these developments, which appeared mostly in the eighteenth century, in Chapter 12. But there were mighty impediments to this kind of development, including the disinterest of landlords, the lop-sided tax structure, the impoverishment of the majority of the peasantry, the persistence of feudal law and seigneurial arrangements, the fragmentation of landholding, and the devotion of traditionalists to archaic crop rotation and field patterns. If we concentrate on the typical situation in most places, and look at overall averages and persistent patterns, we will conclude that, unlike England, France was still immersed in a very traditional, age-old way of growing its food, and one which would not disappear before the middle of the nineteenth century.

Suggestions for further reading: *prélèvement* and village community

Peasants and *prélèvement*

Bloch, Marc, *French Rural History: An Essay on its Basic Characteristics*, trans. Janet Sondheimer (Berkeley, CA, 1966).

Dewald, Jonathan and Liana Vardi, "The Peasantries of France, 1400–1800, in Tom Scott, ed., *The Peasantries of Europe from the Fourteenth to the Eighteenth Centuries* (London, 1998).

Goubert, Pierre, *The French Peasantry in the Seventeenth Century*, trans. Ian Patterson (Cambridge, 1986).

Hoffman, Philip T., *Growth in a Traditional Society: The French Countryside, 1450–1815* (Princeton, NJ, 1996).

Hufton, Olwen, "The Seigneur and the Rural Community in 18th Century France: The Seigneurial Reaction, a Reappraisal," *Transactions of the Royal Historical Society*, 5th series 19 (1979), 21–39.

Le Roy Ladurie, Emmanuel, *The Peasants of Languedoc*, trans. John Day, (Urbana, IL, 1974).

The French Peasantry 1450–1660, trans. Alan Sheridan (Berkeley, 1986).

Le Goff, T. J. A., *Vannes and its Region: A Study of Town and Country in Eighteenth-Century France* (Oxford, 1981).

Moriceau, Jean-Marc, *Les Fermiers de l'Île-de-France: l'ascension d'un patronat agricole (XVe–XVIIIe siècle)*, rev. edn (Paris, 1994).

Gendered family relations

Collins, James, "The Economic Role of Women in Seventeenth-Century France," *French Historical Studies* 16 (1989), 436–70.

Flandrin, Jean-Louis, *Families in Former Times: Kinship, Household and Sexuality*, trans. Richard Southern (Cambridge, 1979).

Hufton, Olwen, "Women and the Family Economy in Eighteenth-Century France," *French Historical Studies* 9 (1975), 1–22.

Lebrun, François, *La Vie conjugale sous l'Ancien Régime* (Paris, 1975).

3 | Domination by the nobility

The French nobility had many of the characteristics of a ruling class. These included special access to the country's productive forces; political power in the provinces and at court; and a collective sense of superiority and mission that was conveyed to the rest of the population, sending a strong message to the effect that its rightful place was at the head of society. But other characteristics complicate the picture. France's 40,000 noble families possessed vastly different levels of wealth, ranging from the poorest rural farmers to the grandest princely figures, with the majority of nobles situated at the low end of the spectrum. The composition of the nobility also changed considerably between 1350 and 1750 and there was turnover within the ranks as ancient families were replaced by newcomers. In addition there was a considerable change in the nobles' cultural identity. The archetypical noble in 1350 was a chivalric knight primed for battle, whereas by 1750 his counterpart had become a cultivated, landlord–aristocrat. To add a final complication, the traditional nobility was transformed in the sixteenth and seventeenth centuries by the rise of a whole new category of nobles, the "robe nobility."

What then did nobility mean, and what was the nobles' role in society? We need to look at several different aspects of this question: the idea, or ideological justification, of noble superiority; the legal definition; and the place of the nobles in the larger society. In ideological terms, the concept of nobility was constructed out of various contradictory elements. Its foundation was a myth of hereditary superiority. Nobility was thought of as something that could be earned, but it was also considered a hereditary trait. Nobles were supposed to be courageous warriors who shed their blood defending a just cause to which they gave allegiance – the Catholic faith, their lord, society in general. They supposedly lived according to the moral precepts of their class, at all times defending their honor and that of those close to them. This noble ethic was a somewhat contradictory amalgam of ideas from military procedures, medieval chivalric romances, and (as time went on) the Renaissance ideal of the perfect courtier. Ideal nobility was something one traced as far back into the obscure darkness of the medieval past as possible. To be truly noble was to be connected to a family line that was associated with glorious deeds in the past. Nobility was taken to be a sort of inherent superiority that matured with time and proved itself repeatedly across the generations. It was not something instantly acquired by particular deeds or formal documents. Also important was the residual sense, inherited from the middle ages, that only nobles were truly "free," and commoners, like serfs, were unfree.

In material terms the nobles had privileged access to the wealth produced in the countryside. Their seigneuries provided them with food and cash along with coercive power over the peasant inhabitants of their villages. The idea of being noble was intimately associated with lordly "rule" over territory and subjects. As an echo of the declining feudal system, this landed foundation was also closely tied to the concept of military service. In the feudal past great lords had provided their followers (vassals) with estates (fiefs) in return for such service. This system left behind residual ties of obligation between lesser nobles and higher lords. The fiefs had gradually become hereditary, and the king had managed to make himself the lord of most of the great vassals. Over time the fiefs, as seigneuries, had become almost like hereditary private estates. But the fact remained that the nobles were able to go to war because they were supported by their landed revenues and by the services provided by their peasants.

The concept of nobility had developed gradually, since at least the twelfth century. It was a combination of several basic concepts: the phenomenon of a knight being dubbed on the battlefield because of his glorious deeds; the idea of a "gentleman," that is a man of honor, derived from chivalric and humanist sources; the idea of command over subordinates, either as a lord of feudal vassals or as a lord over peasant subjects; and the negative concept that nobles were unsullied by degrading manual labor, which in practice meant that a noble was expected to be able to live off the proceeds of other people's labor on his estates. To this can be added the related idea that only nobles were truly "free," that is, unencumbered by humiliating obligations. In France nobility was held in law to be hereditary. It passed through the father to all of his legitimate children. Younger sons could establish collateral lines, if they had the means to support a noble lifestyle.

At first the concept of nobility was a matter of custom, not law. You were noble if those around you considered you a noble, and it was possible to become noble by being dubbed a knight on the field of battle. Nobility could also be acquired by adopting the noble lifestyle (that is, by *prescription*). After accumulating a fortune, a commoner could buy a rural estate, retire there with family and servants, exercise all the prerogatives of a lord of the manor, and at some point start calling himself "écuyer" or "seigneur de" in notarial documents. He could establish a military reputation, marry his children to distinguished partners, and avoid any activity that would be considered degrading, such as engaging in retail trade. This lifestyle would have to continue for four generations or about a hundred years. Then legal nobility could be established by having witnesses swear that within living memory the family had always lived nobly.

This customary, peer-centered approach was gradually suppressed by the monarchy, as nobility became transformed into a legal category. In the reign of Saint Louis (1226–70), jurists had already begun to assert that only the king could create a noble. By the 1280s the king had begun ennobling certain of his loyal followers, and by 1312 his agents were prosecuting false claims of nobility.[1] These actions demonstrated that the king could instantly create nobles. He could judge the legitimacy of existing nobles and dictate the way nobility would be defined. As the centuries passed, the rules became more and more legalistic.

By the sixteenth century, entrance into the nobility was possible in several ways. One could slip in by prescription, as we have seen. This door was gradually closed by the crown between 1550 and 1667. There was also the path of ennoblement by letter from the king. One would petition the royal council for this status, and official papers would then be issued that had to be registered by the royal courts. Such documents supplied firm legal proof of nobility, but they had the unfortunate drawback of stating the date on which nobility had been acquired, which made it all too clear that the recipient was an *anoblis* and not a true *gentilhomme*. Such letters were issued in relatively small numbers, starting in the mid fourteenth century. There were about five to thirty per year, with peaks in times when military campaigns were afoot, notably between 1574 and 1588, 1593–99, and 1609–15.[2] The impact of royal letters on the size of the nobility was not great because many of the recipients who were being honored for service by the king were already noble; some of them had purchased letters anyway as insurance against lack of documentation. Certain posts in the king's household and the royal government were also considered ennobling, largely because of their proximity to the monarch, but once again they were mostly held by personages who were already noble. The other important avenue to nobility was purchase of royal office, a very important phenomenon of the sixteenth to eighteenth centuries, which will be discussed later.

Meanwhile, in response to the rising costs of the Hundred Years War, kings began negotiating with representative bodies of their subjects to obtain grants of extraordinary taxes. Summoned for consultation, the nobility, or at least its leaders, began to become conscious of its existence as a corporate body and to demand exemption from tax levies as a condition of consenting to the king taxing other groups. Their argument was that the nobility bore the brunt of service in the king's army, and those who did not fight should pay for their own defense. This momentous development meant that ultimately, in the 1440s, the king would be able to start taxing the peasantry without consent, largely because the nobles showed little interest in demanding further consultations once their own exemptions were assured. But now that being noble had become a legal way to escape royal taxes, it became all the more necessary for everyone, especially local tax collectors, to be clear about who was noble and who was not.

As a result, kings and their advisors became more interventionist. A process gradually developed in which the state increasingly monitored the nobility, partly in response to complaints by legitimate nobles against usurpers, but also as a money-raising device to force usurpers to pay the *taille* and to charge violators with fines. In 1461, for example, Louis XI ordered an investigation into usurpers of nobility in Normandy. Commissioners were sent to requisition family records; 1,024 noble families from Lower Normandy were approved, and 301 were rejected. These rejections violated a Norman custom which stated that commoners who had possessed a noble fief for forty years without challenge could claim noble status. The rejected parties protested and a compromise was reached, but in 1579 Charles IX nevertheless abolished this Norman practice of ennoblement through possession of a fief. Such intervention was becoming normal. The crown instigated investigations of the Norman nobility again in 1523, 1540, 1555, 1576, 1598, 1624, 1634, 1641, and 1655.[3] In 1667 Louis

XIV and Colbert proclaimed a kingdom-wide "reformation" of the nobility which tightened up the requirements for written documentation and fined a number of nobles who had allegedly slipped through illicitly.

Two examples can suggest the way families had been stealthily working their way into the nobility and the effects of the 1667 crackdown. First, the case of Pierre Piguerres, *écuyer*, seigneur de Loinville. In the first generation around 1500, his ancestor was a merchant–draper–stocking-maker in Chartres. The second generation continued that occupation but also purchased two fiefs. Around 1548 the third generation had produced a seigneurial officer and a royal prosecutor in the *prévôté* court of Chartres. These were minor legal positions that would have been unsuitable for a noble. In 1565 the fourth generation continued in the same situation. But the fifth, sixth and seventh generations (1571–1667) styled themselves "seigneurs de" la Bouteillerie and de Loinville. They arranged marriages with the authentic local nobility and no longer pursued any profession. They left no record of letters of ennoblement or military service. Nevertheless, the commissioner approved their nobility in 1667, rather indulgently, according to historian Jean-Marie Constant.[4]

Second, the case of Jean Petit-Coeur, sieur de Saint-Vast. His grandfather was Pierre Petit-Coeur, a physician who was listed as a non-noble in the survey of 1576. However this man adopted the title of *écuyer* for himself. His son Pierre acquired a post of *élu*, which was a royal financial office, in the *élection* of Bayeux and similarly called himself an *écuyer*. His son was Jean, now the third generation, who was called before the commission of 1667. Jean, who must have been a very old man, had fought at the siege of Bordeaux in 1616 and served as lieutenant of light cavalry in 1630; his sons were all serving in the army. The commission conceded that the family had been living nobly since 1576 and had even held an office, but their final ruling was that they had clearly usurped the title of *écuyer* because they had never proved the origin of it or received letters of ennoblement.[5]

Thus, by the end of the middle ages, the idea was well established that nobles were persons of superior status who had the right to enjoy special privileges fixed in law. To be sure, nobles were not the only group to have privileges. The clergy had a parallel set, as did anyone who resided in a privileged town, belonged to a corporate body like a guild, or lived in a favored province. But the nobles' privileges were distinctive in that they were hereditary and they were attributed to whole families by the simple fact of being noble, without anyone having to take any action or join any organization.

Those legally designated as noble enjoyed specific rights before the law. The first was *partage noble*. Special clauses in customary law codes established distinct rules for noble inheritance which generally were designed to favor the eldest son and keep intact a central core of the patrimony to transmit to the next generation. These rules varied from place to place, but they generally treated nobles differently from commoners.

Tax exemptions were second. Nobles were not exonerated from all taxes, but they were explicitly exempted from the basic land tax, the *fouage* or *taille*, and the produce of their estates was exempted from duties levied on goods entering cities. Nobles claimed, and sometimes obtained, exemption from urban hearth taxes and income taxes tied to urban residence and from urban responsibilities like militia duty. They were exempted from *corvées* (labor services) and troop lodgings. On the other hand, they were expected to serve in the royal army when called to the muster (*ban et arrière ban*), and much of the cost of equipment and training fell on their shoulders. In the late seventeenth and eighteenth centuries, new income taxes such as the *capitation*, the *dixième*, and the *vingtième* included the nobility, but nobles still were treated differently from commoners. Nobles also had the privilege of owning noble estates (seigneuries) without paying the *franc-fief*, a tax on commoners who acquired noble estates.

Nobles received special treatment from the judicial system. Their cases went automatically to certain higher judges, and they were not subject to execution by hanging. The alternative punishment, decapitation, was considered more dignified. As one of the three estates of the realm, the nobility had the right to be represented in meetings of provincial or national Estates, and where there were lower assemblies, they also played a prominent role in them. They had honorific privileges such as the right to have family coats of arms, to be treated differently in sumptuary laws (mainly to wear finer clothing), to march in designated spots in processions, and to sit in designated seats in churches and at official gatherings. Certain offices in the royal household, command posts in the royal army, cathedral chapters and religious sodalities, were restricted to nobles. Local customs differed in detail, but the exclusive right of nobles to hunt wild game using dogs and falcons was generally recognized.

Thus the early modern concept of nobility was a mixture of realities and illusions, incorporating three underlying characteristics. First and foremost was lordship over seigneurial estates, which implied a rural lifestyle, the exercise of public authority over other people, and the idea of living without engaging in degrading labor. Second was the connection to military activity, usually in service to an overlord. Military skill, with all that it implied about courage, strength, and loyalty, was a reserve source of status and respect. A third characteristic was the connection between the nobility and the crown. Part of the noble ethic was military service to a lord, and that lord was increasingly the king himself. Kings needed the nobles because of their influence in the countryside and their military aid. In turn, the nobles needed the king as a source of prestige and glory, service, and advancement.

The nobility in society

What was the overall impact of the nobility on French society? Philippe Contamine estimates that, around 1300, the kingdom had twenty million people, including 70,000 noble households. This would constitute 1.75 percent of the population at five persons per household. Other measures of the size of the nobility produce figures from 1 percent to 3.4 percent at various times and places. The exact percentage is not important. What we should note is that although the nobles made up only 1 or 2 percent of the population, they were numerous enough to be a presence in most peasant villages.

We can get some idea of their impact by looking at the county of Champagne around 1250 when feudal relations were still at their height. In twenty-three local districts (*châtellenies*) the comte de Champagne had 1,182 direct vassals, in other words noble followers, of whom 205 were women. Below these vassals were 1,519 subvassals, 304 of them women; most of the rest are unidentified. Contamine estimates that, for the whole province (thirty-seven *châtellenies*), the count might have been able to call on 1,700 or 1,800 "knights" or "sirs," that is, actual male vassals in a condition to serve. In this territory, the size of Massachusetts, there were thus some 3,000 holders of fiefs, probably one or two per village, although only half of them were

Table 3.1 *Levels of wealth of the eighteenth-century French nobility*

Level of wealth	Annual income (livres)	No. of families	Percentage of families		
1. Court nobility, princes, financiers	50,000 or more	200	0.75%	}	*Fantastically rich 13.85%*
2. Rich provincial nobility, parlementaires	10,000–50,000	3,500	13.1%		
3. Comfortable country life	4,000–10,000	7,000	26.2%	}	*Modest to prosperous 67.4%*
4. Modest, decent, frugal	1,000–4,000	11,000	41.2%	}	*Poor 59.9%*
5. Barely decent to desperately poor	below 1,000	5,000	18.7%		

Based on Guy Chaussinand-Nogaret, *The French Nobility in the Eighteenth Century: From Feudalism to Enlightenment*, trans. William Doyle (Cambridge, 1985), 52–3.

potential soldiers. These 2,701 seigneuries were widely distributed. Out of the 1,182 vassals, 80.9 percent had just one fief; 15.5 percent held two, and only 3.6 percent held three fiefs or more. Thus Champagne was populated by a swarm of local knights and squires. Most of them lived very modestly. Although the powerful comte de Champagne had an annual revenue of 27,000 livres tournois, an average knight received 36 livres and a squire received 22.[6]

This pattern of noble implantation did not change much in later centuries, despite fluctuations in the general population. In Brittany in 1710, Jean Meyer estimates that 9 percent of the nobility were very rich, 31 percent were well-off, 14 percent had middling fortunes, and 54 percent were poor, 38 percent of them *very poor*. Chaussinand-Nogaret's estimates for the whole French nobility in the eighteenth century suggest a similar pattern (see Table 3.1). The fantastically rich aristocrats in the top two categories are the people we normally encounter in history books – at most 14 percent of the noble popu-lation. The next category (26.2 percent) represents the well-off nobles in the provinces. If it is combined with the fourth category, making jointly 67.4 percent, it suggests how many modest to prosperous noble families lived on their estates in the country. But if we combine the fourth and fifth categories, making 59.9 percent, we get a group comparable to the "poor" in other studies. The lowest echelons, some 19 percent of all noble families, were desperately poor, some to the point of begging.

These dramatic figures tell us that the nobles were a minuscule percentage of the population. The vast majority of nobles – some 40 to 60 percent – were local notables of modest means whose importance was limited to their own villages. Many of them were not seigneurs in the sense of having seigneurial courts. We cannot establish a clear picture without remembering these legions of petty landowners who perpetuated the ethic of privileged difference outside aristocratic circles and who personified "the noble" in many communities. Nor can we appreciate the position of the nobility without noting the extreme disparity of wealth and lifestyle that separated the upper crust from these run-of-the-mill country seigneurs.

An important question is the degree to which the nobility was transformed by the influx of new blood in the early modern period. On the one hand, we now know enough to reject the old stereotype of the nobles as spendthrift consumers of luxuries who squandered their fortunes and therefore dropped out of the nobility. On the contrary, most nobles were careful managers of their inheritances. On the other hand, we also know that over time circumstances did cause some noble families to disappear and that their places were taken by a steady stream of new recruits. The French nobility was relatively open and, though it took time and patience, families were always making their way into it.

These two conclusions are actually complementary. They suggest a complete revision of the old idea of the decline of the old warrior nobility and its replacement by a new bourgeoisie. What we now see is a powerful class renewing and perpetuating itself in keeping with changing times, and in conjunction with a collaborative monarch. Many old families continued; others were replaced by newcomers who brought new resources to old roles.

Louis XIV's investigation of noble titles in 1667 is a good vantage-point from which to explore this question because of the extensive documentation it provided. Exploiting it for his study of the Beauce region south of Paris and around Chartres, Jean-Marie Constant

Table 3.2 *Origins of noble families in the Beauce in 1667*

Certified duration of family's nobility	Number of families	Number of fiefs held	Seigneurial courts held
Gentilshommes back to the 11th century	4 (1.5%)	4 (1%)	2%
Gentilshommes back to 12th–13th Century	7 (3%)	27 (6%)	10%
Gentilshommes back to 1300–1560	76 (29%)	151 (35%)	29%
Anoblis (1560–1660)	42 (16%)	69 (16%)	11%
Nobles from elsewhere	45 (17%)	89 (21%)	39%
Roturiers	77 (29%)	84 (19%)	3%
Unknown	8 (3%)	9 (2%)	
Totals	259 families	433 fiefs	87 justices

Source: Jean-Marie Constant, "L'Enquête de noblesse de 1667 et les seigneurs de Beauce," *Revue d'histoire moderne et contemporaine* 21 (1974), 548–66.

found that in 1667 only 4.5 percent of the 259 families who were lords over 433 fiefs could trace their nobility back to before 1300 (see Table 3.2). Another 29 percent went back to the period 1300 to 1560, and 16 percent were newcomers (*anoblis*) dating from 1560 to 1660. An additional 17 percent were old nobles who had moved in from another region, and another 29 percent of the fief holders were not noble at all (*roturiers*). Thus a respectable core of old nobles, or "gentilshommes," survived, but greatly augmented by newcomers.

In the sixteenth century, 71 percent of the nobles were considered "new," that is, ennobled within the last hundred years. Clearly there had been a major turnover during the crisis of the fourteenth century. These sixteenth-century arrivals had mostly entered by prescription. But after 1560 that route became increasingly difficult, and letters of nobility or purchase of office became the norm – yet another sign of the authority of the state. Like Wood, Jean-Marie Constant found that military service was rare and, curiously, many old families had waited until the third to sixth generation of nobility before sending anyone to war. The "gentlemen" (that is, older families) were holding their own nicely. Although they represented 33.5 percent of the families, they owned 41 percent of the fiefs and 41 percent of the seigneurial justices.[7]

Other provinces yield similar results. In the *élection* of Bayeux in Normandy, James Wood finds that, between 1463 and 1666, the number of noble families increased from 211 to 592 and that, of the 381 new arrivals, 57 percent were old nobles who had moved in from somewhere else and 35 percent were new nobles: these newcomers were not statistically richer, more urban, or more prone to bankruptcy than the old-timers. In other words, they were not some dynamic bourgeoisie. They came predominantly from royal offices of finance or justice (two-thirds), and the learned professions (16.9 percent). In each generation only about 20 percent of all these nobles pursued real military careers, a third participated in one or two campaigns, and more than half never went to war at all. This picture may have changed after 1660. Guy Rowlands believes that as many as half of all eligible male members of the nobility were enlisted in Louis XIV's later wars in the 1690s.[8]

These figures and others[9] reveal that the majority of nobles had very modest means; that many of them never went to war; that most nobles were relative newcomers without ancient pedigrees; and that most nobles were solvent, effective managers of their property. What then caused the decline of those families that did disappear? Genetically, some inevitably failed to produce the requisite male heirs, although this problem can be exaggerated. Others fell on hard times, especially during the crisis of the fourteenth century when population decline, roving bands of soldiers, and deaths in battle took their toll. We saw in Chapter 1 that seigneurial revenues suffered a severe decline during that period, but we also saw that enterprising lords rapidly reconstructed their inheritances. Success required a long-term strategy for the perpetuation of the lineage, and a lot of cooperation. Families got ahead by taking advantage of their alliances with other families, by pursuing successful marriage strategies which established alliances and collected dowries, and by sensible handling of inheritances. All of these strategies had to be coordinated, and timing had to be right. Assets were accumulated over time by means of marriage contracts for sons and by the acquisition of royal posts, pensions, and favors which would lead to further revenues or more prestige. Assets were dissipated by marrying off daughters or giving support to younger sons, by distributing the family wealth too widely in wills and testaments, by overextending the purchase of seigneurial estates, offices, and titles, or by borrowing excessively for any of these things. They were also dissipated by engaging in military operations, although this commitment was very desirable from the point of view of establishing a noble reputation. Equipping for war cost big money, and actually engaging in it cost even more. Not only was there the danger of having to support one's efforts out-of-pocket, but there was always the possibility of death or injury, which would be an asset to the family's noble reputation but a liability in terms of financial gain. It is no wonder that some failed at this game, while others advanced.

Levels and lifestyles

We must try to imagine these nobles in their social environment. At the low end of the spectrum were the petty gentry of limited resources, the most numerous group. Above them were the families with some regional prominence, sometimes called the "secondary nobility." At the summit were the great families of "grandees" or "aristocrats" whose members spent much of their time at court and enjoyed extensive property and influence in more than one province. We will explore the environment of these nobles, starting at the bottom. The most accessible evidence can be found in records of their possessions, houses, and relationships.

The local nobility

The simple country gentlemen had limited resources. Some were very poor, but many were reasonably prosperous, at least at the level of the richest peasants in the village. Our country squire would be a rustic figure, living on a farm and engaging in agricultural pursuits just like his peasant counterparts. His "manor house" would simply be one of the larger farmhouses in the village, but it would stand out because of its rooms on two floors, and possibly because of the visible remnants of ancient fortifications. The property would consist of a complex of connected buildings looking very much like a barnyard: the main dwelling would be a rectangular structure standing at one end of a large square courtyard flanked by stables, sheds for animals, storage for grain, and a dovecote. The entire complex would be surrounded by a wall with a large entrance gate opposite the main residence. On the ground floor of the residence would be a large hall, a kitchen with a massive fireplace, and a pantry. Upstairs would be a master bedroom, several other sleeping rooms, and a storage place for grain. Furnishings would be spartan, but there would be a few luxury items that would not be found in a peasant dwelling, possibly some silver dishes, a portrait of a family member, a tapestry, or some well-crafted pieces of furniture.

A useful example is Gilles de Gouberville, a rustic nobleman from Normandy who is well known to historians because he kept a detailed daily record of his activities between 1549 and 1562.[10] Gouberville was comfortably well-off and probably the most important man in a small rural community. He spent his life managing the estates he had inherited from his father. Gouberville never married, but he fathered three illegitimate daughters. He lived in the sort of house described above, along with a household of about twelve people, among them his half-brother and half-sister Symmonet and Guillemette, who were his father's illegitimate offspring; Cantepye, a loyal servant–agent who eventually married Guillemette; Arnoul, Symmonet's half-brother (by their mother), who kept the accounts; Lajoye, Gouberville's male servant; and three female servants. He was thus surrounded by an inner circle of relatives and servants, all of inferior status, who enhanced his importance by their presence and provided companionship, even as they hurried to carry out his wishes. Outside this inner circle was a group of some twenty villagers who were regularly seen performing agricultural tasks, and various craftsmen who were called in for specialized repair work, all of whom Gouberville knew by name. At peak moments in the agricultural cycle as many as a hundred peasants from nearby villagers were assembled to help in the fields. Some of these men were paid a real wage for doing the heaviest tasks, but when it was haymaking and harvest time (activities in which women played a prominent role), there was no pay, just a free dinner and dancing late into the night. It appears likely that some of this was *corvée* labor owed to the lord.

Gouberville spent much of his time supervising the work around the farm, directing the making of hay, the harvesting of grain, the cutting-down of trees, the reconstruction of his mill. But while he took an interest in these activities down to the last detail, he never personally engaged in any manual labor. What is striking is his intense sociability. Gouberville was never alone, and he had no real privacy. He was constantly surrounded by people below him in status, whom he treated in a friendly manner without ever forgetting that he was their

Figure 6 The baron de Saint-Vidal, as sketched by Jean Burel in his
journal. Burel (ca. 1540–1603), was a modest tanner from Le Puy. His journal
recorded local events, embellished with sketches of things he had seen.
We will encounter him again later. Saint-Vidal is a rustic noble, perhaps
comparable to Gilles de Gouberville. Burel has portrayed him respectfully, on
horseback, with full name and coat of arms.

superior. Associates who arrived at the manor at the first light of day
did not hesitate to barge into his upstairs bedroom to salute him and
present their business while he was still in bed. Gouberville also
socialized on a more equal basis with local figures of similar status,
such as priests, judicial agents, and family members, engaging in after-
dinner conversations that lasted well into the night. Lost travelers who
turned up at his door were invariably invited to stay for dinner, and

often to spend the night, in an expression of traditional hospitality. In 1559 Gouberville had overnight guests on twenty-nine different occasions. The curé of Tourlaville, where Gouberville owned a fief, stayed over sixty times between 1556 and 1558.

Another striking feature is the narrowness of Gouberville's experience. Although a "sword" noble, he never went to war. He spent his life shielded within his circle of familiar servants and acquaintances. His one passion was a fruit orchard, which he designed and planted himself, and where he delighted in grafting branches onto experimental fruit trees. Gouberville was also an extensive traveler, but only within a 10-mile radius of his residence. In the decade covered by his memoirs, he made 352 round trips to nearby Valogne and Cherbourg and sent his servants on 797 other similar trips to visit relatives, pursue law cases, buy provisions, or carry out Gouberville's duties as *lieutenant des eaux et forêts*. Madeleine Foisil has calculated that they jointly traveled almost 16,000 miles over a period of 5,200 hours. Gouberville never traveled alone, since being accompanied was one of the nobility's chief conceits. He went on horseback, while a lackey walked beside him and sometimes another servant on foot carried valises filled with provisions. Gouberville ventured as far as Rouen three times, but to the best of our knowledge he never got to Paris.

The one time he reached out beyond his customary milieu, his efforts were in vain. In 1556 he took a two-month-long trip to Blois to see the king about obtaining an office. He was received at the royal court, where he saw Henry II, Catherine de' Medici, the young princes, and Mary Stuart. He attended Mass with the king, saw a play, and went to a supper and a ball. But, judging from his brief notations, none of these experiences made much impression on him. The one aspect of the trip that moved him was meeting up with "Little Jehan," who worked in the royal kitchens, the brother-in-law of a blacksmith who occasionally shoed Gouberville's horses near Bayeux. So Gouberville spent his happiest moments in the king's kitchen conversing with this compatriot, and when he left Blois, Little Jehan was the only person to whom he said goodbye. He never obtained the office that was the purpose of his journey.

Gouberville seems to be a congenial character because of his simplicity. But consider how he might have looked to the people from his community. Here was a man who supported bastards in his household and produced three of his own, no doubt to the shame of unknown local families. He was a seigneurial lord who owned the mill and dominated the local labor market, who was pleasant to everyone so long as they did what he wished, who paid low wages or none at all, and who saw the world as revolving around himself. He always served meat at his table when other people went hungry, and he had the leisure to experiment with fruit trees. His authority was paternalistic. Like patrons in other times and places, he was no doubt appreciated at some times and denounced at others.

There were nobles like Gouberville all over France. A comparable example was Aimé Du Claux, seigneur of L'étoile in the Brionnais, near Lyon. A major local figure and an important owner of land, he spent his time like Gouberville tending to his own affairs. At the time of his death in 1677, his "chateau" was a small building with a principal room, a kitchen and a chapel on the ground floor, over a cellar. On the upper floor were the seigneur's bedroom, two other furnished rooms, a wardrobe, and a tiny room above the chapel. The only place in the house to display any luxury was the master bedroom, which contained several pieces of tapestry, two plain mirrors, a bed and some *argenterie*. It accounted for half of the meager 725 livres listed as the value of the entire contents of the chateau.[11]

Another example of middling nobility can be found in the lesser nobles described in Jonathan Dewald's study of the barony of Pont-Saint-Pierre, in Normandy, some hundred years after Gouberville. In the late seventeenth century this barony, which consisted of two communities under the lordship of the baron de Pont-Saint-Pierre, contained four lesser noble families, the Landaults, the Rassents, the Cottons, and the Bigots.[12] All four had originated in the milieu of royal judicial officers in Rouen, but by the late sixteenth century each family had established its nobility and was pursuing life in the country. These nobles lived the traditional life and produced men who served with distinction in the royal army. They were moderately prosperous, with incomes of around 2,000 livres. Each had only one servant.[13]

Like Gouberville, these families had a close relationship with their tenants, consisting of a mixture of violence and paternalism. In 1685 two Bigot brothers and their servant beat up a sharecropper who accused them of stealing his share of the harvest. The same accusation about the crop was repeated in 1715 and 1717. There were also instances of close ties between local nobles and their peasant neighbors. In the mid eighteenth century one noble family, the Rassents, made a habit of asking servants from their household to serve as godparents to their children, and some were known to witness and attend the weddings and baptisms of their tenants. Unlike Gouberville, who was largely independent of feudal ties, these families had a relationship with a higher lord who was close at hand, the baron de Pont-Saint-Pierre. In the shadow of the barony, they enjoyed very little seigneurial power of their own, but they made up for the lack of it by becoming clients of the baron and obtaining posts as forest judges, legal agents, and officers in his household, positions which gave them the power to enforce seigneurial rights on his behalf.

The "secondary" nobles of regional distinction

The Roncherolles family, which held the barony of Pont-Saint-Pierre from 1400 until 1765, provides a good example of the "secondary nobility." These regionally important nobles differed in several ways from the local nobles we have been observing. The Roncherolles were among the top ten noble families of Normandy in terms of wealth and influence, and over the centuries their influence grew as they expanded their land holdings and established collateral branches of the family. They also had a broader perspective on politics. Through the centuries they made themselves known to the crown and played a vigorous role in royal military operations. In return, family members were given army commissions, which included the capacity to sign up other nobles, and they received royal offices which conveyed a certain regional power of command, serving as seneschal of Ponthieu, military governor of the frontier town of Landrecies and military governor of Abbeville. They received pensions from the king and honorific positions at court, until ultimately they became dependent on royal munificence for a considerable portion of their income. The earlier generations of Roncherolles arranged good marriages to prominent regional families; in the seventeenth and eighteenth centuries they began making connections with ministerial and robe families in Paris. The family ultimately moved to the capital and abandoned their Norman homestead.

The residences of these regional noble families were thus a mixture of old medieval fortifications, pseudo-military elements like turrets and ramparts, and late Gothic flamboyant or Renaissance decorative elements. For example, the Roncherolles lived in an ancestral chateau that had been built some time after 1377 next to the ruins of an older castle. It had a moat, a drawbridge, and imposing towers. Unlike the more modest home of a country gentleman, this chateau was surrounded by an enclosed park. The chateau of La Rochejacquelein in Poitou was rebuilt by Louis du Vergier, a loyal friend of Henry IV, at the end of the sixteenth century. The entrance led to a vestibule onto which the other rooms opened. An imposing staircase led to the second story, where the master bedroom contained a great bedstead, a grand oak sideboard with four doors and two drawers, a trunk to hold clothing, a chest for linen, and two old suits of armor as a reminder of the ancestors. Du Vergier had a library of sixty books. His wardrobe included several complete outfits made of silk, eighteen shirts, nine pairs of tights, socks, stockings, twenty handkerchiefs made of Dutch linen, two white saddles and a third saddle covered with green velvet and decorated in gold. We are a long way here from Gouberville's kitchen.[14]

Kristen Neuschel offers insights into the social world of these regional nobles using evidence from the households of three important families in Picardy.[15] Like Gouberville, but on a higher plane, these nobles moved in a world of intense sociability. Their households, consisting of around thirty servants, pages, clients, and hangers-on, imitated on a lesser scale the establishment of the king and the magnates. Official, paid household members might include five to eight nobles in residence, several secretaries, and a battery of skilled and unskilled workers such as almoner, cook, baker, tailor, furrier, head groomsman, stable hands, coachmen, valets and lackeys. Then there were wives, young pages placed in the household by other families, young women serving as ladies-in-waiting, and various menial assistants. There were also local artisans who lived at the chateau temporarily while they were performing specialized tasks.

These families of regional importance might own chateaux on several of their estates and possibly a town house in the city. They spent much of their time on the road, traveling from one chateau to another, visiting the chateaux of their friends, being visited in return, or on military campaigns. Even in transit, the lord and lady took part of their retinue with them and entertained guests. When they were at home, pages came and went to deliver messages; noble men or women left on side trips that lasted a day or two to acquire horses or hunting birds; clerks went off to see to the management of outlying properties. The staff of a chateau thus had to be prepared to accommodate a fluctuating population that shifted dramatically in size from day to day.

Castle life was still very public in the sixteenth century. Even in "modern" wings, most rooms were arranged without connecting passages, so that you had to walk through intervening rooms to get from one place to another. In these larger chateaux, there were usually ten to fifteen rooms, including a great hall that might also be used for dining, equipped with benches and large tables, and a master bedroom. In addition there were antechambers, guard rooms, pantries, and cellars. Most rooms were multipurpose. There were extra beds and cots tucked everywhere so that servants and overflow guests could sleep in places such as the kitchen, the guard tower, or the granary. There were also trunks which were used to store clothes, weapons, or papers, and which could be taken along on voyages or used to sit on. Squires and ladies-in-waiting often slept in the room with their master or mistress, sometimes in the same bed. Most of the furnishings had to be portable because they would regularly be packed up and moved, along with the people.

Along with sociability, food was an important indicator of status. Feeding up to one hundred people was no small task. Without refrigeration much of the food had to be obtained on a day-to-day basis. Servants were constantly acquiring wine, bread, cheese, meat, and vegetables, either at markets or from the estate's own supplies. Secretaries recorded every expenditure, including the success or failure of hunting parties. Enjoying this "free room and board" was a privilege attached to being a member of the household, and sometimes lists had to be drawn up to determine exactly who had that right and who did not. Meals were ceremonial events presided over by the lord. On fancy occasions there would be displays on a sideboard of the lord's best dishes: platters of Italian ceramics, serving bowls, candelabra, salt cellars, and goblets. When there were distinguished guests, delicacies like nuts, fruits, and pastries would be added. There was usually one large dining table at which the lord and his principal guests sat. Then there would be subordinate tables for other categories of lodgers, and trestle tables could be set up in other rooms to handle the overflow. As if to underline social differences further, three grades of wine were served, one for commoners, one for gentlemen, and one "pour Monsieur." The master and mistress of the house drank from silver goblets, while everyone else used wooden or pewter mugs.

Living in this environment was an experience that created lasting bonds between those involved. The noble men and women who accompanied the lord guarded his money, distributed alms, paid for rooms at the inn when traveling, maintained clothing and weapons, and supervised artisans. There was also a large amount of time spent in diversions such as the hunting of game, falconing, and riding through the countryside. These experiences tied lesser nobles to greater ones on a personal basis, heightening the sense of hierarchy among the participants.

These regional or "secondary" noble families played a direct role in political relations that eluded the Goubervilles of the local nobility. Their services were useful to the king because they intimately knew their region, both the physical terrain for military purposes and the social terrain for mobilizing support. The king was useful to them because he could supply army commissions and positions that conferred greater local prestige on them. A good example is provided by Laurent Bourquin.[16] In the mid sixteenth century, Champagne was dominated by the Guise family. If a magnate such as the duc de Guise cooperated with the crown, that was fine. But during the religious wars when the Guises headed the militant Catholic opposition, the king needed other support. In 1580 he turned to Joachim de Dinteville, who was named lieutenant-general of the province while Guise was governor. Dinteville came from an old family that had made its fortune by serving the dukes of Burgundy. After the death of Philip the Bold in 1477, the family transferred its allegiance to France, built up its land holdings in Champagne, and established a virtually hereditary hold on the position of *bailli* of Troyes. Dinteville was a man who knew the court and the larger political scene and maintained close ties with ten or twelve similarly influential families of Champagne, all connected by marriage. For the king he could serve as a conduit to the second-level nobles of the region and thereby circumvent the power of the Guises. This pattern was also followed in other provinces. A great magnate who had many followers among the local nobility would be counteracted by an alternative block of middle-rank provincial nobles with deep roots in the province.

The magnates

The greatest nobles, whom we can call princes, magnates, or grandees, were in a category all their own. They were major players on the political horizon. They dominated whole provinces and maintained international connections. In the best of times they attended the king and lent glamour to his court. In troubled times they withdrew to their lands and led rebellions against the crown. The rise of the monarchical state in France was largely the story of the king's efforts to disarm and co-opt these major figures.

In the middle ages feudal magnates had ruled their territories like sovereigns, raising armies, taxing subjects, minting coins, dispensing justice. They acknowledged the king of France as their overlord, but his claims on them were weak and difficult to enforce. Gradually, over many centuries, the Capetian kings increased their control of the magnates using strategies involving conquest, marriage, and diplomacy. By the end of the Hundred Years War, most of the kingdom had been drawn at least nominally into the king's direct jurisdiction. By the mid sixteenth century the remaining holdouts – Provence, Burgundy, and Brittany – were also incorporated into the realm. But once the feudal rulers were out of the way, the king still had to deal with great nobles who were only somewhat less powerful. Eminent families had extensive properties and numerous followers concentrated in key regions, and their influence could not be ignored. Kings dealt with such powerful subjects by employing them as military commanders and governors of provinces and by getting them to participate in the royal court and the life of the royal family.

In fact, the old aristocracy was gradually being drawn into the orbit of the king by the creation of special dignities which only the king could bestow. The process had begun in the middle ages. By 1216 the concept of "peers of France" had appeared. The peers were men of especially high status who advised the king in his council. There were originally twelve of them, six ecclesiastical peers (the prelates of Reims, Laon, Langres, Beauvais, Chalons, and Noyon), and six lay peers, the dukes of Burgundy, Normandy, and Guyenne, and the counts of Toulouse, Flanders, and Champagne. This concept of hereditary peerage was as much an acknowledgment of preexistent power as it was an honor bestowed by the king. These were men too powerful for the king *not* to consult them. As the original families disappeared, additional peers were named by the crown. By 1505 there were twenty-four lay peers. In 1588 there were forty: twenty-one duke-peers, three count-peers, and sixteen plain dukes. Every peerage was attached to an estate bearing its name. Usually the title was taken from the recipient's principal estate-residence, but sometimes a group of lands assembled by the recipient was explicitly raised to the status of a duchy by the king on the occasion of a noble's promotion to ducal status.

The old medieval system was considerably modified in the sixteenth and seventeenth centuries. Jean-Pierre Labatut finds that, between 1589 and 1723, the number of newly created titles greatly increased, especially during times of governmental insecurity in the period before 1660. These honors were not given out lightly. In order to be named, one needed to belong to an ancient and praiseworthy lineage, to have a hereditary tradition of service and loyalty to the crown, and to have accomplished glorious deeds, usually of a military nature. It was also necessary to own estates vast enough to be worthy of the title which, for contemporaries, meant seigneuries conferring traditional powers of command with revenues substantial enough to maintain the status of a peer. Wealth was thus a necessary condition, but it was not sufficient. Family history and personal achievement were also factors, and there was an element of political maneuvering. The most successful candidates were those who caught the eye of the king early on in their lives and managed to survive the storms of intrigue at court, in addition to making a name for themselves. A few were recognized for administrative achievements such as Cardinal Richelieu, but the usual price of admission was military glory. In addition, a few women were selected, mostly because they were favorites of the king or the queen who had served loyally as governesses, mistresses, or ladies-in-waiting.

Once conferred, the title of duke or duke-peer was hereditary by direct male succession. Thus the monarchy was in effect creating a new aristocracy linked to landed estates but not directly derived from domination over the land. This was a select company. Between 1589 and 1723 Labatut counted 396 persons who held the title of duke or peer. This aristocracy consisted of 62 "Capetian princes" (members of the royal family), 67 foreign princes (nobles with princely status outside France, such as the prince of Monaco), 43 ecclesiastics, and 224 mere "gentlemen." This last group represented a significant change. The peerage was no longer limited to princes of the blood and a few foreign dignitaries, because now there was a prestigious mechanism for involving the most important noble families in the life of the court and enveloping them in the king's regulations.

The prerogatives of the dukes and peers were carefully defined. At major ceremonies they marched immediately after the king and his family, in order of seniority of their titles. They were addressed in notarial documents as "very high and powerful lord milord." They played a special role in *lit de justice* ceremonies in the Parlement of Paris, and they could attend the royal council (but, said Louis XIV in 1667, only when invited by the king). Compared to the rest of the nobility, they were extremely wealthy, but they enjoyed a wide range of incomes, running from 300,000 to 500,000 livres on the low end, to highs reaching 3,600,000.[17] These fortunes consisted predominantly of land. For 16 percent of the dukes and peers it was all land, and for another 48 percent mostly land. They all had at least half of their wealth in land. Other resources included cash, loans to the king or to private parties, and ownership of offices.

We can appreciate the shifting weight of the influence of the greatest families of the realm by examining one dynasty's sources of power in each of the three centuries. In the sixteenth century the best example was the Guise family, known for seriously threatening the monarchy itself during the religious wars. Claude, the first duc de Guise, was given the title in 1527 by King Francis I as a reward for his family's military prowess and his loyalty during the captivity of the king in Spain. He made a strategic marriage with Antoinette de Bourbon, daughter of the duc de Bourbon-Vendôme, from the junior line of the Capetian royal family. This stunning alliance produced ten children, all of whom were skillfully deployed in strategic fashion. François, the eldest son, destined to be the second duc de Guise, was raised at court as a companion to the future Henry II. Their friendship helped the family stay in favor when Henry II succeeded to the throne in 1547. Two daughters established strategic international connections: Mary married the king of Scotland and gave birth to the future Mary, Queen of Scots; Louise married the prince of Orange, head of the leading family of the Netherlands. Two sons (Aumale and Elbeuf) became dukes of collateral lines. Three others gained major posts in the church: François became Grand Prieur de France, a powerful ecclesiastical position that was essentially a sinecure; Charles became cardinal of Lorraine, an immensely influential position inherited from his uncle; and Louis, who had been named bishop of Troyes at age eighteen, became cardinal of Guise. Two other daughters became abbesses.

Figure 7 This painting by an anonymous artist portrays a ball held at the court of Henry III in 1581 in honor of the marriage of the duc de Joyeuse. It illustrates the aristocratic styles of the era of the religious wars.

By the mid sixteenth century, the Guises were strategically placed at court, in the church, and in three or four provinces. In the 1570s they were the richest family in the kingdom. The duc de Guise had an estimated annual income from all sources of 235,507 livres.[18] He owned twenty-six estates in six provinces concentrated in Champagne, the Île-de-France and Picardy. Aumale had eighteen estates, five abbeys, and two priories in Normandy and a few estates in Picardy. Elbeuf had four estates in Normandy and three elsewhere. All three dukes were bolstered by honors from the king. Their military commands provided revenue and positions to give out to followers; the governorships of Champagne, Burgundy, and Bourbonnais provided annual stipends and public authority; Guise and Aumale received annual pensions of 16,000 livres and Elbeuf received 6,000. The Guises also held offices at court, received royal gifts, and lent money to the king in return for claims on certain tax revenues. Jean, the first cardinal of Lorraine, had at his disposal six abbeys and six bishoprics, including the archbishopric of Reims, which conferred on its prelate the status of "first peer of the realm."

The Guises managed their affairs like an extended business or even a "shadow" government, holding great family meetings at Joinville to map out strategy. In 1556 the duke had a ceremonial household of 159 persons that mimicked the royal court. He had intendants to oversee the management of his many properties and bankers poised to mobilize credit when large sums were needed. Councils of judicial experts in Paris and Rouen handled the family's legal affairs. Many of them were Guise clients who brought his influence to the Parlement of Paris. In wartime his army company contained 100 lances, or 250 men, most of them personal followers who looked to him as patron. His properties were managed by seigneurial agents who were knowledgeable about the local communities, in which they were often themselves prosperous farmers. These same individuals were frequently selected to represent the third estate, and thus to promote Guise interests, at meetings of provincial or national Estates.

By the sixteenth century, power like that of the Guises had become a combination of independent landed wealth and increasingly important ties to the crown. In the seventeenth century such royal ties were becoming indispensable. The trajectory of the Condé family is a case in point. The Condés were a junior branch of the Bourbon dynasty, descended from Charles de Bourbon, duc de Vendôme. They fought on the Protestant side in the wars of religion and emerged from that long conflict deeply in debt. Yet, by the time of his death, Henry II, prince de Condé (1588–1646) had acquired a fortune of at least 16 million livres, with an annual income of 1,187,000 livres, and by the beginning of the eighteenth century, his grandson enjoyed a fortune of 31 million livres.

This spectacular growth in family wealth was the result of excellent management and clever politics. Henry II was a devout Catholic who abandoned his family's Huguenot roots. As heir to various childless Bourbon relatives, he acquired a substantial inheritance by the early seventeenth century. At the same time he exploited political situations. He attracted gifts from Henry IV and extorted favors from Marie de' Medici by rebelling during the minority of Louis XIII. Then, in a clever about-face, he allied himself with Cardinal Richelieu at a time when many aristocrats were caballing against the cardinal, and led the royal forces that put down a number of rebellions. He was appointed governor of Burgundy, governor of Berry, and Grand Maître de France. In 1641 he arranged the marriage of his son Louis II (1621–86), the

future "Great Condé," to Claire-Clémence de Maillé-Brézé, Richelieu's
niece. His own marriage to Charlotte-Marguerite, sister of the duc de
Montmorency, led to an unexpected windfall in 1632 when Montmorency was executed for rebellion, leaving no male heir. With the
support of Richelieu and Louis XIII, much of Montmorency's confis-
cated property passed to Condé, including the chateau of Chantilly,
which became the family seat.

Condé's position was thus greatly improved by support at court, on
which he was much more dependent than the Guises had been. In
1646 almost 60 percent of his income came directly from royal
appointments and royal taxes.[19] But his prominence was also the
result of his family name and personal reputation. Condé's stunning
military successes, starting with the battle of Rocroi in 1643,
enhanced his reputation as a gallant fighter and a true leader. Unlike
his father, Henry II also became something of a libertine, and his *hôtel*
in Paris became a meeting place for the leading artists and intellectuals
of the day. During the Fronde this immense prestige was undermined
by competition with Cardinal Mazarin, who was building his own
circle of clients while undermining Condé's credit by denying key
requests for positions and army posts. After being imprisoned by
Mazarin, Condé raised a military rebellion and ended up in exile in
Spain, only returning when the king pardoned him in 1660.

Although his "party" had fallen apart, his household organization
proved amazingly solid in the face of treason and disgrace. In 1657
when Mazarin's agents tried to confiscate all the property of Condé
and his followers, loyal aides hid the titles to his Paris *hôtel*; his
furniture vanished from all his country estates; and his monetary
reserves were spirited off to safe locations a few days before the arrival
of the royal commissioners.[20] When Condé returned to favor, he was
8 million livres in debt and he had to lavish pensions and favors on his
loyal followers to reestablish his reputation as a good patron. But the
continuing strength of his client support facilitated his recovery. Soon
he had turned the chateau of Chantilly into a center of aristocratic
patronage, putting on lavish festivals that rivaled even those at Versailles and cultivating artists like Molière, Le Nôtre, and La Fontaine.
Condé's comeback was possible because he abstained from further
political activism and because his military prowess was still valued.
His son, Henri-Jules (1643–1709) continued the tradition with self-
congratulatory banquets and obedience to the point of marrying his

son to Mademoiselle de Nantes, the bastard daughter of Louis XIV by Louise de La Vallière. This was a degrading marriage in terms of status, but it furthered the family tradition of accommodating the king and cultivating ties with the state.

In 1660 the Grand Condé's household included 546 servants and agents, 58 percent of whom actually lived in the Hôtel de Condé on the Parisian left bank. The rest had lodgings in nearby streets, creating a "Condé compound" which is still remembered in the name of the rue Monsieur le Prince. Condé's household included gentlemen with honorific titles, ladies of honor, real servants of many stripes, and professional administrators and secretaries who handled the prince's external affairs. The prince rewarded and protected these people. They, in turn, distributed favors and appointments to lesser clients, often in the provincial regions where the Condés held sway. The magnitude of this patronage system can be grasped in Béguin's study of church appointments. Between 1660 and 1689 the Condés made no less than 743 appointments to 463 different church benefices, most of them subject to direct intervention by an influential party acting on behalf of the prince. Condé was constantly using his influence by interceding with ministers, confessors, and other secondary parties. He arranged advantageous marriages for important personages, exerted considerable influence in the army, and worked with royal officials in the provinces. Condé's success demonstrated that, within certain parameters, a magnate could still be independently important under Louis XIV's absolutism, provided he maintained good relations with the king.

These activities project a different picture from the traditional idea of great magnates being turned into hapless courtiers and made dependent on revocable pensions from the crown. It is true that dignitaries like Condé were largely removed from political decision-making at the center, and that they no longer had the power base or the motivation to lead further rebellions. But they were still immensely rich managers of complex portfolios of resources and patrons of large numbers of people.

The parallel case of Philippe of Orléans, the brother of Louis XIV, also deserves a mention. Shut off from meaningful involvement in warfare or government by the king and forced to live on royal subsidies, Philippe is usually seen as the effeminate, hapless symbol of aristocratic uselessness. But a recent study by Nancy Barker shows that Philippe also laid the foundations of his family's rise to prominence in the eighteenth century by sound financial management. His revenues consisted of an annual allowance of 1,212,000 livres from the king plus a lordship (*apanage*) over the duchies of Orléans, Valois, and Chartres. In 1693 Orléans received the substantial inheritance of his aunt, Mademoiselle de Montpensier. His council of sixty administrators combed through documents looking for neglected property rights, commissioned land surveys, reorganized the collection of seigneurial dues, reviving many forgotten fees, systematically recovered mortgaged lands, and organized the exploitation of timber in the extensive forests of the Orléanais. Whereas in 1672 the revenue of the *apanage* was about 200,000 livres, by the 1740s it was yielding more than a million, an increase of 600 percent, half from seigneurial fees and half from lumber sales. While seeming to be absorbed in jewels and paintings, Louis XIV's brother had laid the foundations for a fortune which would propel the Orléans dynasty to new prominence during and after the Revolution.[21]

Condé and Orléans were princes of the blood whose influence was guaranteed by their place in the line of succession, regardless of their management skills. Our eighteenth century example came from outside that inner circle. The Saulx-Tavannes family from Burgundy was a distinguished lineage with a long pedigree dating back to 1234. Their fortunes had been ruined by the expenses of the religious wars, but the marriage of the family heir, Claude de Saulx, to Françoise Brulart, daughter of the wealthy first president of the Parlement of Dijon, in 1613 revived their prospects. She brought a dowry of 120,000 livres and an expertise at managing the family fortunes that was reminiscent of the role played by Antoinette de Bourbon in the Guise family. We should take note of this role of powerful wives in promoting the advancement of aristocratic families.

The next two generations of Tavannes were increasingly drawn into the royal orbit. Claude's son Jacques was a loyal follower of Condé in the conflicts of the Fronde. But his son Charles-Marie established a reputation as a successful officer in the army of Louis XIV and took up residence in Paris, where he could stay in touch with sources of credit and marriage prospects and make an impression at the royal court. The result was his lucrative marriage to Catherine Daguesseau, the intelligent and diligent sister of the future Chancellor of France. This new prominence opened up important positions for their children.

The eldest living son, Henri Charles, served for many years as lieutenant-general of Burgundy, and his brother Charles Nicolas became
archbishop of Rouen, a cardinal, and Grand Almoner of France. Still,
the consequence of such eminence was dangerous indebtedness. When
Henri Charles ceded management of the family fortune to his son in
1754, it amounted to 50,000 livres in revenues and 600,600 livres of
accumulated debts. Over the years the family had built up 45,000
livres in debts to merchants for clothes, jewels, wines, and perfumes –
luxuries needed to maintain their station in society – and large sums for
the cost of military service. The payoff was the position of Henri-
Charles' grandson, Casimir, who became *chevalier de la reine* and thus
an intimate in the circle of Louis XV's wife. He also managed to survive
the changing of the guard after 1774 and make his way into the
household of Marie Antoinette. These connections earned the family a
suite of six rooms at Versailles. They rented a townhouse in the rue du
Bac in Paris and persuaded the king to raise their lands in Burgundy to
the status of a ducal *baillage* in 1786 so that they could become hereditary ducs de Saulx-Tavannes. That same year the family heir was
married, at age sixteen, to fourteen-year-old Aglaé-Marie-Louise de
Choiseul-Gouffier, from one of the most influential courtly families.[22]

The family had reached the inner sanctum of the royal court, but
they paid a heavy price. All this influence at court required vast
expenditures to maintain status. The personal expenses of the duke in
1788 amounted to 62,000 livres per year, including 20,000 for
clothing, jewelry and gifts, 7,000 for rent on their townhouse, 10,000
for servants, 3,000 for residence at Versailles part of the year for food,
entertainment, furnishings, repairs, and carriages (room and board at
the palace were free), and 5,000 for legal fees. Another annual
120,689 was owed as interest on loans. This partial list probably does
not include 73,000 livres of debts related to provisions for other
members of the family, making a total annual cost of 257,689. His
gross income was 165,504, 25.6 percent of which came from royal
appointments. Thus he was running a deficit of 192,185 per year.

In the sixteenth century the Guises had dominated several provinces
and maintained a network of connections that supplied allies in town
councils, meetings of the provincial Estates, and influential law courts.
Their power was such that they could bargain for additional favors
from the royal government and, if they liked, even challenge the whole
power structure. In the seventeenth century the Condés had similar

influence, but their fate was tied closely to royal favor, at least after 1654. In the seventeenth and eighteenth centuries the Saulx-Tavannes had to draw on the wealth of less eminent administrative families through marriage in order to maintain an eminence at court which they bolstered with military and governmental service. But the price of success in high society was estrangement from their provincial origins. They sunk all their wealth into maintaining their status at court.

Such was the typical profile of the greatest families in France. They maintained and nurtured their landed wealth, but they gradually traded their regional autonomy and direct local management of resources for life in Paris and dependence on lucrative marriages and royal favors. Their estates, which might have been a source of investment as well as a center of regional influence, became revenue providers to be milked through intensified but traditional means, in order to support the luxurious life at the top.

Conclusion

The French nobility formed the backbone of traditional society. Enjoying special legal and social advantages that set them apart from the rest of the population, they claimed to epitomize the standards and aspirations of the entire society. These standards were intimately tied to assumptions of superiority and advantage developed over centuries of domination. But the nature of the nobles' advantage had shifted dramatically between the fourteenth and the eighteenth century. They had initially ruled by virtue of their control over rural agricultural production, including the individuals who did the producing, and by their superior mastery of military skills and the weapons of warfare. Gradually they had transformed themselves into landlords relying more on rent collection than on coerced labor. They depended increasingly on their political ability to ingratiate themselves into the burgeoning royal administration, and on their skill at managing fortunes and arranging marriages with new sources of wealth. Out of their experience came a mentality which set the tone for the rest of society. It favored ancient pedigrees, valued special privileges, and endorsed an ethic of refinement, first in terms of chivalric values, later in terms of artistic taste and polite manners.

But despite these common class advantages, the nobility was not a unified group. They occupied a tremendous range of wealth and status, with the vast majority, like Gouberville, enjoying nothing more than a shade of superiority in their local communities and a petty claim to a few seigneurial rights or a modest fortune. Many had even less than this. Such nobles could not afford to establish a military reputation or go to court, and many slipped into *roturier* status. Furthermore, the nobility as a group was constantly evolving, as new families fought or bought their way into the group, and others slipped away, died out, or lost their status.

When we say "nobility," what we usually mean is the higher, well-placed nobles – those who had connections with regional authorities and marriage alliances with comparable families, such as the Bigots of Pont-Saint-Pierre who served as local anchors in the system of political networks, or the Dintevilles and Roncherolles who were regional brokers. The great magnates, such as the Guises or the Saux-Tavannes, were named by the king to province-level positions of authority. They increasingly focused their careers on attendance at court and immersed themselves in the ostentation and luxury of the Parisian or provincial aristocracy. Like the society as a whole, the nobility formed a strict hierarchy in which only a few controlled most of the power.

Suggestions for further reading: noble fortunes and lifestyles

Béguin, Katia, *Les Princes de Condé: rebelles, courtisans et mécènes dans la France du Grand Siècle* (Seyssel, 1999).

Bohanan, Donna, *Old and New Nobility in Aix-en-Provence, 1600–1695: Portrait of an Urban Elite* (Baton Rouge, LA, 1992).

Bourquin, Laurent, *Noblesse seconde et pouvoir en Champagne aux XVIe et XVIIe siècles* (Paris, 1994).

Carroll, Stuart, *Noble Power during the French Wars of Religion: The Guise Affinity and the Catholic Cause in Normandy* (Cambridge, 1998).

Dewald, Jonathan, *Pont-St-Pierre 1398–1789: Lordship, Community and Capitalism in Early Modern France* (Berkeley, CA, 1987).

   Aristocratic Experience and the Origins of Modern Culture 1570–1715 (Berkeley, 1993).

Eurich, Amanda, *The Economics of Power: The Private Finances of the House of Foix–Navarre–Albret during the Religious Wars* (Kirksville, MO, 1993).

Forster, Robert, *The House of Saulx-Tavanes: Versailles and Burgundy, 1700–1830* (Baltimore, MD, 1971).

Gallet, Jean, *La Seigneurie bretonne 1450–1680* (Paris, 1983).

Harding, Robert A., *Anatomy of a Power Elite: The Provincial Governors of Early Modern France* (New Haven, CT, 1978).

Jackson, Richard A., "Peers of France and Princes of the Blood," *French Historical Studies* 7 (1971), 27–46.

Labatut, Jean-Pierre, *Les Ducs et pairs de France au XVIIe siècle* (Paris, 1972).

Major, J. Russell, "Noble Income, Inflation, and the Wars of Religion in France," *American Historical Review* 86 (1981), 21–48.

　From Renaissance Monarchy to Absolute Monarchy: French Kings, Nobles and Estates (Baltimore, MD, 1994).

Meyer, Jean, *La Noblesse bretonne au XVIIIe siècle* (Paris, 1972).

Motley, Mark, *Becoming a French Aristocrat: The Education of the Court Nobility, 1580–1715* (Princeton, NJ, 1990).

Neuschel, Kristin, "Noble Households in the Sixteenth Century: Material Settings and Human Communities," *French Historical Studies* 15 (1988), 595–622.

　Word of Honor: Interpreting Noble Culture in Sixteenth-Century France (Ithaca, NY, 1989).

Salmon, J. H. M., "Storm over the Noblesse," *Journal of Modern History* 53 (1981), 242–57.

Schalk, Ellery, *From Valor to Pedigree: Ideas of Nobility in France in the 16th and 17th Centuries* (Princeton, NJ, 1986).

Wood, James B., *The Nobility of the Election of Bayeux, 1463–1666* (Princeton, NJ, 1980).

4 | *City life and city people*

Towns were centers of action. Sitting as they did in the midst of the vast countryside, they were points of attraction to which people came and went to sell their produce, look for work, settle law cases, acquire commodities not made in local villages, attend *collège* or university, or transact business. There men with power made important decisions: the law courts, the companies of royal officers, the bishop's seat, the residences of the royal intendant and the military governor were all located there. As time went on, increasing numbers of country nobles acquired urban living quarters and spent more time there. Skilled trades were practiced by artisan craftsmen (and women) whose shops lined the streets of certain quarters. It was in town that information about the outside world circulated. Royal regulations were plastered on public walls, and trumpeters announced new edicts in public squares. News of distant markets and international events arrived with consignments of merchandise. Tales of gallantry on the battle front and the latest court gossip were eagerly eaten up and repeated by the inhabitants.

Still, town and country were closely intertwined. Rustic peasants could be seen coming to do business with a creditor or a potential buyer. Streets were often unpaved and muddy just like those in the village. Farm animals were kept by city residents. When the gates opened at dawn, there was a daily exodus of peasants who lived in the city but cultivated fields or vineyards outside the walls. Servants headed out to acquire provisions, along with all sorts of stewards, estate managers, and tax collectors who were on missions to collect dues, arrest miscreants, or manage the properties of absentee lords.

In 1550, when the population boom of the sixteenth century was well under way, Paris was one of Europe's largest cities, with 250,000 people. The second-largest French city, Rouen, was only a third as big, with 75,000. Lyon had 54,000, Toulouse 50,000, Orléans 47,000, Bordeaux 33,000, and Marseille 30,000. These were major cities, but

Figure 8 View of Lyon about 1650, looking south. The Saône River is on the right and the Rhône on the left. In the foreground fortifications protect the land access. The old royal castle of Pierre Scize is visible on the far right. Lyon was one of France's largest cities, but the general appearance is similar to that of smaller cities.

they were very small by modern standards. Below these seven, about ten other cities had over 10,000 inhabitants. The towns were islands in a sea of twenty million peasants. Perhaps 10 percent of the French lived in towns of any size in 1400 and that figure rose to maybe 15 percent in 1550, and 20 percent in 1789.[1] Four-fifths of the people lived in villages and small hamlets throughout the period.

By 1700, there was a modest shift toward urbanization. France now had forty-three towns with populations over 10,000 and at least twenty-one more with populations of between 1,000 and 10,000.[2] Paris had mushroomed from 250,000 to 510,000, but the next largest city, which was now Lyon with 97,000, had lost ground by comparison with the capital. The next most populous were Marseille, Rouen, Lille, Orléans, Bordeaux, and Rennes, in that order. Even in 1700, only Paris was big enough to compete on a European scale with metropolises like Rome, Seville, London, or Amsterdam. The influence of the city would spread farther into the countryside in the eighteenth century through books and newspapers, and ultimately by means of the Revolution, but it still did not reach most people.

Cities had different atmospheres, depending on their function and social composition. First, there were administrative centers, including Paris and the regional seats of sovereign courts such as Aix, Toulouse, Dijon, or Rennes. These were cities with an aristocratic air. They housed proud judicial companies of robe nobles who lived in elegant accommodation, supported large numbers of servants, and consumed quantities of luxury goods. Second were diocesan centers built around a cathedral and the palace of the bishop or archbishop, for example Reims, Bourges, or Béziers. They were populated by large numbers of priests, many of whom were attached to the multiple shrines, altars, and chapels that clustered around a bishopric. Third were manufacturing and trading cities like Lyon, Amiens, or Troyes in which dominant industries, usually textiles, employed thousands of artisan workers, and the prominent men were merchants and bankers.[3] In the late seventeenth century a fourth type emerged: the prosperous port cities that profited from the Atlantic trade, such as Bordeaux, Nantes, and Saint-Malo. Such places were dominated by men of new wealth who were involved in the slave trade or made money by importing and processing sugar, tobacco, and cotton.

Life in the city

Each city had its own personality, but there were common elements. First was the wall. Sometimes it consisted of thick medieval ramparts punctuated by tall round towers. Sometimes that wall had been replaced by the low, sloping star-shaped bastions of the seventeenth century. Sometimes the wall was in ruins, with perhaps breaches where it had collapsed or houses built against it. Whatever the wall looked like, it created an almost magical barrier between the citizens and the outside world. It defined a territorial jurisdiction, and it channeled traffic through a limited number of gates, facilitating the taxing of merchandise entering or leaving. The wall limited the amount of available inside land, causing competition for ownership of the desirable plots which were laid out narrow and deep so that as many owners as possible could enjoy facades opening on the street.

Figure 9 View of the "Paris gate" in Troyes: a massive relic from the past, but still functioning.

Other prominent features can be seen in the many engravings which convey a "bird's-eye view" of a given city. Standing out above the indiscriminate mass of small houses crammed inside the walls are the towers of the major churches, possibly a castle or an old fortress or a palatial residence, the main gates, and any bridges over rivers. Monuments like these stood as more or less permanent landmarks. Constructing a bridge or refurbishing a belfry were massive projects requiring major funding and years of effort. City council meetings brought them up year after year as they tried to shift the cost to the bishop or the king, and they quarreled over the taxes needed to fund each stage. In Agen in 1514, when the city council tried to raise money to repair the bridge over the Garonne, an opposition group opposing the move organized a massive protest in which "a thousand" people gathered in the main square.[4] In Toulouse the construction of the graceful Pont de Pierre, begun in 1544, only had four of its eight piles in place by 1560, and the bridge was not finished until the mid seventeenth century.

A building that is rarely visible in the aerial engravings was the city hall, called an *hôtel de ville* or a *maison de ville*. City halls ranged from ramshackle old piles of stone to elegant public buildings in Renaissance or classical style. They were the focal point for civic pride and self-government. They contained meeting chambers, archives, munitions rooms stocked with gunpowder and firearms, and prisons. Near the city hall was often the market square, where goods and news were exchanged on designated market days. In large cities there might be several markets devoted to different commodities. In the market square venders could hawk their wares on designated days from tables and stands rented from the city in the ground-floor arcades surrounding the square.

Most towns had a medieval core that is usually recognizable on a map of the modern city. It is the crowded district at the center with a maze of narrow winding streets, often lying near to a river port or surrounding a cathedral or a fortress. Outside this core the map will show newer zones, extending up to the boundary created by a later wall. The streets here will be a little straighter and wider, but only slightly less cramped. Around the edges, in the space left open between the inner streets and the outer wall there would be more space to breathe. Private estates with courtyards and gardens would appear, along with monasteries and other foundations that required more room or more calm. The inner city walls are mostly gone today, although remnants can be seen here and there, such as the gate towers that survive in Bordeaux. The site of the final, outer wall is usually easy to spot because the ramparts have been replaced by a wide, circular boulevard. Many hospitals and schools today occupy the spaces which show up on the old maps as religious establishments.

Cities had tortuously winding streets, often no wider than 13–16 feet, with the largest barely reaching 40 feet. In 1455, one of the most frequented streets in Rennes was 7.5 feet wide, and the two main north–south arteries in Paris, the rue Saint-Denis and the rue Saint-Martin, were only about 19 feet wide. Very few passages were wide enough for two horse-drawn vehicles to pass one another. Traffic jams were colossal, and great bottlenecks developed at crucial points like market squares, roads leading to gates, and passages across rivers. To make matters worse, some landlords built higher stories projecting out over the street, leaving only a narrow passage for sunlight. Others added towers and balconies, or bridges across the street from the

Figure 10 A typically narrow sixteenth-century street in Troyes.

upper floors of one building to another. Walking was perilous. Most streets were built with sloping sides and a trough in the middle to catch rainwater. This made movement precarious, as people balanced themselves on the edges to avoid the foul center. In Rennes in 1475, carpenters who were repairing the roof of the hall of the haberdashers' confraternity threatened to quit unless the drunken revelers in a tavern across the street stopped harassing them: "the men at the windows were pissing at them and throwing stinking garbage."[5] In eighteenth-century Paris Louis-Sebastien Mercier was still complaining that the city's gutters "are as dangerous dry as when flushed with water, for the people who live in attics use them to save their own legs and throw every kind of ordure down them ... You may be walking quietly with the sun on your shoulders when some stinking liquid or other comes soundlessly out of the blue and soaks you."[6]

Parisian streets were treacherous in other ways. Traffic jams and encounters between carriages and flocks of animals were frequent, as were accidents caused by holes in the road, stones bouncing up to hit passers-by, and the collapse of carriages whose wheels would be sent rolling into the crowd of pedestrians. The air was filled with the sound of hawkers shouting out their wares, children screaming, and people in the street shouting to people in windows. Country folk were as struck by the noise of the city as they were by its animation.

Improvements were gradually introduced. City councils spent much time discussing the placement of houses that impeded traffic and regulating property owners who wanted to build additions. There was no legal right to appropriate the land for public purposes, so any widening or reconstruction required negotiations with every property owner involved, making it especially difficult to consolidate plots or cut through new streets. The best prospects lay in developing outlying areas, and it was usually some higher authority that took the initiative to do so. Henry IV set a precedent by developing the Place Royale (today Place des Vosges) in Paris. It was a public square surrounded by arcaded buildings with uniform facades. The plots were parceled out to private contractors with the proviso that they observed the standards set by the king. Henry used the same procedure for the Place Dauphine and the construction of the Pont Neuf. These squares, which introduced a moment of air and light into a crowded city, were elegant settings with human dimensions. Other cities followed this model, creating the Place Bellecour in Lyon, the Place du Capitole in Toulouse, and the Place Ducale at Charleville.

Starting in the late seventeenth century, cities began to follow the lead of Louis XIV by creating aristocratic promenades, broad avenues, and grandiose monuments. In Paris, the king created the first boulevards by demolishing the ramparts on the northeast side of the city. He erected classical victory arches at several gates and began to develop the grand axis that stretches today from the Louvre to the Arc de Triomphe and beyond. The esplanade leading up to the Invalides, Louis's military hospital, is another example. Other cities created elegant new public spaces where fashionable citizens could see and be seen, such as the esplanade called the Peyrou in Montpellier, the Cours la Reine in Paris or tree-lined avenues like the Cours Mazarin in Aix. These newer features were usually outside the old core of the city, which remained largely unchanged.

Town governments

Cities were run by an oligarchy of leading families. Each city had its own personality and its particular way of selecting its collective leadership. The city fathers were prominent merchants, resident nobles, lawyers or other professionals, and in certain cases representatives of the most influential guilds. In their heyday during the first half of the sixteenth century, these elite families, most of them connected to profit from trade, passed the chief city posts around among themselves almost at will, and enjoyed considerable autonomy. Although they could be disdainful toward the citizens below them, they felt a deep loyalty to the larger community and their responsibility to protect it. Service was a matter of duty as well as self-interest.

Each town had a collective leadership consisting of a council of members called *échevins, consuls, jurats,* or something else. Some had a single *maire* or first consul who presided over the council. Sometimes there were larger committees of respectable citizens who met less frequently when particularly serious decisions needed ratification. Most city councils served for one year, or in a few cities for two. The *échevins* might represent particular districts of the city, or they might be tied to specified occupations or trades.

Election procedures were infinitely varied, but they all added up to some sort of co-optation, sometimes tempered by an element of chance. In Bordeaux the *jurade* consisted of twelve *jurats* chosen annually and representing particular districts. Each sitting *jurat* named two *prud'hommes* from 'his district, and these twenty-four *prud'hommes* then selected the new *jurats*. In Lyon, after 1595, the king named the *prévôt des marchands* each year. The *prévôt* presided over a committee of four *échevins*. Each year the sitting *échevins* chose a representative from each of the 102 guilds elected by an assembly of former *échevins* and guild representatives. The old *échevins* and the *prévôt des marchands* then chose the new *échevins*, upon his recommendation. In Poitiers there was a city council consisting of 100 members: the *maire*, twenty-four *échevins*, and seventy-five bourgeois. The *maire* changed annually, but the other posts were held for life, and when one was vacant, the council of 100 selected the successor.

A city's *échevins* directed a very small staff of employees, most of whom were kept on for life: a secretary, a *procureur-syndic* to pursue judicial business, some guards and process-servers. Town councils regulated what they called "police," which meant rules concerning market practices, pubic morality, guild regulations, and compliance with religious dictates such as prohibiting the eating of meat during Lent. They defended the privileges of the city against any infraction by means of lawsuits; they managed the municipal budget and handled the protocol of greeting arriving dignitaries with the appropriate parades, speeches, or fireworks; and they responded to threats to the community such as approaching armies, an epidemic of plague, or popular rioting. Serving on a city council was an onerous job, but it had limited personal responsibility because decisions were always collective.

Meeting as a group in their matching robes and bonnets, or processing down a street, the *échevins* could be quite intimidating. But their power was ephemeral. They had no real police force, and they were volunteers on a one-year assignment. Their influence was largely dependent on the degree to which they could use their own personal reputation to get disobedient forces to comply.

Between 1550 and 1650, two developments began to challenge the notables' stranglehold on municipal power. The first was the rising status of royal officers. Their infiltration into municipal affairs followed a different timetable in each city, but it occurred almost everywhere. By 1640–50, in Lyon, the royal officers were occupying over 59 percent of the municipal posts and the merchants 38 percent.[7] In Montpellier's city council the six posts of consul had all gone to merchants and artisans from 1440 to the early sixteenth century. From 1566 to 1599, robe nobles, urban nobles, and lawyers held every post of first consul.[8]

The second development was the intrusion of the king's direct agents, the provincial intendant and his sub-delegates, into municipal affairs. These resident agents first appeared in the 1630s as rather powerless outsiders, but by the 1680s and 1690s they had been empowered to monitor the city finances and approve all new taxes and expenditure. Then, in 1692, Louis XIV created the venal posts of *maire* to head the administration of each city. Each municipality had to buy off this office or allow a rich purchaser to head its government. The initiative of the traditional elected bodies was quite severely curtailed, and they increasingly looked to the intendant and the royal council for approval of their projects.

Merchants and professional "middle classes"

Within these towns and cities lived a diverse population which we must now examine, starting at the top and working down toward the working majority. The top of the pecking order was inhabited by merchants and "bourgeois." This last term requires some explanation. We might expect to find a progressive bourgeoisie, bringing about change through business and education. Cities did produce people who were different from peasants, people not tied so closely to the soil and the seasons, some of whom understood account books and how to make a profit. But the majority of urban inhabitants practiced traditional mechanical skills in small shops, or they served as servants or day laborers. If "bourgeois" is precisely defined as a capitalist entrepreneur who invests capital in increasing production, then France only saw the first hints of a bourgeoisie. If we mean simply a merchant who bought and sold things for profit, we will find a much larger group, but we still will not have captured the important people in most towns. The term "bourgeois" was used by contemporaries to mean a "city person" or, more narrowly, a *citizen* of a town, when "citizen" was a legal category referring only to a designated group of male heads of households, and not to everyone who lived within the walls. The term "bourgeois" was also used to designate a much smaller group of urban citizens who lived off their income from land and loans and did no productive work.

These last bourgeois, who today would be called "independently wealthy," sat high in the traditional urban hierarchy, along with some resident nobles and the richest merchants. To find the most important merchant bankers – the ones with international connections – we would have to go to a city like Lyon, which was the financial hub of France in 1569. In that year a register of goods imported into the city recorded the activity of 532 merchants. Most of their business was dominated by the ones at the top. Ten importers controlled 36.6 percent of the total value of imports, and the top forty-three controlled 74 percent. That left 26 percent of the business for the other 489 merchants, most of whom were obviously small operators. Most of the biggest importers were Italian, including fourteen from the top twenty, from Lucca, Milan, and Genoa. The other six were Lyonnais drapers (cloth merchants) and *épiciers* (spice merchants) whose specialty was supplying the interior of France and who could hardly compete with the Italians in international trading.

The same patterns prevailed in sixteenth-century Rouen, which was another merchant center. Gayle Brunelle identified 144 merchants who had invested in trade with the New World between 1559 and 1630. This was again a minority, compared to the estimated 500 genuine merchants in the city. In Rouen, as in Lyon, the market was controlled by foreigners, in this case, Dutch and Italian merchants, while resident Spanish and Portuguese played a major role in contacts with the Spanish Empire. Most of the Portuguese were Sephardic Jews who had migrated to escape the Inquisition. Among all these merchants, the New World traders were the more daring, risking long voyages and unpredictable mishaps. But they still hedged their bets by cautiously buying shares in many different voyages and backed their enterprise by acquiring landed estates and private loans.

Smaller-scale merchants were more typical. To become a major merchant capitalist required skills that few French merchants were capable of providing. You would need, first, a mastery of knowledge about international markets and prices. Second, you would need large amounts of capital that could be committed for a year or longer, which was the time it took to reap the returns of a distant transaction. Third, you had to be able to transfer large amounts of money across long distances without physically moving sacks of heavy coins. Fourth, you needed safeguards against the considerable risk that the merchandise would be lost, stolen, or damaged in transit. The key to mercantile activity was contacts. If you wanted to sell goods to any individual in another place, you needed someone there to demand payment for you and to get the money back to you. Establishing personal relations with a variety of people in many places was therefore essential. Foreigners had the advantage of arriving in France with such contacts already in place. To transfer funds, the best connected merchants had access to letters of credit, which enabled a customer in one city to deposit money with a banker, and a payee to retrieve it from another banker in a different city at a later date. These letters required sophisticated relations between bankers in both places and a good deal of trust. They were not widely used in France until much later.

Most French merchants' methods were more primitive. A characteristic sixteenth-century example was Jehan Pocquelin, merchant-draper in Beauvais, a small episcopal town north of Paris. When Pocquelin died in 1572, the inventory of his property shows shelves in his shop loaded with bolts of cloth worth a total of 2,000 livres. All kinds of fabric were represented, including lightweight *estamets*, *rases*, and *serges*, in a broad range of colors. His clients were local citizens: an attorney, an apothecary, the innkeeper of the "Swan," some local tailors, some nuns and some cathedral canons, plus farmers and poor nobles from the surrounding region. Pocquelin was quite wealthy, but his income came from many small and greatly diversified activities. He owned a house in town. He undertook forays to the nearby towns of Rouen, Amiens, and Saint-Quentin to buy merchandise at fairs, but he also frequented the textile markets of Paris. He owned extensive lands near the city, with vineyards, pasture, and good grain-producing fields. His woods produced almost as much revenue from the sale of lumber as his shop. He was stockpiling grain in his attics to sell when the price peaked. He possessed 857 promissory notes totaling 11,035 livres of debts owed to him by individuals in 134 towns and villages scattered throughout the Beauvaisis within a radius of 30 miles. His house was filled with furniture, robes, bonnets, belts, sheets, and napkins which people had deposited with him as security for small, interest-bearing loans.[9]

In Amiens in the early seventeenth century, the richest merchants were men like Pierre Hemart, who died in 1608. Hemart was essentially a regional distributor with excellent connections to sources of supply. He had contacts in Rouen and Middelburg and dealings with Danzig, Antwerp, Amsterdam and Bilbao. He dabbled in goods acquired from all over and sold them wholesale or retail, whatever came along. He imported butter from Frisia, cod from Flanders, cheese from Holland, wheat and rye from Danzig, dyes from all over the world, via Spain and Rouen, honey from the Baltic, and yarn from England. His shop was crammed with foods, apothecary items, thread, wax, tar, hemp, and needles. He was a rich man. His wife owned diamonds and he owned two rural estates.[10]

These merchants were small players compared to the great international figures. They rarely used letters of credit. They regulated payment by accepting a simple signed note from the purchaser, promising to pay in six months or a year. Enforcing payment was difficult. Often they had to send a trusted employee to another city to collect payment in coin and literally carry the money back home. There is little evidence that they kept formal accounts, and they never took inventories.

Joining the merchants at the top of urban society were the officials holding royal offices. In major cities there was likely to be a Parlement or another sovereign court, whose judges outclassed city leaders by virtue of their jurisdictional superiority and their role of acting on behalf of the king. The judges in these royal courts owned their offices, which represented a major investment in prestige and influence, and many had nobility or were in the process of acquiring it. They might be local men on the rise, or they might be interlopers from elsewhere. In either case their jurisdictional challenges and attempts to regulate local affairs were likely to antagonize the local magistrates. We will meet them again in Chapter 5. Below the sovereign judges were the officers of lesser royal courts and fiscal agencies whose members were more a part of the distinctly urban scene. District capitals usually had a royal appeals court, called a *bailliage* in the north and a *sénéchaussée* in the south. In that case the titular head of the court, the *bailli* or *seneschal*, or in his place the court's *lieutenant-général*, usually played an important role in overseeing municipal elections on behalf of the king. The most important *bailliages* and *sénéchaussées* had an added chamber called a *présidial*. It was an intermediate court designed to settle certain petty cases as a final court of appeal, eliminating them from the workload of the Parlements.

These middling royal officers were usually local men very much tied to the community, yet their modicum of royal influence made them roughly equivalent in authority to the city magistrates, and their royal offices made them assertive. In some cities they participated directly in council meetings and stood for office. In others they were excluded. But the existence of a bureau of *trésoriers de France* or a *bailliage* or *présidial* court meant that another company of robed dignitaries would march in processions, intervene in elections, and arrest rioters, often to the dismay of the *échevins*, disrupting their authority.

All these courts required legal practitioners. Attached to each court was a crowd of *avocats* (barristers) and *procureurs* (solicitors).

Avocats were professional lawyers whose specialty was delivering long oral arguments before the court. In the seventeenth century the Parisian avocats had formed an unofficial association, the Order of Barristers, which looked after their interests. To obtain the title *avocat* one had to pursue a three-year *licence* in law from a university and take an oath, but to plead before the court (to be *avocat au parlement*) it was also necessary to be placed on an official roster. In the 1660s the Order formalized these requirements. They required two years of observation in the courtroom and stated that the association was the body that admitted new candidates. In 1705 they founded a law library in Paris, and in 1710 they established legal seminars. By 1700 the Order was made up of some 300 to 500 lawyers, who were becoming confident enough to take up public issues and stake out political positions.[11] The regional Parlements had similar organizations.

Procureurs were similarly registered by the Parlement, but their status was decidedly inferior to that of the *avocats*. They were legal consultants who worked for private parties, helping them draw up petitions in legal form, getting them hearing dates, and leading them through the complicated process of bringing a case before the Parlement. *Procureurs* might have some legal training, but they did not have a *licence* and they were not qualified to argue before the court. They employed clerks who were undertaking the ten-year apprenticeship required to learn the ropes of legal recording. In sixteenth-century Paris there were 300 *procureurs* and 500 clerks attached to the Parlement, thus representing a sizeable interest group. The clerks, ranging in age from sixteen to twenty-five, had their own unofficial youth association known collectively as the Basoche. They were famous for their pranks and bawdy satirical skits.

A characteristic member of this legal "middle class" was René Felot, whose 200 letters analyzed by Joanna Virginia Hamilton give us a window on his activities. He was a *procureur* attached to the Parlement of Brittany in the 1690s.[12] Felot was from Vannes, where the Parlement had resided during its exile from Rennes from 1675 to 1690. In 1701 he was living in Vannes as a "bourgeois," having resigned his judicial post to a colleague. He was well-off financially, judging by his capitation tax, and he lived with his family in the two nicely furnished upper stories of a building in the professional quarter of Vannes. He also owned an estate in the countryside where he housed his mother. Like most people of the day, Felot operated entirely through personal contacts. He did business through his sister in Rennes, her son, his cousin in Croisic, a priest in Vannes, a rector in Sarzeau, and more occasionally with about thirty other correspondents, all within a certain radius around Vannes. Although "living off his rents," Felot was involved with a variety of economic activities. He did legal work on behalf of his successor in Rennes when legal actions in Vannes were part of a case before the Parlement. He bought and sold grain. He served as receiving agent for a priest in Nantes who was importing shipments of wines, housewares, bricks, starch, lime, prunes, grapes, tapestries, clothing, and shoes. He contemplated investing in a company to buy and sell wood from a nearby forest, and he was involved in selling serge (cloth) in Vannes. He bid on a tax farm. He lent out money. Here is a lawyer who becomes a "bourgeois" but who is involved in activities typical of a merchant or a rural landowner.

Another category of legal practitioners was the notary. Notaries were centrally important to families as legal and financial consultants and advisors. Their principal function was to record legal documents such as wills, business agreements, and marriage contracts, which they listed chronologically in a large register. The notary's copy was considered the original, which could then be consulted to prove the authenticity of the document by comparing it to other copies. Each document was signed by two notaries and a variety of witnesses. Although a few notaries were very wealthy, especially in Paris, most had modest incomes and worked in small shops very much like other artisans. Their families did not advance very much socially. They were usually poorer than the *avocats* and *procureurs* and they tended to marry within their own circles. They were not trained in the law but they were familiar with the appropriate legal formulas needed for each occasion. Since they came in contact every day with property transfers, inheritance issues, business arrangements, and the constitution of *rentes* (loans), they tended to become financial advisors and served as mediators in personal feuds and arrangements to borrow money.[13]

All these practitioners were middling urban professionals with little hope of upward mobility. Below them every court had a series of *greffiers* (chief clerks) who recorded transactions and scheduled sessions and a team of *huissiers* (process-servers) and *sergents* (guards). The *greffiers* were influential facilitators of court business. The *huissiers* and *sergents* were basically armed guards who delivered summonses and maintained order.

The world of artisans

Bourgeois, merchants, royal officers, and lawyers made up the cream of urban society. But the most important citizens were the artisans. It was they who did all the processing of raw materials, the making of commodities, the constructing of buildings, the decorating of churches and palaces, in short, all the skilled, non-agricultural work. Artisans worked with relatively simple tools, using jealously guarded techniques passed down from previous generations. It was no small task to construct a shoe or make a wagon wheel or a barrel. Virtually everything one needed in this society to dress, pray, plow, furnish, build, or travel, was laboriously made to order, by hand. This meant that consumers had direct, personal relations with the person who made them a table, or shoed their horses, and that they valued the final product because it was not easily replaced.

This economic activity was organized around the concept of distinct "trades" or "crafts" (*métiers*), each with its own guild or legal association. Specialization was the rule. Each town had a long roster of resident crafts, some of which became obsolete and disappeared with time (armor-makers), while others appeared and multiplied (wig-makers). In 1550 Rouen had seventy-two guilds. Dijon had seventy-six in 1643. Toulouse had sixty-four chartered guilds and forty-five independent guilds in 1673, involving 3,329 master guildsmen.[14] A good way to capture this richness of association is simply to list examples. In 1545, Lyon guilds included butchers, bakers, saddle-makers, gatherers of fresh fish, cheese-venders, innkeepers, millers, mustard-makers, pastrycooks, fishmongers, meat-roasters, poultrymen, tavern-keepers, barrel-makers, tripe-sellers, vinegrowers, vinegar-makers, needle-makers, bleachers of cloth, hosiers, harness-makers, embroiderers, carders, candle-makers, stocking-makers, cobblers, clothing-sewers, tailors, makers of sheaths for knives, glove-makers, leather-workers, silk-throwers, perfume-makers, lace-makers, furriers, dealers in plumes, saddle-makers, taffeta-weavers, tanners, upholsterers, silk-dyers, weavers, and velvet-makers. In 1725, the membership of the 117 *métiers* of Paris ranged from ten to over two thousand, with an average of 270 members each, totaling 331,583 artisans. As we might

Figure 11 Anonymous, eighteenth century. Saint Crespin as a shoemaker. There are very few images of artisans at work in their shops. This page from an almanac honoring Saint Crispin, patron saint of shoemakers, captures the atmosphere well.

expect, the largest associations, with more than a thousand members, were the providers of basic necessities: mercers, winesellers, market gardeners, tailors, shoemakers, seamstresses, and cobblers. But elegant Paris had quite a few purveyors of luxuries: 47 furriers, 500 goldsmiths, 180 watch- and clock-makers, 50 makers of musical instruments, 229 bookbinders.

The guilds to which these artisans belonged were proud organizations, considered pillars of the civic community. They were always town-based. They set standards for their craft and regulated who was allowed to practice it. Each guild had a distinct personality expressed by banners bearing its emblems, veneration of a particular patron saint, and maintenance of the chapel dedicated to that saint. Guilds marched together in civic processions. They selected officers, issued statutes, and named inspectors, often called *jurés*, to tour the shops and inspect the merchandise. *Jurés* could confiscate defective merchandise and issue fines for infractions. Often there were fierce rivalries between guilds whose skills overlapped. In 1742, for example, the locksmiths of Toulouse drew up a detailed list of exactly which objects they had a monopoly on producing in order to protect themselves from the competition of the nailsmiths, the blacksmiths, the edge-tool-makers, and the cutlers.[15]

Guilds enforced standards by regulating the hiring of apprentices and the employment of journeymen. This system had originated in medieval towns. The idea was to protect the public from shoddy merchandise and overpricing, while protecting the masters by limiting their competition to the number of shops that the community could effectively support. This interdiction made some sense in a small, isolated community, but it sat less well in larger cities.

Guilds were sometimes self-governing organizations, but usually they had a specific connection to the constituted authorities. The tradition was established early that royal approval was needed to provide the authority for a guild to become a legal entity capable of exercising jurisdiction over its own rules. Day-by-day governance was carried out by the members themselves. In many places, guilds or certain trades were written into the municipal constitution in the form of representation in the city council or consultation by city officials when serious decisions were contemplated. Sometimes they chose their own officers and inspectors, but more often these were named by the city council.

Guilds ranged greatly in importance. There were always relatively simple services provided by neighborhood artisans such as bakers, locksmiths, or winesellers. There were also highly influential guilds of merchants with international reach. Their members were elite figures who played an important role in municipal politics: for example, the "six corps" in Paris, namely the drapers, *épiciers*, mercers, furriers, hatters, and silversmiths. Louis XIV's minister Colbert began an ambitious campaign to intervene in guild affairs and turn them into semi-independent organs of the state. His motives were mixed. He firmly believed that by setting standards he could make the French economy more competitive, but the king also wanted him to create solvent corporate bodies that could be taxed and induced to take out loans on behalf of the king.

Historians have traditionally presented the guild system as an orderly but rigid framework encompassing all production. By limiting competition and banning innovation, they argued, guilds presented serious impediments to economic progress. Their policies kept prices high and quantities low, producing products of superior quality, but resisting change and putting a brake on expansion. Recent studies see urban economies as far more flexible and market-oriented. The guilds were important in regulating and policing artisans' shops, but they were never capable of dominating the entire economy.

Guilds were organized around strict control of the work force. Apprentices were carefully selected at age ten to twenty and assigned to live and work with a master for two to six years. The master was paid a fee, and a contract was drawn up stipulating the boy's obligation to serve and obey the master and the master's duty to train the boy. This was a socialization process designed to introduce the newcomer to the skills and secrets of the trade. Apprentices as young as ten were sometimes placed in shops away from home, where their closest role models might be other apprentices or older journeymen from the shop. Others learned the trade in their father's shop. Either way, they were often in the streets running errands or getting into trouble, and their presence was part of the pageant of street life, especially in the largest cities. Ménétra, the Parisian glazier who wrote an account of his life, spent his youth evading work in his father's shop and instead setting off firecrackers under the seats of venders, playing hide and seek under the Pont Neuf, and sleeping out overnight in boats docked along the Seine. Many apprentices ran away or were fired by their masters.

Those who finished their training became journeymen, that is, young adults working as a hired labor force in masters' shops. The tradition was that they were to travel on a *tour de France*, hiring themselves out as needed to masters in different cities to get experience and see the world. Then they were to settle down in their home city and find a wife. After fees had been paid and many formalities had been accomplished, they would be admitted to the guild as a master and allowed to open their own shop. One of the entrance requirements was often that they demonstrate their skills at their craft by creating and displaying a "masterpiece." The reality was quite different from this idyllic progression. Masters and journeymen were adversaries. They had conflicting interests and they were competitors for the limited number of available livelihoods. It was in the interest of guild masters to restrict membership and save the best spots for their sons. They scrutinized the morals and family background of aspiring members and set high standards. Few journeymen made the grade; the rest became a skilled labor force subject to downturns and layoffs.

Cracks were appearing in the guild system. The guild typically restricted the number of looms one master weaver could operate in his shop, but faced with competition, masters added extra looms and hired journeymen to operate them. Masters fallen on hard times might be reduced to working for piece rates. A growing industry could in effect proletarianize many masters and hundreds of auxiliary workers by turning them into dependent employees.

Manufacturing luxury goods for an international market required large capital outlays. Artisans could not afford this, so processes like silk weaving came to be organized by merchants with capital. In such cases, master artisans were increasingly drawn into various roles in a larger system of production that they did not control. Their fortunes depended on luck, circumstance, and cleverness. Some rose, some crashed. A few became merchant-entrepreneurs who organized textile production by hiring employee-artisans.

The next logical step was to move production to the countryside where there were no guilds or restrictions, and hire peasants to do the spinning, weaving, and finishing in their cottages. For example, in 1708 in the region around Beauvais, at least 5,000 of the 8,000 working looms were in rural cottages. All this cloth was bought up and taken back to the town of Beauvais, where 30,000 pieces of finished cloth were processed per year. Export to Spain and the New World via Rouen was handled by a tiny, closed elite. As the weavers put it, "The whole business is in the hands of seven or eight families who have made immense fortunes in the last fifteen or twenty years and who are fattening themselves up at the expense of the artisans." This "cottage industry" or "proto-industry" took advantage of the peasants' lower standard of living and the absence of guild restrictions to force down labor costs.

Faced with these challenges, many guild masters defended their livelihoods by resorting to defensive name-calling. Pierre Ignace Chavatte, a poor weaver who lived in Lille at the time of Louis XIV, was a master in the declining guild of *sayetteurs*. He was aware of the competition from the countryside, which he irascibly dismissed by evoking a superior lifestyle: "the inhabitants of this town do not live as frugally as the people in the countryside, and we would never be able to get used to eating nothing but porridge and drinking only water as the peasants do."[16]

A typical case of industrial expansion was Lyon's silk industry, launched in 1536, which grew to become the city's major source of employment. Tax records in 1575 show 200 masters, of whom 138 were velvet-weavers, 31 taffeta-weavers, 15 spinners, 15 dyers, and two unidentified. In 1660 the silk trade had expanded to encompass 2,076 looms worked by 841 masters, 809 journeymen and apprentices, around 800 sons of masters, plus a great many women and children who were used for spinning and milling the silk thread.[17] In an industry like this, the inevitable slumps in international demand would now put thousands of citizens out of work because they had become dependent on employment by merchant-entrepreneurs who could cut back whenever it was financially desirable to do so.

The results could be catastrophic. In Lyon in January 1627, the city council was besieged with appeals concerning a rumor that the use of silk in clothing was to be banned. Four hundred silk workers burst into the council room and complained that "20,000 people" were out of work because of this rumor. A week later they returned, and despite a stern warning from the council that such gatherings were illegal, the clamor was so great that a group of spokesmen was allowed to present their case. "Five or six began screaming all at once that they were miserable, they had no work for their craft, that it was because of the law about dress, they could not earn their livelihoods, they were reduced to starvation, and in the name of God they implored the consulate to *do something* about it."[18]

For all these reasons the traditional guild system could never uphold its monopoly on production. Competition from journeymen, subordination to merchant capitalists, and the inability to police effectively all took their toll. The result, in Paris at least, was what Michael Sonenscher calls the "economy of the bazaar," a free-for-all of self-help and improvisation. The guilds were still immensely powerful institutions with hundreds of members. But by that very fact they could not keep track of all their people. Much work was done on the sly by unaffiliated workers. Some guilds were poorly managed or driven by bribes. New techniques discovered independently by workers on the job were ignored by the traditional guilds. Journeymen shut out of the official guild system struck private deals to produce extra units in unauthorized locations, often by farming out the work to other unemployed weavers. The larger the city and the more diverse the population, especially in the eighteenth century, the more "the underground economy" prospered. As Sonenscher put it, "There was, in other words, no clear or rigid separation between a corporate world consisting of master artisans secure in the enjoyment of their rights and privileges, and an unenfranchised world of journeymen divested of any rights or privileges at all."[19]

Women's work

Women also played an essential role in the work life of the city, but their contribution was half hidden behind the more visible, institutionally reinforced activity of the men. French society was profoundly patriarchal in nature, meaning that virtually everybody thought that men had a superior claim to authority and should always be in charge. Women were treated before the law as minors under the guardianship of first their fathers, then their husbands. The husband controlled the management of the wife's dowry. She could not legally sign contracts, take out loans, or initiate lawsuits without his consent. Caught being unfaithful in marriage, wives could have a separation forced upon them, whereas unfaithful husbands were not prosecuted.

Women's influence in the workplace seems to have deteriorated during the early modern period, largely as a result of the increasingly hierarchical nature of social relations. Women had participated more completely in many medieval guilds, but they were gradually forced out of most of them or else lost status and rights. The jobs that were left to them were either low in status and poorly paying or involved skills that were considered too feminine for men to perform. Gender roles dictated that the wife was to manage the household and raise the children. When she did work, it was in the context of supporting the household as an economic unit. She was essentially relegated to the home, whereas the husband's place was out in the world dealing with the public and engaging in politics with other men.

This bleak picture painted by the first women's historians needs some modification. Women were indeed subject to all these constraints, but they also had a central role to play in families and businesses, and there is growing evidence of women acting independently, running shops, and looking out for their own interests in legal cases and in daily life. Artisans' wives hardly led passive, secluded existences. A wife might work side by side with her husband in the shop, take over when he had to go out, keep the books, or direct servants and apprentices. A weaver's wife might prepare the loom for her husband to weave, but she might also fill in for him and carry on with the actual weaving.

Although most women had no formal training, they often knew the business as well as, or better than, their husbands. Guild rules usually did not allow them to become masters in their own right, but they were allowed to step in and take over if their husbands died. Many guilds also gave favored treatment to a son, allowing him to become a master without as many years of apprenticeship as an outsider, or by simply paying a fee. Widows who married a journeyman in the same trade as their former husbands could transfer their status as "provisional" master to the new husband. In this way guilds protected the family unit against newcomers and even acknowledged some influence on the part of the wife.

These women knew how to look after themselves. Julie Hardwick gives us the example of Louise Lecocq, daughter of a baker, mother of seven children, and wife of a notary in Nantes, whose husband fled from the city in 1656, accused and apparently guilty of embezzling the money of his clients. Faced with tough questioning from a roomful of city officials, Lecocq defended her husband, engaged in delaying tactics, hid and then revealed that she had the keys to the books, got herself a lawyer, and initiated legal proceedings to assert her claims as a creditor of her husband. She was aided in these defensive moves by her sister and her sister-in-law, both of whom were also married to notaries – evidence of professional ties, blood ties, and gender ties.[20] Women like Lecocq could be fierce defenders of their turf and vehemently urged on their husbands. When an *échevin* tried to requisition some horses from an inn in Dijon in 1644, the innkeeper protested that this was not right, but his wife screamed, "Devil take me, you won't get them." She announced that "she wished the Devil would take the *maire*, the syndic and the *échevins*," and brandishing a knife which she grabbed from the kitchen, she swore that "If you come near me I'll plant this knife in your chest to give me something to feed on, you starving beggar."[21] This was the same sort of feminine indignation that instigated riots.

Further research has revealed that women held jobs outside the household. Often these were menial positions such as servants or laundresses, but sometimes they were mistresses of trades in their own right. To be sure, the occupations they took up fitted contemporaries' views of what constituted "women's work." Besides the inevitable midwifery and prostitution, women were involved in textiles, where they spun thread, unwound silk, and became drapers and weavers of linen. Linen was a rough cloth made from flax and hemp, which was in demand for underclothing, napkins, and bed sheets. Some varieties were used to make sails. The association in people's minds of linen with "crude and utilitarian," "less skilled work," "making beds," and "setting tables" resulted in a gendered prescription that linen workers be women. Provision of food was also gendered feminine: women sold fish and vegetables in markets, peddled all sorts of edibles in the streets, and were known for running hostels and taverns. In metal work they were relegated to making pins. In the design and creation of clothing, they were limited to women's and children's clothes.

Nancy Locklin's study of the major towns in Brittany uncovers an impressive number of self-employed women who were heads of households. In the early eighteenth century she finds 516 such women in Nantes, 872 in Rennes, and 160–600 in each of five other towns. These are small numbers compared to the male artisan population, but there are enough to make it impossible to hold onto the idea that women were restricted to the household. In one instance 19 percent of these women were widows carrying on their husband's businesses, but the rest were unmarried women on their own or women married but pursuing a separate occupation.[22] These independent *bretonnes* were heavily concentrated in the usual categories, mostly low-paying jobs such as the retailing of foods and merchandise, clothing, and menial textile jobs such as spinning. Their trades were highly gendered. Linen, lace, buttons, bleaching, and spinning were for women; tailoring, weaving, combing and dying were for men.[23]

Carol Loats has found similar evidence in Paris in the mid sixteenth century. Studying apprenticeship contracts, she found many cases where the wife trained apprentices in the shop of her husband, or where a woman alone or a widow trained new employees without any husband. In eighty-five cases the husband and wife had entirely separate professions, with combinations such as a butter-seller and a cloth-shearer, or a fish-seller and a printer.[24] In some places women held their own. Rouen in the 1770s had 700 female masters, or 10 percent of all the masters in the city, and women had enjoyed almost equal rights since the middle ages in seven of the city's 112 guilds. Four guilds were exclusively feminine, including, typically, the linen drapers of new clothes, the linen drapers of old clothes, the *bonnetières* (knitted wear) and the seamstresses. Women collaborated with men in four other guilds. One guild, the ribbon-makers, had 160 members, 64 percent of them women. This ratio came as close to equality as the old regime could imagine. Women participated in the ribbon-makers' initiation rite, a practice which was highly unusual. Like the men, they presented masterpieces in order to be admitted, served as guild inspectors, and acquired the capacity, by virtue of their guild membership, to initiate lawsuits without a man's permission.[25]

An interesting example of gendered differentiation concerning the tailors and seamstresses of Paris is provided by Clare Crowston. In 1675, as part of the move to incorporate all of France's trades, Louis XIV granted an exclusive charter to the Parisian seamstresses to make children's clothing, along with dressing gowns and undergarments for women, thus taking that business away from the tailors. The women would have their own autonomous guild, but they were forbidden to hire male journeymen, and in return their former colleagues in the tailors' guild could no longer make these items or hire female workers. In subsequent disputes, both sides used gender stereotypes to their advantage. The tailors portrayed themselves as patriarchs defending their families by allowing their daughters to carry on the business and transmit it to a journeyman-husband. The seamstresses saw themselves as virtuous women protecting other women by keeping the masculine tailors away from the delicate matter of dealing with children and women. They also claimed to be giving women the opportunity to pursue an independent occupation free from the influence of men.[26]

These examples, taken from recent research, are certainly not typical and do not alter the situation of the vast majority. What they do tell us is that working women were capable of adapting to circumstances and fighting for their rights, and that some always did. Women were profoundly unequal to men. Even when they had a guild they were usually deprived of the rituals and ceremonies that reinforced the pride of their male counterparts. They were capable of anything, but their actual opportunities were limited to low-paying activities governed by negative gendered assumptions.

The urban poor

In major cities, as many as 60 percent of the total households were headed by poor working men who did not appear on lists of occupations or taxes. This very rough estimate refers to people in a variety of situations. The essential question for those on the low end of the social scale was whether their families could survive on the income of their working members. Skilled artisans in the lowest-paying occupations pulled through in good years but fell below subsistence in bad times.

Manual laborers who lived from day to day were the worst off. They made ends meet by scrambling after supplementary income in any way possible. A rented strip of farmland might yield 10 livres per year. Some makers of pottery and candles also sold eggs and butter. A part-time postman, town crier or fireman could also make shoes, make soap, or work in people's gardens. Mothers wove lace in their rooms while babies played on the floor. If someone fell sick or more babies arrived, the family would have to take to the road and beg.[27] Servants and journeymen, who jointly may have made up 20 percent of the population, were slightly better off. They were at the mercy of their employer, but while they were employed they were at least housed and fed. Still lower on the scale were whole families of beggars, or abandoned women and children who had no livelihoods. There were the *pauvres valides*, those who could work but had no job. Then there were those who could not work because they were crippled or mentally ill, or too old. Olwen Hufton has calculated that a working family of three in eighteenth-century Bayeux would need 20 sols per day to provide a basic subsistence.[28] The highest wage for carpenters, joiners, and textile workers was less than 14 sols, and the most their wives could earn from making lace, spinning cotton, or washing clothes was 6 sols. Thus if both parents worked and they had no additional children, their 20 sols might barely suffice. But this estimate assumes that they both had the best possible jobs, and it fails to take into account the many holidays when there was no pay.

If a series of bad harvests shot the price of bread skyward or there was a slump in the local industry, many of the marginally employed slipped into poverty. Swarms of beggars seemed to flood the streets and "vagabonds" and thieves threatened public order. "These miserable bands include men and women of all ages, couples with their children, abandoned infants and adolescents, journeymen without work, cripples, old men, and of course professional vagabonds," complained the city council of Amiens in 1717. Such people sometimes came from far away. In a sample of 302 vagabonds arrested between 1615 and 1640 in Amiens, about 42 percent came from surrounding provinces, 12 percent from the Paris region, and 35 percent from as far away as Franche-Comté, Auvergne, and the southwest.[29] Gascon estimates that in sixteenth-century Lyon in a normal year 6–8 percent of the population were destitute, and in a year of bad harvest that number rose to between 15 and 20 percent. An estimate of the numbers of beggars haunting the streets of Lyon was 8,000 in 1531. In 1597 nourishment was distributed to 6,746 paupers for four months.[30] In the late eighteenth century, one-third of the 10,000 inhabitants of Bayeux were on the edge of subsistence and another sixth were dependent on relief. At the same time a tenth of Parisians was destitute.

Faced with beggars accosting them whenever they went outside, and disreputable-looking vagabonds moving in threatening gangs through the countryside, respectable citizens began to change their view of the poor, seeing them as lazy bums and dangerous criminals instead of innocent souls requesting handouts in the name of Jesus Christ as they would have done in earlier times. In Lyon the consulate created one of the first new institutions to deal with this problem, the Aumône-Générale, in 1534. A board of rectors was established to manage poor relief in the city. Endowments for charity from a variety of church foundations and private charities were pooled and contributions were accepted. Instead of allowing the poor to beg or the rich to give them donations, the authorities drew up a list of the legitimately needy in the community, a sort of census of the poor, and those parties received a weekly allotment of food delivered to their door. Three thousand of these handouts were delivered per week for thirty years in Lyon. Rouen adopted a similar plan the same year, and every town soon had the equivalent. The novelty lay in the pooling of

Figure 12 Three beggars by Jacques Callot. Beggars, homeless families, pilgrims, and thieves, all of them poor, frequented the highways and begged for alms at city squares and outside the doors of the wealthy. Callot, from Lorraine, was a sympathetic chronicler of both high and low life who frequented the courts of Italy and France in the 1620s and 1630s.

resources and the rational, secular administration. The dark side was that the program only applied to certified "worthy" residents. "Unworthy" vagabonds and beggars from other places were to be whipped and sent out of town.

These measures did not solve the problem, and the numbers of beggars on the roads constantly increased. The more typical solution that emerged everywhere was the arrest of vagabonds and their incarceration in what were called hospitals but were really work houses, where the inmates were forced to do productive work and given minimal nourishment and places to sleep. The prototype for this solution was the Hôpital-Général of Paris, founded in 1656, which was a state-mandated pooling of the resources of ten existing hospitals and prisons into one organization dedicated to caring for the sick and locking up the beggars. In 1662 a royal edict stipulated that a similar process be undertaken in every town in France, and the towns gradually complied.

The shape of the urban population

Each French city had a distinctive personality created by its particular combination of social types. In a few cities, tax rolls provide enough information to perceive the composition of the population. For example, in 1545 Lyon was an international banking center whose international fairs were a meeting ground for merchants from all over Europe. The city had about sixty foreign bankers in residence, plus forty-seven less important foreigners who dealt with money. Its 237 native merchants included merchant-drapers, book-sellers, bankers, and international traders in merchandise and commodities. Middling merchants did a modest regional business, and local merchants managed shops which sold items retail. Also in this category were the nineteen "bourgeois." This whole banking and merchant sector comprised 13.2 percent of the taxpayers and included most of the richest citizens. Collectively they paid more than 25 percent of the total tax.

In the absence of a university or a sovereign court, other "professions" were poorly represented. These included doctors, barbers, surgeons, "writers," and one "extractor of teeth." The sixty-seven royal officers were only of middling stature because Lyon had no high court. The legal practitioners included notaries, who registered official papers, and *avocats* and *procureurs*, who handled

Table 4.1 *Social distribution of taxpayers in Lyon, 1545*

Category of Taxpayer	Number of households	Percentage of households	Percentages grouped	Hypothetical % of total households
Clerics	–	–	–	–
Bankers, handlers of money	52	1.7	} 13.2	2.7
Merchants large and small	333	10.9		
Bourgeois (*rentiers*)	19	0.6		
Liberal professions, medical	101	3.3	} 9.9	2.0
High royal officers	67	2.1		
Lower royal officers				
Legal professions	137	4.5		
Lesser functionaries	80	2.6	2.6	0.5
Artisans/crafts/ shops	2,104	68.6	} 70.6	14.4
Agriculture	0	0.00		
Unskilled labor	62	2.0		
Miscellaneous or unknown	112	3.7	3.7	0.8
Rest of 15,000 households	–	–	–	79.6
Total	3,067	100.0	100.0	100.0

Source: Richard Gascon, *Grand commerce et vie urbaine au XVIe siècle: Lyon et ses marchands*, 2 vols. (Paris, 1971), I, 357–404.

business before the local courts. This whole "middle class" adds up to only 9.9 percent of the households taxed. Then the many lesser functionaries such as *greffiers* and *sergents* add another 2.6 percent. The largest segment of taxpayers was made up of artisans, who constituted nearly seven-tenths of the working population, and represented the real life of the city. Their trades were extremely varied, ranging from highly skilled and highly paid craftsmen to persons involved essentially in acquiring and selling at retail. Finally, below the artisans and their employees were large numbers of day laborers who were too poor to be taxed.

Thus we may consider Lyon as having about 13 percent bankers and merchants (not counting the foreign bankers), 10 percent "middle class" citizens, 3 percent lesser functionaries, and 71 percent artisans and taxpaying unskilled labor (see Table 4.1). Priests and resident nobles were not included in the tax rolls. If we reinsert these categories of people into a total population of about 15,000 households, according to Richard Gascon's rough guess, we will have merchants making up 3 percent of the total households, the "middle class" 2 percent and the master artisans 14 percent. This means that 80 percent of the households were headed by wage workers and other poor inhabitants. Lyon was a working-class city in which a thin upper crust of wealthy banking and trading families collaborated with a larger minority of artisanal craftsmen and ruled over a vast majority of poor weavers and day laborers.

Other cities produce comparable figures. The artisans and the laboring poor always represent the largest group, although the latter are under-represented in most cases. Clergy, when noted, are 5–10 percent. The merchants are most numerous in the commercial cities, such as Lyon and Amiens, but they are never more than 12 percent. In cities with sovereign courts the robe nobles make up 3–5 five percent, and there are more legal practitioners. Servants are also numerous in centers of the robe nobility, or so it appears in Aix, the only available case. Once again, the preponderance of artisans and menial laborers is overwhelming.

The rise of seafaring ports

In the eighteenth century major port cities such as Nantes, Saint-Malo, Bordeaux, and Marseille came to life in a new way. Their spectacular growth was built upon Europe's colonial expansion and the rise of the Atlantic economy. In Saint-Malo privateers made fortunes attacking British ships during the wars of Louis XIV, and soon they were undertaking the 20,000 kilometer voyage to the Pacific coast of South America, bypassing the Spanish middlemen and bringing home 200 million livres of New World silver between 1703 and 1718, reaping profits of 136 to 306 percent.[31] The beneficiaries built themselves rows of elegant mansions overlooking the sea. Meanwhile Nantes, the emerging capital of the French slave trade, was building a new city next to the old medieval one, and its merchants were constructing grand *hôtels* in the new district called the Île Feydeau.

The change was probably best exemplified by Bordeaux. Its population rose from 55,000 in 1715 to 109,500 at the end of the century. Bordeaux had a long tradition of producing and exporting wine, and rich *parlementaires*, among others, were grabbing the best lands and developing the fine crus that still exist today. But these were traditional, inward-looking developments focused on the land and dependent on foreigners to export the results. The new exciting commerce was with the Antilles, where sugar and tobacco plantations were producing new fortunes and enslaving thousands of Africans.[32] In 1717 the commerce of Bordeaux was valued at 13 million livres; by 1789, it was 250 million. In 1730, 115 ships per year left the port. In 1786, there were 265, including 23 slavers heading for Africa and a dozen going to the Indian Ocean. In fact, the eighteenth century saw 411 slaving expeditions leave the port of Bordeaux, carrying 150,000 slaves to their fate.

Soon the city harbored seven to eight thousand sailors, carpenters, and ship builders, and the port was employing 17–18,000 persons, including merchants, bankers, agents and bookkeepers. European exports were mostly handled by resident communities of German, Portuguese Jewish, Dutch, and Irish merchants. Any semblance of orderly regulation was lost. As one foreign observer commented; "No matter who settles here, whether he is Jewish or Greek, he buys, sells, or engages in commerce [freely]; and no one asks where he came from or what he wants. As long as he stays within the accepted rules, the authorities ask nothing of him."[33]

This new prosperity made the fortunes of successful businessmen who, unlike their counterparts in earlier times, showed less interest in purchasing royal offices or retiring to their county estates to lord it over their tenants. They constituted a genuine bourgeoisie of planters and repatriated manufacturers. They sailed back and forth to the Antilles, acquiring plantations and slaves, or getting involved in the new industries that processed colonial products in Bordeaux for export to other European countries.

Flush with success, Bordeaux transformed itself into a more open, elegant city adorned with monumental architecture in the latest classical style. The same urbanism was taking place in other regional capitals, making life more pleasant for persons of fashion who wanted to live in town. In Paris Louis XV was constructing the enormous Place Royale (today Place de la Concorde). Dijon had its own Place Royale centered on the site of the Estates of Burgundy and the remnants of the old ducal palace. In Toulouse the Place du Capitole acquired uniform facades on three sides of the square and an elegant facade to hide the old ramshackle Capitole (the city hall of Toulouse). In Bordeaux two energetic intendants, Claude Boucher and Louis-Urbain Aubert, marquis de Tourny led the way in the beautification of the city. It is not surprising that it took determined royal agents from outside to modernize the urban landscape because they were used to thinking in national terms, and from their perspective Bordeaux and other regional capitals needed to reflect a broader civilization. Many of their reforms were opposed by the more conservative city government. And the architecture, in what was becoming a national style, was designed by Gabriel and other well-known architects, mostly borrowed from their work at Versailles.

In the course of a generation, the city was opened up by building new monumental portals at the gates of the old wall, most of which was demolished, and the complete reconstruction of the entire expanse of the port, or river front, which was now lined with impressive public buildings and uniform facades. Bordeaux too had its Place Royale, complete with its statue of Louis XV. The Grand Theatre, designed by Victor Louis, was much admired. The Allées Tourny, a tree-lined promenade, was complemented by a public garden and a number of private mansions designed by major architects. Monuments like these, often in the latest neo-classical style, left their imprint on many regional capitals. The Place de la Concorde in Paris, framed by the facades of the Hotel Crillon and the Ministry of the Navy on the north, and opposite, across the river, the Grecian facade of the National Assembly on the south, are the most familiar examples of this legacy.

Suggestions for further reading: towns and town life

General Studies

Benedict, Philip, ed., *Cities and Social Change in Early Modern France* (London, 1989).

Finley-Croswhite, Annette, *Henry IV and the Towns: The Pursuit of Legitimacy in French Urban Society, 1589–1610* (Cambridge, 1999).

Konvitz, Josef W., *Cities and the Sea: Port City Planning in Early Modern Europe* (Baltimore, MD, 1978).

Studies of particular cities

Benedict, Philip, *Rouen during the Wars of Religion: Popular Disorder, Public Order, and the Confessional Struggle* (Cambridge, 1975).
"Faith, Fortune and Social Structure in Seventeenth-Century Montpellier," *Past and Present* 152 (April 1996), 46–78.
Deyon, Pierre, *Amiens, capitale provinciale: étude sur la société urbaine au 17e siècle* (Paris, 1967).
Farr, James R., "Consumers, Commerce, and the Craftsmen of Dijon: The Changing Social and Economic Structure of a Provincial Capital, 1450–1750," in Benedict, *Cities and Social Change*, 134–73.
Hufton, Olwen, *Bayeux in the Late Eighteenth Century: A Social Study* (Oxford, 1967).
Holt, Mack P., "Popular Political Culture and Mayoral Elections in Sixteenth-Century Dijon," in Mack P. Holt, ed., *Society and Institutions in Early Modern France* (Athens, GA, 1991).
Monahan, W. Gregory, *Year of Sorrows: The Great Famine of 1709 in Lyon* (Columbus, OH, 2000).
Robbins, Kevin C., *City on the Ocean Sea: La Rochelle, 1530–1650: Urban Society, Religion, and Politics on the French Atlantic Frontier* (Leiden, 1997).
Schneider, Robert A., *Public Life in Toulouse, 1463–1789: From Municipal Republic to Cosmopolitan City* (Ithaca, NY, 1989).
Wallace, Peter G., *Communities and Conflict in Early Modern Colmar: 1575–1730* (Atlantic Highlands, NJ, 1994).

Merchants and urban elites

Adams, Christine, *A Taste for Comfort and Status: A Bourgeois Family in Eighteenth-Century France* (University Park, PA, 2000).
Beam, Sara, "The 'Basoche' and the 'Bourgeoisie Seconde': Careerists at the Parlement of Paris during the League," *French History* 17 (2004), 367–87.
Beam, Sara, *Laughing Matters: Farce and the Making of Absolutism in France* (Ithaca, NY, 2007).
Bell, David A., *Lawyers and Citizens: The Making of a Political Elite in Old Regime France* (Oxford, 1994).
Breen, Michael P., *Law, City, and King: Legal Culture, Municipal Politics, and State Formation in Early Modern Dijon* (Rochester, NY, 2007).
Brunelle, Gayle, *The New World Merchants of Rouen, 1559–1630* (Kirksville, MO, 1991).
Gascon, Richard, *Grand commerce et vie urbaine au XVIe siècle: Lyon et ses marchands*, 2 vols. (Paris, 1971).

Artisans, crafts, guilds

Farr, James R., *Hands of Honor: Artisans and their World in Dijon, 1550–1650* (Ithaca, NY, 1988).

Hauser, Henri, *Les Compagnonnages d'arts et métiers à Dijon aux XVIIe et XVIIIe siècles* (Paris, 1907).

Kaplan, Steven Laurence, "The Luxury Guilds in Paris in the Eighteenth Century," *Francia* 9 (1981), 257–98.

  The Bakers of Paris and the Bread Question, 1700–1775 (Durham, NC, 1996).

Ménétra, Jacques-Louis, *Journal of My Life*, ed. Daniel Roche, trans. Arthur Goldhammer (New York, 1986).

Safley, Thomas Max and Leonard N. Rosenband, eds., *The Workplace before the Factory: Artisans and Proletarians, 1500–1800* (Ithaca, NY, 1993).

Sonenscher, Michael, *The Hatters of Eighteenth-Century France* (Berkeley, CA, 1987).

Sonenscher, Michael, *Work and Wages: Natural Law, Politics and the Eighteenth-Century French Trades* (Cambridge, 1989).

Truant, Cynthia Maria, *The Rites of Labor: Brotherhoods of Compagnonnage in Old and New Regime France* (Ithaca, NY, 1994).

Gendered work

Coffin, Judith G., "Gender and the Guild Order: The Garment Trades in Eighteenth-Century Paris," *Journal of Economic History* 54 (1994), 768–93.

  The Politics of Women's Work: The Paris Garment Trades 1750–1915 (Princeton, NJ, 1996).

Crowston, Clare, "Engendering the Guilds: Seamstresses, Tailors, and the Clash of Corporate Identities in Old Regime France," *French Historical Studies* 23 (2000), 339–71.

Davis, Natalie Zemon, "Women in the Crafts in 16th Century Lyon," *Feminist Studies* 8 (1982), 46–80, reprinted in Barbara Hanawalt, ed., *Women and Work in Preindustrial Europe* (Bloomington, IN, 1986).

Fairchilds, Cissie C., *Poverty and Charity in Aix-en-Provence, 1640–1789* (Baltimore, MD, 1976).

Gullickson, Gay L., *Spinners and Weavers of Auffay: Rural Industry and the Sexual Division of Labor in a French Village, 1750–1850* (Cambridge 1986).

Hafter, Daryl M., "Female Masters in the Ribbonmaking Guild of Eighteenth-Century Rouen," *French Historical Studies* 20 (1997), 1–14.

Hardwick, Julie, *The Practice of Patriarchy: Gender and the Politics of Household Authority in Early Modern France* (University Park, PA, 1998)

Loats, Carol L., "Gender, Guilds, and Work Identity: Perspectives from Sixteenth-Century Paris," *French Historical Studies* 20 (1997), 15–30.

Locklin, Nancy, *Women's Work and Identity in Eighteenth-Century Brittany* (Aldershot, 2007).

Maza, Sarah C., *Servants and Masters in Eighteenth-Century France: The Uses of Loyalty* (Princeton, NJ, 1983).

Poverty and charity

Adams, Thomas McStay, *Bureaucrats and Beggars: French Social Policy in the Age of the Enlightenment* (Oxford, 1990).

Gutton, Jean-Pierre, *La Société et les pauvres: l'exemple de la généralité de Lyon 1534–1789* (Paris, 1971).

Hickey, Daniel, *Local Hospitals in Ancien Régime France: Rationalization, Resistance, Renewal, 1530–1789* (Montreal, 1997).

Hufton, Olwen, "Begging, Vagrancy, Vagabondage and the Law: An Aspect of the Problem of Poverty in Eighteenth-Century France," *European Studies Review* 2 (1972), 97–123.

  The Poor of Eighteenth-Century France (Oxford, 1973).

Jones, Colin, *Hospitals and Social Welfare in Early Modern France* (New York, 1988).

Meuvret, Jean, *Le Problème des subsistances à l'époque de Louis XIV*, 2 vols. (Paris, 1978).

Monahan, Gregory W., *Year of Sorrows: The Great Famine of 1709 in Lyon* (Columbus, OH, 1993).

Norberg, Katherine, *Rich and Poor in Grenoble 1600–1814* (Berkeley, CA, 1985).

Roche, Daniel, "A Pauper Capital: Some Reflections on the Parisian Poor in the Seventeenth and Eighteenth Centuries," *French History* 1 (1987), 182–209.

Schwartz, Robert, *Policing the Poor in Eighteenth-Century France* (Chapel Hill, NC, 1988).

5 | *The monarchy and the new nobility*

In the sixteenth and seventeenth centuries the French nobility's traditional position at the top of society was challenged by new men whose rise to wealth and influence was built upon professional expertise and administrative service instead of hereditary superiority and warrior skills. This new group was once interpreted by historians as a "rising bourgeoisie" whose emergence infused the monarchy and the state with new values. Their rational, more business-like influence, so the story went, was instrumental in transforming France's medieval monarchy into a proto-modern state, in effect replacing an obsolete warrior class with a new set of educated, legal-minded statebuilders. This view needs revising. These newcomers did not look like a new class because they had so much in common with the old nobility, and they were still dependent upon the traditional monarchy for their success. It makes more sense to think of them as a new branch of the nobility. Both old and new nobility enjoyed the same sources of wealth derived from privileged access to the produce of land and peasants, and both espoused the same belief in the merits of royal service and in a social system built around a divine-right monarch and a hierarchical society. Most important, neither showed much interest in profit-making from agricultural improvement, merchant trade, or business enterprise.

The newcomers are generally referred to as the "robe nobility" after the long robes worn by judges, to distinguish them from the traditional "sword nobles" who were defined by ancient pedigree and military skill. The differences between the robe and the sword were largely a matter of lifestyle and attitude. Robe nobles built their identity around professional and administrative skills instead of military gallantry. They were looked down upon by the traditional nobility as vulgar newcomers with little honor. But the two groups nevertheless intermarried and collaborated in the same financial dealings. As time went on each became more like the other. Robe nobles scrambled to acquire landed estates with the seigneurial honors and lordly attributes of the sword nobles, and tried to emulate the fashions of society's upper crust. Sword nobles became better educated, learned the self-discipline needed to function at court, and took a more businesslike approach to managing their fortunes.

The new elites' rise was brought about through two closely related activities: acquisition of royal offices and management of royal finances. Both meant exploiting the opportunities provided by the expansion of the monarchical state. The families pursuing these strategies had begun their rise several generations earlier with money made in trade. Rather than continuing in business, at some point they had tied their fortunes to the crown and raised themselves up by tapping into the royal state machine either as officers wielding royal authority, or as financiers managing the royal tax flows. It was better to be affiliated with the state than to rely on feudal authority over land or profit from commerce, because the state was the principal distributor of wealth. Even traditional nobles were turning more and more to royal appointments and favors to supplement their landed influence. Thus the state was important, and we need to understand its two distinctive features: venality of office and the system of royal finance.

The world of venality and royal office

Medieval monarchs ruled in direct, personal ways, in conjunction with a council, the *curia regis*, consisting of royal family members, powerful regional nobles, and churchmen. In the late twelfth century, when the royal zone of control began to expand into provinces beyond the Île-de-France, Philip Augustus created districts the size of a county called *bailliages* and appointed loyal followers as *baillis* in each one.[1] Assisted by legally trained prosecutors, the *bailli* ran a court that looked out for royal interests and prosecuted certain kinds of royal crimes. Appeals from these courts began to pour in to the royal council. Swamped with business, the royal council began to assign the more technical cases to a group of legal experts. Their meetings were at first improvised, but by the mid thirteenth century they had evolved into a permanent institution. By the early fourteenth century, the Parlement of Paris had ceased to follow the king and took up permanent residence in the old royal palace on the Île de la Cité in Paris, which came to be known as the Palais de Justice.

By 1400 the Parlement had evolved into a highly distinguished court consisting of some one hundred councilors (*conseillers*) and presidents (*présidents*), divided into three to five separate chambers devoted to various kinds of cases, and presided over by a First President. Half the judges were nobles and clerics, and the rest were commoners with legal training. Thus, from its early days, the Parlement was a very aristocratic company. By virtue of their position close to the king, even non-noble judges enjoyed most of the lifetime privileges of nobles. These included exemption from most regular taxes, and freedom from militia duty and from the obligation to lodge soldiers in their homes.

By the second half of the fifteenth century, the Parlement was developing into a proud institution unified by its own rituals, internal procedures, and common outlook. It had a system of ranks, promotion by seniority, and distinctive attire. Lay councilors wore a long scarlet judicial robe with a fur-lined hat; clerics' robes were vermillion. The First President wore three golden stripes and three bands of white fur on each shoulder and a black velvet beret with a border of gold.[2] The company marched as a body in a privileged place in civic processions. It attempted some control over its membership by promoting a system of election whereby the company could name three candidates to a post and the king could chose one of them. The court also began to have political ambitions. Using the process of registering new laws, it began to issue remonstrances to the king which asked for modification of distasteful measures.

The Paris Parlement was a "sovereign" court, meaning that it dispensed the highest level of justice, issuing judicial decisions in the name of the king unless he took over a case by intervening personally. In the fourteenth century the king also created other, more specialized sovereign courts – the Chambre des Comptes to judge cases concerning the king's finances on appeal and the Cour des Aides to audit tax records and handle appeals. There was a Cour des Monnaies for cases about counterfeiting and devaluation of currency. All these high-level sovereign courts sat in the Palais de Justice, creating a dense concentration of judges who acted in the name of the king.

When it was fully developed, the Parlement consisted of a number of separate chambers, each with its own councilors, presidents, and royal prosecutors. The Grande Chambre was the most prestigious chamber, where important cases were tried. Its councilors, seated by

Figure 13 *Lit de justice* at the Parlement of Paris. This view by Nicolas Lancret (1690–1743) of the plenary session held on February 22, 1723 for the coming of age of the young Louis XV, gives a clear picture of the chamber, the decor, and the robed judges, more or less as they had looked for centuries.

seniority, were called *conseillers à mortier*. A Chambre des Enquêtes was staffed with junior judges who carried out inquests into the circumstances of crimes. A Chambre des Requêtes handled cases concerning certain categories of privileged defendants. The Tournelle, which handled criminal cases, was made up of selected judges from the other chambers, serving in rotation. Attached to each sovereign company was a roster of *avocats*, certified lawyers who argued cases before the court, and a body of certified *procureurs*, who performed more routine administrative procedures on behalf of clients. There were also clerks, process-servers, and sergeants (guards).

The original Parisian sovereign courts were eventually replicated in a number of other provinces. As Charles VII and Louis XI were reintegrating peripheral provinces which had been lost during the Hundred Years War, they renegotiated each province's "privileges," thereby redefining the nature of its relations with the state. An aspect of this "Renaissance decentralization," which was a way of winning back loyalty, was the creation of regional Parlements, using the Paris court as a model. Parlements were set up in Toulouse (1443), Grenoble (1456), Bordeaux (1467), Rouen (1499), Aix (1501), and Brittany (1553). The Paris Parlement continued to be more important than the others, with a district covering most of northern and central France. In other areas the new courts offered advantages for both provincial elites and crown. On the one hand, the transfer of influence to regional leaders as participants in the dispensing of royal justice was a way of co-opting them into support for the monarchy. On the other hand, this same process gave provincial leaders strong corporate institutions which could become centers of resistance. Regional Cours des Aides and Chambres des Comptes were also set up in peripheral provinces, with similar results.

A Parlement always occupied a building at the heart of the city. In Paris, the Palais de Justice occupied the site of the old castle of the medieval kings, thereby making a statement about the continuity of royal authority and the close connection between judges and the crown. In Aix, all the sovereign companies were crammed into the old palace of the counts of Provence. In Toulouse, they used the ramshackle premises of the medieval counts of Toulouse. Dijon and Grenoble had nicer Renaissance buildings, while in Rouen, the Palais, begun in 1499, was decorated with glorious flamboyant tracery. Rennes had a newer building in the classical style of the seventeenth century. All these *palais* were places of bustling activity and surprising worldliness. In Paris the great hall was crammed with *procureurs* and *avocats* looking for clients, hawkers of printed broadsheets, booksellers, and prostitutes. In Toulouse the judges faced a constant ruckus from gamblers and brawling students. The fact that it was in a special zone outside the jurisdiction of the regular city authorities made it a haven for thieves. Matters were no better in Rouen. As an observer remarked around 1550, "Ought one to see in a Palace of Justice so many hawkers, men and women alike? So many pages and valets? So many messengers? And then there are the fruit sellers, who come whether wanted or not... all of these have to be kept out to assure that the commonality stops coming to piss beneath this vault."[3]

The Paris Parlement and its ten provincial counterparts were impressive companies of somber judges who represented the highest ideal of the robe nobility. In Paris, the Parlement was a focal point for the concentration of wealth, talent, and prestige, but it was counterbalanced by the presence nearby of the king, his court, and a great many resident magnates. In the various provinces the other Parlements had no equivalent rival. Their predominant place at the center of social and regional influence was therefore assured, and would only occasionally be challenged by a regional magnate who commanded a strong following.

Dispensing justice in the name of the king was serious business, and the judges' proceedings and demeanor suggested gravity and discipline. They followed an austere schedule, working from 6 a.m. until late morning in small closed sessions and larger hearings; then after a leisurely meal at home, they would return at 2 p.m. for another couple of hours. The long robes and other insignia that they wore outside the courtroom and all around the city lent an aura of authority, not unlike that of priests, as they walked or rode to the Palais de Justice, accompanied by lackeys and followers. The company heard Mass every morning before they started work. They marched as a company in processions and sat together in a designated place in church. They presided personally over the public rituals of execution in which those condemned to death made amends before being executed.

All of them had at least minimal training in the law, and some were exceptionally learned. Their education often consisted of tutoring at home in Latin, followed by residence in one of the *collèges* of the

University in Paris around age twelve, often accompanied by the tutor. Later the student would study law at a more distant university, often while traveling abroad. The more serious judges were dedicated to nurturing and developing the mixed body of Roman law, customary law, and legal precedents that provided the context for their decisions. Each Parlement had its eloquent orators who could deliver lucid summaries of complex cases without consulting their notes. Some of them wrote learned treatises or handbooks of cases. Many were deeply interested in humanist study.

The judges also imposed their influence in political matters of governance, It was their duty to review, register, and promulgate royal edicts, and this function provided them with the opportunity for remonstrances to the king and tactical delays if the new law was not to their liking. Finally, they were expected to fulfill the rather nebulous and poorly defined obligation of looking out for the public well-being and the maintenance of public order. This function set them on a collision course with other local authorities which had more or less the same mandate. Parlements could issue *arrêts* which intervened in matters that were really the job of lesser authorities such as the defense of the city, the grain supply, or the order of march in a procession. These were issues on which *échevins*, military commanders, or the *présidial* courts might already have ruled. But because the Parlements, for all their posturing, had no police to enforce their decrees, such occasions often turned into duels of prestige and public display between *parlementaires* and consuls or *échevins*.

Alongside the sovereign courts, the monarchy also developed a network of financial officers to deal with the immense task of administering tax collections. Tax levies had been undertaken before, but the regular collection of the annual *taille* was begun by Charles VII in 1438. The *taille* was a basic land tax levied on the non-privileged, meaning essentially the rural peasantry. Soon after, the *gabelle*, or salt tax, was instituted, along with excise and sales taxes (*aides* and *traites*). Gradually a system of financial officers was created. The country was divided into province-size financial districts called *généralités*, with receipts managed in each by a *receveur-général* who handled the funds and a *controleur-général* who audited the accounts. A company of *trésoriers de France* provided the administrative oversight. Each *généralité* was divided into smaller county districts called *élections* in which there were *receveurs* and *contrôleurs particuliers* for handling the funds and a company of *élus* for administering them. The *gabelle* and royal domain revenues had a similar hierarchy. At the top, the monies coming in from these agencies were channeled into the royal treasury (the *épargne*), managed by a *trésorier-général de l'épargne*. There were other financial agencies too complicated to describe here.

The important point is that by 1525 the king was being served by powerful companies of royal officers in major provincial cities. On the judicial front, every district had a *bailliage* court staffed with a noble *bailli* and a small team of royal prosecutors. At the higher level each area fell under a near or distant Parlement and an array of other sovereign courts. A parallel hierarchy of financial officers handled the revenue flows.

Under Francis I this whole system was dramatically transformed by the general extension of venality of office. This term means "sale of offices." It was not a new phenomenon, in as much as kings had always treated government offices as personal possessions that could be given as gifts, used to pay off debts, or simply sold for money. As early as the fourteenth century, offices had occasionally been sold, even by one officer to another. Nevertheless, around 1525, Francis I, desperate for additional revenue in his wars against the Emperor Charles V, put the whole range of governmental offices up for sale and created a new treasury, the Parties Casuelles, to handle the revenue. Purchasers of offices were guaranteed to hold the post for life, and the king was guaranteed a substantial source of revenue. In a sense he was mortgaging his authority to private parties who would then exercise it in his name. In return for a large initial sum, the investor received the office and the promise of an annual return, or *gage*, to pay for his services. Another way to put it would be that the officer was making a loan to the king (the price of the office), with the actual office as collateral, and the *gages* as annual interest payments.

Venality of office was not as outlandish a practice as it might seem at first. Granted, the king was selling off authority that might better have been retained and deployed to develop state power, but that option was not available because the king did not have much control over the officers in the provinces and what they did or did not do. He had to rely on local people to collect taxes and enforce laws, and pushing them beyond what they perceived as their personal or regional interest was next to impossible. Selling them their offices was a way of committing them to collaborate with the government. Institutions like the Parlement were filled with officers related by blood, judges who belonged to the client systems of the great, and family dynasties whose members managed to pass the office from father to son despite royal ordinances to the contrary. Thus the generalized sale of offices did not radically transform the composition of royal companies. Francis I merely regularized a system that existed already. As an added bonus, by selling and taxing offices, the king was able to tap the funds of privileged individuals who paid very little in regular taxes.

Venality struck a responsive chord in French life. The more offices the king created, the more persons came forward to buy them. From the point of view of the officer, the office was worth much more than the modest annual stipend (*gages*) paid by the king because it conferred prestige and authority where it counted – within the person's own community. In addition, many offices afforded their holders substantial benefits in the form of fees, bribes, and in the case of financial officers, percentage shares of the proceeds. The purchaser was in effect loaning the price of the office to the king. But unlike a regular loan, he got back in return not just interest payments but decision-making power and an irresistible increase in authority. Now he could wear judicial robes, march in the best positions in public ceremonies, and issue commands and rulings that affected his fellow citizens.

Once this process had begun, the king faced an irresistible temptation. Why not create new offices and sell them to raise additional money? This practice was widely used by Francis I and his successors, who were faced with the soaring costs of the wars against the Habsburgs and the religious wars in France. It was tempting to create more offices than were really needed. Francis added three new presidents to the Paris Parlement, along with fourteen councilors and two new Chambres des Enquêtes of twenty councilors each. Henry II added twenty-two more presidents and 110 more councilors. In 1552 he created and staffed a *présidial* chamber in every *bailliage* court. Soon he began issuing duplicate and triplicate offices for the same post. The two or three incumbents would then have to share the post, with each serving for a half or a third of the year. Lesser offices were invented and sold in great numbers. Within a generation, the whole administration had become bloated with offices, many of them superfluous.

One estimate is that in 1515 there were 4,081 royal officers in the kingdom and in 1665 there were 46,047. A great majority of these held petty, local positions, but the numbers are significant. The Parlement of Toulouse grew from twenty-four officers in 1515 to about a hundred by 1600. The Parlement of Rouen rose from thirty-five to eighty-six in the same period. In the city of Dijon there were 700 officers at the beginning of the century and 1,200 at the end.[4]

As the sale of office became commonplace, the issue of final ownership loomed large. When an officer died, the post reverted to the king, who could sell it all over again. But this meant the loss of a serious investment on the part of the family of the deceased. Predictably, families began to lobby for the right to leave an office to a designated heir. Documents called *résignations* and *survivances* that allowed the holder to pass on their offices to someone else were soon invented. But these dispensations were expensive. They required someone with influence at court to intervene on your behalf, and they were periodically revoked by the king, who could then collect the fees all over again. They were also a mixed blessing for the royal administration because the constant lobbying at court gave powerful individuals a way to develop a private following. In 1604, Henry IV regularized the situation by creating the famous *droit annuel* tax, commonly called the *paulette*. By paying an annual tax of one-sixtieth of the value of an office, the property rights were guaranteed. This meant that the office could be passed on to a minor son, transferred temporarily to a third party until the heir was ready to take it over, or sold outright. This tax removed the uncertainty from officeholders in return for a regular payment by individuals who were otherwise exempt from basic taxes. In addition, because the *droit annuel* was granted only for a specific number of years, the king could pressure the Parlements by threatening not to renew it.

This regularized venality took on added significance because of its connection to the acquisition of nobility. Over the course of the sixteenth century the tradition developed in the sovereign courts that councilors and presidents became personally noble by owning their offices and that their families acquired hereditary nobility in the third generation.[5] This rule was confirmed by an edict in 1600 and eventually extended to the other sovereign courts.

Offices became key elements in the financial planning of families. Their value soared. A councilor in the Paris Parlement who bought his office in 1597 for 10,000 livres could sell it in 1606 for 36,000 livres. An office of councilor in the Parlement of Aix that was worth around 5,000 livres in 1610 had risen to 64,000 in 1684. A post of *président à mortier* at Aix that sold for 75,000 in 1643 was worth 120,000 in 1674.[6] These major offices were lending new prestige and legal nobility to a group of rising families, all based upon their connection to the authority of the monarch.

The seventeenth century was a golden age for the high *robins*. They now constituted an important element in the structure of power. They were noble; they had fortunes grounded in offices; they enjoyed connections with the great aristocracy, the financial world, and the royal ministers. Collectively they shared an institution which gave them a voice in political affairs. But they constituted an *element* in the power structure, not a *constitutional opposition*. They only spoke with the king's voice and issued rulings in his name. Their resistance could have impact, as it did during the days of Richelieu and Mazarin. Later, Jansenist sensibilities and growing criticism of arbitrary government would give rise to the resistance of the eighteenth century. But the *parlementaires* were also vulnerable. The king could threaten their fortunes, now heavily invested in offices. He could change the rules of the game. He could demand additional tribute. Two clashing views of the power relationship – the king claiming absolute authority and the sovereign courts insisting on a collaborative role in decision-making – represented two ways of defending the same upper-class interests. One or the other made headway, depending on circumstances. Sometimes events favored the king, sometimes the courts had room to maneuver.

When Louis XIV unleashed his massive military force on Europe in the wars after 1672, his overriding need became revenues. Increasingly, reform and economic initiatives were put aside as the king desperately tried to cash in assets. He turned to the financiers and revived all the expedients of the past. As John Hurt points out, the robe officers were hard hit. The king used the renewal of the *paulette* tax to impose *augmentations de gages* on the Parlements in 1674, 1683, 1692, and 1701. These were essentially forced loans at a fixed interest rate, which netted the crown four to six million livres each time. The king also resumed the sale of offices and created them at the fastest rate since Henry III. Between 1665 and 1695, 179 new offices in the various Parlements were created, bringing in almost 7.5 million livres. The new positions eroded the value of the old ones, and credit was drained from affluent *parlementaire* circles. Resale prices of offices dipped. In 1702, an *augmentation* milked the *parlementaires* of 5.67 million livres; then, in 1703, the king demanded another 5.67 million. In 1705, seventy-two additional offices were created. In 1708 each *parlementaire* was charged a sum in lieu of the *capitation* (head) tax, and the money was taken right out of their *gages*. In 1709 the *paulette* was abolished with the proviso that each officer pay sixteen years of *paulette* tax in advance. Some judges had trouble raising this money. Some families were ruined. In 1709 the king suspended payment of all *gages* and *augmentations*.

Thus, offices were vulnerable to royal interventions as well as market fluctuations. But, as David Bien points out, the king and the officers were trapped in mutual dependency. To underwrite his loans, the king was dependent on corporate bodies with independent control over their finances such as the Assembly of the Clergy, the provincial Estates, and the judges in the sovereign courts. The judges' collective credit was superior. They could borrow substantial sums from wealthy individuals at much better rates than those the king had to pay, because his ability to nullify debts and change the rules arbitrarily made him a more risky prospect. On the other hand, the king could force royal officers to borrow on his behalf by threatening their offices. They would have to come up with funds for the king by taking out loans, pledging their offices as security. Thus by selling offices that offered prestige, revenues, and nobility, the king was creating a kind of intangible property that could then be mortgaged to underwrite his loans. The officers could not easily refuse because he could jeopardize their offices, which were valuable family investments. The more the king extracted loans secured by the value of offices, the harder it would become to abolish venal offices, because attacking them jeopardized loans. The officers needed his protection, but he needed them to back his growing debt. Both sides were locked in a dependency that made them mutual beneficiaries of the status quo.[7]

To add another complication, a particular office, that of *notaire et secrétaire du roi*, took on a special usefulness for social climbing. These were positions as clerks in the royal chancellery. In 1485 Charles VIII decreed that because of their closeness to the royal wishes, all *secrétaires du roi* would acquire immediate and hereditary nobility. These offices had few responsibilities and could be purchased for a large sum by almost anyone, so they became the most direct route to nobility for wealthy individuals who wanted to upgrade their status.

The financiers and the royal fiscal system

Meanwhile close relatives of these distinguished robe nobles were achieving similar success through finance. By the sixteenth century, the crown's burgeoning fiscal machine was producing flows of money and credit that required handling. Financiers profited from this situation in three ways. The first was by acquiring a financial office. One might begin as a receiver or controller on the level of a province or a subdistrict, in an *élection* or *généralité* or the *gabelle* administration, or the royal domain. The essential job would be taking in and paying out tax monies. Receivers saw quantities of money pass through their hands, and they collaborated closely with investors and financiers. Currency at that time took the form of silver and gold pieces that had to be physically transported from place to place at considerable expense and some danger of theft. The only alternative was transfer of credit on paper, which was essentially an exchange of IOUs between bankers in different places. This was the function of financiers and bankers. Privately they might handle money transfers and arrange loans. If they held a royal office, they got, in addition, access to the royal tax flows. Receivers took in the money and saw to its disbursement; controllers audited the accounts.

This royal financial process was greatly complicated by the practice of assignment of revenues. Because of the difficulty of transporting bullion, the government often paid its bills by instructing its creditors to apply for payment to a designated financial officer at a particular location. This "assigning" of payments to regional collection points obviated the necessity of transporting all the money to Paris and then sending it back to pay for agents or services. The trouble with this practice was that the authorities in Paris might issue multiple claims on the same funds, and a scramble would then ensue over who was actually to receive the money. Meanwhile, the receiver would be taking in tax payments from each district in installments, some of which might come in late or not at all. He would be responsible for producing the entire sum on the date due, and if there was a shortfall he would have to come up with the difference out of his own pocket. But he also had to pay out sums to assignees who presented him with

Figure 14 *The Money-changer Orazio Lago.* He is actually Italian, but the painting gives a rare glimpse of the milieu of professional money-handlers and bankers who rose to influence in France. They were men of account books and notarial contracts.

legal orders to pay. Given this inflow and outflow, he would try to arrange for as much of the tax money as possible to be in his possession for as long a time as possible so that he could put the money to use for short-term loans of his own. His life was an endless sequence of legal cases in which he sued those who had not paid him and fought off suits by claimants demanding that he pay them. No sharp distinction was made at that time between a receiver's private and public funds, as long as he met the required disbursements. For his trouble he was entitled to a percentage share of the total receipts.

The second way financiers profited was by extending loans to the crown. All French kings borrowed money, but during the religious wars and most of the seventeenth century their debt mounted to colossal proportions. Most of it took the form of short-term loans borrowed by contract between the king and an individual who represented a cartel of investors. Since the king had the power to renounce his debts at any time, his credit was shaky, and he generally had to pay higher interest rates than a private person. To make the loans palatable to creditors, they were normally secured by granting the lenders access to a sure source of tax revenue from which to draw their repayment. In this way *taille* receipts were committed for many years into the future.

These sums loaned to the crown represented the pooled resources of an impressive array of France's elites. Françoise Bayard studied 1,539 lenders to the crown from the first half of the seventeenth century. She was able to identify 595 of them and of these, 77 percent were Parisians, 18 percent were from the provinces, and 4.5 percent were foreigners from Württemberg, Swiss cities, Italy, and England. Of the 606 whose occupations are known, 50 percent were bourgeois or merchant-bankers, many of whom were from Lyon; 30 percent were royal officers (including four judges from Parlements, five from the Chambres des Comptes, two from Cours des Aides, and 37 persons connected to the royal household and the king's council); 8 percent were tax farmers; 7 percent were *taille* receivers; 2.6 percent were nobles and 2.3 percent were the agents of nobles.[8] Officers, bankers, connected people from the royal household – here is a road map to the people who had disposable income in the seventeenth century and were willing to invest it in the state enterprise.

The third way of profiting was through tax farms. While the *taille* was collected by royal officers, other indirect taxes were beyond the state's capacity to collect because they required continuous monitoring of a great many points of sale or transit. Collection of particular fees and sales taxes was a day-by-day proposition, and the revenues were highly variable, depending on economic conditions. But because the king always needed the money right away, the solution was to farm the tax out to a company formed for that purpose. After an auction had been held to determine the highest bidder, a contract would be drawn up with the winning cartel, under the name of a figurehead organizer, specifying the exact terms of the deal. The cartel would advance the expected revenue to the king and receive the necessary royal authorizations. It would then subcontract the collection of the tax to subordinate participants.

In 1619, for example, Antoine Feydeau, the man responsible for the company farming out the Aides de France for the whole country, signed a subfarming agreement with three associates, Guérin, Le

Comte, and Delahaye, who would undertake the collections in a section of northern France. They listed another man, Le Cocq, as the underwriter who would guarantee the funds. These partners then subdivided the territory, granting Laon to two men named Royer and Jouet for 27,000 livres, Soissons to a certain Fautrier for 26,500, Noyon also to Fautrier for 25,000, and Guise to a man named Variclair for 10,000. Guérin and the associates paid Feydeau 73,917 livres for the contract. But the sums collected from the subfarmers totaled 88,500 livres. Thus between them they made a profit of 19.7 percent, not counting their expenses. If each of the subcontractors in turn had collected a modest 5 percent more from the public than they had paid for their contracts, and Feydeau had made a similar profit, the raising of 70,221 livres for the king would have cost the taxpayers 92,935 livres, the difference of 22,714 livres or 32.3 percent, representing the total profit of the various participating financiers, not counting their expenses.[9] The king would have his money right away, he would not face any collection problems, and the cost of financing would be transferred to the taxpayers. These high financing costs were necessary because the venture was extremely risky for those financing it. On each level they would have to guess how much they could actually collect and write their predictions into the binding contract. If their projections were wrong, they stood to lose their investment, or they might have to engage in lengthy negotiations to get the king's agents to modify the contract.

In addition to the well-established tax farms such as the *gabelles* or the *aides*, there were contracts to collect special fees and one-time taxes. In the seventeenth century special levies made up an increasing proportion of the king's budget. Royal administrators, desperate for more revenues, searched the records for new fees that could be levied on officeholders, uncollected sums that could be recovered, or new items to tax. "Advice-givers" were constantly presenting petitions suggesting such operations. For example, in 1617, Benoit Bernardet suggested creating hereditary offices of "commissioners to draw up the taille roles" in Bresse, Bugey, and Gex. He was granted a contract offering him one-sixth of all the proceeds of the sale of the offices if he would undertake the expenses of getting the edict registered in the courts.[10] The instigators of these special contracts (*traités*) or tax farms (*parties*) were commonly called *traitants* or *partisans*, both derogatory terms when uttered by the people in the street.

The financiers who made these deals were involved in complex chains of indebtedness to one another and to other wealthy investors, with obligations due at variable dates and everything dependent on successful grain harvests and accurate predictions of the amounts to be collected. It was a house of cards that frequently collapsed when a central figure went bankrupt, pulling down others with him. This informal credit network was unwieldy and expensive, but it took the place of a central bank and allowed the king and the aristocracy to do without a modern credit system. The flow of credit and money created an important community of interest linking the royal tax system to the leading elites.

In the period from Henry III to Louis XIV, the financiers received what we would call an extremely bad press. Pamphlets, placards, slogans, and political tracts blurted out the same opinions that were uttered in popular revolts. Financiers were considered effeminate and ugly, "Their tongues are double like a seal, sharper than a venomous sword and deadly as a forked-tongued serpent." Their vanity, insolence, and greed were proverbial. They brought fear and dread to every town and village. They were "vipers who chew our entrails," they were "ulcerous... bubonic sores," "miserable traitors," "sorcerers," "devils condemned to Hell." They "rise from the scum of the people." They wore splendid clothes while their wives displayed emeralds, sapphires, rubies, and diamonds in their hair, collars of gold, and expensive pearls. They amused themselves with visits to "kept women whom they support on a level that could feed a hundred families." They were sucking the blood of the people, eating them alive. They rose too fast.[11]

Françoise Bayard's magnificent study concerning 367 of these financiers who operated between 1598 and 1653 gives us a better look at the truth behind this hate literature. Of course, fortunes varied, and many bankers died poor. But the big guns were extremely wealthy. For ninety financiers for whom we have records, about 7 percent were destitute when they died, and the rest left behind modest to substantial reserves of cash. In terms of property left to heirs (in sixteen known cases), nine left 100,000 to 500,000 livres; two left 500,000 to a million. Five had more than a million, including Jacques Morin (2,253,000), Nicolas Camus (2,700,000), and Claude de Bullion (7,826,864). These immense fortunes, acquired by newcomers without traditional noble pedigrees, might well have aroused shock and envy in the everyday world. They did not, however, equal the fortunes

Figure 15 Wealth of the robe and finance. The most blatant manifestations of the seemingly ill-gotten wealth of financiers and their royal officer relatives were the town houses they built. Figures 15 (a)–(d) are from Dijon. The facade and the elegant staircase in Figures 15 (e) and (f) are from the so-called Hôtel Salé in Paris (now the Picasso Museum) which was associated in the public mind with a seventeenth-century farmer of the salt tax.

of the greatest magnates. Princes of the blood generally had more than 4,000,000 livres. The prince de Condé had more than 10 million. Cardinal Richelieu amassed 20 million and Cardinal Mazarin 36 million. The composition of these fortunes varied, but it is probably correct to say that the fortunes of financiers were more liquid and better diversified than those of the old nobility. Some financiers owned substantial amounts in land, but this was rarely more than a third of their fortunes. The rest would be concentrated in offices, loans to individuals, loans to the state, and houses. But each profile was different. Mathieu Garnier had 66 percent in loans to the state. Pierre LeClerc had 53 percent in loans to individuals. Pierre Sainctot had 41 percent in buildings. Claude Cornuel had 23 percent (the highest for this) in offices.[12]

Thus a sizeable contingent of these financiers were indeed ostentatiously wealthy. The most notable financiers owned one to five carriages and many fine clothes. Sebastien Zamet had 214 shirts. Most lived in elegant townhouses with several stories, a courtyard, sometimes a garden, five or more bedrooms, often a gallery for paintings. Many of these elegant townhouses can still be seen in the Marais district of Paris, with their eighteenth-century counterparts scattered throughout the Faubourg Saint-Germain. In addition, 53 percent of the financiers owned a country house or estate, and twelve of them owned from two to eight country estates. They had many servants, cellars full of wine from their estates, stocks of linen (Claude de Bullion had 221 tablecloths and 256 dozen napkins). Ceilings were decorated with murals by the finest artists. Collections of shells or rocks betrayed scientific hobbies. Inventories of the 367 financiers revealed that 26 of them owned a total of 384 statues of marble, bronze or ivory, and 137 owned 3,088 paintings between them, including works by Titian, Carpaccio, Mignard, Poussin, Caravaggio, and van Dyck.[13]

Rise of a new robe-ministerial elite

The emergence of these judicial and financial families was an important force in the development of French society. Their rise began in the 1520s and accelerated until around 1620. At that point, the most successful families were moving into key positions in the government, the courts, and the financial establishment, and the doors were closing to newcomers as offices became expensive and harder to get, and the effects of hereditary venality began to be felt. Some of those who had reached the top became powerful advocates for absolute monarchy and served the crown in the royal councils and on missions to the provinces. Others consolidated their influence in the Parlements and contributed to the forces resisting the streamlining of royal authority. The same professional–administrative families dominated both camps – those with members who became royal officials and those with members who led the sovereign judicial companies. In fact, many families had individuals in both camps as well as strong connections to finance. The top families emerged by the 1660s as part of a new ministerial–judicial–financial aristocracy bound together by ties of kinship and common interest.

In the provinces a similar consolidation of rising families was taking place. Rouen, Bordeaux, Dijon, and Toulouse, all seats of Parlements and thus provincial capitals, saw the same emergence of a province-level 'high society" of interconnected robe families. The increasingly haughty sovereign judges gained power at the expense of the traditional municipal authorities, and the competition between judicial companies and city consuls or *échevins* led to a heightened standard of elegant display and a new sensitivity to issues of precedence and rank.

Provincial families had a fairly predictable ladder of success to climb. First they would accumulate wealth through trade, then undertake financial dealings, then acquire minor offices. They prepared at least one of their sons with appropriate training and set him up in an office. Less fortunate sons rose no higher than the *présidial* or *bailliage* courts or the *gabelle* administration, or they wielded influence in local city halls. The more successful undertook legal studies and obtained positions as *trésoriers de France*, receivers-general of various taxes, and ultimately counselors or presidents in one of the sovereign courts, where they aspired to seats in the *grande chambre* or presidencies of Parlements and appointments as royal prosecutors in sovereign courts.

We must not forget the social and economic influence these men had over the countryside in the region they dominated. Around Bordeaux the *parlementaires* had bought up most of the best wine country by the end of the seventeenth century. Around Rouen, as the *parlementaires* grew richer, they gradually shifted their investments from loans and commerce to land. They bought and sold seigneuries readily, and regrouped them without legal difficulty. Most of their land lay scattered in many pieces throughout upper and lower Normandy. As a result, the *parlementaires* were mostly absentee landlords who made little attempt to consolidate or modernize.

Around Toulouse it is possible to arrive at a picture of the *parlementaires'* vast influence in the region. During the first half of the seventeenth century, *parlementaire* families produced twelve bishops, all but one with sees in the immediate vicinity. Lesser clerics, some of whom actually sat in the Parlement as clerical counselors, held a number of abbeys and clerical posts in the region. In the nearby diocese of Montauban alone, *parlementaire* families controlled three out of the seven abbeys. Seigneurial influence has also left its mark. In a single month, July 1645, the royal council received complaints from the inhabitants of Fossert in the diocese of Rieux against the oppressions of their seigneur, Counselor François Papus, and from the inhabitants of Montaljat in the county of Rodez against the intervention of President Philippe de Caminade in their local election. The bishop of Cahors complained in the 1660s that many individuals from his diocese were acquiring posts in the Parlement to buy protection against his influence, and that most of his priests were in league with the counselors in Toulouse whom they knew from their student days.

An example of such regional prominence is Alexandre Bigot de Monville, who became First President of the Parlement of Rouen in 1666.[14] He and his family virtually dominated the Norman political scene. From the late fifteenth to the mid seventeenth century, six generations of Bigots, up to and including Alexandre himself, produced forty-four male descendants who lived, thirty-four of whom were royal officers, every one of them in the home region. Five others were priests, two were "sieurs" living on their estates, and two were goldsmiths. Alexandre grew up knowing that, in addition to having a father who was councilor in the Parlement, he had uncles who held the positions of president and councilor in the Parlement, *correcteur* in the Chambre des Comptes, controller in the war treasury, controller in the *généralité*, *trésorier de France*, lieutenant in the *bailliage* court of Rouen, and finally officer in the city militia. He had family in every sector of local government.[15]

As venality spread through the system, critics began to react. Nobles complained that their natural role as advisors to the king was being undermined by men of low birth. Distinguished *parlementaires* decried the loss of wisdom and erudition caused by the packing of the king's courts with inferior candidates. Many observers attacked what appeared to them to be the pernicious rise of upstarts and fortune-seekers. The debate came to a head in the Estates-General of 1614 where the clergy and the nobility denounced venality of office and the spokesmen for the robe nobles claimed the right to sit with the nobles, not the third estate (commoners).

The change in urban society was no illusion. In the southern city of Montpellier, which had a population of some 15,500 people in 1600, commerce had been a major activity since the fourteenth century. The city had a prosperous cloth industry, produced dyes and perfumes, and housed a venerable university. During the sixteenth century, however, facing a decline in trade, the merchants took their money out of commerce and began investing in land, noble titles, and offices. There were plenty of the latter. Montpellier recevied a Cour des Aides in 1467, a Chambre des Comptes in 1523, a tax-receiving bureau (for the *généralité*) in 1542, a *bureau des finances* in 1577, a seat of the *gabelle* administration, and a number of other financial offices. The number of royal offices in the *généralité* rose from 111 in 1500 to 441 in 1600. Between 1549 and 1640, the share of local taxes paid by sword nobles inched up from 7.32 to 9.37 percent, that paid by the bourgeoisie (meaning merchants and notable citizens living from their rents) fell from 25.14 percent to 21.40 percent, and that paid by robe nobles rose from 7.10 percent to 20.16 percent.[16] Another measure of prosperity is the size of dowries given by fathers in a given profession to their daughters. Here there was also a dramatic shift.[17] Average dowries of bourgeois and merchants between 1550 and 1610 declined around 25 percent, while those of lawyers more than doubled, and those of robe officers rose by more than 2.5 times. Studies in Dijon, a city with a Parlement, illustrate the same tendency.[18]

These shifts produced two notable changes in urban governance. For one, all the sovereign courts were increasingly being filled by sons whose fathers had already been royal officers and less by sons whose fathers had been merchants. The high robe was moving toward becoming a closed caste. For another, legal professionals and robe nobles were taking over the city governments. Dijon, a typical regional capital, shifted from being a manufacturing city of artisans, guilds, and merchants in 1450 to being an administrative city

Figure 16 Anonymous, *Louis XIV Holding the Seals*, 1672. This rare representation of Louis XIV in a royal council meeting is in reality a judicial session held in the spring of 1672 when the king had temporarily assumed the post of Chancellor. The painter is unknown.

dominated by wealthy sword and robe nobles in 1750. Artisanal activity meanwhile shifted from textiles and basic commodities to luxury industries and services.[19]

Meanwhile, elite families were also conquering Paris and the royal government. The king's central institutions were now more fully developed. At the core, the medieval *curia regis* had evolved into the Conseil d'État, which was really a set of overlapping royal councils. They each met on different days of the week with different combinations of members to discuss their particular categories of business. Four secretaries of state were really the king's right hand men. A *surintendant des finances* was something like a finance minister, and under him were four *intendants de finance*. The king's highest court, the Grand Conseil, was rather like a prerogative court that took cases of special interest to the king out of the hands of the Parlements. There was also a company of fifty to a hundred *maîtres des requêtes* (masters of requests). They were a pool of experienced lawyers used to examine governmental issues and draw up position papers which they presented in royal council meetings.

In the period 1620 to 1789, the rising *parlementaire*-ministerial dynasties began to rival the great sword nobles. This was a triumph for men of education and wealth. Take, for example, André Lefevre d'Ormesson, a member of a prominent robe family whose father had been president in the Chambre des Comptes of Paris. Born in 1577, André was sent at age nine to the Collège du Cardinal Lemoine, where he studied Virgil, Cicero, and Terence. The siege of Paris (1590) interrupted his studies. He continued at the Collège de Navarre where he mastered ancient literature, rhetoric, and history; then attended the Jesuit Collège de Clermont. By age sixteen he was being tutored in the *Institutes* of Justinian, and after studying law at the University of Orléans, as well as with a tutor back in Paris, he received his *licence* in civil law in 1596. In 1598 he already held an office in the Grand Conseil, which he left at age twenty-three to fill his brother's office of councilor in the Paris Parlement. In 1604 he purchased a position of master of requests for which he paid 42,450 livres. The age requirement was thirty-two and he was only twenty-eight, but he obtained a dispensation. He performed many important missions and financial investigations for the crown and served as intendant in Champagne. He died greatly honored as dean of the royal council in 1665. Meanwhile his brother Olivier had been president in the Chambre des Comptes like their father, and André's three sons held the posts of councilor in the Parlement, master of requests and intendant in Picardie and Soissonnais, and councilor in the Grand Conseil.

But how did families like the Ormessons reach such heights? Their actual origins, contrary to the trumped-up genealogies showing ancient noble ancestors that so many of them had concocted, lay in provincial cities and merchant commerce. A family's social ascent usually took three or more generations and required backup support from a whole range of relatives. Many emerged from provincial obscurity in the aftermath of the fifteenth-century economic recovery, especially in the Loire region, which was the stamping ground of the monarchy during much of the sixteenth century. When we first see them in the records they are already prosperous urban citizens. Their takeoff is always facilitated by a burst in wealth from marriage, inheritance, or trade. Frequently it is connected to profits from the handling of tax revenues. The rise to prominence of a particular individual was usually the result of collaboration among members of an extended family group. It frequently involved sacrifices on the part of collateral lines and the transfer of offices back and forth to the best-placed candidate. Patronage was also very much in play, usually in the form of service to the great nobility.

Consider another example. The Selve family[20] can be traced back to the fourteenth century as prosperous local merchants in the remote town of Marcillac in the Bas-Limousin. Around 1455 Fabien Selve married the daughter of a prosperous notary and took over his father-in-law's practice and lands. A second marriage brought him more lands and rents. His eldest son founded a branch of the family that joined the local nobility and helped fund the younger son, Jean, to study law at the University of Toulouse. There Jean de Selve became a professor of law as a very young man. His reputation as a legist must have attracted the attention of the king, because in 1514 Louis XII sent him on a mission to England. In 1515 Francis I chose him to be First President of the Parlement of Bordeaux. By 1520 he had become First President of the Parlement of Paris, where he established a long and distinguished career. His daughters married First Presidents of Parlements, two of his sons became bishops and the third was *maître d'hôtel* of Catherine de' Medici. This solid robe nobility had been achieved in only the second generation.

A more typical pattern was the case of Pierre Séguier, Chancellor of France from 1635 to 1672. Five generations back, around 1465, at the same time that Fabien Selve was launching his family's fortunes in the Limousin, the Chancellor's great-great-great-grandfather Étienne Séguier was an apothecary in Saint-Pourçain in the Auvergne. Somehow Étienne's children made the transition to Paris, no doubt through apothecary connections, since around 1510 we find his son, Bluet, identified as "apothecary, grocer and bourgeois of Paris." Bluet's son Nicolas followed in his footsteps and became an important figure in Parisian municipal affairs. Eventually he made his strategic move into finance with a minor post in the *gabelle* administration, and by his death in 1583 he had become receiver of the *aides* tax for all of Paris. In the third generation, Nicolas's son Pierre Séguier studied law and became a renowned jurist who acquired the prestigious post of *avocat du roi* (royal prosecutor) in the Parlement in 1550. There he eloquently defended the integrity of the court against the spread of venality: "Justice is something so excellent, so sacred, so divine, so properly belonging to God that it appears entirely reasonable to assert that it should not be profaned, polluted, or soiled by sale or money."[21] These views did not prevent him from purchasing a newly created office of president in 1554. He began building contacts with the aristocracy. He lent money to the duchesse de Nevers and Henriette de Clèves and took over ownership of their estates when they could not repay their debts. He acquired the family's principal seigneurie in a similar manner by calling in loans he arranged for members of the Montmorency family, and began consolidating his farms into large titled estates.

Pierre Séguier had six sons and four daughters, whose marriages created a vast network of relations. Three sons became presidents in the Parlement; another was *grande audencier* in the royal chancellery. Louis, a priest, started out in the Parlement and ended up as dean of the Paris clergy. Jean, the father of the Chancellor Séguier, was judge and administrator of the *prévôté* of Paris. Two of the daughters married councilors in the Parlement. Pierre Séguier and his sons made their reputation with the king by becoming highly visible defenders of the crown and the church during the takeover of Paris by the radical Catholic League. Parisians resented the Séguiers for siding with Henry III when he moved to repress the radical leaguers. The family defended the king's enforced toleration of Protestants and supported his new taxes. In 1588 in the midst of the Parisian rebellion called the Day of Barricades, someone scrawled in large letters on President Séguier's door, "valet for hire." It was no doubt this "valet" loyalty which opened doors for Pierre, the son of Jean. Pierre started out as councilor in the Parlement, became master of requests in 1618, and received governmental commissions through the patronage of the noble Épernon family. In 1624 he inherited his uncle Antoine's office of president in the Parlement. In 1633 he became keeper of the seals, and in 1635 he was named chancellor with the blessing of Louis XIII and Richelieu. He married his daughters to members of the old aristocracy and died with a fortune estimated at almost 1,300,000 livres.[22] But it had taken six generations, 200 years, and a good deal of luck and good timing to get there.

Distinguished seventeenth-century ministerial families, such as the Phélypeaux, the Colberts, and the Le Telliers, followed similar patterns. The Phélypeaux family had been merchants in fifteenth-century Blois, where they had opportunities for relationships with royal agents during the king's frequent sojourns in the Loire Valley. Jean-Baptiste Colbert, Louis XIV's most famous minister and *contrôleur-général*, stemmed from well-off "merchant-bourgeois" of Reims in Champagne, where they had been plying various trades since the 1490s. Colbert's father Nicolas moved to Paris in 1630; became a banker; began lending money at a cleverly concealed interest rate of 13 percent to 17 percent; acquired an office of *receveur-général et payeur des gages de la ville de Paris* and established good financial connections. His son Jean-Baptiste, the future minister, was not the lowly shopkeeper's son of legend, since his family had already held posts in sovereign courts and they were very well connected. A cousin, Saint-Pouange, who was assistant to Sublet de Noyers, the secretary of state for war, got Colbert a post as *commissaire ordinaire des guerres*, travelling around the country inspecting royal troops. Saint-Pouange was married to the sister of Michel Le Tellier who became secretary of state for war in 1643, bringing both Saint-Pouange and Colbert into his bureau. All three worked for Cardinal Mazarin.

Thus by the age of Louis XIV these families had risen to powerful positions, but not on their own. They were the beneficiaries of much cultivation of personal relationships during the previous generations, backed up by a century or more of strategic family manipulation of money and offices. There was no single formula for success. In 1588–9 the Séguiers were in Paris supporting Henry III, while the Le Telliers were in the camp of Mayenne and the Catholic League. The Phélypeaux were in Blois establishing ties with the people around Henry III who were rallying to Henry of Navarre. The Ormessons were toeing a cautious neutral line between loyalism and Catholic extremism. Loyalty to one side or the other was not sufficient. What the winners all had in common was the legal or financial training and extensive experience that made them effective political players. All of them made their way by means of wealth from offices and finance, along with family connections.

This group of family dynasties was no longer a rising bourgeoisie, because they had abandoned their family roots as locally based merchants, shopkeepers, and urban dignitaries and based their social advancement on ties with the crown and skillful management of the king's resources. Banking on good education in the professional worlds of the law, finance, and the church, they worked their way over multiple generations into positions of prominence. What distinguished them from a classic bourgeoisie was their close dependence on the monarchy as a source of influence and advancement and their relative disinterest in genuinely capitalist enterprises. It was through investment in royal financial contracts and royal tax collections that they accumulated the fortunes needed to acquire high positions in the state. It was by exercising royal offices that they were able to acquire political influence, and it was through the purchase of offices that they acquired hereditary noble status. Their identity was closely tied to professional competence, but their participation in the monarchical enterprise was parallel to that of the old nobles. Both grounded their wealth on landed estates producing revenue, and their social position on royal favor. Both relied on the royal system of tax collection and distribution to support their lifestyle. Both shared family ties and collaborated in underwriting the royal fiscal system. But the nobles of the sword relied on royal pensions and military commands and considered themselves superior. The nobles of the robe relied more on administrative competence, financial deals, and venal offices.

Suggestions for further reading: robe, finance, and office

Parlements and robe officers

Bien, David D., "Offices, Corps, and a System of State Credit: The Uses of Privilege under the Ancien Régime," in Keith Michael Baker, ed., *The Political Culture of the Old Regime* (Oxford, 1987), 89–114.

Dewald, Jonathan, *The Formation of a Provincial Nobility: The Magistrates of the Parlement of Rouen, 1499–1610* (Princeton, NJ, 1980).

Doyle, William, *The Parlement of Bordeaux and the End of the Old Régime* (London, 1974).

Venality: The Sale of Offices in Eighteenth-Century France (Oxford, 1996).

Farr, James R., *Authority and Sexuality in Early Modern Burgundy (1550–1730)* (Oxford, 1995).

A Tale of Two Murders: Passion and Power in Seventeenth-Century France (Chapel Hill, NC, 2005).

Hamscher, Albert, *The Parlement of Paris after the Fronde, 1653–1673* (Pittsburgh, PA, 1976).

"The Conseil Privé and the Parlements in the Age of Louis XIV: A Study in French Absolutism," *Transactions of the American Philosophical Society* 77 part 2.

Hurt, John J., *Louis XIV and the Parlements: The Assertion of Royal Authority* (Manchester, 2002).

Kettering, Sharon, *Judicial Politics and Urban Revolt in Seventeenth-Century France: The Parlement of Aix, 1629–1659* (Princeton, NJ, 1978).

Levine, Frederick M., "From Renaissance City to Ancien Régime Capital: Montpellier, c.1500–c.1600," in Philip Benedict, ed., *Cities and Social Change in Early Modern France* (London, 1989).

Mousnier, Roland, *La Vénalité des offices sous Henri IV et Louis XIII* (Paris, 1971).

Roelker, Nancy Lyman, *One King, One Faith: The Parlement of Paris and the Religious Reformations of the Sixteenth Century* (Berkeley, CA, 1996).

Rogister, John, *Louis XV and the Parlement of Paris, 1737–1755* (Cambridge, 1995).

Swann, Julian, *Politics and the Parlement of Paris under Louis XV, 1754–1774* (Cambridge, 1995).

Ministerial dynasties and agents of the crown

Beik, William, *Absolutism and Society in Seventeenth-Century France: State Power and Provincial Aristocracy in Languedoc* (Cambridge, 1985).

Bonney, Richard, *Political Change in France under Richelieu and Mazarin 1624–1661* (Oxford, 1978).

Chapman, Sara E., *Private Ambition and Political Alliances: The Phélypeaux de Pontchartrain Family and Louis XIV's Government, 1650–1715* (Rochester, 2004).

Collins, James B., *Classes, Estates, and Order in Early Modern Brittany* (Cambridge, 1994).

Gruder, Vivian, *The Royal Provincial Intendants: A Governing Elite in Eighteenth-Century France* (Ithaca, NY, 1968).

Kalas, Robert J., "The Selve Family of Limousin: Members of a New Elite in Early Modern France," *Sixteenth Century Journal* 18 (1987), 147–72.

Kettering, Sharon, *Patrons, Brokers, and Clients in Seventeenth-Century France* (Oxford, 1986).

Murat, Ines, *Colbert*, trans. Robert Francis Cook and Jeannie Van Asselt (Charlottesville, VA, 1984).

Potter, Mark, *Corps and Clienteles: Public Finance and Political Change in France, 1688–1715* (Aldershot, 2003).

Ranum, Orest, *Richelieu and the Councillors of Louis XIII: A Study of the Secretaries of State and Superintendants of Finance in the Ministry of Richelieu 1635–1642* (Oxford, 1963).

Swann, Julian, *Provincial Power and Absolute Monarchy: The Estates General of Burgundy, 1661–1790* (Cambridge, 2003).

Taxes, finances and financiers

Bayard, Françoise, *Le Monde des financiers au XVIIe siècle* (Paris, 1988).

Bonney, Richard, "The Failure of the French Revenue Farms 1600–1660," *Economic History Review* 32 (1979), 11–32.

　The King's Debts: Finance and Politics in France 1589–1661 (Oxford, 1981).

Collins, James B., *Fiscal Limits of Absolutism: Direct Taxation in Early Seventeenth-Century France* (Berkeley, CA, 1988).

Dessert, Daniel, *Argent, pouvoir et société au Grand Siècle* (Paris 1984).

Kaiser, Thomas, "Money, Despotism, and Public Opinion in Early 18th Century France: John Law and the Debate on Royal Credit," *Journal of Modern History* 63 (1991), 1–28.

Kwass, Michael, *Privilege and the Politics of Taxation in Eighteenth-Century France: Liberté, Égalité, Fiscalité* (Cambridge, 2000).

6 | *Ecclesiastical power and religious faith*

Priests and religious symbols permeated life more completely than we can possibly imagine today. The Catholic church influenced French life on many levels. As an institution it was part of the power structure. The top ecclesiastics who controlled it were well-connected members of prominent noble families with influence at court or in Rome. They enjoyed lifetime stipends, ranging from comfortable to spectacular, and immense authority in their spheres of influence. But the church was also a sort of umbrella organization loosely encompassing many overlapping, sometimes competing, bodies and many diverse practices. It included hundreds of religious houses, peopled with monks and nuns sworn to observe strict regimens, sometimes with saintly dedication. The landscape was teeming with tonsured priests of all sorts, most of them poor and without their own churches. All of these groups collectively constituted the first estate of the realm. This privileged status exempted them from regular taxation and entitled them to special protection before the law and other legal advantages.

But the church signified more than just a common legal identity. It was deeply immersed in the rural world of agricultural production by virtue of its ownership of vast tracts of land, its lordship over villages, and its role in taxing directly the produce of the land. It was also a powerful institution exploited by the crown to provide patronage and impose authority. Finally, it was an international body, headed by a foreign potentate, the pope. Since the eleventh century kings and popes had quarreled over control of this major source of wealth and influence.

There was potential conflict within the church as well. A vast gulf existed between the church hierarchy and the ordinary priesthood. The church supported the power structure by providing sinecures for aristocratic families and by reinforcing the king's claim to be acting in the name of God, while it channeled much of the revenue to its top clerics, disadvantaging the parish clergy. Conflict between the rank and file and the hierarchy was always a possibility. Corruption was also an issue. Those enjoying luxury and power could easily lose sight of their mission. This problem became acute in the sixteenth century when the Renaissance church, following the lead of the pope in Rome, was deeply compromised at a time when Protestantism was introducing a critical alternative. In France skillful proselytizing and Catholic demoralization led to the rapid growth of the Calvinist, or Huguenot, church. Soon Huguenot communities were confronting Catholic communities and the result was a generation of religious wars (1562–1629).

Of course the church was also a genuine spiritual force. High prelates might live in luxury; priests might hold church positions without demonstrating any real calling; monks and nuns might fail to live up to their vows, but there were always others who were sincerely dedicated to promoting the work of God. For the population at large such details were less important than the fact that the church was simply their only direct contact with the sacred. Most people believed, at least intuitively, that the true church had been founded by Saint Peter on direct orders from Christ himself. It was the manifestation of God's will on earth and, as such, the only means of salvation for all humankind. The local priest's celebration of the Mass and the familiar rituals of birth, marriage, and death offered comfort during life's most intimate moments of sorrow and joy. But even here, at the most personal point of contact between local communities and the church, there was a political dimension. Local priests could serve as moral policemen by calling for denunciations of criminals from the pulpit, and they could serve the state by promulgating important royal messages from the pulpit. In cities the celebration of Te Deum services to honor royal military victories and major events such as royal births and deaths was a way of reinforcing the reputation of the monarchy in the eyes of the population.

The church was a powerful influence in many other aspects of French life. Besides animating cathedrals and parish churches, maintaining monasteries that were viewed by locals as centers of holiness and prayer, and offering salvation to the penitent, certain clerics played a major role in the agrarian economy, in the maintenance of the nobility, and in the construction of royal patronage networks. The rise of the Huguenots presented new challenges, first in the form of a power struggle, then in the form of a Catholic revival. The intensity of the passions aroused during the religious wars stimulated a dramatic revival of devout Catholicism in the seventeenth century. We need to examine each of these sacred and secular influences.

But first, an observation about faith. The French population was overwhelmingly Catholic, and for about a century the Calvinist minority played a major role as well. However, Protestants and Catholics do not tell the whole story. Jewish communities held on in a few places. The papal territories of Avignon and the Comtat Venaissin in the southeast harbored around 3,000 Jews in the sixteenth century. In the southwest, so-called "New Christian" or "Portuguese" merchants began to settle around Bordeaux in the mid sixteenth century, eventually reaching 15,000. They arrived in Nantes around 1590. A few could be found in Saint-Jean-de-Luz, Bayonne, and Montpellier. In the northeast, areas which had been acquired from the Holy Roman Empire saw some 480 Jewish households in Metz by 1717 and ninety families in Nancy. By 1700 Alsace had about 6,000 Jews. At that time Paris had only 350 Jews, mostly from Bordeaux or Metz.[1]

Social background and role in society

The principal figures in the French church were the bishops, who were the administrators of each of the 113 dioceses (bishoprics). The dioceses were grouped into provinces or archdioceses, each administered by one of their bishops, who then became an archbishop. The dioceses were divided into local parishes, organized around a parish church served by a curé (vicar). Parishes often encompassed entire villages, but some extended parishes spanned several communities. Larger towns were divided into multiple parishes. Curés assigned to parishes, who consequently enjoyed a steady income, were the elite of the priesthood. There were other lower levels of priesthood, and tonsured clerics were everywhere.

The bishops were essentially nominees of the king. In 1516 Francis I concluded the famous Concordat of Bologna with the pope in which the two parties agreed to share the nomination process between them, leaving out in the cold the religious organizations that had formerly held elections. Henceforth the king would name almost all the French bishops, abbots, and abbesses, with certain exceptions, and the pope would have the final power of confirmation or rejection. This agreement gave the king a vast arena for patronage.

Figure 17 View of the bishop's palace in Béziers in 1616 by Étienne Martellange. Photo of the archbishop's palace in Albi. These two sees, both in Languedoc, were among the wealthiest in France. Both had impressive cathedral compounds and an episcopal palace situated on the river.

Bishoprics were lifetime positions supported by an endowment that returned an income based on a mixture of rent-producing seigneurial property, jurisdictional rights, tithes, and "spiritual" fees charged for various services. They varied immensely in importance. The smallest encompassed as few as thirty parishes, while large ones such as Rouen had 1,388. Their annual revenues ranged from 6,000 to 100,000 livres in the mid seventeenth century, with the majority falling into a middle range of between 8,000 and 30,000 livres. The worst off was Vence (6,000); the richest were Albi (100,000), Auch (90,000), and Paris (90,000).[2] The king doled out high positions in the church as if they were pensions. The recipients treated them like investments and had no hesitation in openly discussing their monetary worth. Contemporaries did not see any contradiction between spiritual commitment and selection by patronage because the deal-making took place among persons of high birth who considered themselves naturally suited for positions of authority. Some churchmen were dedicated to their calling; those who were not could always employ substitutes.

The well-placed used every means in their power to acquire bishoprics or other major church posts for family members, often second sons who would not be in line to inherit the family estate; or sometimes relatives who had a natural leaning toward a spiritual calling. Some families considered their right to fill certain church posts as hereditary. Once a bishopric was in their hands, they employed all kinds of stratagems to hold onto it. A common method of designating one's successor was to appoint a coadjutor to take over the functions of an ailing or infirm bishop. The coadjutor was then favorably placed to step in when the incumbent died. Another revealing practice was the diversion of diocesan revenues into pensions. When an elderly bishop retired, he would be granted a pension drawn from the revenues of the diocese, at the expense of the successor bishop. When Silvio de Santacroce replaced his uncle Prospero as archbishop of Arles in 1574, Prospero retained most of the revenues of the see for himself. In 1583 Prospero ceded the pension to the duc d'Angoulême. When Angoulême died in 1586, Henry III transferred the pension to the sieur de Crillon, a secular military commander.[3]

Who were the bishops and archbishops? Under Louis XII and Francis I, the appointees were almost exclusively old nobles. During the rest of the sixteenth century, newer sword families, and members of the financial–judicial robe began to join the ranks. Bergin's study of

the social origins of all the appointments from 1589 to 1661 shows
that 63 percent were nobles, 25 percent were commoners, 6 percent
were foreign dignitaries (mostly Italian), and 6 percent are unknown.
Generally speaking, the episcopacy evolved from an almost totally
noble membership in the late middle ages, to an aristocratic mix
between 1560 and 1640, with one-fourth to one-third consisting of
influential commoners. Then, under Mazarin and Louis XIV, the
nobility, old and new, staged a comeback, reaching between 78 percent
and 87 percent depending on how one defines noble origins. In the
eighteenth century the episcopacy returned to almost total nobility.[4]

Becoming a bishop meant stepping into a position of considerable
prestige and influence. After being formally nominated by the king,
the candidate would have to consult specialized bankers who knew
how to navigate the maze of bureaucratic steps needed to obtain the
necessary papers from the pope in Rome. He would have to negotiate
large loans to finance the whole process. There would be a fancy
consecration ceremony, sometimes in Paris. When the prelate actually
entered his episcopal city, there would be a welcoming procession and
a formal ceremony by which he took possession of his cathedral.
These formalities could be performed by a stand-in. In some cases the
bishop might never appear at all in his diocese.

If he did reside there, the new bishop would settle into his episcopal
palace not far from his cathedral. He would have to get acquainted
with his cathedral chapter, a rather intimidating committee of independently endowed priests called canons. In Amiens the bishop faced
a chapter of forty-three canons whose combined annual revenue was
three times larger than his own. They were the collective lords over
three local abbeys, seven convents, and thirty-one parishes.[5] In the
diocese everyone would be watching to see what path the new bishop
would take. He might spend most of his time at court. He might
engage in power struggles with the local town authorities or the
canons of his cathedral. Or he might arrive full of ambition and initiate a major program of reform which would severely shake up the
local establishment.

Ordinary priests lived in a different universe from bishops. Those
who had their own churches and congregations were the fortunate minority. Most clerics served in menial positions and had little
more than their privileged clerical status to distinguish them from
the masses of poor. It was not difficult to become a low-level priest.

The first step was simply to be tonsured, that is, to have the head shaved in a certain pattern under the direction of a bishop. Some parents had their sons tonsured as early as seven years old in hopes of directing them toward an honorable calling that could provide a little financial security. In the 1520s the bishop of Mende tonsured three hundred boys per year.[6] Local society must have been accustomed to the sight of these tonsured boys, most of whom eventually went on to other vocations. The ones who persisted received a modicum of training from a priest and passed through a series of minor titles before becoming a subdeacon, a deacon, and finally a full-fledged priest. It was only in this final stage that the priest received the *sacerdote*, that is, full power to celebrate the Mass and perform the sacraments. Only fully qualified priests were expected to be celibate. Other requirements existed, but they were frequently compromised. A formula published in 1525 stipulated only that:

priests must be knowledgeable enough to read distinctly well and under-stand, at least grammatically, all the words contained in the mass and the [church] offices. They must be able to distinguish what is a sin and what is not. They must be familiar with the number of the sacraments and the way they are administered. They must at least know the Decalogue and the articles of faith, in order to be able to teach them to others.[7]

This minimal standard did not require the priest to know Latin, master the Bible, understand theology, or have the capacity to preach. Church leaders often worried about the poor training of priests, but there was literally no way to provide thousands of rural parishes with qualified candidates.

Short of becoming a bishop, the most prestigious role for a priest was to serve as a canon in the cathedral chapter. The chapter was a per-manent self-renewing committee of clerics who administered the cath-edral or another major church. They oversaw the life of the city's parishes and chapels, the schooling of young children, the hiring of preachers, and the management of their collective properties and rev-enues. The chapter was a formidable body. Chartres had ninety canons, Notre Dame de Paris had fifty-one, many cathedrals had about twenty. Most chapters enjoyed substantial revenues derived from endowments that the canons distributed among themselves by seniority. Canons were required to be at least fourteen years old. Most, but not all, had priesthood status.

Collectively, cathedral chapters were powerful institutions made up of locally connected notables who were there for life, whereas the bishop was often absent. The chapter frequently quarreled with the bishop and with municipal authorities, and constituted one of the power centers of the local elite.[8] The highest ranking canons were the *prévôt*, who was second only to the bishop in stature; the archdeacon who was next in line; then the *sacristain*. The canons directed lesser priests called *bénéficiers* whose job was to perform all the services in the cathedral. The post of canon was essentially a sinecure that provided attractive positions for sons of well-to-do families. In some places, such as Lyon, membership required a long noble pedigree.

The majority of priests formed a kind of proletariat, performing minor services for monasteries, or supporting themselves by celebrating the many Masses for the dead stipulated in the wills of important individuals. They tended to congregate in the cities. In the single diocese of La Rochelle in the late seventeenth century there were 580 to 615 resident priests. About 49 percent of them were parish curés. Another 27 percent were curates assisting or replacing the curés, along with a few almoners attached to convents or to the retinue of military men. The rest (23 percent) were retired or attached to one of the many lesser altars or chapels.[9] Nantes contained forty-six endowed chapels, and the celebration of Masses on behalf of the dead by low-grade priests was a major industry.[10] In short, there were many more priests than benefices.

The lucky ones became pastors of a parish. In rural settings parish priests were prominent figures, more so than in cities, where they faced competition from confraternities, special shrines, and mendicant friars. The village curé had usually grown up in the community or nearby, and his habits were little different from those of his neighbors. He participated in festivities, hunted or fished with other villagers, and frequented the local tavern. During most of our period, rural clerics were poorly educated and their manners were considered crude. Visitation reports from the archbishopric of Lyon in the early seventeenth century found that a small minority of curés still lived with concubines and uncovered many other instances of behavior not fitting for a priest. Pierre Morard, pastor of Pasin, had "greasy linen" on his altar and was clothed "in an extremely indecent costume, with a huge mustache like a soldier – which we made him shave off on the spot." The curé of Couzance was familiar with neither "the form of absolutions nor how to administer the other sacraments."[11] This sort of backwardness typically persisted in rural areas through most of the seventeenth century, but gradual improvement was noticeable as the reforms of the Council of Trent trickled down to the local level. By the eighteenth century, rural priests were generally better educated and usually came from urban backgrounds. As a result, they tended to be unsympathetic to rustic customs, and their constant scolding alienated them from their parishioners.

Another holdover from the past was the degree to which the nomination of parish clergy was in the hands of a non-resident party called a *curé primitif*. This external authority might be an abbey, a cathedral chapter, a priory, or a lay patron. Authority might be inherited from a predecessor who had created or endowed the parish long ago or who had been granted these rights by some higher authority. Ownership then passed down like property to subsequent generations. This appropriation by private parties of authority that should have belonged to the community was typical. In the face of powerful local interests, neither the church nor the crown was able to abolish this obviously undesirable influence. The most they could do was to regulate the dimensions of it. The *curé primitif* filled the position of parish priest in absentia, and appropriated a substantial portion of the revenues of the tithe, which was the share of the crops in the fields that went to the church. He then appointed a substitute to perform the actual clerical functions, and assigned him only a fraction of the tithe revenues. The priest's smaller share, fixed by law at a minimum of 200 to 500 livres, depending on the era, was called the *portion congrue*.

This seemingly counterproductive practice, which was widespread, meant that few curés assigned to parishes actually resided in them. In Rouergue in the early sixteenth century only 15 percent did. In Toulouse it was 12 percent.[12] We can observe the extent to which the rural church was underwriting the urban elites by looking at the figures for the Paris region in the seventeenth century. Of the 388 parishes in question, twenty-four were under the control of Parisian church chapters, twenty-two were held by the priory of Saint-Martin-des-Champs, twenty more by Parisian abbeys, eighty-one by rural abbeys, priories and chapters, and thirty-two by religious establishments from outside the diocese. Thus, almost half (45 percent) were in the hands of external ecclesiastical agencies. Nine were in the hands of lay seigneurs.[13] The remaining two hundred – a little more than half – were named directly by the archbishop of Paris.

The members of religious communities, often called the regular clergy, played a separate and distinctive role in French society. They belonged to many separate orders, each with its own culture. In the early sixteenth century it is estimated that France had 99 Carmelite houses, 367 Franciscan, 148 Dominican, 102 Augustinian, 600 Benedictine, and 200 Cistercian.[14] The original monastic orders had been founded as places of seclusion dedicated to prayer. Their religious men or women swore to observe the three vows of poverty, chastity, and obedience, and to follow a particular monastic rule. In dedicating their lives to prayer and to serving God, they became "dead before the law," giving up the right to inherit or bequeath earthly goods. Each religious order was made up of a network of local houses with some sort of central direction. For example, the Carmelite houses were grouped into provinces, each presided over by a provincial prior elected for three-year terms by the local chapters.

Monasteries and convents had a decided impact on the populations around them. In cities, the best-established houses were enclosed compounds containing chapel, cloister, refectory and dormitories. Smaller groups might simply take over a building that had been built for another purpose. Townspeople would hear the periodic ringing of their bells signifying daily prayers, and they would take comfort in the thought that these centers of holiness were protecting the city through constant prayer. The monks might appear to be distant saintly figures, or they might be familiar figures if they served actively in the community as preachers or confessors. Communities of nuns were less visible because most of them were cloistered. Convents were familiar to affluent residents because they frequently sent their daughters there to take the veil. Some nuns felt a strong calling. Others were there simply because their fathers did not want to undertake the expensive prospect of marrying them. Convents also took in young girls as *pensionnaires* to board and train. Monastery churches were often the finest in the city, and since they were often closed except on special occasions, it was considered a sign of distinction to have your family buried in the chapel of a favored monastery or, even better, to have a family tomb there. In troubled times the monastery walls might serve as a sanctuary from tax collectors or angry crowds. In the countryside, contact with monks and nuns was not as intimate, but peasants would also be conscious of the tocsin ringing and aware that prayers were being sent to heaven in the neighboring abbey. Quite possibly they would know the monks as landlords, crop inspectors, or *curés primitifs*.

Monks and nuns might be admired as saintly figures, but they might also come to be hated as greedy seigneurs. Traditional monasteries, usually far out in the country, were primarily places of seclusion and prayer. The monks followed a rigorous schedule that involved seclusion within the walls, continual prayers, Masses said around the clock, and austere living conditions such as meager diets, hard beds, and deprivation of all comforts. In extreme cases, talk itself was restricted. Sister houses overseen by the monks subjected nuns to similar regimes.

Monasteries and convents were funded by pious donations, usually from important persons who wanted recognition or hoped for salvation through good works. Through time, many of the oldest houses had accumulated extensive property from donations and came to be known for their luxury. It was in reaction to this departure from their original goals that the mendicant orders had been founded, based on the principle that poverty and immersion in the real world, not seclusion and comfort, would best serve God. The Franciscans, Dominicans, Augustinians, and Carmelites relied on alms and public charity for their support. Their mission was to live among the people, bring them to the faith through preaching, and set an example by helping the poor and the needy.

Each religious order had its own history and distinctive personality. Its identity was built upon a successful mixture of spiritual inspiration and aristocratic patronage. For example, the new order of Minimes was founded by François de Paule, a saintly Neapolitan hermit who came to be known for his ability to cure diseases. In 1481 the French king Louis XI, on his death bed, summoned de Paule. The monk was not able to cure the king, but Louis's son, Charles VIII, who was deeply impressed by this holy man, gave him a monastery at Amboise and asked him to baptize the Dauphin. De Paul soon gained the confidence of the royal women, Anne of Brittany, Anne de Beaujeu, Queen Jeanne, and Louise of Savoy. With their support, additional communities of Minimes were established. By 1550, there were eight houses of Minimes in northern France.[15]

Sometimes the initiative came largely from the patrons. The Carmelite monastery in Nantes was founded in 1318 by Thibaut, head of the Rochefort dynasty in Brittany. John II, duc de Bretagne, had just founded a Carmelite house in nearby Plöermel, and Thibaut did not want to be outdone. So Thibaut imported six monks and a prior from the Plöermel establishment and gave them the use of a house in Nantes. This move so threatened the Franciscans and Dominicans of Nantes that they induced the bishop to excommunicate the Carmelites for not getting his prior approval. The conflict went on for many years, but the house survived, thanks to repeated donations from subsequent generations of the ruling families of Brittany.[16]

The monastic tradition gave aristocratic women their greatest opportunity for creative leadership outside the home, even before the religious upsurge of the seventeenth century. Consider the Benedictine abbey of Saint-Georges in Rennes, founded in the eleventh century by a Breton duke for his sister to run as abbess. In 1434, the abbess was directing the home convent, six subordinate priories scattered in different directions, and thirty parishes and chapels, while administering seigneurial rights over many properties around Rennes, including mill, fishing and boating rights, and shipping and market tolls.[17]

Royal power and Catholic decadence

Unlike today, France had no separation between church and state. The various groups that made up the French Catholic church – prelates, priests, monks, and nuns – played an influential part in matters we would consider secular. At the same time, the royal state was deeply influential in the management of the church. The monarchy had always tied its fortunes closely to the Catholic faith. The Valois and Bourbon kings were anointed with holy oil at their coronation. They saw themselves as successors to Louis IX, raised to sainthood by the church. They attributed the salvation of France in 1432 to a divinely inspired peasant girl, Joan of Arc. But the French had just as long a tradition of insisting on a certain independence from Rome. After all, the church owned possibly as much as a third of the land of France. The local parishes probably had greater influence and enjoyed closer relations with the general population than any royal agents.

In the sixteenth century, as a result of the Concordat of 1516, the principle of kings determining appointments to the episcopacy weakened the moral reputation of Catholic institutions just at the moment when the Protestant Reformation was challenging their validity. The rapid success of Calvinism presented major problems for the king. In political terms, what was at stake was his control over positions entailing vast revenues, and the loyalty of men who wielded a great deal of influence over the population. In religious terms, the king had to stop the spread of Calvinism because it encouraged the people to deal directly with God, rendering the saintly reputation of the crown irrelevant and bypassing the king's role as God's agent on earth. But Calvinism was successful, in part precisely because the church, led by royal appointees, was failing to meet the needs of the population. Three problems emerged which took a century of conflicts to resolve. The first was the decadence of the church and its connection to the state. The second was the immense success of the French Huguenot (Calvinist) church. The third was the lively, often extreme, Catholic response, which led first to a generation of religious wars, then to a forced coexistence on the level of practical daily life, and ultimately to the elimination of the Huguenot threat by Catholic repression.

The French church, which called itself "Gallican," meant different things to different parties. To the king, it was an organ of the state, guided, to be sure, in spiritual matters by the pope, but managed in temporal matters by the king. To church leaders, Gallicanism meant an autonomous organism that bowed to neither pope nor king, and leaned at times to a conciliar view of church governance. Within the Gallican church there was some disagreement about who spoke for the church. Was it the bishops or the various assemblies of clerics? Or was it the Sorbonne, the theological faculty of the University of Paris? The Parlement of Paris, as the highest corporate judicial body, also claimed jurisdiction over issues touching on faith, and sided sometimes with the king, sometimes with the church.

Thus the ties between king and church were close. Were they detrimental to the faith? Certainly the church's vast wealth was protected by privileges granted by the crown. Ecclesiastical property was tax-exempt, and all priests, noble or commoner, were exempt from the *taille* on their personal lands and freed from many other burdens. They were also exempt from taxes levied for repayment of community debts and for poor relief. On the other hand, the king was not going to leave this vast sector of privilege and wealth untapped. In the Concordat of 1516, Francis I was granted a *décime* by the pope. This was a tax on church revenues, the weight of which was distributed by a general formula drawn up by royal commissioners. Between 1516 and 1561 this tax was frequently levied, sometimes with the assent of various kinds of assemblies of churchmen. Between 1561 and 1580 this process was regularized. Every ten years an Assembly of Clergy would debate the king's request for money and grant a large sum called, euphemistically, the "free gift." The illusion of autonomy was preserved by having the assembly collect the money using its own financial agents.

These obvious bonds of interest between flamboyant Renaissance monarchs, worldly Roman popes and aristocrats, and a church run by royal appointees, offered reformers much to criticize. The picture, as it appeared to moralists and Protestants, was not pretty. Church officials were appropriating the tithe paid by the rural masses and using it for their own aggrandizement. The church was underwriting the enterprises of the crown. Some bishops lived like princes, while others scraped by on barely adequate incomes. In the late sixteenth century a Bordeaux chronicler described the gallery in the archbishop's palace as "filled with the most beautiful, grand, and rare paintings and an infinite number of devises and emblems...with a cabinet decorated with the most exquisite rarities and things of beauty imaginable."[18] Many bishops also enjoyed country estates to which they retired in the summer.

Political appointees gave the church a bad name and provided Huguenots with easy targets. In the wake of the Concordat, royal favorites, many of them Italians, were allowed to accumulate benefices. This pluralism meant that one individual could be bishop or abbot of several places at once. Subordinate priests would perform the actual functions of their posts, while the titular head drew the revenues. Julien de' Medici never resided in his archbishopric of Aix, but he was also bishop of Albi and abbot of Saint-Victor. When eminent foreign names such as Strozzi and Medici appear on the list of appointees to the see of Aix, it is not surprising to learn that during the forty-two years between 1551 and 1593, an archbishop of Aix was only in residence for fourteen of them.[19]

This episcopal irresponsibility can be exaggerated. Absentee bishops often named competent substitutes to run their affairs. Many royal appointees came from noble or professional families and were well educated. According to the terms of the Concordat of 1516, nominees "should have a doctorate or licentiate in canon or civil law from a famous university and, after proper examination, be otherwise suitable." On the other hand, the agreement also allowed "those related by blood to the king and other high-ranking officials" to be accepted "for legitimate and reasonable causes to be expressed in their nominations and papal provisions."[20] Thus nominees were ordinarily to be well trained, but members of the royal family and agents of the king could be exempted from these qualifications.

This mixture of talent and nepotism is supported by Bergin's statistics. Of the 351 bishops holding office between 1589 and 1661, 53 percent had law degrees and 31 percent had theology degrees; thus 84 percent had some sort of advanced preparation. About one-fifth had performed clerical duties at the royal court. Those who came from secular careers were predominately important royal officers. On the other hand, one-third of them were not even priests at the time of their nomination.[21]

Thus the church never succumbed completely to decadence, but its growing dependence on the state made it vulnerable to attack. Even worse, worldly bishops were not likely to do much to improve the quality of parish life. We have seen that parish worship was often conducted by an underpaid, appointed vicar, while its revenues were siphoned off to higher clerics. Local curés were often ignorant and superstitious. Concerns about their training did not bear fruit. In 1551 a royal declaration required priests serving in a walled town to have at least a secondary education, but this rule did not apply to the countryside. Before the seventeenth century, many country priests had little or no education, or learned the ropes by assisting a practicing priest. It would take a hundred years of efforts to implement the reforms of the Council of Trent (1563) before the parish priesthood could be considered properly educated. Studies suggest that, around 1500, from 10 to 25 percent of them were living with concubines.

Many religious houses also faced crises of conscience. Dedicated monks began leaving the church and joining Huguenot communities which seemed better able to satisfy their spiritual needs. Monasteries could be holy places inhabited by saintly individuals, but they were often little more than residences for the younger sons and unmarriageable daughters of the upper classes. The result could be a lowering of standards and a lapsing of vows. At the abbey of Notre-Dame des Anges in rural Languedoc in 1644, an investigation found that the Clarisse nuns "had abandoned their duty." Neither "religious exercises" nor the principle of closure, or other "holy practices" were being observed. Commissioners sent by the king called for a general shakeup. The nuns were to dismiss their numerous servants, start wearing more modest habits, repair the entrance doorways, fill in holes in the walls which permitted conversations with outsiders, and regulate their manner of speech. In the future no nun was to have her own resident *pensionnaire* or be the recipient of any pension.[22]

Resistance to this sort of reform was common on the part of the rich families who supported the institutions. As the city council of Marseille wrote to the intendant in 1719, "we beg you to consider, Monseigneur, that installing the reformed Benedictines in the Abbey of Saint-Victor would deprive poor gentlemen and bourgeois of the haven they now use [to support] their younger sons. It could bring about the ruin of many respectable families of this city."[23] In convents, the belligerence of women was a dramatic aspect of this resistance. The sisters of the Benedictine convent of Saint-Sauveur in Marseille required as an entrance fee a dowry of 300 gold écus, plus a trousseau and some furniture from its postulants: clearly they were from wealthy families. By 1610 their discipline had collapsed. They were not observing the rules concerning food, clothing, silence, or family visits, and there were rumors that the monks from Saint-Victor were sneaking into the convent in the evenings, playing cards with the nuns, making jellies, and causing other "scandal." In 1612 the bishop sent Catherine d'Allemand to become abbess at Saint-Sauveur and initiate reform. She tried to restore the nuns' decorum, but the majority of old-timers hated her reforms. They got their families to appeal to the Parlement of Aix against her procedures and initiated a whole series of underhanded intrigues that forced d'Allemand to leave the convent. In 1626 a more determined bishop sent his grand vicar, escorted by a company of priests and masons, to reinstate d'Allemand by force. They marched up to the gate and set about forcing open a door to the church, whereupon the fourteen nuns who opposed reform put up a spirited and violent resistance. Several nuns were wounded, and the screaming combatants were dragged out of the convent and deposited in the street. As word spread, the belligerent nuns were joined by wives and mothers from the "best" families who had rallied in support of their daughters. The consuls and the militia captains appeared, but seemed uninterested in enforcing the royal orders. Equally unsupportive, the Parlement charged the grand vicar with exceeding his authority and ordered his arrest.[24]

Monastic orders – especially the mendicants – displayed their own potential for resistance when they rallied to support the extremist

Catholic League during the religious wars of the second half of the sixteenth century. Faced with the prospect of the monarchy making deals with the Protestants, agitators like the Franciscan Melchior de Flavin "cried with full vigor against the magistrates, sparing not even the king or his council, encouraging the people to all disobedience."[25] They took up arms and marched through the streets of the capital during the siege of 1590, and they stockpiled weapons for three years in their friary on behalf of the League.[26]

Monks could also be on the side of order. In Bordeaux during the Fronde from 1651 to 1653, a rebel party called the Ormée had taken over the city and joined the rebellion of the princes Condé and Conti. Pierre Berthod, a Cordelier monk, was sent to Bordeaux by Cardinal Mazarin to find out the situation and try to get the Ormée over-thrown. Berthod naturally used the local Cordelier monastery as a base for his counterinsurgency, with the assistance of one of its monks, Father Ithier, and the advice of Mère Angelique, the mother superior of the nearby Carmelites. But he soon discovered that the monastery was not safe because many parish priests and some of the monks sympathized with the Ormée.[27]

The challenge from the Huguenots

The advent of Calvinism challenged the religious sensibilities of the population, presenting wrenching moral choices and calling forth both courageous expressions of faith and vicious acts of violence. The Huguenots were always a minority, and they probably never had any chance of winning over the Catholic majority. But their strength was strategically concentrated in certain regions, and their adherents included key figures in positions of power ranging from urban magis-trates and *parlementaire* judges to grandees at the royal court. They were too powerful to defeat, but not strong enough to win. They did, however, leave a permanent impact on both the church and the state by forcing compromises that challenged both institutions to change.

As we have seen, the mid sixteenth-century church was vulnerable to charges of decadence. Meanwhile, the arrival of humanist learning from Italy was breathing fresh air into the world of education and scholarship. Christian humanists such as Jacques Lefèvre-d'Etaples and Erasmus of Rotterdam were applying their new standards of criticism to the history of the church and discovering that forgeries, mistranslations, and undocumented practices had distorted the original message of the Bible. They began trying to revive the spirit of the primitive church when Jesus was the evangelist and the message was communicated directly to the believers. This meant rejecting superstitious medieval practices and replacing decadence with commitment. At first such reforms were well received, but when news arrived of the Lutheran Reformation in Germany, any call for reform began to look subversive. For Lutherans, the whole Catholic belief in good works, including pilgrimages, the worship of saints, and the power of relics as a means to salvation, seemed a sham.

Lutheranism had very little influence in France. The real threat only emerged in the 1550s with the rise of Calvinism. John Calvin, born in 1509, was French and had followed the early discussions of Protestant reform as a young man at law school in Paris and Bourges. In 1536 he published the first edition of his *Institution of the Christian Religion* in Latin, which came out in French in 1541. That same year he moved to Geneva, just outside the kingdom, and persuaded his followers to take over the city and establish a base from which Calvinist ideas could be disseminated throughout France. Calvinists infused the basic Lutheran doctrine with an added dimension of activism that filled their movement with intense energy and enormous commitment. They believed that their duty as potential chosen ones was to bring order to a world riddled with sin and corruption. They must discipline themselves and then form congregations of the disciplined, eradicating sinful activity such as blasphemy, quarrels, usury, dancing, lechery, ostentation, and other forms of frivolity.

Once his followers had firm control of Geneva in 1555, Calvin organized a subversive campaign to spread the new belief to France. His ideas arrived in the form of pamphlets, broadsheets, and missionaries. Dedicated individuals, often noblemen and conscientious priests, fled their posts and secretly made their way to Geneva, where they underwent training in Calvin's academy to become ministers. The annual number of such immigrant proselytizers registered in Geneva rose from 8 in 1549, to 24 in 1553, to 119 in 1555.[28] Their message valorizing hard, honest work, and indignation at the failings of the Catholic church took root. In 1557 Geneva's Company of Pastors began to fill the many requests for ministers that were pouring in from Huguenot congregations begging for leadership. The clandestine nominees, often disguised as merchants and bearing false passports, made their way into France using obscure mountain passes. In Castres in Languedoc, the initial contact was made in 1559 by a bookseller and several others who visited Geneva to hear sermons and buy Bibles. Later that year the congregation in Castres wrote to Geneva requesting a minister. They sent an escort that met Geoffry Brun and unobtrusively brought him back to Castres. Eventually the city consuls were converted, and then the whole town turned Huguenot.[29]

All over France, as numbers grew, the Huguenots ventured into the open by holding public processions, loudly singing psalms, and invading Catholic churches to overturn the holy water, smash the images of saints, and occupy the buildings. In Paris, between 1556 and 1559, hundreds, if not thousands, of converts began gathering regularly at the Pré-aux-Clercs, an open space on the Left Bank across the river from the Louvre. Outside several gates to the city, "persons of all classes and every station of life: men, women, old men, youths, boys, girls, gentlemen, plebeians, and craftsmen paraded peacefully around, loudly singing psalms in French in the manner of Geneva."[30] Catholic Parisians were appalled.

Henry II had once proclaimed, "I swear that as soon as I can get my external affairs in order I will see that the streets are flowing with the blood and heads of these infamous swine the Lutherans."[31] Now that moment had come. On April 3, 1559, the king signed the Peace of Cateau-Cambrésis ending a generation of wars with the Habsburg emperors. On May 18, the Parlement decreed against public demonstrations by Huguenots, and the king arrested François D'Andelot, a leading Protestant noble. On May 25, a few blocks away from the psalm-chanting crowds, the first national synod of the Protestant church was meeting in secret to hammer out a common confession of faith that would join the emerging congregations into a national Calvinist church. Two months later, Henry II was killed in a jousting match, throwing the royal government into turmoil just at the moment when Huguenot communities were going public and seizing power all over France.

For the next thirty-five years, the citizens of French towns had to deal with the fact that they were split between two irreconcilable religious communities. Eight civil wars were fought over religion between 1562 and 1593. Each war pitted royal forces led by Catholic grandees against Protestant forces led by Huguenot grandees. Each

war was followed by a shaky peace that accorded a limited, legalis-
tically defined, toleration to Huguenots, only to lead to a new blowup
and another war. As the conflict grew more desperate, moderate
aristocratic leaders were replaced by angry, militant crowds. Meanwhile, Huguenot churches multiplied, and wherever there were sufficient numbers, they took over municipal governments, set up Protestant
schools, and reorganized charitable activities. A major turning-point
was reached in 1572, when the massacre of Protestants on Saint Bartholomew's Day in Paris initiated a wave of fear and hatred that stifled
the growth of the Calvinist church. Further wars culminated in the
parallel assassinations of the leader of the ultra-Catholics, the duc de
Guise in 1588 and Henry III in 1589.

During this long tumultuous period, Catholics and Protestants in
local communities had to deal with one another. Direct, often violent,
confrontations were frequent. Calvinists were offended by the crosses,
rosaries, and figures of saints they saw everywhere, signifying for them
superstition and error. Catholics were offended by the stark plainness
of the Huguenots, by the apparent arrogance with which they flaunted
their severe morality, and by their rejection of the beautiful ceremonies and artifacts of Catholic worship. Huguenot crowds demolished images of saints, trampled on the wafer used in the Catholic
Mass, polluted holy water, ate meat on Fridays, and mocked Lenten
fasting. Catholic crowds, usually in the majority, invaded prayer
meetings, betrayed by the sound of loud psalm singing. They harassed,
jailed, and murdered Huguenots. For each side, the presence of the
other threatened to bring the wrath of God down upon the community.

These conflicts, in many different localities, left behind a complicated
pattern of directed violence. Catholic bias against Huguenots was
manifest. In Amiens, in 1562, a Protestant minister complained to the
authorities that "every day, when he or other members of the reformed
religion walk through the streets, small children and other men and
women harass them in high voices and insult them greatly."[32] In
Troyes, where Huguenots were a minority in the 1560s, militant soldiers from the urban militia, usually artisans, were known to drag
Huguenots out of prison, kill them, and dump their bodies onto dung
heaps, a tactic that was intended to humiliate and degrade. When the
Peace of Amboise in 1563 required that Protestant worship be legally
tolerated at one location in every *bailliage*, the spot designated by the
city of Troyes was 20 miles away. Loyal Protestants who made this

Figure 18 Just one example of the sorts of atrocities that occurred during the religious wars, the massacre of Protestants by Catholics at Sens in April 1562. One of a set of engravings published by two Protestant authors, Jean-Jacques Perrissin and Jacques Tortorel. They were far from impartial, but their representation of the massacre appears to be based on solid facts.

long commute on Sundays were harassed by the residents when they returned in a group.[33]

This sort of discrimination was evident everywhere on both sides. In Nîmes, in 1567, when Catholics had regained power from the insurgent Huguenots, prominent Protestant leaders executed a coup. They closed the gates, arrested the leading Catholic figures, including many priests, and locked them in a dank basement for over twenty-four hours without food or water. Those on a prepared list of enemies were then dragged to the courtyard of the bishop's palace, killed in cold blood with swords, daggers, and pistols, and dumped down a well. Accounts reported that about a hundred had been so murdered, including a group of Catholic city officials and at least eighteen priests and monks.[34]

When crowds engaged in religious violence, they tended to invoke a common language of ritual humiliation. In Provins in 1562, when a Protestant was hanged for committing various crimes, his corpse was

Figure 19 Massacre at Le Puy, October 16, 1594. Here Jean Burel (see Figure 6), a loyal supporter of the Catholic League, triumphantly sketches the corpses of men he calls "the politique traitors," that is, royalist Catholics who had died while trying to take over the city.

cut down, allegedly by children twelve years old or younger. They dragged the corpse through the streets, tried it for heresy, and ultimately built a fire and immolated it. Adults supposedly watched approvingly. In Toulouse a certain François du Mas was dragged alive through the streets, stoned and burned, also by children. The same thing happened to the merchant Joseph Guerin in Marseille. The repeated mention of children has been interpreted by Denis Crouzet as an expression of the Catholic belief that children, as innocents, were carrying out God's divine retribution. There are enough reports of similar atrocities to guarantee that events of this sort did take place. But some of these episodes are highly implausible and come from Protestant sources that were intended to outrage public opinion. "Children" in such sources were often the adolescent males who habitually carried out community rituals.

These stories, accompanied by graphic engravings of mass disembowling and naked bodies floating in rivers, were part of the first extensive struggle in printed media to sway "public opinion," by addressing an early sort of "public sphere." Protestant books of martyrs contributed to the development of a common Huguenot identity, while

Catholic descriptions of the Protestant demolition of cherished churches and their cruelty to nuns and priests fired up Catholic animosities. Floods of pamphlets and cheap engravings inflamed public opinion, while a few dispassionate authors made a more analytical attempt to understand the wrenching experiences everyone was going through. Certain Protestant authors struggled to justify some kind of constitutional check on the tyranny of kings who were destroying their own subjects.[35]

The religious wars climaxed in 1589, when the Huguenot Henry of Navarre became the legitimate king. He had to win his kingdom by first defeating the army of the Catholic League and then becoming Catholic in 1593. In 1598 he issued the Edict of Nantes which established the right to worship and a limited legal status for Huguenots, hedged with restrictions and ambiguities. They lived under this set the rules until the Edict was revoked in 1685, but there were episodes of armed Protestant resistance until 1629.

Confessional interaction on the local level

During the era from 1560 to 1685, Huguenot congregations were able to put their beliefs into practice and develop their own traditions in areas under their control. Calvin and his followers had imagined the outlines of a different kind of society. Ministers would marry and have families like other members of the community. Authority would rest not in a holy priest, set apart by ordination and celibacy, but in the community of believers. The church would be built from the ground up, starting with local cells, all considered equal. Each local church would be governed by a consistory made up of elders who would oversee the righteousness of the members and discipline or expel offenders. Each consistory would send representatives to a colloquy of nearby churches, which in turn would send representatives to a provincial synod, and then to a national synod. These arrangements, the reverse of the top-down Catholic church hierarchy, threatened the very fundamentals of Catholic daily life.

At its height, the Huguenot population never represented more than 10 percent of the total population of France. Geographically, there were about 1,200 Protestant churches in 1560. They existed in every province, but their strongest numbers were in Normandy and the southern provinces of Guyenne, Languedoc, and Dauphiné, with major clusters around La Rochelle, Montauban, Agen, Toulouse, Montpellier, and Nîmes.

The social origins of the Huguenot population have been much discussed. The movement attracted educated urban individuals of the sort who would be receptive to their stern insistence on order and sobriety and who were able to read their literature. This included former priests, men of law, royal officers, other professionals, and a great many artisans, especially in skilled trades such as printing, which facilitated receptivity to ideas, and newer trades that were more open to innovation. In Montpellier in 1560, 90 percent of the Huguenots were professionals or artisans. In Amiens, poor textile workers formed the basis of the movement, most of whom were first-generation immigrants to the city. Many nobles were attracted by the self-confidence and the sense of leadership which Calvinism conveyed to them. Calvinism was less appealing to artisans in traditional trades such as winegrowers, butchers, and bakers, and especially to the rural peasantry, all of whom were deeply committed to their traditional Catholic rituals. Another factor in recruiting was the example set by regional nobles who carried their clients and servants with them when they converted, as the Bourbons did in Navarre and Bearn.

Women from these same circles were attracted by the dedication and sobriety of their men and by the recognition given to the importance of reading the Bible in the home and strengthening family ties. Possibly they also enjoyed the sense of community in a small congregation where women could participate, although they sat apart from the men in services and had no more place in church governance than Catholic women.

The local consistory was managed by elders drawn from the more distinguished members of the church. Studies suggest that although Protestant congregations were democratic in the sense of crossing the boundaries of professions and status, and considering everyone equal before the Lord, there was a tendency for the more eminent to dominate the proceedings. In the important consistory of Nîmes, the vast majority of those sanctioned were artisans of lower status than the elders who sanctioned them. These somber, business-like elders were dedicated to making God's world more orderly. They kept registers of marriages, baptisms, and burials. They also kept track of which members were considered unworthy to participate in the Lord's Supper, those boys needing employment as apprentices, and members who could be hired out as servants.[36]

Under the regime of the Edict of Nantes, communities with mixed religions had to learn to coexist. A good example is the consistory of Layrac-en-Brulhois, which has been expertly analyzed by Gregory Hanlon. Layrac was a small town in the Agenais with a population of around 1,500, half of whom, including most of the notables, were Protestant. Despite this relatively favorable situation, running the church was no easy task. A succession of pastors seemed always to be struggling with the elders. They received a substantial salary and a house to live in, but they were never paid in full or on time. Pastors were considered to be employees who were expected to deliver inspirational sermons and live exemplary lives, but they were never satisfied with the congregation, or the congregation with them. The first prominent pastor was Izaac Sylvius, who married locally into a leading family. He had studied in Geneva with Théodore de Bèze. His son, and later his son-in-law, succeeded him as pastor, and in fact seven pastors from this church were related to one another, creating a sort of dynasty. Sylvius served until his death in 1638, but his later years were sullied by a nasty dispute with his wife's family over inheritance.[37]

However committed the Huguenots in this rural town may have been to their beliefs, Calvinist orthodoxy did not take precedence over other kinds of community solidarity. Hanlon has shown that Catholics and Protestants interacted daily, of necessity, without building any strong barriers between the two confessional communities. They collaborated in business deals, lent money to one another, trained apprentices and hired servants of the opposite faith, arranged mixed marriages, and witnessed one another's wills and contracts. Neighbors helped neighbors across confessional boundaries.[38] Such interaction does not necessarily mean that the inhabitants were tolerant. They were being pragmatic about their options, and given the numerical importance of the local Huguenot bourgeoisie and the isolation of the Huguenot townspeople in the surrounding Catholic countryside, collaboration was a necessity on both sides.

In cultural terms, it appears that the Calvinists clung formally to their strict beliefs but could not entirely overcome the social and cultural milieu in which they lived. The consistory was constantly reprimanding its members for dealing too closely with monks and priests, marching in processions displaying Catholic symbols, and administering Catholic oaths. Officially the Protestant church had nothing to do with carnival celebrations, charivaris, or masked balls. But members, especially youths, could never entirely be kept from singing bawdy songs, wearing costumes, dancing, frequenting taverns, drinking, and gambling. In these respects, the traditional practices of community and craft solidarity won out over sectarian identities.

Calvinist communities were gradually put on the defensive by resurgent Catholic forces, not least of which was the determination of the royal government to eliminate their faith. The king, egged on by assemblies of the clergy, the Jesuits, and most of the French people, gradually took the offensive. There were Huguenot wars of resistance in 1621–2 and 1625–9. During this period the Protestants held their own. But after 1660 Louis XIV and his agents began imposing more and more stringent constraints. Royal agents paid bounties for Protestants who converted, harassed ministers, insisted that Catholic priests have access to the death beds of Protestants, limited Huguenot participation in guilds, abolished whole congregations on the grounds of some petty infraction, and took children who claimed they wanted to convert to Catholicism away from their Protestant parents. Even in Layrac there were signs that the tide was turning in favor of the Catholics: fewer mixed couples, more conversions to Catholicism, eventual demolition of the temple in 1671.

As Catholic society pressed them harder and harder, many Huguenots fought back with plans for resistance, or just with manifestations of public contempt. In 1678, Protestants in Saint-Hippolyte, a small town in the mountains above Nîmes, jeered at a Catholic procession in which the local priest, carrying the holy sacrament under a canopy, led a group of Catholic well-wishers carrying lighted candles to the bedside of a sick parishioner. Refusing to remove their hats, the Protestants' taunts sound like the defensively assertive expressions of a group feeling very insecure: "Poor blind people, you can't see anything even at high noon." "The papists must be blind to have to carry candles in broad daylight." "The priests are as stupid as dogs." The wife of the pastor was seen at a window making grimaces and scornful gestures. Someone was heard to say that, if the king pushed them much farther, they would emigrate to England and return with an army of more than fifty thousand men.[39]

Times got harder for the surviving Protestant communities. Some families emigrated; some advocated resistance. In 1683 a report from the royal intendant in Languedoc described the panicky state of the

Protestant axis around Nîmes and Montpellier. He spoke of nocturnal meetings on the estates of prominent local nobles, of efforts by royal agents to disrupt the consistories by fomenting internal quarrels, of a decree prohibiting children whose parents were of mixed religion from entering the Protestant temple, and of the removal of all Protestant attorneys and solicitors from their royal offices. He went on,

> Nîmes and Uzès are the centers of heresy in Languedoc... These two consistories, especially Nîmes, are animating all the rest of the province and have sent emissaries everywhere to dissuade those who are thinking of converting. They encourage them to borrow as much as they can and then flee to foreign countries, where they promise them great assistance.[40]

When the Edict of Nantes was revoked in 1685, troops and the royal dragoons were mobilized to occupy the houses of those who refused to convert; the result was massive conversions, few of them very sincere. Although the borders were closed, thousands emigrated to England, Prussia, and other parts of Europe. Many of the converts rejoined the Catholic fold more or less permanently, but a minority retained the memory of their Huguenot heritage, and some even worshipped secretly. One last holdout in the Cévennes mountains of Languedoc suggests the desperation of those who remained. The so-called "Camisards" were poor mountain dwellers guided by men with prophetic visions. They rose up against royal troops and fought desperately between 1701 and 1704. An underground Calvinist movement survived until Protestantism was legalized in 1783.

Resurgent Catholicism

One of the most lasting impacts of French Calvinism was its role in forcing the Catholic church to regroup and fight. Although Catholicism was already reviving in other countries, the energy released in France by intense Catholic revulsion toward Huguenot activism was especially virulent. It took the form, first, of militant attacks on Huguenots and military intervention. Later, when the religious wars were over, radical Catholic sentiment settled down into intense apolitical piety.

The Bourbon kings Henry IV, Louis XIII, and Louis XIV benefited from the religious disorders by successfully asserting a more powerful, more absolute style of ruling that was acceptable to the major elites as an alternative to endless conflict. They continued to tax the church and make full use of their powers of nomination and their ability to exploit ecclesiastical resources. But all three of them were surrounded by ministers and courtiers, many of whom were considered *dévots* in that they were deeply committed to the new piety that was sweeping over France, and all three were themselves influenced by the Catholic revival. As a result, their manipulations of the church were less disruptive and somewhat more conscientious.

In the seventeenth century the monarchy continued to draw on ecclesiastical revenues for its own purposes. Henry IV used pensions drawn from clerical incomes to conciliate former enemies and reward faithful followers. Joseph Bergin has calculated that during the reign of Henry IV (1589–1610), 66 of the 116 available episcopal appointments were burdened with pensions. These stipends were used by the king to conciliate powerful regional figures, buy off rival claimants to a position, or reward personal service to the king. During the subsequent reign of Louis XIII and the years before 1661, pensions continued to be used in this way. However, there is evidence that they were going increasingly to clerics rather than laymen, and although Cardinal Mazarin turned again to their use for political patronage, the long-term trend was for them increasingly to be used for legitimate clerical purposes.[41]

In the personal reign of Louis XIV (1661–1715), the king's nominees were more aristocratic, but probably also better qualified. A look at these 250 bishops shows that almost half of the nominees were related to bishops who had served during previous regimes, and 120 of the group were related to one another. As many as 71 percent had fathers who were royal ministers or important officers from the sovereign courts, 14 percent of their fathers were financiers or financial officers, and only 12 percent came from the rest of the population. Unlike his predecessors, Louis XIV never nominated a non-priest to a bishopric. On the other hand, not a single nominee had ever served as a parish priest. Thus his bishops were better trained and better qualified, but they were drawn from the highest, most privileged circles, and they had little contact with the parish world of everyday life.[42]

An inventory of the possessions of the bishop of Béziers in 1702 gives us a glimpse of how one of these aristocratic prelates lived. The bishop's recently built town house opened onto a ceremonial courtyard. It contained a chapel and about twenty rooms, counting servants' quarters and utility spaces. Each room was decorated with tapestries on the walls and Turkish carpets on the floors. Each had candelabras and chandeliers, a fireplace with fancy andirons and screens, small and large tables, lavish curtains, and a large mirror. Tapestries from Bergamo, Flanders, and England decorated the walls, accompanied by other wall hangings that often matched the uphol-stered chairs. The bishop owned at least eight ceremonial beds with canopy, curtains, and all the trappings. His walls displayed paintings framed in gold depicting the four seasons, the bishop's coat of arms, with a large painting of Louis XIV on horseback in one room, and, in another room, Louis XIV accompanied by portraits of the whole royal family. The palace also contained a sedan chair upholstered in red velvet bearing the late bishop's coat of arms, a stable full of horses, a library of 2,500 volumes, a complete silver service for twenty-four, platters, some portraits of saints, and some religious articles. In his country chateau of Lignau, the bishop's orangerie contained fifty-one orange trees and 153 pots of roses, carnations, and fig trees.[43]

All this was a far cry from the confessional ferment of a century earlier. The traumatic 1590s had left a residue of bitterness and dis-satisfaction. In one generation heretical insurgents had polluted the true faith, torn down churches and monasteries, uttered innumerable blasphemies, and rebelled against their legitimate monarch. In Paris, the Catholic party called "the Sixteen" had taken over the city in the midst of eschatological panic and widespread calls for repentance. Moderates who supported a compromise with Navarre in the interests of orderly government had to flee. All over France the same drama was playing out. In the distant Massif Central, Jean Burel, merchant tanner of Le Puy, described in his journal how his city harassed and expelled the "politique" supporters of Navarre and sold their property at public auction. Like the Parisians, the citizens of Le Puy swore a collective oath to defend the Catholic League in 1591 and recognized "King Charles X," the Guise candidate. In 1594 they lit bonfires of joy and displayed the colors of enemy Spain when they heard a rumor that Henry IV was dead.[44]

The dramatic swing of allegiances during a single lifetime must have produced wrenching conflicts of loyalty for those who lived through them. Consider just one example, the story of Henri de Sponde, born in 1568 in Protestant Béarn. Henry's father was secretary to Jeanne d'Albret, queen of Navarre. His godfather was Henry of Navarre himself. As a Huguenot youth, Sponde participated in the collective desecration of Catholic churches, personally demolishing tombs, altars, and statues. He received an excellent humanist education, first in the Protestant *collège* of Orthez, which was installed by the Huguenot regime in a former monastery, then for three years in Calvinist Geneva. At age nineteen, he was sent by Navarre on a diplomatic mission to the British Isles where he conversed with Queen Elizabeth in Latin and impressed James VI, king of Scotland. Here was a man destined for high places in the Protestant world. But in 1593 his mentor and godfather, now king of France, converted to Catholicism. Sponde's world must have been turned upside-down. He later claimed that he had been struggling for a long time with "doubts and anxieties...but however many steps forward he attempted to take, the Devil made him take twice as many backwards." About a year later he too converted and plunged into the study of Catholic theology. Obviously still well connected, he pursued a law degree in Bordeaux and accompanied the archbishop of Bordeaux on a trip to Rome, where he was ordained a priest in 1606 and where he lived on and off until 1616. He became a prominent Catholic scholar and held various papal offices. In 1626 he was named bishop of Pamiers by Louis XIII, who gave him gifts and attended Mass at his side. On May 22, 1627, Sponde entered his new seat at Pamiers and was formally greeted by the consuls, all of whom were Huguenots. Sponde would now have to reform a diocese in which all the priests were in exile and all the churches were in ruin. He celebrated his first Pentecost in a tent. Sponde had successfully changed with the times, but he was publicly vilified in Protestant pamphlets for doing so, and when he became a bishop he had to get a special papal dispensation because of his past. Then he had to cope with a city full of heretics, and they had to accommodate an unwanted, turncoat prelate.[45]

Out of such wrenching experiences emerged a Catholic spiritual revival among members of the robe–financial elite. This wave of devotion was influenced by three circumstances. Some had tasted the collective religious fervor that had prevailed in the streets of Paris during the siege of the city in 1590 and the subsequent regime of the Sixteen. Franciscan friars had delivered fiery sermons and held forty-hour prayer vigils. Daily processions of penitential monks and barefoot laymen had marched through the city, often at night carrying candles. The second factor was the trauma experienced by many

Figure 20 François de Sales blessing the Sisters of the Visitation.

families. These successful robe dynasties, often on the verge of acquiring important posts in the councils of the royal government, suddenly found their future threatened by factional splits and loyalty tests. The third circumstance was the already flourishing Catholic revival taking place in Spain and Italy as a result of the decrees of the Council of Trent. New saints and religious orders were proliferating, and the militant Society of Jesus was reaching out to win Europe over to the reformed Roman church.

These *dévots* were in the vanguard of a burgeoning movement for renewed faith that swept through French upper-class society between 1600 and 1640. It involved, on the one hand, the creation of new religious orders attuned to the revived spirit of devotion and, on the other hand, a multitude of lay charitable associations in which elite men and women could channel their spiritual energies without abandoning their aristocratic lives. It was also literally an age of saints. Saint François de Sales (1567–1622), the bishop of Geneva, who was renowned for his ability to convert Protestants through his oratory, came to Paris in 1602 and became a preacher in the queen's chapel. Saint Vincent de Paul (1581–1660), was concerned for "the poor people who are incurring damnation from ignorance of the things necessary to salvation and for want of confessing their sins."[46] He founded missions to instruct and convert the rural peasantry. The most typical figure was perhaps Pierre de Bérulle (1576–1629), typical because he was from a prominent French robe family. As almoner to the king, he provided a link between the court and *dévot* circles. He founded the Oratory, another society of priests dedicated to teaching in *collèges* and seminaries as well as rural missions, and wrote several influential treatises on the necessity of reaching God through contemplation of the humanity of Christ.

These leaders were only the tip of the iceberg. Between 1600 and 1639, the number of monasteries and convents in Paris jumped from about fifteen to seventy.[47] Provincial cities experienced the same influx of new establishments, patronized and populated by their local elites. In Lyon in the first half of the century, nine new men's houses and eleven new women's houses were created. In Toulouse eighteen new male and female houses were established between 1563 and 1662.[48] To this bourgeoning movement must be added the many traditional monasteries that underwent rigorous reforms and the efforts of many bishops, through visitations of their dioceses, to monitor the performance of their parish clergy and to assess the quality of local religious practices. Meanwhile, congregations of lay volunteers were organizing charitable activities, and the Jesuits were introducing humanist learning with a decidedly Catholic twist in *collèges* in many cities.

One of the more interesting aspects of this movement was the central role of powerful women. After the murder of Henry, duc de Guise in 1588, Guise's wife, Catherine de Clèves, and his mother, the duchesse de Nemours, both assumed direct public roles in raising funds and rallying support for the League. Guise's sister, the duchesse de Montpensier, paid large sums to induce priests to preach against

Henry III. When the king was murdered, the mother and sister rode
through the Paris streets in their carriage, shouting out to passers-by,
"Good news, the tyrant is dead!"[49] A decade later, it was one of these
women, Barbe Acarie, a relative of the Bérulle and Séguier families,
who was the motivating force behind the spiritual movement in Paris.
Her recollections of the days of the League suggest a psychological
link between the League experience and *dévot* spirituality.[50] Acarie
was personally guided by Carthusian monk Richard Beaucousin, her
spiritual advisor, and by Capuchin monk Benoit de Canfield. Her
Parisian residence became a meeting place for noted preachers,
theologians from the Sorbonne, and spiritual leaders like Pierre de
Berulle, François de Sales, and Michel de Marillac, the future chancellor of France. They regularly discussed spiritual reform and
sometimes attended five or six Masses a day in her private chapel.
Devotions, they thought, should focus on the humanity of Christ on
the cross and his very human suffering. To share this suffering meant
abandoning all personal desire and giving oneself up to Christ. Their
moment of greatest transcendence came during the celebration of the
Mass, at the moment of the elevation of the host, when the body of
Christ and his passion were actually present. "The Eucharist is thus a
marvelous epiphany of the passion, a renewal of the sacrifice on the
Cross, rather than a sharing or communion."[51]

Acarie was prone to fainting spells during which she experienced
religious ecstasy. In one of these, Saint Teresa of Avila, the Spanish
mystic, appeared to her in a vision and told her that she should
introduce the Spanish order of reformed female Carmelites into
France. With the aid of her many influential allies, Acarie devoted
her life to fulfilling this wish. The initial funding was supplied by
Catherine d'Orléans, princesse de Longueville, who pledged 2,400
livres per year for the convent's upkeep. This pattern of *dévot* direction and aristocratic funding became typical. The Carmelite convent
in Paris was inaugurated in 1604, and by 1668 there were sixty-two
chapters in France.[52]

The impulse to seek purification through suffering was shared by
other aristocratic women. All of these well-connected ladies were
driven by an urgent need to annihilate their self-will and become totally
dependent on the will of God. Mortifying the flesh was considered
necessary to subdue the body's sinful urges and to use it as a vehicle for
being at one with Christ. In 1599 Antoinette d'Orléans-Longueville

abandoned her children and family to join the rigorous Feuillantines convent in Toulouse. Marie Sevin ventured into dangerous parts of the city to rescue the souls of prostitutes. Louise Gallois followed the instructions of her Capuchin spiritual director, who made her give up everything she held dear. First, she had to abandon the use of a crucifix to which she was closely attached, then – threatening her very religious identity – he made her abstain from the spiritual comfort of receiving the Eucharist. Finally, when she accomplished even this sacrifice with difficulty, he prescribed the ultimate challenge: to send her servants to Mass while she did their chores! She passed all of these tests.

Meanwhile, additional cloistered communities were being created through the intervention of other aristocratic women. Marie de Luxembourg had acquired long experience managing her extensive properties in Brittany while her husband, the duc de Mercoeur, was away fighting for the League. Widowed in 1602, she devoted her attention to establishing a convent of Capuchin nuns. She purchased a Parisian site for the convent and spent two years directing its construction. She also monitored the selection and training of candidates, and the design of the rule they would follow.[53]

A number of other newly created orders followed, as the reformers experimented with different formulas. The Order of the Visitation (Visitandines, 1619), created by François de Sales and Jeanne de Chantal, was intended to admit women whose age, health problems, or family obligations prevented them from entering other orders. The congregation of Sainte-Marie Madeleine took in repentant prostitutes.

As time passed, the memories of the 1590s became more distant, and the mystical zeal of the original founders faded for those of the next generation. Another element in the moderating of original expectations was financial. The new religious houses proved very expensive to maintain, and when the founders' funds were depleted, they had to compromise by accepting rich daughters as *pensionnaires*.

The interests of the *dévots* shifted to doing charitable work, and cloistered nuns tended to be replaced by lay groups of well-to-do ladies and gentlemen who could participate without abandoning the other aspects of their lives. Vincent de Paul collaborated with Françoise-Marguerite de Silly, wife of the commander of the royal galleys, in establishing the Congregation de la Mission (1625) as a community of priests dedicated to bringing better knowledge of the rudiments of the faith to peasants in the countryside. In the 1630s,

Louise de Marillac, Michel de Marillac's illegitimate niece, organized the Filles de la Charité, a group of lay women who went out into local communities in small groups to aid the needy.

Another movement, emanating directly from elite men, was the highly secret Compagnie du Saint Sacrement founded by Henri de Lévis, duc de Ventadour, around 1630 with a membership of high nobles, bishops, *parlementaires*, and provincial dignitaries. Its purpose was to promote devotion to Christ by secretly intervening in political and religious affairs. Its statutes contain both charitable and repressive impulses: "the focus of the members' charity will be the hospitals, the prisons, the sick, the afflicted poor, all those who need help, and they will monitor whether the magistrates observe Christian regulations and whether the heretics observe the edicts."[54] With chapters in many provinces, they intervened behind the scenes to promote charitable works that disciplined the poor and spread orthodox Catholic worship, while converting or subverting the Huguenots.

Despite these masculine activities, the Catholic revival was the particular domain of women. They had to confront strong gender barriers. Women were not allowed to celebrate Mass or run religious houses without male supervision. They were legally subordinated to husbands, fathers, and spiritual counselors. A society with deep-seated attitudes concerning gender remained convinced that independent women on their own were dangerous, and very likely prone to error and disorder. It was difficult for the Visitandines to innovate when they could not get approval for nuns to leave the convent for service in the community. As the archbishop of Lyon argued, women of good family "needed the cloister to preserve their reputation, and to save themselves and their relatives from dangers, fears and anxieties."[55] He might have added that family fortunes were threatened if nuns had the power to abandon their calling and appear at their parents' houses claiming their inheritances. Nevertheless, *dévot* women demonstrated an impressive degree of initiative. Barbara Diefendorf notes that even while they were subordinating themselves to men, these women were asserting their own independent course of action. They accepted their dependency, but at the same time they were asserting their spiritual independence by choosing a course that had not been prescribed by husbands or confessors.

Figure 21 Part of a series by Abraham Bosse (1602–76) depicting acts of mercy. Well-dressed ladies and gentlemen visit prisoners, in the spirit of the Catholic revival.

This broad *dévot* movement was an expression of the quest for identity and legitimacy on the part of the aspiring families who were profiting from venal officeholding, state officialdom, and royal finance. Many of these families were also enjoying the advantages of an era when the rural economy was channeling a greater share of the agricultural produce toward landlords and away from tenant farmers and rural laborers.[56] Although these *dévots* were perfectly sincere in their spiritual and charitable interventions, they were at the same time contributing mightily to their own status and reputation. Holiness was another much-respected form of eminence and a way of establishing credibility, especially for upwardly mobile families lacking in ancient pedigrees.

The French church had undergone a sea change between the time of Louis XI and the age of Louis XIV. From a medieval collection of diverse organizations, each deeply immersed in local connections and corrupt practices, it had been reborn as a more modern institution. It had been subjected to a large dose of royal control; but it had withstood the major shock administered by the Huguenots. At the same time it found new strength in the intense spirituality and pious activism generated by prominent elites. It had also reformed many abuses and improved its practice through education and better oversight. It did so at the expense of becoming more aristocratic and more susceptible to royal intervention. And it was still subject to internal conflicts. The eighteenth century would see the intensification of a battle between Jesuits and Jansenists that revolved around two conflicting strains of the new piety. A legacy of the seventeenth century was that religion was still intimately intertwined with politics.

Suggestions for further reading: Catholic institutions, sectarian conflict, and the Huguenots

Catholic institutions

Armstrong, Megan C., *The Politics of Piety: Franciscan Preachers during the Wars of Religion, 1500–1600* (Rochester, NY, 2004).

Baumgartner, Frederick J., *Change and Continuity in the French Episcopate: The Bishops and the Wars of Religion, 1547–1610* (Durham, NC, 1986).

Bergin, Joseph, *Cardinal Richelieu: Power and the Pursuit of Wealth* (New Haven, CT, 1985).

The Making of the French Episcopate 1589–1661 (New Haven, CT, 1996).

Crown, Church and Episcopate under Louis XIV (New Haven, CT, 2004).

Briggs, Robin, *Communities of Belief: Cultural and Social Tension in Early Modern France* (Oxford, 1989).

Dolan, Claire, *Entre tours et clochers: les gens d'église à Aix-en-Provence au XVIe siècle* (Aix, 1981).

Edelstein, Marilyn Manera, "The Social Origins of the Episcopacy in the Reign of Francis I," *French Historical Studies* 8 (1974), 377–92.

Hayden, J. Michael, "Social Origins of the French Episcopacy at the Beginning of the 17th Century," *French Historical Studies* (1976), 27–40.

Hoffman, Philip T., *Church and Community in the Diocese of Lyon 1599–1789* (New Haven, CT, 1984).

McManners, John, *Church and Society in Eighteenth-Century France*, 2 vols. (Oxford, 1998).

Nelson, Eric, *The Jesuits and the Monarchy: Catholic Reform and Political Authority in France (1590–1615)* (Aldershot, 2005).

Parsons, Jotham, *The Church in the Republic: Gallicanism and Political Ideology in Renaissance France* (Washington, DC, 2004).

Phillips, Henry, *Church and Culture in Seventeenth-Century France* (Cambridge, 1997).

Tackett, Timothy, *Priest and Parish in Eighteenth-Century France: A Social and Political Study of the Curés in a Diocese of Dauphiné 1750–1791* (Princeton, NJ, 1977).

Tallon, Alain, *Conscience nationale et sentiment religieux en France au XVIe siècle: essai sur la vision gallicane du monde* (Paris, 2002).

Wanegffelen, Thierry, *Une difficile fidélité: Catholiques malgré le concile en France, XVIe–XVIIe siècles.* (Paris 1999).

Religious orders and Catholic revival

Bruneau, Marie-Florine, *Women Mystics Confront the Modern World: Marie de l'Incarnation (1599–1672) and Madame Guyon (1648–1717)* (Albany, NY, 1998).

Diefendorf, Barbara, *From Penitence to Charity: Pious Women and the Catholic Reformation in Paris* (Oxford, 2004).

Mellinger, Laura, "Politics in the Convent: The Election of a Fifteenth-Century Abbess," *Church History* 63 (1994), 529–40.

Rapley, Elizabeth, *The Dévotes: Women and Church in Seventeenth-Century France* (Montreal, 1993).

Ultee, Maarten, *The Abbey of Saint Germain des Pres in the Seventeenth Century* (New Haven, CT, 1981).

Calvinism

Benedict, Philip, *The Huguenot Population of France 1600–1685: The Demographic Fate and Customs of a Religious Minority*, Transactions of the American Philosophical Society XCI, pt. 2. (Philadelphia, 1991).
  Christ's Churches Purely Reformed: A Social History of Calvinism (New Haven, CT, 2002).
Butler, Jon, *The Huguenots in America: A Refugee People in New World Society* (Cambridge, MA, 1992).
Chappell, Carolyn Lougee, " 'The Pains I Took to Save My/His Family': Escape Accounts by a Huguenot Mother and Daughter after the Revocation of the Edict of Nantes," *French Historical Studies* 22 (1999), 1–64.
Elwood, Christopher, *The Body Broken: The Calvinist Doctrine of the Eucharist and the Symbolization of Power in Sixteenth-Century France* (Oxford, 1999).
Kingdon, Robert M., *Geneva and the Coming of the Wars of Religion in France 1555–1563* (Geneva, 1956).
Mentzer, Raymond A., "Ecclesiastical Discipline and Communal Reorganization among the Protestants of Southern France," *European History Quarterly* 21 (1991), 163–83.
  "Organizational Endeavour and Charitable Impulse in Sixteenth-Century France: The case of Protestant Nîmes," *French History* 5 (1991), 1–29.
Nichols, David, "The Theatre of Martyrdom in the French Reformation," *Past and Present* 121 (November 1988), 49–73.

Confessional interaction and religious conflict

Benbassa, Esther, *The Jews of France; A History from Antiquity to the Present*, trans. M. B. DeBevoise (Princeton, NJ, 1999).
Cameron, Keith, Mark Greengrass, and Penny Roberts, eds., *The Adventure of Religious Pluralism in Early Modern France* (Oxford 2000).
Crouzet, Denis, *Les Guerriers de Dieu: la violence au temps des troubles de religion (vers 1525–vers 1610*, 2 vols. (Seyssel, 1990), I, 77, 83–5, 86.
Davies, Joan, "Persecution and Protestantism: Toulouse 1562–1575," *Historical Journal* 22 (1979), 31–51.
Diefendorf, Barbara, *Beneath the Cross: Catholics and Huguenots in Sixteenth-Century Paris* (New York, 1991).
Hanlon, Gregory, *Confession and Community in Seventeenth-Century France: Catholic and Protestant Coexistence in Aquitaine* (Philadelphia, 1993), 127–32.

Heller, Henry, *Iron and Blood: Civil War in Sixteenth-Century France* (Montreal, 1991).

Mentzer, Raymond A., *Heresy Proceedings in Languedoc, 1500–1560.* Transactions of the American Philosophical Society, LXXIV, pt. 5 (Philadelphia, 1984).

Miskimin, Patricia Behre, *One King, One Law, Three Faiths: Religion and the Rise of Absolutism in Seventeenth-Century Metz* (Westport, CT, 2002).

Meyer, Judith Pugh, *Reformation in La Rochelle: Tradition and Change in Early Modern Europe, 1500–1568* (Geneva, 1996).

Monter, William, *Judging the French Reformation: Heresy Trials by Sixteenth Century Parlements* (Cambridge, MA, 1999).

Luria, Keith, *Sacred Boundaries: Religious Coexistence and Conflict in Early Modern France* (Washington, DC, 2005).

Taylor, Larissa Juliet, *Heresy and Orthodoxy in Sixteenth-Century Paris: François Le Picart and the Beginnings of the Catholic Reformation* (Leiden, 1999).

Tulchin, Allan A., "The Michelade of Nîmes, 1567," *French Historical Studies* 29 (2006), 1–35.

7 | Warfare and society

War was a powerful influence. It was the primary preoccupation of the king, the court, and the nobility. It played a major role in providing the often fabled, sometimes real, exploits that fueled the pretensions of great noble families. Service in the army drew innumerable people from home towns and villages and plunged them into the exterior world. When they were discharged en masse, they became a menacing army of ragged beggars, threatening local residents and stealing along the roads. Even more menacing were the ravages of troops on the march through the countryside or stationed in winter quarters on some hapless town or village. And, of course, the horror for civilians caught in an actual war zone was incomparably worse.

The French monarchy was at war much of the time. Military activity troubled the peace during close to half of all the years between 1400 and 1789. Of course, these were not years of continuous fighting because warfare was seasonal, and many wars consisted of sporadic episodes rather than continuous fighting. During our period, weaponry shifted from pikes and longbows to muskets, rifles, and artillery. Armies mushroomed and became better coordinated. Louis XII and Francis I fought the Italian wars (1490–1525) with about 40,000 men. Henry II battled the Habsburgs (1543–59) with 70,000 men, and France mobilized 125,000 troops during the Thirty Years War (1635–48). Under the personal reign of Louis XIV the size of the army grew from a theoretical 134,000 in 1668 to 279,600 in the Dutch War (1678); 420,000 in the Nine Years War (1689–97); and 380,000 in the War of Spanish Succession (1701–14). The actual numbers in the field, given losses and false reports, were somewhat lower. Louis XIV's peak was probably reached during the Nine Years War, when the realistic totals on all fronts may have approached 340,000, compared to the 70,000 of the sixteenth century.[1] Mobilizing and directing such a force was the most ambitious enterprise undertaken by the state.

Consider the elements of a fully mobilized army of the mid six-teenth century. In December 1567 a field army led by the duc d'Anjou set out against the Protestants in the first religious war. His army consisted of about 25,500 infantry and 9,500 cavalry. But the entire assemblage numbered around 50,000, including 3,000 civilian porters and crews attached to the artillery units, all sorts of servants of indi-vidual commanders, teams of artisans such as carpenters, ropemakers, wheelwrights, and blacksmiths, and many camp followers, including prostitutes and the wives and children of soldiers. They were accom-panied by 25,000 animals, including the horses of the cavalry, mules to pull the heavy wagons, and all kinds of livestock. Two large com-panies – an advance force and the main body of the troops – marched several miles apart, in columns several hundred yards wide and almost two miles deep. A bystander would have had to watch for most of a day to see the whole procession go by.[2]

In front of the whole army was a group of light cavalrymen wearing open-faced helmets and breastplates and carrying pistols and swords. Then came the heart of the king's army, the *gendarmes*, who constituted the main cavalry force, made up of nobles armed with wooden lances and wearing full armor. Behind them marched a large contingent of French infantry. These were mostly pikemen wearing helmets, cuirasses, and leg armor. Their sole weapon was the 10-foot-long pike resting on their shoulders. At their flanks were arquebusiers, infantry soldiers carrying the arquebus, which was a primitive rifle with a very long barrel. Behind the infantry were several hundred conscripted peasants called "pioneers," who cleared the roads and pulled an enormous baggage train consisting of two-wheeled carts, freight wagons, mules, and horses, along with personal effects, tents, weapons, munitions, and two days' worth of victuals. And then there were the sounds:

to the visual spectacle ... would be added the sounds of thudding hoofbeats and tramping feet, rolling wheels, bumping and jarring vehicles, the jingling of spurs and harness, the clash of weapons against armor, the crack of whips, shouts of teamsters, the sounds of drums, fifes and trumpets, and a babble of speech and song including snatches of most European languages – English, German, Italian, Flemish and Spanish – and many varieties of French, as well as Breton, Gascon, and Provençal.[3]

An army like this was the sum of many different elements that were thrown together rather than developed as a coordinated whole.

Figure 22 Jean Paul, *The Siege of Maastricht*, June 29, 1673. This unusual painting shows Louis XIV's troops dug in for a siege. Although the details are hard to make out, the infantry and cavalry have pitched tents in the order of march. The field is bustling with activity.

Functionally speaking, there were four kinds of units: light cavalry out in front, heavy cavalry (*gendarmes*), infantry, and artillery. The cavalry and infantry were made up of separate companies of around fifty to a hundred men, each commanded by a captain who had recruited, hired, and paid his own soldiers. Many were hired mercenaries, German *reiters*, or Swiss infantry. The army as a whole marched, camped, and fought using the same formations all the time; consequently, no elaborate maneuvers were required to begin a battle. The various units just ranged themselves along a front, with the artillery grouped in the rear, and they were ready to fight. Companies spoke different languages, but there was little need for communications between them because each one functioned more or less autonomously.

The entire field army was commanded by the constable or by an appointed *lieutenant-général*. For decision-making, the field commander was assisted by a council of other commanding officers, who would all be important nobles experienced in war. No more than forty officers higher than captain were in charge of this army of 36,000 combatants and 50,000 individuals. These included three marshals of camp, eight masters of camp who commanded infantry regiments, two colonel-generals, and three colonels of infantry. Another 200 salaried civilian appointees performed clerical, accounting, and messenger services (thirty-six), medical services (seventeen), police functions (seventy-seven), and lodging and transport arrangements (forty-eight).

This sixteenth-century-style army had serious flaws. Using a simple additive principle, an army could be pieced together out of diverse units that did not necessarily match: experienced French infantry units, newly formed companies of inexperienced recruits, companies of gendarmes, foreign mercenaries, and artillery. The army's officers did not necessarily know one another, and the various units had little experience working together. Units were always being disbanded and reassembled.

By the time of Richelieu, the army was expanding rapidly and straining to fulfill the cardinal's ambitious plans for asserting Louis XIII's influence in Europe. It appears, however, that the forces just got larger, without much improvement in organization. This was the era of the so-called "military revolution" pioneered by Maurice of Nassau in the Netherlands and Gustavus Adolphus in the Thirty Years War. Their new style of warfare required intensive drilling of infantry, a better-trained officer corps, and heavy fire from lighter, more mobile artillery. Broad, shallow lines of soldiers, capable of rapid maneuvers, would be reinforced by increased cannon fire and swift charges by light cavalry. But although this "new" warfare was being adopted elsewhere, there is little evidence in France of attempts to adopt the same procedures, or even of discussion of them in published manuals. Troops numbered many fewer than their official size. In fact, David Parrott has shown that the massive French army was somewhat hollow because troop musters were distorted by the presence of stand-ins and the number of unreported desertions was high. Cavaliers were expensive and hard to recruit. France suffered from a major shortage of artillery.[4]

Progress was also impeded by social constraints. Royal tax collection was crippled by the cuts taken out by middleman-financiers and by the exemptions of most of the richest subjects. Incoming receipts were closely tied to the rhythms of the fields, which accorded badly with the needs of the military. The year's revenue would arrive at fall harvest time when military campaigns were already winding down. To fund a springtime war, these revenues would have to be anticipated by borrowing, and the king's lack of a bureaucracy to administer collections meant relying on tax farmers who siphoned off a fair amount of the proceeds. Collection costs and corruption also reduced receipts. As we saw in Chapter 5, these financiers operated through private credit networks that could not be easily interfered with because the bankruptcy of one might cause the whole house of cards of interlocking credit and debt to collapse.

Finally, there was the identity of the officers themselves. Most of the company commanders were nobles of some importance, usually known personally by the king. Their prominence at the front of each unit was built on status more than talent. The cavalry companies were almost exclusively made up of nobles – light cavalry, archers, and *hommes d'armes* – the main difference between them being their level of armor and weaponry. Although infantry companies were usually commanded by nobles, the foot soldiers were mostly peasants, along with occasional young nobles, trying to make their way, but too poor to buy a commission.

This venality of military offices was a major factor. The captains and colonels who commanded the basic units of both cavalry and infantry were required to buy their commissions. Then they were expected to defray some or all of the costs involved in organizing the unit. This meant that they might have to come up with bounties for recruitment or supply clothes, equipment, and arms. Cavalry officers had to provide horses. The officer's commission from the king included a certain sum for each recruit, but the amount was always inadequate, and it did not cover the replacement of shoes, clothes, and weapons. The state paid a wage to the soldiers, but in many cases it was late to arrive or lacking altogether, and the officer would have to come up with the funds on his own, or risk desertions and non-cooperation. Keeping the men supplied was essential for morale. Noble commanders, or their families, often took out loans to cover these expenses which might never be reimbursed. A company or regiment was thus an investment which was unlikely to be profitable and might indeed lead to financial ruin. If it was demobilized or destroyed in battle, there would be no compensation for the owner.[5]

As John Lynn points out, the officers were in effect pouring their personal resources into the king's war effort, in what might almost be considered a tax on the nobility.[6] But if this was a tax, it was a very unequally distributed one. A large percentage of the provincial nobility never went to war, and thus never paid. Those who did purchase commissions were the higher placed, more affluent nobles. A tax on them might have been socially justifiable. Within the army, state money to pay wages and replenish equipment was always in short supply. The result was a competition by officers for funds and supplies that was won by those with the most influence. Status at court and family name were therefore determinants of success. Companies and regiments were not operating on a level playing field. Faced with ruin, some commanders became desperate. In 1705 one captain wrote to Chamillart, "I have employed all that I have in the world to reestablish my company and have put thirty two men in it, one better than the other, who cost me 2,700 livres. It is all complete. I am now obliged to live on bread alone because it is necessary that I spend my wages on their clothes."[7]

This system of selling commissions meant that king and officers were collaborating in an uneasy alliance of mutual convenience. It was the only way the king could guarantee that his officers would be affluent enough to support the troops once they were in the field. A grant of a commission was also useful as a source of favors that the king could bestow upon ambitious young colonels. The officers continued to volunteer for such potentially damaging commissions because they were seeking glory of the sort that would permanently enhance the reputation of their lineage. They needed the attention of their patrons, or later the king himself, to win better positions in the hierarchy of esteem. Here, as at court or in the world of finance, one's advancement was partially dependent upon reputation and personal contacts.[8]

A danger for the king was that independent commanders might retire to their provinces, taking their soldiers with them, as some did during the religious wars and the Fronde. Another was that officers with an investment in their troops were likely to want to preserve that investment. They might shy away from open battle or favor siege warfare because they could milk the surrounding countryside for resources when they held a strategic fortress. When there were losses in battle, it was the commissioned officer's duty to replace the men, but this was a difficult and expensive proposition. There was always the temptation to conceal the losses or employ stand-ins at musters. The French king and his military officers were exchanging prestige in a joint venture that tied the officers loosely to the state and precluded the kind of independence that was enjoyed by the true mercenaries of the Thirty Years War in Germany; they were free to sell their services to the highest bidder.

Thus, throughout the seventeenth century, the army flourished and grew, but within social constraints. Its high command was chosen as much for reasons of prominence as for talent. Its captains and lieutenants had motives that did not always coincide with the best interests of the crown. The financial system provided a clumsy but necessary method of funding the wars. The administrative agents who managed the wartime administration were tied up in client networks that made the system work, but only while protecting their own vested interests.

Under Louis XIV, there was unquestionably a change of tone, with much better administration and more effective discipline. During the years of peace between 1659 and 1667, the king decided to maintain a standing army of 60,000 to 70,000 troops, and the famous ministerial team of Michel Le Tellier and his son and successor Louvois set out to improve the management of these forces. Over time the officer corps was enlarged, with a greater contingent of provincial nobles, and the need for more trained officers induced the system to tolerate up to 20 percent of men of common origin. More money was supplied for recruiting troops. Officers were still financially vulnerable, but their pay was more adequate than before, and the king applied his famous personal attention to helping some of them maintain their positions. Louis offered them gifts and bonuses and intervened to issue moratoriums on the debts of noble families in need. He provided furloughed officers with pensions and civilian positions so that their talents would not be lost when war resumed. He experimented with methods of training the uninitiated. A newly created company of royal musketeers made up of the sons of selected noble families was highly successful. The king's attempt to rescue the sons of impoverished provincial nobles from oblivion by subsidizing and training companies of cadets was wildly popular in the provinces, but proved less successful in practice, and was abandoned.[9]

New units were added to the military machine. The king's own infantry regiment, the Régiment du Roi, was created as an attempt to set an example for other commanders. Royal dragoons – light cavalry armed with carbines – were created in 1669. A regiment of fusiliers armed with flintlock muskets called *fusils*, appeared in 1671. Standard uniforms were adopted, and regular drill was instituted. Bayonets were introduced in the 1680s. After much foot-dragging, the lighter, more accurate flintlock muskets replaced the older matchlocks. The king issued a table of ranks to clarify the confusions between personal status and military seniority, but he continued to violate his own rules by using army commissions as favors to reward loyalty and friendship rather than to reward only military talent. There were still serious conflicts over the hierarchy of command when those with superior military rank topped those with superior noble rank. Field commanders continued to build personalized units by filling their subordinate posts with their own clients. After 1690, the king gave in to a shortage of effective officers for his burgeoning forces and the pressure of ambitious young nobles to obtain commissions, by creating new infantry regiments for them. The number of regiments rose from 88 in 1691 to 238 in 1714, the majority of which were new commissions sold to ambitious social climbers.[10]

As Guy Rowlands points out, institutional support for Louis XIV's army was greatly improved over previous regimes, but it was far from becoming an effective bureaucracy. Louvois used twenty *commissaires des guerres*, civilian agents attached to regiments, to enforce better conformity to established standards. They conducted frequent musters at which the troops were inspected and counted, and unfit soldiers were rejected. They traveled with troops, arranging for stopovers and monitoring the way troops treated the local citizens. In the 1690s, with a much larger army, these posts were replaced by 180 venal offices of *commissaires ordinaires des guerres* and 180 offices of *contrôleurs ordinaires des guerres*. *Intendants de l'armée* were now assigned to armies in the field. They audited accounts, arranged payments, and worked on stocking magazines, repairing fortifications, and hearing complaints. This proliferation of agents reporting back to the War Ministry did force company commanders to behave themselves better or face consequences. There is also evidence that common soldiers were more frequently punished for crimes against civilians.

However, the system of civilian managers faced a serious contradiction. When the cost of war forced the king to create and sell these civilian offices in large numbers, many of them were acquired by investors who simply named a substitute to perform the administrative duties of the office, thus divorcing it from its primary purpose. These military intendants and commissioners certainly brought more order and rationality to poorly disciplined troops. But, like the provincial intendants, they were overworked, and they had great difficulty enforcing their orders when they were countermanded by noble commanders of superior status.

In fact, the War Ministry was run by Louvois as a vast family patronage network, and his successors did likewise. Thus, even under Louis XIV, despite considerable progress, the military administration was structured by personal ties within administrative frameworks. Commanders pulled rank on commissioners and filled their subordinate posts with allies. Fraud and corruption were widespread. Books were badly kept, and audits dragged on for years. The same was true of the other ministries such as the office of controller-general which was infiltrated by clients of the Colbert family. But the greatest nonbureaucratic influence was the king himself, who was more concerned about maintaining a large war machine and protecting the pedigrees of favored noble lines than about discipline or efficient execution of programs. His table of ranks still gave weight to titles of nobility instead of prioritizing military skills. The king continued to treat army commissions the way he handled the courtiers at Versailles. He recognized merit, but he overlooked incompetence when it involved a key figure. He wanted his favors to be regarded as arbitrary gifts, granted out of pure grace, and this principle clashed with the awarding of merit.[11]

Life among the troops

For a simple foot soldier, to enroll in the army was to enter a different life. He would be removed from all the collective bonds that defined his existence – family, parish, village – and plunged into a masculine world of hardship, rootlessness, and violent camaraderie. For this very reason, it was generally believed by the authorities that the best solution was to enroll marginal persons such as orphans, vagabonds, and beggars, whose removal would also benefit the sedentary population.[12] Recruits were always poor commoners who had no better options.

The law stated that enrollment must be voluntary. Recruitment abuses were sometimes punished, but the king was more interested in getting recruits than in worrying about how they were signed up. Troops were recruited by captains trying to fulfill their commissions. Traditionally, these enrollees might be the tenants of a local lord or at least villagers who knew each other from the same vicinity. Familiar or not, their commanding officers would be nobles of superior status, and commentators invariably argued that the foot soldier should only be chosen from the dregs of society. Thus the social gulf between powerful elites and subordinate underlings was reproduced in the army.

Sometimes the task of recruitment was delegated by lieutenants or captains to recruiting agents who were in it for profit. They were likely to use questionable techniques such as getting men drunk and then inducing them to sign a contract. In the sober dawn they would be told that the deal was irrevocable because they had drunk at the king's expense. Sometimes recruits were promised places in an elite unit, places that never materialized. The more unscrupulous recruiters might ensnare twelve-year-old sons of affluent parents in order to extract ransoms to get them free. A complaint in 1656 stated that recruiters "take children, students, artisans, pickpockets, servants, and laborers under the pretext of finding them positions in which they can work at their profession or of having them carry packages or other jobs ... and, after having locked them up for some time, they make them leave during the night and hand them over to the said captains."[13]

New recruits were enticed by a bounty, the amount of which depended on the moment. In times of famine, this money could provide an incentive for enrolling. Once committed, enrollees were conducted to their regiment in small groups led by an officer. Contingents of recruits were sometimes chained like convicts. Officers were known

Figure 23 In 1633 Callot published a series of engravings depicting the miseries of the Thirty Years War. Here we see troops being recruited outside the town walls. Companies are forming in the background, while in front, recruits are being signed up at tables.

to sell them like slaves to another recruiter who proposed a better deal. These unfortunates were sometimes rescued by angry neighbors and relatives as they were led away from the village. Despite these coercive tactics, most soldiers signed up voluntarily because they were hungry or had no viable alternative to serving.[14]

In 1688 Louis XIV decided to create provincial militias in order to provide 25,000 troops to supplement the regular armed forces. Parishes were to meet in the church after Sunday Mass, and name one qualified recruit for every 2,000 livres the village paid in *taille*. This kind of service was especially unpopular. At first married men were exempted, but this led to such a flurry of hasty marriages that the provision was dropped. Nobles were exempt from serving, as were most townspeople. This selection process aroused so much antagonism that it was changed in 1691 to a lottery system. Soon the practice of buying substitutes to take the place of those selected appeared. Militia recruits were grouped into regiments under a commander from the region. They were sent away from their home province as reinforcements for active forces, out of fear that the militiamen would desert. They were to serve for the duration of the current war, but during winter quarters they were sent home to their villages to save expenses.

These poorly prepared provincial militias failed to live up to expectations, and the system was abandoned in 1697, only to be revived in 1701, when fifty-seven battalions of thirteen companies each were created to meet the extreme pressures of fighting the War of Spanish Succession. Parishes were again assessed and the draftees chosen by lot. But this was no longer a force with a provincial identity, since the soldiers were incorporated into regular regiments. They had become just another tax, an assessed human tax, and in the end even a monetary tax, because in 1708 communities were encouraged to buy off the obligation by paying 100 livres per soldier to exempt local men from serving.[15]

Thus recruitment practices recapitulated the social relations of the time. Assessments for the militia were tied to the lopsided assessments for the *taille*, and the physical conscription of men was soon translated into just another pretext for raising revenue. This military draft, which recurred periodically throughout the eighteenth century, was extremely unpopular. Able-bodied men from surrounding communities would gather in a designated village where an agent of the intendant would preside over the drawing of lots. Young men took extreme measures to avoid being chosen, such as cutting off fingers, inducing skin diseases, or running away. In 1726 in the Gatinais, twenty-five young men armed with clubs declared "that they were prepared to march wherever the king commanded" but that they "refused to draw lots for the militia," and a rock-throwing riot ensued. In Nevers in 1705, during a festival, a large crowd chased the mayor's deputy through the streets and pillaged his house for having recently presided over a militia lottery. In Dijon in 1766 rioters attacked the *hôtel de ville* and tried to break into the prison. Shots were fired. A participant was reported as saying that "if all the young men would get together there would be no militia, and that the only thing to do was to throw those who wanted to get them killed out the window."[16]

The composition of the common soldiery is difficult to determine. However, the figures provided by André Corvisier for various years during the reign of Louis XV, and the additional comments of John Lynn, give us a rough idea. Soldiers were recruited 65 percent from the countryside and 35 percent from towns and cities. Certain traditional regiments, such as those of Picardy and Navarre, drew many of their soldiers from those regions, thus maintaining a regional tradition. Other regiments changed composition as their commanders changed. Recruits tended to come more from the north than the south, and especially from border provinces. There were height limits which may have disqualified a greater proportion of southerners, who were traditionally shorter of stature. Socially, some 3 percent were noble, 10 percent were from the professional middle classes, and the vast majority, perhaps 70 percent, were half artisans, half peasants, with a small percentage of laborers. Thus, as one might suspect, recruits were predominantly from the lower strata of the population but they were not the beggars and thieves of contemporary opinion. Elites and nobles were rare, except at the higher ranks.[17]

Life in the army was brutal. There was no clear tour of duty. Most soldiers were there for life, or until their company was disbanded because of the return of peace. Troops often went without food, shoes, clothing, or pay. Mutinies were frequent, especially before 1661. They were usually caused by famine or lack of pay. Soldiers were looked down upon by their officers, and infractions were subject to military discipline which entailed severe penalties. Under Louis XIV the army intendant, in collaboration with the military officers, was put in charge of judging infractions, and the king got better control over punishments. Desertion, which reached rates of 25 percent at times, was punishable by death. Other common penalties were whipping, cutting off noses, ears, or hands, branding, death by firing squad, hanging, burning, breaking on the wheel, or sentencing to the galleys for life. Like most old-regime justice, military courts were erratic in their sentencing. Needing bodies for the army, they frequently issued amnesties and exemptions from rules, while punishing a few scapegoats severely.

Despite all the crudity of the soldier's existence, army life became better organized and more tolerable by the time of Louis XIV. Before that, the chief advantage for the common soldier was the coveted opportunity to pillage captured towns and to requisition supplies by force in the countryside. After 1661, this option was diminished by royal regulations being more effectively enforced, although robbing and pillaging were still authorized at certain times. As supply became better organized under Louvois and his successors, the army could at least promise regular meals most of the time and fairly regular pay. Regiments included at least one surgeon and one chaplain. Military hospitals began to be officially provided to care for the curable wounds of soldiers. Deals were made for the maintenance of prisoners held by the enemy and for prisoner exchanges to bring them home. The opening of the Hôtel des Invalides, a hospital residence for wounded veterans in Paris in 1674 symbolized a new concern for the permanent casualties of war. By 1715 more than 27,000 infirm veterans had been serviced.

It is probably safe to say that, by 1715, the royal army was better organized and inspired more loyalty, if only because groups of men who lived together bonded and became fiercely loyal to one another and to charismatic commanders. Lynn hypothesizes that this might have something to do with the fact that women, children, and families were gradually removed from the army. At the end of the seventeenth century, many units still had fifteen to twenty women accompanying them, but the state had taken over many of the service functions that the women had previously provided.[18]

Civilians and the scourge of war

Contact with military activity was without question the worst thing that could happen to a civilian population. Those trapped in a war zone, especially peasants in the open countryside who had little defense, were of course vulnerable in the extreme. Towns with walls were safer and townspeople behind walls had more room to maneuver. If they were properly fortified, they might temporarily even withstand a siege. But they could not hold out forever against a real attack, and the consequences of not surrendering promptly would likely be pillage and devastation for the inhabitants. The majority of inhabitants living in the interior of France were spared the horrors of occupation by foreign armies, but civil wars and regional rebellions, such as the religious wars and the Fronde, also brought military action.

When troops were not actively fighting they were still a burden to local citizens. Supporting the troops inside the country was a perennial problem that grew exponentially in the seventeenth century because of the burgeoning size of the army. Troops had always lived off the land, and kings had always attempted to regulate their excesses. Charles VII had stationed his forces in border fortresses or distributed them among fortified towns that could handle them. Troops were to pay their way when garrisoned, he declared, and provinces and towns could buy exemptions from military lodgings. Francis I introduced a system of support for troops on the move. Itineraries (*routes*) were established with designated stopover points (*étapes*), each a day's march apart, prepared to receive them. Henry II followed suit by issuing numerous ordinances forbidding troop excesses, and he established a system of judicial appeals to local judges as a recourse for civilians with grievances. But none of these measures was effectively enforced, and with the advent of the religious wars, all semblance of control was lost.[19]

In the era of the Thirty Years War the problem once again became acute. As John Lynn notes, "the soldiers … robbed and pillaged because the state that employed them lacked the resources to maintain them."[20] He calls this phenomenon the "tax of violence." Troops of crude, badly trained, often tired or hungry soldiers were not likely to be polite when they encountered fields of ripe grain or villagers stocked with provisions and hoarding caches of money. Their violent requisitions were part of a system and not just irresponsible exceptions. Just as the crown induced its commanders to pay part of the cost of troop recruitment and maintenance by not providing adequate funding, the peasants in the vicinity of troops were induced by the threat of superior force to replace provisions that the king had not supplied.

The province of Burgundy offers a prime example of repeated devastation. A stronghold of the Catholic League, it was the theater of repeated campaigns during the religious wars. It became a center of operations once again during the Thirty Years War because of its proximity to Spanish Franche-Comté. From 1636 to 1656, the province was subjected to repeated devastation, leaving behind countless particular instances of brutality. A notary from Beaumont-sur-Vingeanne recorded one such incident:

8 November 1636, enemies numbering more than 6,000 men, horsemen and infantry alike, entered Beaumont for the third time, took the chateau, killed those whom they met, whether men, women, or children [and] threw the sick and poor out of the windows. The woman Bilbaudet, wife of the notary Gaillet and more than sixty years old, was forced to leave her home for the chateau where she was savagely beaten and raped by the enemies, even though she had given them all she had. Then they led her back to her house, beating her along the way, [and] when she had given them all she could find, money and other things, they murdered her with hammers.[21]

In 1651, 1,400 men from the regiment of Burgundy who lodged in the province "not content to act prudently ... pillaged houses, killed all the livestock, burned possessions and houses, raped the women and killed the men."[22]

Such violent requisitions were much rarer after the 1670s, when discipline within the ranks was better enforced and Louvois began to punish officers for the crimes committed by their men. In addition, the state intervened in occupied foreign territories by introducing the system of *contributions* in which the army imposed a formal tax on the residents that was rationally assessed and collected and channeled to the state coffers instead of going directly to rampaging soldier bands.

Certain regions were also severely hit during the worst years of the War of Spanish Succession. In 1705 and 1707 an invasion of Provence caused repeated raids: As the bishop of Vence reported, "there were five to twelve passages [of troop contingents] per day, first came the houssards, then the dragoons, then detachments from the garrisons of Saint Paul and Nice.... The fields are left fallow; the men have been kept away by construction work to defend the Var river or frightened away by the fear of invasion." In 1708–10, the northern frontier was periodically occupied by foreign troops, while the French army under Villars requisitioned all the available grain in the region without any reimbursement for the peasants. In 1709 there was no seed for planting, and typhus swept the region, along with famine. "Unable to rescue a single blade of hay from foraging and all the furies of war, the people in the countryside are surviving on grass and a bit of milk," wrote the intendant. In 1712 the inhabitants of Maretz in Burgundy were burned alive in their church while soldiers pillaged their houses.[23]

The system of *étapes*, perfected in the seventeenth century, where contractors were supposed to be prepared to supply the basic necessities to troops on the march, was another considerable improvement. When a troop arrived, the commanders were to meet with the local authorities and distribute the soldiers equitably among local householders who were to put them up for the night. The host was to supply a place to sleep, firewood to cook a meal, and candles for lighting. Soldiers were to pay for their own food. But letting an unknown, possibly brutal, soldier into your household must have been an unpleasant prospect at best, and there was every likelihood that he would extort money, rob the family, or mistreat daughters and servants. This might be tolerable for one night, but the standard routes dictated that the same places would be hit over and over again. And although winter quarters were better in the sense that the troops were stationary and therefore better organized, any longer stay might only exacerbate the problem. When the army of Harcourt stayed at Neubourg in Normandy for twelve days during the Fronde, they "burned more than 200 buildings besides losses of animals, wheat, and other grains such that the majority of the inhabitants were forced to abandon the area and are reduced to begging."[24]

The tension between organization and license in the mid seventeenth century was illustrated by the experience of Languedoc in handling the winter quarters of the army of Condé in 1639–40. A royal ordinance dated July 24, 1638, with eighty-two separate articles, detailed a plan for orderly winter quarters in the province "so that the people can not only supply them with sustenance without being excessively burdened, but can also cultivate the land in complete freedom and still meet their obligations to pay the regular taxes." Royal officers were to apportion the total cost among all the communities, arrange with leading citizens to collect the money in six installments, and have them stock strategically distributed magazines with supplies. The troops were to be evenly distributed in walled towns. Each soldier was restricted to his assigned house and supplied with specified payments and food. Officers were to stay in town and monitor the behavior of their men, and local civilian judges were to try infractions.

Such arrangements were fine on paper, but it was difficult for local people to get them enforced. As a privileged province with Estates, Languedoc was theoretically exempt from troop lodgings by virtue of the *don gratuit* it paid annually to the king. But several years of skillful lobbying in the Estates had failed to keep the army out of the province. The province did have its own officials who administered the regular tax collections and could at least serve as facilitators for appeals against abuses. Overwhelmed, the syndic-generals of the province and the syndics of each local diocese spent the year desperately collecting evidence of infractions, extortions, and illicit changes of venue. Towns and individuals had not been compensated for advances of food and credit. Soldiers had refused to pay their way when on the road. They had crawled along at their own pace, moving little each day, and collecting ransoms wherever they went. There had been murders and excesses committed at Castelnau in the diocese of Montpellier. In the diocese of Uzès, at Vendargues and Castelnau, there were demands for reparations after the citizens had been terrorized by the troops. In the second Castelnau no one dared leave their houses. Long itemized lists of towns and the troops they had received were drawn up. In 1640 the syndic of Toulouse filed papers charging the army of Condé with excessive damage in nine specified villages that had been ravaged, milked for advances of funds, and deprived of nearly all their livestock "to the extent that most of the inhabitants and their families have deserted their house and left their fields unplowed and taken refuge in the city of Toulouse and other cities to try to earn their living and have been reduced to such misery that most of them are reduced to eating bad bread."[25]

Legal recourse was difficult. On March 8, 1640, the Parlement of Toulouse issued warrants for the arrest of Captain Damont and Ensign Teyssier from the regiment of Poitou stationed in Montastruc. But the sergeant sent to apprehend the two found that Damont had been absent for several days. Teyssier was holed up in the regimental headquarters with a corps of soldiers guarding the door. Neither man was arrested.[26]

Direct occupation and supplementary tax payments did not exhaust the impact of an army. When it entered a region, orders would be issued requisitioning all available carts and mules for transporting supplies. There was no guarantee that they would ever be returned. Sometimes the work force itself was drafted to reinforce fortifications, pull carts, or dig ditches. Cannons, the pride of walled towns, were seized and had to be transported to where the army was stationed. When battles were won, the captured Spanish prisoners were distributed among the prisons of Languedoc, amid great disputes about whether towns like Toulouse had to pay for their upkeep. Military commanders and royal agents had a habit of imposing special funds on local populations that could not be refused, such as the 100,000 livres imposed on certain dioceses by the intendant of Languedoc in 1643 to pay for the "embarkation of troops from Beaucaire to Barcelona." Local garrisons were likely to demand subventions from the town where they were based.

The army in the eighteenth century

By the end of Louis XIV's reign, the army had become a colossal, highly organized institution with established procedures and values. It continued to evolve, but the basic parameters did not change much before the Revolution, or at least until the reforms of Choiseul after 1763. Its peacetime strength of 110,000 soldiers of French origin rose to 135,000 by 1763. In wartime the numbers grew by adding foreign troops and drafted militias. The militias became permanent after 1726 and continued to be levied like a tax on each community, with the drawing of lots and paid substitutes. In 1744 the army of 133,200 men had 68,230 militiamen, or slightly more than half of the total force. In wartime the older, more traditional local militias of towns and provinces were sometimes called up to perform local defense functions.

Eighteenth-century wars were fought mostly on foreign soil and on the high seas. There were none of the wrenching conflicts that so disturbed civilian populations. The military administration created by Le Tellier and Louvois was finally bearing fruit in the form of supply depots and better management of food suppliers and munitioneers. Troops on the move were well disciplined. They were still lodged in towns during winter quarters, and this was still unpopular. Towns began to build barracks to house the troops, but only in some places.

The royal intendants played an ever larger role in monitoring the troops, regulating *étapes*, and managing military hospitals. There were still requisitions of local men and materials for transporting necessities near military fronts, and in 1746 the peasants of Lower Languedoc had to provide carts and mules just as they had done in 1640. Military affairs were increasingly unpopular with writers and intellectuals. Artisans and laborers still detested the militia system and continued to resist it at call-up time, but they nevertheless contributed the majority of enrollees in the regular army.

The army had become enveloped in the state, which in turn grew in response to the needs of the military. In form the army was a hybrid institution, better managed and regulated by royal officials. But it served the purposes of a favored nobility. It requisitioned the lives and labors of countless subordinate subjects, and served as a vast patronage network for the powerful. Warfare had become less intrusive toward civilian populations, but it still raised their taxes, perpetuated expensive land wars fought for possibly irrelevant diplomatic objectives, and bolstered the class consciousness of a favored aristocracy.

Suggestions for further reading: army and society

Blaufarb, Rafe, "Noble Privilege and Absolutist State Building: French Military Administration after the Seven Years; War," *French Historical Studies* 24 (Spring 2001), 223–46.

Corvisier, André, *L'Armée française de la fin du XVIIe siècle au ministère de Choiseul*, 2 vols. (Paris, 1964).

Lynn, John A., "Tactical Evolution in the French Army, 1560–1660," *French Historical Studies* 14 (1985), 176–91.

  Giant of the Grand Siècle: The French Army, 1610–1715 (Cambridge, 1997).

Martin, John, "Recalculating French Army Growth during the Grand Siècle, 1610–1715," *French Historical Studies* (1994), 881–906.

Parrott, David, *Richelieu's Army: War, Government and Society in France, 1624–1642* (Cambridge, 2001).

Rowlands, Guy, *The Dynastic State and the Army under Louis XIV: Royal Service and Private Interest, 1661–1701* (Cambridge, 2002).

Wood, James B., "The Royal Army during the Early Wars of Religion, 1559–1576," in Mack P. Holt, ed., *Society and Institutions in Early Modern France* (Athens, GA, 1991), 1–35.

  The King's Army: Warfare, Soldiers, and Society during the Wars of Religion in France, 1562–1576 (Cambridge, 1996).

8 | *Social bonds and social protest*

Early modern society was conceptualized by philosophers as an organic "body" made up of categories of people enjoying differing levels of status, each group with its own niche in the hierarchy and each with a different functional purpose. Everyone from the king at the top to the lowliest beggar at the bottom had a place. All these hierarchically arranged groups fell into three broad categories: the priests who prayed for the community, the nobles who fought for the community, and the peasants and craftsmen who worked by the sweat of their brow or applied their manual labor to particular crafts. These were the three "estates" – the clergy and the nobility, both of whom enjoyed special arrangements, and the "third estate," which meant the rest of the population. More detailed accounts, such as that of Charles Loyseau published in 1610, subdivided each of the three orders into every possible profession, office, or title, each of which had a distinct set of privileges, creating a society organized according to the principle of the inequality of persons before the law.

This was, of course, a very conservative approach. It suggested that inequality was the natural state of affairs and everyone should embrace the station into which he or she had been born without questioning the advantages of the higher placed. It implicitly accepted the idea that the system, as part of God's plan, provided justice for all; that the built-in privileges enjoyed by those at the top were legitimate, and that the toils of the lowly were deserved. While they were not familiar with learned theories, most ordinary people accepted some intuitive version of these messages, at least in the normal course of affairs, barring extraordinary circumstances.

This conception of an unchanging, organic society did not do justice to the complicated nature of actual social relationships. Drawing confidence from everyday experiences, common people often stretched the boundaries of the corporate society and found the strength to struggle, protest, and defend common interests. Membership in formally constituted bodies gave them a certain collective voice. Patronage networks provided channels for influencing the power structure. People's loyalties developed out of daily habits of sociability. Their everyday exchanges established circles of contact which could serve later as groups for mobilizing protests or conflicting with rival groups. It is more useful, therefore, to approach social structure by asking what bonds tied people together and what conflicts set them against one another. Individuals were profoundly unequal, and the cards were still stacked in favor of the elite segments of society because they had more connections and greater influence.

This chapter asks what networks of personal connections reached across the fixed categories of the society of orders and made change possible. We will investigate these various communities of solidarity and sociability, starting at the lowest unit, the family, and proceeding upwards towards the centers of social power.

Family relations

The family was the basic unit of society. Each marriage represented an alliance between two extended families which was formalized in a written contract. Among aristocrats negotiations over marriage alliances took on the appearance of high diplomacy. Extended discussions and even orders from the king were usual. Among commoners it was more likely that the fathers of the couple would meet to draw up and sign a contract before a notary, in the presence of multiple witnesses from both sides, and cement the deal with glasses of wine. If there was no father, a brother or uncle would take his place, since men were very much in charge. At all levels of society marriage was a calculated strategy in which personal preference was not considered important. Aristocrats could not even think of marrying someone without the sanction of the family. In everyday life mutual attraction between the two partners certainly came more into play, but material interests were still more important than love. Marriages were eagerly awaited opportunities for families to buy offices, repay debts, establish patronage connections in high places, or annex the farm next door. We read with some surprise the terms of a marriage contract from the town of Lucq in Béarn in 1580:

Today Gaillard de Saint Martin from the Saint Michel quarter and Gaillard de Maisonave from the Affites quarter have declared that owing to their desire to strengthen their friendship, they have agreed to the following covenant, that Saint Martin has promised to give in marriage one of his sons named Jean, age ten or eleven, exclusively to Jeanne, age six, the daughter of Maisonave.[1]

These children might not marry until they were older, but their lives were already determined by a deal designed to strengthen the alliance between two fathers.

There was an implicit conflict between this desire to arrange marriages and the doctrine of the Catholic church. Since the twelfth century the church had taught that marriage was an indissoluble sacrament created when the bride and groom exchanged vows by mutual consent and then consummated the marriage by sexual intercourse. Its sacramental nature meant that divorce was out of the question. According to this doctrine, if a couple of legal age (fourteen for boys, twelve for girls) eloped without parental consent, the marriage was completely valid in the eyes of the church. The doctrine threatened parental control of property because it meant that sons and daughters could choose inappropriate partners out of love, regardless of the parents' wishes. The church was also concerned about youthful mistakes. In 1215 it added further restrictions. The bride and groom were instructed to signal their intentions by publishing banns a certain length of time before the wedding, and they were to be married by the parish priest of at least one of the parents and not by some unknown cleric, in front of proper witnesses. Marriage between close relatives, which included cousins up to the "fourth degree" and godparents, was prohibited.

By the sixteenth century it was becoming clear to government officials that the church was not adequately protecting the interests of families and that papal rulings were encroaching on the authority of the king. Cases of elopement or kidnapping went to church courts where the family's concerns were treated as less important than upholding the church's doctrines. Concerned, the French monarchy began to encourage the Parlements to evoke marriage disputes to royal courts. In 1556 Henry II issued an edict abolishing clandestine marriages and disinheriting any men under thirty or women under twenty-five who married without their parents' consent. This royal crackdown, which Sarah Hanley calls the "family–state compact," combined protection of the authority of a patriarchal king with protection of the interests of a patriarchal father. Further edicts in the seventeenth century elaborated on the king's position and made it clear that the state, not the church, decided these matters in France.

Social relations in the community

Outside the family, the most immediate bond was loyalty to the neighborhood where one lived. This was an informal allegiance that had no institutional existence, but it was formed and reformed every day by personal contact. The neighborhood was made up of the people you saw regularly because they lived or worked nearby. In a small village this could be the entire community. In larger villages, and especially in cities, it would more likely be your street or the part of town where you lived or worked. Neighbors knew each other's daily habits; watched everyone's comings and goings; rushed up when someone started a fight, or screamed "Help!" Neighbors were always judging you. There were observers at windows, lounging around the well, or gossiping in the marketplace. If you cried out, or collapsed, or got into a fight, your neighbors would swiftly come to your aid. However, if they thought you deserved what you got, they might stay aloof. Neighbors exchanged favors, and lent dishes and cash to one another. Everyone kept an eye on children playing in the street. Peasants conversed as they walked to their fields. Women and girls, and sometimes young men observing them, talked things over in their *veillées*, which were evening gatherings in a barn or around a fireplace for spinning and sewing.

In the city open space was scarce, and human interaction more frequent. People lived in small rooms and apartments above shops, or in the back of courtyards reached by a narrow passageway. Laundry was hung out of windows and doors were left open. A marital quarrel or a secret rendezvous was no secret to the neighbors. Business transacted in shops easily spilled over into the streets. The master artisan would sit inside at his workbench, in plain view of the customers, plying his skill. In front, a half-open counter displaying merchandise would connect the shop to the outdoors. Market stalls and street vendors would gather a crowd.

These sorts of contacts formed the basis for the exchange of information among the common people. Residents in the neighborhood observed each other's behavior. They discussed the news, sometimes distorted or exaggerated, of events in the province and the kingdom. Ideas were exchanged during daily activities in the street, but also in wineshops where men gathered (and women were largely excluded), or at bakeries and pastry shops. Artisans' shops could serve as intermediaries between the neighborhood and broader guild associations. A workshop could generate a sense of family between the master and his employees if they were reasonably intimate and worked together. Certain trades were clustered together in a few streets, creating a feeling of solidarity. In Lyon the printers and the hatters were concentrated in single neighborhoods, while textile workers were widely dispersed. Artisans, such as confectioners and jewelers, who catered to the rich, tended to live close to the elegant parts of town and identified more with their customers than with their guild or the people in the street.

Men dealt with neighbors differently from women. Men viewed the family as a private domain that they should rule without interference. They felt free to beat their wives and considered this a privilege of their station.[2] The neighbors were keen observers of domestic conflict, but they would only intervene if the beating went beyond accepted practice. Women were more likely to intervene in a marital quarrel because men were reluctant to encroach on the husband's right of "moderate correction." Women were seen as managers of the household, raisers of children, and outspoken defenders of basic moral values. When the husband was away at work, no man was permitted to enter a woman's house. The wives gathered at the well, the washhouse, or local shops. They defended their children blindly. They filled the air with gossip and did not hesitate to intervene to break up violent fights by men, but if their husband's honor was at stake, they were also perfectly capable of cheering on the combatants.[3] When women fought, at least according to Yves Castan in Languedoc, they used childish tactics, stabbing one another with pins and needles and dishonoring the adversary by knocking off her headgear or inflicting scratches and bites. When they won, women burst into sarcastic songs and danced around the loser.[4]

Legal records from Marseille in 1694 give us precious glimpses of women monitoring and censuring the morals of neighbors, especially those of other women. A certain Anne Martine had entertained ten male visitors the previous day, reported Anne Lamer and her father who had both been keeping count, and men shouting obscenities were constantly pounding on Martine's door. Anne Raguce was accused of taking gifts of clothes from priests, one of whom got her pregnant. But Anne Bellanger whose father considered her a "libertine" for running away twice with young men and getting pregnant, was *defended* by the neighborhood women, who pleaded on her behalf that she had been faithful to her first lover and should not be locked up. Neighbors often tolerated these situations for a long time or tried to get them resolved quietly before they finally denounced their neighbors. Ultimately they reported them to the authorities.[5]

Beyond the neighborhood, people belonged to a variety of locality-based associations. The most elusive were the youth abbeys. As we noted in Chapter 2, late marriage at age twenty-five or six left adolescent and young adult males in an ambiguous, dependent position. They were physically adults but were still under the rule of their fathers, and they had no professional identity or personal household to give them full status in the community. Nevertheless, they were accorded a distinctive role by society. Youth "abbeys" or "kingdoms" were informal organizations of the unmarried men of a village.[6] Their role, which was embedded in folk traditions, was to serve as the voice of the community in censuring perceived misbehavior and enlivening local festivals. The terms "abbey" or "kingdom" imply jurisdiction over a constituency, and this is how the youths thought of themselves – as the voice of the community in monitoring the marital relations of local couples. Their officers adopted titles like "abbot," "king," "emperor," or "patriarch." It was they who animated the maypole dancing on May Day. On Midsummer Night (St. John's Day, June 24) they lit the bonfires and performed dances while leaping over the flames. On All Souls' Day they went door to door, coercing inhabitants to pay them off with coins in a variation of what we would call "trick or treat."

The youth groups were primary organizers of charivari and other kinds of "rough music" (see Chapter 9). They led the community in expressing displeasure at any violation of unspoken norms, such as a husband who allowed his wife to dominate him, or a man who married a much younger woman. When weddings did take place, the youths had further tricks, ambushing the wedding party on its way to the church, or interrupting the bedding ritual. Youth groups also competed with their counterparts from neighboring villages in raids and violent sports contests.

In the city, youth groups continued to exist, but they tended to become street gangs. Many lost their close attachment to community values and spent their time fighting one another, often in the clearing just outside the city walls. They might throw rocks and jeer at unpopular dignitaries in times of disorder. These local groups continued to be populated by unmarried adolescent males, but broader, more organized societies, often called "abbeys of misrule," took on a more witty function as clubs dedicated to mocking the authorities on festive occasions and chastising violators of community norms. Lyon had twenty such groups in the sixteenth century. These societies included married men of a variety of ages, with a membership that was more socially respectable and educated than the rural abbeys. Whereas in the countryside all the young men, rich and poor, banded together, the city groups tended to be more socially uniform, with membership lists and entrance qualifications. Their jokes were literary as well as visual, and their festive mockery merged in style with the topsy-turvy world of carnival celebrations when men wore masks and the lowly changed places temporarily with the exalted. Abbeys of misrule ridiculed authority, made jokes about leading citizens, and staged large parades with floats representing "the world turned upside down." This phenomenon was more sophisticated than traditional merrymaking. It combined the same spirit of ribaldry with learned allusions to classical mythology and elaborate symbolism. Some such organizations, such as the Basoche of the law clerks, were limited to a single profession.

Urban militias also offered important opportunities for organization. The citizen guard was theoretically made up of all heads of households residing in the city. For example, in 1483 Troyes was divided into four *quartiers*, each of which was subdivided into sixteen *sixaines* consisting of fifteen to twenty wealthy armed citizens who guarded the gates during the day; and sixteen *dizaines* of thirty to forty unarmed common soldiers who did the night watch. All heads of household were expected to serve. There were about 1,100 militiamen in Troyes in 1483 and 4,000 in the 1630s. The company on duty, led by its officers, would assemble, march to the *hôtel de ville* and take custody of the keys of the city in a formal ceremony, then march to the various gates of the city and stand guard all day.

These militias were important for several reasons. Although they were made up of civilians with no serious military training who had other jobs to fill their time, they were built around organized neighborhood units whose officers, sometimes elected by the troops, were prominent residents of the same streets. The officer corps provided a chain of command that enabled the *hôtel de ville* to reach down into each neighborhood through its captains. Lyon was divided into thirty-six *pennonnages*, each commanded by a captain *pennon* and several subordinate officers; each *pennonnage* was divided into companies called *dixaines*. These neighborhood officers were enlisted to compile reports on the numbers of poor families in their precincts and the addresses of Protestants. The existence of a militia also meant that many citizens were armed and had at least rudimentary experience in mobilizing forces to resist an intruder.[7]

Militia service entailed a great deal of pride, especially for officers. When they marched in public ceremonies, they were joyfully expressing both the town's loyalty to the crown and the secure hold its prominent commanders enjoyed over their lesser neighbors. But at the same time the units were strictly local and not well integrated into a city-wide force. René Duchemin, a notary in Rennes, kept a journal of his militia service. In 1662 he recounts how his street and five other trusted companies were called to arms from 7.00 a.m. to noon because of the city council's "fear of the rabble from the lower town who wanted to revolt." In 1664 he notes that his company was one of the seven allowed to take part in the marriage ceremonies of the young governor, and later that year he records that his street marched third in the ceremonies for the entrance of the duc de Mazarin into Rennes.[8]

Up until the mid sixteenth century, most urban militias were healthy components of largely self-governing cities. The religious wars undermined them considerably, and by the mid seventeenth century they were becoming vehicles for ostentation and ceremony rather than effective military forces. The medieval principle that everyone should serve was gradually abandoned as privileged individuals withdrew from service, claiming exemption. By the 1630s, many militias had become poorly disciplined collections of badly trained, half-hearted soldiers who goofed around and shirked their duties. The city of Troyes received complaints that "from the closing of the gates until three or four in the morning men from the companies gather in groups and shoot off salvos with their muskets up and down the streets, which inconveniences the inhabitants."[9] And when riots broke out it was often hard to get the troops to muster: either the bulk of the soldiers sympathized with the rioters, or the officers were reluctant to face the risk of confronting an angry crowd.

The Parisian "bourgeois militia" was an important force in the power politics of the city. In 1559 the medieval *guet* (watch) based on participation by all the guilds was abolished and replaced in 1562 by a territorially based militia in which all bourgeois, including relatively poor residents, were expected to participate through their local neighborhood. This system produced a local civic consciousness in which citizens identified with their street and their captain and fought the hardest when at home. Paris was, militarily speaking, a set of micro-districts, each fiercely patriotic in the face of a threat and determined to keep out opposing forces, even the king's. This arrangement made it easier for religious extremists to take over neighborhoods during the religious wars and for the city to resist the forces of the king during the Fronde rebellion of 1548–52. Clearly it was in the royal interest to break down this system of local cells, and Louis XIV did so by tearing down the ramparts of Paris and taking the policing of the streets away from the militia.[10]

The next association to link town citizens in alliances broader than neighborhoods was the guild, which we have already examined in Chapter 4. Guilds could bring together tradesmen from all parts of the city, or, if the membership was too large for familiarity, they could at least link a smaller core of powerful masters. Every guild had a strong identity built upon devotion to a particular patron saint and participation in various bonding rituals. Banquets were the occasion for admitting new members, who would be required to take the oath and shell out the funds to pay for the banquet. The members drank and ate amid toasts and comments.

Many guilds set up religious confraternities that were dedicated to devotion of their patron saint. They would hold services in the saint's chapel, donate funds for the chapel's maintenance, and organize festivities on the saint's day. Confraternities also served as benevolent institutions by collecting dues from the members and paying for charitable activities such as helping masters' widows with funeral expenses, and they were convivial societies. In mid sixteenth-century Toulouse there were sixty guilds, each with its own confraternity. In Bordeaux proper, the number went from sixteen to thirty-two between 1600 and 1645, and by the end of the century there were 197 in the entire diocese.[11] These organizations had the effect of shifting the religious center of gravity away from the parishes, towards city-wide trades and eventually toward a broader consciousness. They spoke to the public by means of their traditional processions, which projected an image of the community. The older style from the sixteenth century involved burlesque features and humorous skits. For example, on a stage in Bordeaux the barrel-makers of the Saint-Michel quarter portrayed the baptism of Christ while Christ's apostles doused the audience with water. By the seventeenth century the barrel-makers had abandoned gaiety for a new piety. After banning all levity and profanity from their ranks, they required that their members confess four times a year and attend Mass every Sunday.[12]

Journeymen were excluded from the masters' organizations. The journeymen in certain trades therefore formed brotherhoods, or *compagnonnages*, of their own. These began to proliferate in the mid sixteenth century. As job-seeking employees, the journeymen were in potential conflict with the masters. Their precarious state drew them together and led them to defend customary rights in the workplace against masters who were trying to abolish them. Each trade claimed entitlement to certain customary perquisites beyond their basic pay. Journeyman and apprentice roofers claimed the exclusive right to carry off old slate and lead pipes from building sites. Carpenters and joiners wanted to take wood scraps home with them. There were also disputes over food and drink, since meals provided by the master were among the more valuable benefits of employment. The joiners of Nantes went on strike when their "wine break" at 6 p.m. was abolished.[13]

In their quest for employment, journeymen traveled from town to town on the proverbial *tour de France*. Because their special skills were usually in high demand for only a limited time in one place, they kept moving on from job to job. Soon journeymen were forming broader associations with chapters in different cities. The most common participants were men in the construction, furnishing or clothing trades.[14] Like Masonic lodges or fraternal societies, these *compagnonnages* eventually developed an elaborate mythology of mysterious ancient origins, along with secret initiation ceremonies and passwords, new names for initiates, and special handshakes.

Clandestine associations of laborers were anathema to the masters. They did what they could to keep them repressed. In 1627 the Company of the Holy Sacrament charged certain *compagnonnages* with performing blasphemous ceremonies. In the 1630s the faculty of the Sorbonne condemned, in turn, the shoemakers, saddlers, hatters, and cutlers, and outlawed their meetings. In 1655 the Sorbonne doctors, prodded by the master shoemakers, condemned journeyman shoemakers, tailors, hatters, and saddlers for their independence. The complaint was that the employees were rowdy and were threatening to boycott shops if they heard of a master mistreating his employees.

Although outlawed, *compagnonnages* continued to develop clandestinely, with quite a bit of ritual drama. For example, in 1677 the joiners' *compagnonnage* of Dijon had its own archives, lists of new arrivals, and ceremonies designed, it was charged, to "organize a cabal and monopoly to make themselves masters over the journeymen arriving in this city."[15] When a newcomer arrived, he went to the house of the *mère*, which was usually an inn. The *mère*, who could be either a man or a woman, then helped him get established in his new location. He was temporarily housed, charged a fee (*bienvenue* or "welcome tax"), and entered in a roster of names. He was then expected to pay for a banquet or a round of drinks for his fellow workers, and, if new, might be subjected to an initiation ceremony. Ultimately, he would be assigned a job with a master, and he would work there until he moved on to the next location. Then he would be given papers to present to the *mère* of that place.

To join the saddlers in 1654, the new arrival went to a designated house with all its windows shuttered. There he was met by two men who made him swear on the gospels never to reveal their customs to anyone, not even his wife, his children or his priest, and never to write down an account of them. Passing on to the next room, he encountered a man dressed in a priest's robe who performed a ceremony very similar to the blessing of the bread and wine in the Mass. The novice was then instructed to choose a godfather, and he was "baptized" by the group's "master," after which he passed out the bread and wine to all present.[16] There may have been hazing and other rituals in the following days.

The *compagnonnages* created a cult of belonging that, predictably, led to the denunciation of an "other," in this case a rival association of journeymen. By the late seventeenth century, an intense rivalry had developed between two "families" of *compagnonnages*, each of which denounced the bad attitudes and shoddy workmanship of the other. The original group called themselves the *compagnons du devoir, or* "the children of Master Jacques," and they called their rivals *gavots*, who called themselves the "children of Solomon." The two associations fought bitterly and eventually there was a third contender, the "children of Master Soubise" or *drilles*.[17]

This life of the journeyman was both individualistic and collective. Menetra, the Parisian glazier we met in Chapter 4, spent years walking across France, meeting people on the road and cultivating sexual relationships with a succession of women. His *compagnonnage* provided him with contacts and places to stay in each city he visited, along with recommendations to local employers offering work. His memoirs convey the intensely personal quality of this world of improvised expedients. Menetra thinks in terms of his relationships with particular individuals. It is not the job, the conditions, the institutions that he cites, but the friend who drank with him, the enemy who had it coming to him, the priest who was amazed at his skill with stained glass, the woman who took a liking to him. Menetra is always demanding favors from acquaintances and doing favors for others in a constant exchange of tips about jobs, small loans, retaliatory beatings, places to stay. Wherever he goes, he meets people he knew somewhere else and develops relationships with new friends he will use later on. Menetra describes a quarrel between a locksmith of the *devoir* and some *gavots* that escalated into a pitched battle outside Angers in which 500 *devoirs* (Menetra exaggerates) fought 750 *gavots* with clubs and rocks. Seven were killed, and around fifty were wounded. Menetra and his allies had to flee the city to avoid being arrested.[18]

Above the artisans were the various urban elites. Unlike ordinary citizens, they had their corporate identity firmly established as officers in royal companies, *avocats* or *procureurs* attached to a court, professors or priests with a designated place in the hierarchies of their own institutions. But these people were joined in religious and cultural associations that crossed over professional boundaries and sometimes even made connections with the rest of the population. First of all, there were festive societies like the Abbey of Misrule in Dijon and its counterparts in other cities, or the "Academy of Floral Games" in Toulouse, which sponsored an annual poetry contest, accompanied by parades and merrymaking. Membership in these organizations was limited to the well-to-do, but they held parades and street celebrations aimed at involving the populace.

The Catholic revival of the seventeenth century generated a spectacular revival of pious societies. This flowering has been documented by Robert Schneider for Toulouse. At the end of the seventeenth century, the city had sixty lay confraternities, twenty of which had been founded or reorganized since 1590. Some took charge of the financial management of a particular parish. Others were devotional brotherhoods dedicated to a particular saint or to a certain form of worship. In 1647 a branch of the Company of the Holy Sacrament was set up in Toulouse by a group of secretive dignitaries and began to sponsor moves against Protestants. Other charitable societies were dedicated to charitable work, often donated by women. The Confraternity of Charity founded in the 1670s encouraged "charitable persons of recognized probity," that is, highborn *parlementaires* and other elite figures, to do good works while allowing girls and widows and "other people of mediocre quality" to clean the chambers of the sick and poor.[19]

These lay societies had interesting characteristics. Many were quite large and recruited members from the entire city. Their specialty was staging public processions that dramatically and publicly represented the new, more abstract doctrines of the militant church, such as reverence for the Holy Sacrament and the Immaculate Conception. This expression of a coherent doctrine contrasted markedly with the old style of having multiple, locally based celebrations of particular saints. Many confraternities had a socially mixed membership. For example, in 1643, Our Lady of the Assumption of Saint Étienne's 636 members were 24 percent nobles and *parlementaires*, 13 percent other professionals, 8 percent merchants, 20 percent artisans, and 26 percent clergy, students, soldiers, and artists.[20] Confraternity members were supposed to treat each other like family members, avoid internal quarrels, and join in common devotions. They also had provisions for assisting members in time of need and many of them held genuine elections for officers. These organizations provided another opportunity for poor and rich Toulousains to associate with one another.

Family, neighbors, parish, youth abbey, *compagnonnage*, festive company, guild, confraternity, militia company, lay charitable society – all these groups gave ordinary citizens experience in relating to one another and provided them with multiple identities. Most of them excluded women. The striking exceptions were the charitable societies in which women often dominated. In the countryside the options were fewer, but peasants could still belong to a village community, a parish, and possibly a confraternity. Everywhere people had preexisting groups through which they could act. But almost all these connections were local. They were limited to the space within the town walls. The *compagnonnages* reached out to other cities, and religious organizations were tied to the larger Catholic church. None of them had a direct handle on major political decisions. In this respect the local elites had a real advantage. Their horizons reached as far as universities and business contacts in other cities. They belonged to royal companies oriented towards a whole region, and ultimately towards Paris and the king, the source of their power.

Conflict, protest, revolt

How did common people react when the demands from higher authorities became oppressive and they felt they were being ruined by bad government? They had very few legal options. Organized meetings and demonstrations were outlawed, except for officially sanctioned gatherings such as town meetings and church services. Guilds, village assemblies, even city councils, had very little control over the really important decisions concerning taxes, troops, or religion. It was always theoretically possible for anyone to appeal to the king. There was a long tradition in which a guilty party pleaded for letters of remission that excused the petitioner for a murder or other serious crime on the grounds of extenuating circumstances. But even here any number of impediments – the laws of inheritance, the distribution of property, the structure of taxation, the opportunities for social advancement, gender differences in marriage and public authority – gave the higher placed considerable advantages over the lower placed.

In this climate the best way to obtain protection was to make full use of your family ties and take advantage of the system of privilege by tying your fortune to a powerful patron. Rural villagers might appeal to their seigneur or to royal courts. Anyone could appeal to a royal military commander (sixteenth century) or a royal officer (seventeenth century) such as the provincial intendant or one of his subordinates. These were officials who had regular communication with the ministers at court. The correspondence of such people is filled with petty requests from individuals, some of which did actually reach the royal council or the king. But to make such an appeal you needed a connection with someone in power, which meant that you had to be submissive and loyal to that person. It would be out of the question to challenge privileges that the patron enjoyed, or question the authority of higher-ups. Thus, when it came to fundamental issues of subsistence and faith, most of the people were left on their own. If they were going to oppose what seemed to them to be outrageous burdens foisted on them by corrupt middlemen, they would have to take matters into their own hands.

The French people were extremely sensitive to their rights, especially long-established customary rights, and they had a keen sense of honor. They were fatalistic and long-suffering when it came to natural calamities, such as plague and bad weather, that seemed to be the will of God. But when family survival or the essentials of faith seemed threatened by measures that were man-made and attributable to intruders who could be identified and physically confronted, they were ready to lash out in anger and demand better. This upsurge of popular anger could emerge autonomously if the conditions were right. Popular protest was very common. It could range from quiet grumbling at a tax collector to full-scale urban insurrection. The best way to understand this protest is to see the phenomenon as a continuum of many small acts of daily resistance, a few of which set off larger explosions.

When uprisings occurred, it was because an abuse had struck a responsive chord in the community. There would have been talk for weeks or months in advance about an anticipated offense. The initial outcry by someone in a public place – "here comes the tax man" – rang like a self-fulfilling prophecy in the ears of the bystanders. Often the term used was *gabelle*, which technically meant the salt tax, but the terms was widely used to mean any new oppressive tax. The news would spread that the long-dreaded abuse had arrived and that a certain individual was the bearer of a threat to everyone's well-being. A crowd of angry citizens would form, determined to eliminate the abuse in the simplest and most direct way possible, by tearing up the authorizing documents and chasing away the bearer of the bad news. They would begin by targeting the individual himself and then go on to attack property or persons connected in some way to the abuse or the abuser.

The measure that would set off a revolt would be shocking to the demonstrators because it threatened something fundamental to their existence and because it was a novelty. The crowd did not think abstractly about law and government. Their sense of legality was commonsensical: they were acting in self-defense to protect what they knew was right and what was customary. Their objective was to eliminate the abuse, but more than that to express outrage at the humiliation of being treated in this way and to retaliate by humiliating the offending party. In increasingly violent stages depending on the degree of indignation and the way the events unfolded, crowds typically threw rocks at a tax collector, chased him out of town, beat up him or his servants, attacked and pillaged the inn where he was staying, destroyed papers taken to legitimize the abuse, beat the man to death, tied his body by the heels to a cart and dragged it face down through the streets, mutilated the corpse, and left the remains in the dump to be eaten by dogs. Very few crowds were violent enough to reach these final stages. More often they threatened the offender, who made himself scarce. If they cornered him he was verbally lambasted with curses and insults or kicked and beaten until someone intervened to stop the attack, or his property would be pillaged and destroyed. More developed crowds then turned on the local authorities, either because they had counterattacked, causing injury or death, or because they had arrested some demonstrators who needed to be liberated from prison. In the most serious stage the crowd would attack and pillage the homes of rich citizens because they were seen as complicit in the abuse or simply because they were unjustly rich and ostentatious.

It is common to describe popular revolts as waves associated with centuries. The sixteenth saw religious riots, the seventeenth tax revolts, and the eighteenth grain riots. This schema, which corresponds nicely to a broad explanation for each century – the religious wars, then the "tax squeeze" of the military revolution, then the liberalization of the grain trade – is generally accurate as far as it goes. However, it is important to remember that these incidents were routine events and any type of revolt could happen in any century.

In the sixteenth century many riots had religious objectives. The most famous event, the Massacre of Saint Bartholomew's Day in Paris in 1572, was not a riot in the sense meant here, but rather a mass murder, or massacre, of Protestants by Catholic crowds, stemming from the rumor that spread through the already mobilized Paris militia that the king had ordered the killing of all the Huguenots. This attack on a whole category of people *because of who they were* was different from the attacks on individuals *because of what they*

represented. In the aftermath of the Huguenot leader Coligny's murder, however, the authentic sort of vindictive crowd took over.
Enraged citizens dragged the corpse around the city, set fire to it,
dumped it in the river, hung it from a gallows, and mutilated it. In
doing this they were mimicking the rituals of official executions with
the intent of humiliating the victim and his reputation. Since the body
was already dead, there was no torture involved. More typically,
religiously motivated crowds attacked persons or symbols of the
opposite faith as a way of removing spiritual pollution. Protestants
went after roadside crosses, Catholic statuary, holy water, or sacred
relics. Catholics went after clandestine Protestant services, Protestant
burials, Protestant temples (churches). The religious wars included
other massacres of Protestants. On at least one occasion in the
"Michelade" of Nîmes in 1567, a Protestant faction massacred up to a
hundred Catholics. More typical episodes of attacks on Catholic
targets included monasteries pillaged for their stores of grain and
attacks on monks who were limiting villagers' traditional rights of
access to forest timber. In the eighteenth century, people from the
village of Quernes near Saint-Omer chased a Jansenist priest out of the
church and all the way to the edge of the village, tearing his cassock
into tatters. When the bishop came to the village a few days later to
calm things down, he was met by about a hundred women and girls,
"armed with rocks, clubs and pitchforks, who blocked him from
entering the church," calling him "beggar, filthy Huguenot, heretic,
damned to Hell, Jansenist." The bishop was chased from the village,
while the crowd demolished his litter with rocks and wounded his
assistants.[21]

In the seventeenth century, novel taxes were often the problem,
especially between 1600 and 1660 when the state was inventing many
indirect taxes and special fees that were being collected by private tax
farmers. Not only were articles of common consumption that people
needed being taxed, but many fees were assessed on specific groups for
the renewal of their privileges, and on royal officers who were being
coerced into coming up with money for forced loans to the crown.
These were measures that were bound to antagonize a range of special
interests from targeted guilds to royal officers. Even worse in the
popular eye was the perception that tax farmers were siphoning off
much of the money for their own profit and pouring it into ostentatious palaces and luxury furnishings. The local agents of the tax

farmers fitted perfectly the description of the exploitative outsider that the crowd was looking for. And it was the victims' misfortune that if they wanted to collect an excise or sales tax, they would have to set up an office in a prominent public place and visit the shops of artisans or the cellars of innkeepers in broad daylight to mark the merchandise. Such activities made them an easy target for angry demonstrators.

Every century and every region had grain riots, but they were particularly prevalent in the eighteenth century. A shortage of grain, or its high price, or the cost of flour or bread, would threaten the well-being of families because bread was the main staple of the diet of the poor. Crowds would stop convoys carrying grain out of the city, or invade attics where grain was stored, or seize grain and sell it at a more reasonable price in the marketplace, or attack local dignitaries seen as hoarders or exporters of grain. An early example is the so-called Rebeine of Lyon in 1529 in which a large crowd, prepared in advance by flyers accusing city officials of being grain profiteers, pillaged the houses of four or five eminent citizens and then carried off grain from the municipal stores. In the eighteenth century grain riots were increasingly common because the population was expanding faster than the grain supply, and each local community hoarded its stock, impeding the flow to markets and causing shortages in places where not enough was produced. In 1770 the conflict was intensified when Controler-General Turgot tried to open up a free market in grain by abolishing local tariffs and restrictions. Fearful communities hoarded what they had even more. The result was the "Flour War" of 1774 when a chain of grain riots swept the entire Parisian region.

Popular revolts were directed at a variety of other objectives. Peasants rioted against troop lodgings, smugglers or the repression of smugglers, seigneurial exactions, guild restrictions, field enclosures, attacks on religious traditions. Jean Nicolas and his team studied the 8,528 known incidents from 1661 to 1789. Of these, 39 percent were over state taxes, 17 percent were about subsistence, 14 percent concerned the legal system, 5 percent involved labor issues, 5 percent were against seigneurs, 3 percent concerned religious belief. The rest were directed against noble privileges, the clergy, notable individuals, municipal authorities, regional particularities, and state efforts at reform.

The larger urban riots could be quite serious. To take just a few examples, in 1630 in Dijon mixed crowds of men and women roamed through the streets, threatening elegant townhouses owned by judges of the Cour des Comptes because they believed the court was going to register a mandated change in the Burgundian tax system that was seen as a threat to the poor. They spent the next night meeting on walls and ramparts and at 5.30 the next morning an all-male armed force emerged bearing pikes, swords, and muskets. While drummers rallied support in the neighborhoods, this popular army pillaged the mansions of seven major officials, burning their luxurious possessions on great bonfires in the streets, to cheering crowds. When the city finally persuaded a citizens' force to fire on the crowd, killing seven or eight demonstrators, the rebels retreated into the popular Saint-Philibert quarter and barricaded the streets, creating a stronghold of opposition, with neighbors on every rooftop throwing rocks. On the third day the uprising gradually subsided.

In Rennes in 1675 crowds angry at a shortage of tobacco caused by new taxes stormed and pillaged the tax bureau and went on to sack four other tax offices, making a bonfire of official records and generally causing havoc. A group of noblemen fired on the crowd, killing thirteen and wounding nearly fifty. This stopped the agitation, but left behind simmering anger and people murmuring about burning down the houses of rich merchants. Later, when the governor arrived with three companies of infantry to subdue the city, his forces were met with derision and rock throwing. The bishop's palace, where the governor had established his headquarters, was besieged by three hundred angry women who insulted him to his face, calling him a "fat pig, fat beggar" and complaining "that he had come to enrich himself at the expense of the province, that this was a fine dog of a governor." Meanwhile half of the town's militia companies sided with the rebels and more or less occupied the city. For twelve days Rennes was split into two camps.

In Paris in 1750 the police practice of arresting vagrants off the streets and sending them to populate the colony of Louisiana led to rumors that the police were arresting and deporting children. This was not general policy, but in fact children were being arrested and thrown in prison. Fear mounted, until on May 22 and 23 spontaneous riots broke out all over Paris. None of them was coordinated, but each separately involved an outcry against a soldier or police agent who was thought to be kidnapping a child. Crowds of thousands stoned public buildings and broke into shops to get weapons. On the second day a child was freed from the clutches of a sergeant named Labbé. The indignant crowd pursued Labbé through many streets and in and out of several buildings before he was finally beaten to death and his body dragged and dumped on the doorstep of the lieutenant-general of police, a reproach from the people to the man in charge, who was a direct appointee of the king.

Who participated in all these riots? It is hard to know specific details, but the crowd was usually a cross-section of the middle to lower classes from particular neighborhoods. Participation was not uniform. Some neighborhoods might remain untouched. When rioters are identified, they are usually a mixture of craftsman from various trades, sometimes bringing along their shop employees, day laborers, and petty professionals such as legal functionaries, process-servers, and clerks. There was always a large contingent of women, and they were usually the most vociferous, partly because they were functioning as moral guardians of the community, egging on the men by screaming "this isn't right," partly because they were less recognizable to the authorities and less subject to serious prosecution. Young men and "children" (boys, rarely girls) were frequently mentioned. They would be apprentices or school boys from the local *collège*. Many peasants from the surrounding villages might pour into town if the riot lasted long enough. Absent from the crowd were the more eminent city leaders: royal officers, merchants, resident nobles. The desperately poor might participate, but they were in the minority, contrary to official statements blaming the "scum of the people" or outside agitators. Participation was never unanimous. There were probably just as many people who did not participate as those who did, because they did not approve, were busy, or did not want to take the risk.

When an uprising was becoming serious and expanding to a whole city or into a second or third day, people from the crowd, usually women, would march through neighborhoods beating on a drum to rally a force. As there were minimal forces of order, crowds could form and attack individuals or buildings with relative impunity, at least until the reluctant civic guard could be mobilized. The *échevins* or consuls could command the rioters to desist and arrest isolated individuals, usually not the most deeply involved, but they were relatively helpless to stop a mass movement until a real armed force could be brought in. At that point the lightly armed crowd was easily subdued by soldiers on horseback with superior weapons. Still, until that stage, it was possible to join a revolt with good odds that you would not be caught. When an uprising reached the stage of actually occupying a city, the women and children would disappear and an improvised military force of men with weapons would appear, no doubt using experience from the militia. Some riots were led by workers from particular trades, such as the unemployed journeyman weavers and wool combers in Amiens in 1628 and 1636. Boatmen on the Garonne raised the alarm in Agen in 1635. The revolt in Bordeaux in 1675 began in the shops of pewter-makers.

The local riots described up to this point could be very damaging to property and threatening to the crown and to local authorities. They were brief explosions of intense anger as crowds went after scapegoats and demanded retribution. If the riots went into a second phase and turned from an immediate scapegoat to an attack on local authorities, they could disrupt business for weeks. But they were not as massively threatening to the state as certain other kinds of popular movements because they were confined to one place, and once the outburst was played out, popular anger tended to recede. When troops could be brought in, the outcome was inevitably repression and the exemplary punishment of a few unfortunate rioters.

Large city revolts made a big impression because they caused dramatic damage to the property of important dignitaries, they insulted and humiliated the officers of the town, including the highest royal officers. They also led to spectacular punishments such as the razing of town walls, the exile of royal courts, and the imposition of oppressive troop lodgings on the citizens. There is no official list of them. Perhaps forty or fifty are well known, and others are lost for lack of documentation. They made a lasting impression on the public and were remembered long afterwards. But they did not happen frequently, and they were not as threatening to the state as certain other kinds of popular protest because they were confined to one place, and tended to quieten down fairly quickly.

Another type of rebellion was the seizure of control of a town by an ostracized faction of the local elite. In the process they might enlist the support of common citizens, making their coup look like a popular uprising. They might also join forces with a noble rebellion going on outside, adding support for their cause, but at the cost of losing the initiative to noble leaders. Municipal battles between the in-group and the out-group had the negative effect of polarizing all the local bodies such as sovereign courts, town councils, royal agents, and town offi-cials, compromising law and order, stalling legal cases, and paralyzing local business as each body seized the opportunity to extend its jur-isdictional claims by challenging the others.

Again, two examples will suffice. In Agen in 1514 a group opposing the existing city council's policies, most notably their attempt to raise taxes to pay for the repair of the bridge across the Garonne, staged large public meetings; administered an oath in which citizens swore loyalty to the "commune," a word evoking the historical unity of earlier times; stormed the city council; took over the seats of the consuls; and demanded an audit of the books. A long conflict ensued. Large crowds made threatening gestures and spoke extravagantly of hanging "those thieves of consuls who want to put novel taxes on grains, wines, and other victuals," but no real violence occurred because the popular element was just a tool used by one faction of elites against another.

In the Italianate cities of Aix and Marseille in Provence, factional conflicts took the form of semi-permanent rivalries between clans of urban nobles led by powerful patrons who viewed local politics as an eternal struggle between clienteles. In Marseille, sides formed around the Valbelle family and the Glandèves-Félix group that opposed them. The memoirs of Antoine de Félix convey the way these self-confident aristocrats manipulated a crowd of fishermen angered by a rise in salt taxes that they blamed on the consuls:

We went in a troop as far as Saint Jean where my brothers had some power, and after the party had been expanded by adding Gressy and some fisher-men who carried oars and poles and those long rods that they call *grapes*, we were shouting "Vive le Roy" and the group that was at Saint Victor was shouting that those people were thieves and that we should go and attack them; then we withdrew into the fortress of Notre-Dame de la Garde.

Félix and his fisherman allies were shouting slogans to get a riot started. He noted with satisfaction how the crowd they stirred up had besieged the *hôtel de ville*, where the consuls spent the night barri-caded against "certain unknown persons who appeared with axes and hammers to go and break down the doors and pillage the houses of the consuls allied with Cosme de Valbelle." This sort of rabble-rousing would not have worked if the crowd had not already been angry. Crowds could get out of hand. A month later when royal guards arrived to implement the rise in salt taxes, Félix describes how the soldiers were besieged in the house of the second consul and how his brothers had to come to decoy the crowd away from the building so that the besieged *gabeleurs* could escape over the roofs.[22] This was a typical factional situation. The partisans of Félix enjoyed stirring up a riot against their enemies, but the demonstrators tended to have minds of their own and might go farther than the instigators really wanted. Armed rivalries and near confrontations continued to characterize conflicts in Marseille throughout the seventeenth century.

Much more dangerous were rebellions by dissident nobles with regional followings, because they gave focus to a rebellion and they had the capacity to redirect popular anger toward political objectives. The period 1440–1660 was punctuated by many noble rebellions, including the war of the commonweal against Louis XI, the clashes of the Protestant and Catholic forces during the religious wars, the repeated rebellions of Condé and other princes under Henry IV and Louis XIII, and the Fronde (1648–53). The most alarming thing about these rebellions was that they were led by grandees with significant regional power bases who could mobilize networks of followers and soldiers who were capable of actual battles. Their physical withdrawal from the royal court also split the rest of those attending the king into several camps, as they weighed their loyalties and private obligations. The same process forced royal ministers and agents to take sides, producing contradictory rulings. Meanwhile in the rebellious regions, members of the secondary nobility would also take sides, as would the towns or factions within the towns. The rebels would be tempted to link up with popular movements in "their" towns because doing so was an easy way to gain popularity. Popular protesters led by a local faction leader might be seduced by the illusion that linking up with a larger movement would get results. This was a bad move for the local protesters because their noble leaders would inevitably sell them out when a peace was negotiated. It was also a dangerous strategy for the noble commanders because popular anger could get out of hand and lead to unintended consequences. The prince de Condé found this out during the Fronde, when he used the city of Bordeaux as a base from which to oppose the regime of Cardinal Mazarin. His allies, the so-called party of the Ormée, took over the city and welcomed the rebellious princes. But they also threatened and expelled leading judges from the Parlement of Bordeaux, established a sort of emergency city government, terrorized the opposition, and fought several pitched battles against the usual leaders of the community. The Ormée was a creative attempt to reform the power structure of Bordeaux in favor of the "middling" citizens, but it was an embarrassment to Condé, who could not control the violence or the attacks on persons of importance.

The most dramatic form of rebellion was a regional peasant uprising. This could be a nasty problem for the king because its repression would require a military campaign. If rebel nobles got involved as commanders, the problem would be even worse. Major peasant uprisings were relatively rare events. Militant peasants were perfectly capable of courageous battles and eloquent appeals when sufficiently aroused, although they were no match for an organized army. Many peasant revolts have left their mark, including the Jacquerie of 1358, and the uprisings of the Pitauds of Aquitaine (1548), the Gautiers of Normandy (1589), the Nu-Pieds of Normandy (1639), the Sabotiers of Sologne (1658), the Tard-Avisés of Quercy (1707), and the Great Fear of 1789. One kind of movement took the form of separate disturbances occurring in waves over a whole region in response to a common grievance. An example was the so-called Bonnets Rouges movement in Brittany in 1675. In response to the news that the province's two leading cities, Rennes and Nantes, had risen up against the stamped paper and other excise taxes, peasants in small towns and villages all over the province challenged the rights of their lords, attacked and burned castles, and blockaded the roads. The sum of these riots was a serious regional crisis. On July 23 the bishop of Saint-Malo wrote despairingly to Colbert:

The [tax] agents in all the little towns around here do not dare to use [stamped paper] any more, and most of them have abandoned their houses or been expelled from them by the owners for fear that the houses will be burned down. Almost all the nobles of Lower Brittany and the surrounding districts are leaving their country homes and taking refuge in the principal cities, bringing along what they can of their most precious furnishings and all their papers to keep them from being pillaged or burned, which is what happened at the Chateau of Kergöet, one of the best fortified of Lower Brittany.[23]

Another well-known example of proliferating, autonomous local disturbances is the Great Fear of 1789, which saw villagers responding to rumors of approaching forces of repression by attacking castles and burning records.

A different kind of peasant war was a coordinated military confrontation in which peasants formed armies and fought against the forces of order. In 1578–80, Dauphiné was faced with widespread anger at heavy wartime taxes levied on the province by marauding troops, and outrage at the unfair distribution of these taxes. Peasants were feeling the pinch, while urban bourgeois were angered by a tax system that enabled nobles to remove new land purchases from the tax rolls. Action took place on three fronts. There were urban uprisings from below, including a famous case in Romans.[24] There was a more constitutionally informed legal movement by middle-class reformers in the Estates of Dauphiné to restrict the nobles' *taille* exemptions. This effort gave leaders from different towns some experience in collaboration with one another. There was, third, a Peasant League in which towns joined with rural villages to create an armed force to defend themselves from the destruction caused by marauding troops. By 1580 4,000 peasants had been mobilized, led by village lawyers and notaries, seizing strongholds and opposing troops. Encouraged by the discussions in the Estates, they also began to oppose the idea of noble privilege itself. On March 26, 1580, about a thousand peasants were killed by royal forces in a bloodbath at Moirans, and the rest were defeated by royal troops in September. This combination of separate but parallel levels of agitation had some impact on the future of the *taille* in Dauphiné.

Some of the most renowned peasant rebels were the Croquants of the southwest. This term was loosely used to describe peasant rebels. It was a term of opprobrium meaning roughly "hayseeds" or "bumpkins." The peasants never used it, referring to themselves rather as "the communes." In 1636, deluged with heavy taxes and troop exactions, the peasants of Angoumois and Saintonge began ringing the tocsin and forming local forces to defend the villages from tax collectors and the soldiers backing them up. Meetings of men from all the communes in a traditional district called a *châtellenie* were held in the central market town to coordinate their efforts. The use of the familiar feudal districts indicates that they were modeling their organization on traditional habits. Word of a meeting would be passed around three or four days in advance. Messengers were sent from place to place, notes were exchanged, and a rendezvous point

Figure 24 This is Burel's sketch of 'Croquants' (peasant rebels) in 1595 "who banded together to coerce villages that did not want to join their movement ... all in order to betray our town"

would be announced. On the appointed morning the tocsin would ring for miles around and soon an army would emerge of "around four thousand men armed with arkbusses and pikes, divided into twelve to fifteen companies led by their priests, all marching in good order accompanied by the sounds of fifes and violins, for lack of drums."[25] It consisted of local community contingents acting pretty much on their own. They formed in the late spring when the crops were in and disbanded at harvest time. Their demands were all about taxes: insufferable rates, distorted assessments, violent collection by guards, excessive seigneurial dues and tithes, and the diversion of church revenues to distant owners. They did not question the existence of the traditional *taille* and tithe, only their misuse. They spoke in the name of "the people" or "the communes," meaning all the inhabitants. They expressed a total contempt for measures coming from Paris, and the term "Parisian" was almost as detestable to them as "gabeleur." Besides the local curés, the leaders of the movement were petty local judges from seigneurial or royal courts with their clerks and subordinates. They took command of the troops by haranguing them standing on a makeshift platform built out of barrels. There were incidents of cruelty against cornered individuals, but the movement was without extraordinary violence. Several poor souls were suspected of complicity because of an innocuous letter found in a pocket or an aggressive statement "that [the nobles] should be hanged". In the village of Saint-Savivien, the bodies of tax agents were mutilated and the parts supposedly pinned to doorways. In mid May a large force decided to invade the city of Angoulême during the annual fair, but the city got wind of the plan and blockaded the streets. The peasants withdrew and agreed to send an appeal to the king instead of further military action. The king sent an agent to investigate their demands, and that process seems to have quietened the situation.[26]

In 1637 the Croquants of nearby Perigord set the record for militancy and made the term "Croquant" a feared household word. In that year special military levies increased the *taille* by a third and took unconventional (therefore suspicious) forms. The response astounded the authorities. When an archer who was delivering the tax commissions was asked by an old woman in the village of Notre-Dame des Vertus what he was carrying, he replied jokingly that it was "the gabelle." Seemingly out of nowhere the tocsin rang out and 5,000 men marched forth and besieged the city of Périgueux, which was considered the tax collectors' base of operations. They demanded that they be given the city's cannons and that the *gabeleurs* be turned over to be killed. This was a clear conflict between the towns and the countryside. When the city closed its gates, the peasants proceeded to lay waste the rural homes of known *gabeleurs* and held a great rally in a field outside the city. There they elected Antoine du Puy, sieur de La Mothe La Forêt, as their "general" and sent messengers throughout the province to summon more men. Two other nobles, Antoine de Ribeyreix, "the Turk," and Léonde Laval, baron de Madaillon, emerged as leaders. All three were from the genuine lesser nobility. Ribeyreix was the spokesman for the rebels. Madaillon was an old, experienced soldier. La Mothe La Forêt, fifty-five years old, seems to have believed that when the king learned of the distress of the people, he would moderate his demands. He reported that the Virgin Mary had told him in a vision that their cause was just.

On May 8, 30,000 men gathered in the forest of Vergt. La Mothe La Forêt picked 8,000 of the best of them to form sixty companies armed with pikes, pitchforks, and muskets. Of his appointed captains, six were noble, six were artisans, fourteen were judicial personnel, many others were farmers. The army maintained strict discipline and taxed some 400 parishes for revenues, each for the upkeep of its own soldiers. On May 10 the army marched on Bergerac, which was undefended, and occupied the city for twenty days. Their movement issued a "Protest by the Assembled Communities" that announced their existence and issued regulations for their meetings and a "Request of the Insurrectionary Communes of Périgord to the King" in which they demanded punishment for the *gabeleurs* and a return to the olden days by a revival of the Estates of Périgord which had been abolished in 1611. They treated the people of Bergerac mildly except for those reputed to be *gabeleurs*. The offending tax had been apportioned by Jay d'Ataux, lieutenant-general of the *sénéchaussée*, and the orders distributed by his *greffier* André Alesme. Ataux was arrested by the peasants and would have been executed except for the intervention of La Mothe La Forêt. Alseme had his townhouse pillaged, and his suburban house burned down, his garden ruined, his grapevines pulled up, and his well filled in. He and his family went into hiding until October. Six other officials connected to tax collections received similar treatment. The peasant army under its two noble commanders made plans to advance on Bordeaux while sending for more recruits from all the communes of the province. They moved towards the Agenais, occupying small towns along the way, but when the duc de La Valette approached with a small royal army, they barricaded themselves in a small walled town called La Sauvetat and stationed 3,000 peasant soldiers inside. In a fierce two-hour battle, La Valette's men assaulted the town, overthrew barricades, and set fire to houses where the Croquants had taken refuge. The result was "a bloody butchery because they refused the quarter offered to them and defended themselves with an obstinate rage, street by street, from shed to shed, in the church and in the houses."[27] The death toll was 200–800 royal soldiers and 1,000–1,500 Croquants. The whole country was amazed at this dogged resistance by mere peasants. The remaining forces fell back on Bergerac, where La Mothe decided to accept a truce on condition that there be no reprisals against the rebels.

The Croquants of 1637 had managed to raise the hopes of hundreds of villages, and they had effectively expressed the utter contempt felt in the countryside for the king's oppressive tax measures. But they had focused only on taxes. They had no program of reform beyond the absolute destruction of new taxes and the total elimination of anyone who dared to be involved with them. It had been a genuine peasant war, despite the leadership of La Mothe and Madaillon. The regional nobility wanted no part of it, and the towns were unanimously opposed. The only people who were impressed were the peasants in neighboring regions, who continued to carry out similar uprisings throughout the 1640s.

French society was characterized by a stable, traditional hierarchy of power, grounded in the domination of old and new nobles, the spiritual guidance of a multifaceted church, and the wealth which artisan craftsmen produced, and which merchant middlemen and financial speculators managed. These features were organized conceptually in the tripartite society of orders. It was essentially a class system which channeled wealth and power to those who were born into, or had the ability to acquire, a privileged position. But the system was also built upon an unstable equilibrium between the traditional powers and the more dynamic social and cultural forces that operated within it. A few fortunate families rose from wealthy peasant to merchant fortune or royal office and even ministerial power. Clever individuals developed connections with patrons who favored their advancement. Urban associations promoted piety, managed the poor, protected guild monopolies, and organized to benefit journeymen. Youth abbeys enforced community standards on village recalcitrants and regulated marriage rites. All these connections meant that society was modifying the contours of power in small ways. Throughout the society there was tension between the forces of order and subordinate groups determined to oppose tyranny and demand retribution. This equilibrium was unstable because the pride and repressed anger of individuals and groups were always simmering below the surface. Protests and rebellions were a significant check on the day-to-day rule of the authorities on many levels. The rebels never got the upper hand, but given the weakness of state and local enforcement measures, they consistently challenged and checked the excesses of those in power.

Suggestions for further reading: group loyalties and social conflicts

Classes, orders, social stratification

Collins, James B., *Classes, Estates, and Orders in Early Modern Brittany* (Cambridge, 1996).

Loyseau, Charles, *A Treatise of Orders and Plain Dignities*, ed. and trans. Howell A. Lloyd (Cambridge, 1994).

Mousnier, Roland, *Social Hierarchies 1450 to the Present*, trans. Peter Evans (New York, 1973).

Parker, David, *Class and State in Ancien Régime France: The Road to Modernity?* (London, 1986).

Women and family relations

Davis, Natalie Zemon, "Ghosts, Kin and Progeny: Some Features of Family Life in Early Modern France," *Daedalus* (Spring, 1977), 87–114.

Women on the Margins: Three Seventeenth-Century Lives (Cambridge, MA, 1995).

Edwards, Kathryn A., *Families and Frontiers: Recreating Communities and Boundaries in the Early Modern Burgundies* (Boston, 2002).

Gager, Kristin Elizabeth, *Blood Ties and Fictive Ties: Adoption and Family Life in Early Modern France* (Princeton, NJ, 1996).

Gullickson, Gay L., "The Sexual Division of Labor in Cottage Industry and Agriculture in the Pays de Caux: Auffay, 1750–1850," *French Historical Studies* 12 (1981), 177–99.

Hardwick, Julie, "Seeking Separations: Gender, Marriages, and Household Economies in Early Modern France," *French Historical Studies* 212 (Winter 1998), 157–80.

Phillips, Roderick, "Women, Neighborhood, and Family in the Late Eighteenth Century," *French Historical Studies* 18 (1993), 1–12.

Rand, Richard, *Intimate Encounters: Love and Domesticity in Eighteenth-Century France* (Princeton, NJ, 1997).

Solidarity and conflict within groups

Garrioch, David, *Neighbourhood and Community in Paris, 1740–1790* (Cambridge, 1986).

Castan, Yves, *Honnêteté et relations sociales en Languedoc (1715–1780)* (Paris, 1974).

Cattelona, Georg'ann, "Control and Collaboration: The Role of Women in Regulating Female Sexual Behavior in Early Modern Marseille," *French Historical Studies* 18 (1993), 13–33.

Davis, Natalie Zemon, "The Reasons of Misrule: Youth Groups and Charivaris in Sixteenth-Century France," *Past and Present* no. 50 (1971), 41–75. Also in her *Society and Culture in Early Modern France* (Stanford, CA, 1975).

Schneider, Robert A., *Public Life in Toulouse, 1463–1789: From Municipal Republic to Cosmopolitan City* (Ithaca, NY, 1989).

Social conflict and popular protest

Beik, William, *Urban Protest in Seventeenth-Century France: The Culture of Retribution* (Cambridge, 1997).

Bercé, Yves-Marie, *Histoire des Croquants: étude des soulèvements populaires au XVIIe siècle dans le sud-ouest de la France* (Paris, 1974).
History of Peasant Revolts: The Social Origins of Rebellion in Early Modern France, trans. Amanda Whitmore (Ithaca, NY, 1990) (a translation of sections of the longer work cited above).

Farge, Arlette, *Fragile Lives: Violence, Power and Solidarity in Eighteenth-Century Paris* (Cambridge, MA, 1993).
Subversive Words: Public Opinion in Eighteenth-Century France (University Park, PA, 1995).

Farge, Arlette and Jacques Revel, *The Vanishing Children of Paris: Rumor and Politics before the French Revolution*, trans. Claudia Miéville (Cambridge, MA, 1991).

Golden, Richard, M., *The Godly Rebellion: Parisian Curés and the Religious Fronde, 1652–62* (Chapel Hill, NC, 1981).

Le Roy Ladurie, Emmanuel, *Carnival in Romans*, trans. Mary Feeney (New York, 1979).

Mousnier, Roland, *Peasant Uprisings in Seventeenth-Century France, Russia, and China*, trans. Brian Pearce (New York, 1970).

Nicolas, Jean, *La Rébellion française: mouvements populaires et conscience sociale (1661–1789)* (Paris, 2002).

Pillorget, René, *Les Mouvements insurrectionnels de Provence entre 1596 et 1715* (Paris, 1975).

Tilly, Charles, *The Contentious French: Four Centuries of Popular Struggle* (Cambridge, MA, 1986).

Westrich, Sal Alexander, *The Ormée of Bordeaux: A Revolution during the Fronde* (Baltimore, MD, 1972).

9 | *Traditional attitudes and identities*

The term "culture" often refers to the sophisticated creations of theatre, literature, painting, philosophy – in other words, "high culture." Applied to ordinary people, it can mean customs, practices, and rituals. Here we are closer to the latter than the former. We want to know how the French people or, more accurately, the various subcategories of French people, viewed their world. This is culture in an anthropological mode. It asks what beliefs and customs structured their lives and relationships, how they behaved toward one another, how they positioned themselves in terms of individual or collective identity. This chapter and the next explore these questions, first in terms of traditional cultures and then in terms of change and development.

Historians have rallied around three interpretive ways of thinking about these issues. The first is to make a distinction between popular and elite culture and to see them as evolving separately out of a medieval world in which everyone shared the same mental universe. Popular culture was mostly orally transmitted. It consisted of rituals that gave meaning to daily life, customs governing interpersonal relations, belief in a magical universe with its own processes that could be manipulated by human intervention, and a world filled with devils and spirits who led humans astray. Elite culture was literate and more exclusive. It derived from humanist education, scientific discovery, and upper-class appreciation of the arts. Gradually the more educated and sophisticated elites began distancing themselves from what they now saw as the culture of the ignorant masses.

The second interpretation invokes what Peter Burke calls the "triumph of Lent" and Ronald Po-Tsia calls "social disciplining."[1] In the early modern centuries, under the influence of the Protestant and Catholic Reformations, a variety of forces – the churches, royal administrators, merchant-capitalists, city governments – all undertook to discipline and organize the popular masses beneath them by cracking down on unruly traditional practices. While government bureaucrats developed the capacity to intervene more directly in the provinces to suppress resistance, disobedience, and violence, the church cracked down on seemingly disorderly activities like public dancing, carnival revelry, and concubinage among priests. Towns started locking up beggars and vagabonds in workhouses to get them out of the public view. An extremely negative view of this process is provided by Michel Foucault, who sees it as a phase in the state's mastery of the technology of social control.[2]

The third interpretation derives from the influential work of sociologist Norbert Elias who saw the rise of proper manners as a new style of behavior that originated among the aristocrats in royal courts and trickled down to the bourgeoisie and the rest of the population. This view is more psychological. Maintenance of one's physical autonomy vis-à-vis other bodies, repression of gross bodily functions, emotional self-restraint, assumption of a proper veneer of courtesy toward others – all these were aspects of a civilizing process that gradually changed the ground rules for social interaction.

These three models all focus on different aspects of the same broad process. Whether you see societal change in terms of divergence between elite and popular modes of behavior, discipline through repression from above, or changes in interpersonal relations, you are adopting a cultural explanation of societal movement. All three are broad generalizations requiring closer analysis. They raise the question of how to integrate the way people behaved with what we already know about social groups and conflicts.

The culture of the majority

The basis of everyone's culture was the mentality of the vast rural majority. These people's lives were focused on the village where they lived and died. Even town dwellers were influenced by a continual influx of country people seeking work. But coming from a village did not mean ignorance of the larger world. Seasonal workers migrated long distances to harvest crops; soldiers returned from wars; pilgrims traveled to shrines; and villagers maintained contact with relatives who migrated to the city. News of king and court was generally known and wildly popular. Still, most people's everyday experience was limited to the confines of their home town: its outlying fields, the rival villages on its periphery, and the roads to nearby market towns. Daily reality contrasted "those from here" with "people from outside."

Rural perceptions of quantitative categories such as age, distance, or date were not very precise. People described their ages as "around twenty or so" and distances as "a two day's walk." Their days were marked, not by the time of day, but by references to day or night, dawn or dusk, or by noting the ringing of church bells for services and prayers. There was no need for formal precision, except in cases where some sort of reckoning was needed in buying and selling goods or paying taxes. Rural people measured their lives in terms of temporal milestones. When they thought of past events they linked them not to the year when they happened but to significant occurrences at that time such as a great fire, the rededication of the church, or the passage of soldiers. Distance was thought of in terms of concentric circles of remoteness from the home village.

Local life was held together by a cycle of religious and agricultural events that gave logic to the year and infused life with meaning. Births, marriages, and deaths punctuated the ongoing routine of each family, while the annual sequence of festivities with their accompanying rituals gave a sense of order to the whole community. Both family events and public celebrations involved a set of elements that were similar everywhere, but each region or village embellished them with its own particular habits and customs. Each locality had peculiarities that made the natives feel at home and outsiders feel a little uncomfortable.

As we noted in Chapter 2, the inhabitants of villages belonged to a community which had some form of governance for purposes of tax collection. In most cases the same community also constituted a parish under the direction of the curé or his substitute. Sometimes the boundaries of parish and village did not coincide. But usually the parish priest was a major figure in the community. The church was the only place indoors where the community could hold a meeting, and Sunday Mass was the chief occasion for people to see one another collectively. As God's local representative, the priest was an important member of the community. He was not rich, but he enjoyed a steady income that was greater than that of the average peasant. He had the power to hear confession and absolve sins. This made him privy to much private information. He read directives from the bishop or the king from the pulpit. He mediated quarrels, handled poor relief, and served as a reputable contact when outsiders wanted someone to provide information or vouch for the truth of witnesses' testimony. At the same time, he could be the object of abuse. If the tithe went to him, there would be disputes over rates and payments. If conflicts arose over the management of local affairs, he was likely to conflict with other notable citizens who saw themselves as natural leaders of the community, such as the notary, the lord, or the richest farmers.

The affairs of the parish were managed by the *fabrique*, a committee of the most important village men who were responsible for managing any funds that had been donated to the parish. They saw to the celebration of Masses for the dead, maintaining the church and its outbuildings, providing lamp oil and candles for services, and sometimes hiring the local schoolmaster. These *marguilliers* (members of the *fabrique*) thus had a role similar to that of the canons in a cathedral, except that they were laymen.

Before the seventeenth century parish priests were very much members of the community. They had been born nearby and they had little more education than their parishioners. Their mindset was not very different from that of the other villagers. They were not necessarily celibate, and they did not always dress as priests were supposed to do. Their understanding of church rituals was not generally very great, and they joined right in with the other villagers in celebrating local rituals which were not always entirely orthodox.

Catholic rituals

Most communities were staunchly Catholic in their beliefs. Attendance at Mass, annual confession and communion at Easter, belief in the intercession of saints and the holiness of the Eucharist, were all assured. At least until the early seventeenth century, medieval practices still prevailed. Processions for saint's days, wills that commissioned large numbers of Masses for the dead, the worship of relics, and pilgrimages to shrines were common. As Neil Galpern reports concerning Champagne:

In evil times Catholics appealed beyond their parish to the patrons of towns and regions. To quell a fire in 1530 the clergy of Troyes carried in procession the relics of three protectors of the diocese, Saint Loup, Saint Helen, and Saint Hoylde. The bones of Saint Loup, who was credited with having preserved Troyes from Attila [the Hun], lay in the abbey that bore his name... The remains of Saint Hoylde, a Champenois virgin, graced Saint Stephen's collegial church. During a severe drought in 1556 the peasants of the surrounding countryside marched village by village to the Cathedral of Troyes, in hopes that Saint Mathie, another local virgin, whose relics were housed there, and Saint Helen, would intercede with God for rain.[3]

At the same time most people took the faith for granted and treated everyday rituals with the casualness of familiarity. Christophe Sauvageon, who was a priest in the rather ordinary village of Sennely in the Sologne from 1676 to 1710, gives a down-to-earth portrayal of his parishioners' religious practice. Most of them attended either an 8 a.m. Mass or afternoon Vespers regularly, and many participated actively in confraternities. But during Mass they milled around inside the church, sitting or standing, chatting or doing business. "All sorts of people who only attend the service out of habit or decency – the drunken, the non-devout, the lazy – position themselves behind the [baptismal] fonts, lean against them, or use them as cover so they can talk during the divine service."[4] His parishioners observed the Lenten season scrupulously, but they were reluctant to take communion at Easter because they disliked confessing their sins, preferring to save them up for their deathbed when they would not become village gossip. Loyalty to the Virgin Mary was so intense that villagers caused an uproar in the church when the priest tried to move a silver lamp out of the chapel dedicated to her; indeed "they gave more willingly to the Virgin than to God."[5] The villagers' religious practice had a distinctively local flavor. They ignored Saint John the Baptist who was officially the patron saint of their village and flocked instead to Saint Sebastian, a more practical choice since he was the curer of contagious diseases. They associated names of saints with remedies, for example, Saint Paxent became Saint Paissant who should be invoked when animals refused to graze because "paissant" means "grazing" in French. Saint Firmin became "Fremin" and was invoked if the animals were shaking (*frémir*).

The five hundred inhabitants of Sennely attended almost one hundred processions per year, either within the village, from the church to the cemetery or the public square, or through the countryside to nearby shrines. Led by the priest, the inhabitants would group themselves according to status and rank and march to another town where they would be ceremonially greeted at the boundary by the local priest accompanied by his flock. After five or six hours of services and visits to shrines, they would make their way home, losing thirsty dropouts to taverns passed on the way. Sauvageon thought that his parishioners were "more superstitious than devout." They believed that it would offend God to sift flour on Saint Thomas's Day because Thomas had been martyred with a sieve; that their children would die within the year if they were baptized on the eve of Easter or Pentecost; that salvation was doubtful for anyone who died in bed facing the wall because that was where a demon waited to kidnap souls.[6]

The same religiosity was evident in larger towns, where the strength of numbers and the animosities of the religious wars produced impressive mass movements. An earthquake in 1579 caused 300 citizens of Tours to process through the countryside in midwinter wearing nothing but white robes of penitence and carrying the weight of heavy iron bars. In 1582 thousands of people from 200 villages in Champagne marched to the cathedral of Reims in response to an epidemic of plague. In 1583 peasants who had processed to Notre-Dame in Paris reported that "they had been moved to make these penitences or pilgrimages because of some fires that had appeared in the sky and other signs, like prodigies seen in the sky and on the earth, especially toward the Ardennes.[7]

Returning to Sauvageon in Sologne, we may note that his critical temperament suggests that he was perhaps in the vanguard of a broader movement to improve the quality of parish priests. The dictates of the Council of Trent did not actually produce working seminaries until the late seventeenth century. By the eighteenth century they were turning out a better-trained and educated priesthood. In rural settings the atmosphere changed considerably. The curé was now a product of the seminary and possibly the university. He was from the city and usually from a comfortable middle-class background. Many such curés arrived in their parishes with strict ideas about the proper way to perform ceremonies. They were shocked and appalled to discover the way their backward, superstitious parishioners lived their lives, and so they set out to reform the community. It was becoming common for priests to use confession as a tool for disciplining the population. Thus Sauvageon recommends active probing for sins:

It is also very rare for them to accuse themselves of the sins of sodomy and bestiality except at their death or in times of jubilee. This is why it is necessary to interrogate them on the matter, but it must be done with singular prudence for fear of teaching them sins they have never known.

He is determined to change the habits of his parishioners:

When the priest sees them commit some evil such as swearing, losing their temper and cursing their neighbor, or if he has seen them get drunk, they are under the false impression that in such cases they need not confess, alleging as their reason that they should only tell what the priest does not know.

He even comments on their customary work habits, taking the side of the employer:

They think they have the right to employ a kind of compensation against their masters, taking and keeping on their own initiative as recompense grain and other property of these masters when they have performed what they call *troches* for them ... and they never confess anything of all this.

This focus on confession is a good example of social disciplining, and the reaction of the priests certainly illustrates one kind of withdrawal of certain elites from popular culture.[8]

The inquisitorial gaze of the curé was badly understood by the congregation. For them, confession and the taking of communion were supposed to reinforce community by bringing people together and causing them to lay aside their mutual differences. Now the priest was intruding on their personal identity in an attempt to reform their rustic habits. He was splitting the community apart by criticizing their local saints or denouncing promiscuous dancing by unmarried men and women on Midsummer Night. Perhaps this is why some villagers lost interest in the church in what is sometimes called the "dechristianization" of the countryside.

For a family, the cycle of important religious events centered around births, marriages, and deaths. The most important events were the births of the children needed to perpetuate the line and carry on the necessary work. Once a baby was born, the most urgent concern was baptism, which enrolled him or her in the Christian community. The ceremony was very simple. The parents and godparents brought the baby to the sanctuary where the priest made the sign of the cross, gave it the name of a saint who would serve as its protector, performed various exorcisms, and did symbolic acts which varied from place to place such as placing salt in the mouth to symbolize the savoring of the faith, and touching the child's eyes and nose to open him or her to spiritual regeneration. The godparents would renounce Satan and his works. The child would be dipped in water and then dressed in a white robe. Baptism was considered so important that the church allowed any layman, even a Protestant, to baptize on the spot if a baby was stillborn or lived only a short while and a priest was not available. Like the popular invocation of non-existent saints, unauthorized elements of popular culture could creep into the baptismal ceremony despite all the efforts of the church to eradicate them. In 1608 in Béarn, the church forbade "laughter, games, promenades and kissing" during a baptism and banned "the detestable practice of placing the newly baptized children on the altar and having the godparents redeem them for a sum of money." In 1701 the church attempted to ban the practice of naming four, or even more, godparents that families were using to expand their clientage network. In 1712 the church banned the choice of godparents younger than twelve, "unless they are very well educated."[9]

Marriage was a time for merrymaking and showing off. In 1577 in Lorraine, Jean Le Coullon's 150 guests celebrated for three days at his son's wedding, and this was not unusual. For a family the marriage represented an alliance with another family and an opportunity to flaunt one's wealth. For the unmarried bachelors of the youth abbey, the marriage ceremony represented both the joyous coming-of-age of one of them and the unfortunate removal of an eligible bride from circulation. Tradition allowed them to express symbolic resistance to the marriage, while at the same time joining in the festivities.

A typical wedding would start with a formal procession of the entire wedding party from the bride's house to the church. If the bachelors disapproved, they might erect a barrier of straw to block the parade's progress until a tribute had been paid. In the church the couple would exchange vows, and the priest would bless them. Then he would deliver warnings about "those who attempt to break up the marriage by means of ligatures or other charms," a reference to the custom of bewitching the groom to render him impotent by "tying the knot." The whole party would then proceed to the tavern and from there to the father of the groom's house where they would be served course after course of food, each round followed by lively singing and eventually dancing. At some point, one of the bachelors would hide the bride's shoe, symbolically impeding her departure.

Another would distribute pieces of the bride's garter or auction them off to the company. In the course of the evening the married couple was expected to sneak away to a secret hiding place to consummate the marriage. The bachelors were expected to locate this hideaway and make the couple drink a *soupe à la mariée* which was an extremely spicy drink reputed to be an aphrodisiac. In the Sarladais, it was also customary during carnival season for couples who had been married during the previous year to be assessed a fine toward the costs of the festivities, another compensation for removing a potential bride from circulation.[10]

Like birth, death was an opportunity to think about salvation. Good Catholics underwent carefully scripted confessions and prayers on their deathbeds in the presence of their priest. Their funerals, like their weddings, were occasions to show off the family's importance by means of public processions of weeping relatives and friends, local guilds out in force, congregations of paid orphans or beggars, fancy tombs reflecting the glory of the family of the deceased, and legacies of funds to pay for multiple priests to say hundreds of Masses for the soul of the departed. The most powerful figures would manage to get their remains buried in the church itself, where everyone could see or walk over their tombs.

It was important for the dying to receive the last rites and to be buried in hallowed ground. A heavy emphasis was placed on the last rites and extreme unction because they prepared the soul for the next stage, which for most was purgatory. Dead souls were thought to remain close to home awaiting the Last Judgment when they would be reunited with their bodies. They were part of the community, so to speak, and the cemetery was a public place where open-air meetings and even dancing and merrymaking might take place. On such occasions the living were joined by the dead. For this reason unqualified bodies, those of unbaptized infants, beggars, plague victims, lepers, suicides, and especially Huguenots, were banned from the cemetery or segregated into one sector. During the religious conflicts of the sixteenth and seventeenth centuries, some unfortunate corpses became pawns in confessional disputes. Protestants tried to bury their loved ones in the local cemetery where their ancestors lay. Outraged Catholics would dig them up and desecrate their bodies. Each burial became a debate on the orthodoxy of the departed person, and cemeteries came to symbolize the splits in communities instead of their common heritage.[11]

The annual cycle of rituals

These periodic family events provided a counterpoint to the repeating annual cycle of agricultural duties and church festivals that enlisted the participation of the whole village. Concerns about the fertility of the fields and the fate of the crops were intermingled with religious holidays celebrating the life of Christ and preparing for the salvation of good Catholics. Robert Muchembled describes this rustic calendar beautifully: "The perception of time is a combination of ecclesiastical dictates, of necessities tied to rural existence, of expressions of sociability important for the survival of the community and of festive releases necessary to provide some color to a life that is rough, often dangerous."[12]

The cycle went something like this: in August and September grapes were picked and grain was harvested and processed. By October it was time for plowing the fields and planting winter wheat. Then came All Souls' Eve (Halloween), when the youths of the community went door to door demanding tribute, and All Souls' Day (November 1), when the souls of the dead came out of their graves. This was not to spook the living, as in today's Halloween, but to be close to their families. These two events inaugurated the winter phase, which extended from St. Martin's Day (November 11) to Easter. This was the time of year when work in the fields was minimal and the village was preoccupied with festivities which reinforced community solidarity. It was also characterized by nocturnal gatherings in houses or barns where young and old huddled close to the fire and entertained themselves by telling stories while the women sewed or spun. The Advent season called for fasting; then came Christmas which meant just another church service and not the colossal event it has become today. The "twelve days of Christmas" from December 25 to Epiphany (January 6), were the occasions for additional neighborhood customs; then came Carnival and Lent, culminating in Easter, the climax of the Catholic year. These were moveable feasts which fell between mid February and late April. They were followed in May and June by a whole series of other moveable church holidays: Rogation Days, Ascension Day, Pentecost and Fête-Dieu (Corpus Christi). During these months gardens were planted, and spring wheat was sown. The fasting during Lent made sense because it came at a time when supplies of stored food from the harvest were running short.

Figure 25 This detail from *The Fair at Xeuilley* by Callot depicts not so much a fair as a festival in which people are dancing, wearing costumes, and climbing tress. A real fair might have involved many more people and much selling of merchandise.

Easter, as a festival of spring, brought the promise of fresh vegetables and fruit from trees to supplement the shrinking stores of grain that had been used up during the winter. This religious and agricultural buildup of spring energy culminated in Saint John's Day on June 24, also called Midsummer Night, around the time of the summer solstice. Bonfires were lit, and young couples leaped over the fire in what might be called a fertility rite. Then followed the warm summer months, characterized by intensive work in the fields, culminating in the grain harvest of late July and August.

All these festivities had common elements. There would be religious services. Processions to churches or shrines were frequent. Most of the festivities had what we might call carnivalesque elements, referring to the special forms of playing and mocking connected to the carnival season. These were moments of escape when people gathered to celebrate together, to express the unity of the community, to reinforce feelings against outsiders and deviants, and to imagine for a moment that they were in a "land of cocaigne" where everything was plentiful and cares were non-existent.

The principal expression of this mood was Carnival itself, the week before the beginning of forty days of Lent. Carnival (Mardi Gras) was a time to wear masks and costumes, perform farces, dance, and mock the authorities, hold contests and play games, parade through town in masks or on allegorical floats, and above all to eat and drink to excess. Bawdy, sexual themes were likely to emerge, along with mockery of husbands dominated by wives and the put-down of priests or rulers who behaved arrogantly. At the heart of the celebration was the allegorical "battle of Carnival against Lent," representing the eternal conflict between pleasures of the flesh and the voices of reason and piety. It is best known as portrayed in Pieter Breughel the Elder's painting of the same name. Associated with Carnival were ham, fat, sausages, food delicacies of all sorts, gambling, games, phallic symbols, fertility, basic bodily functions, everything that was down-to-earth and unpretentious. Associated with Lent were emaciated figures, monks and nuns, abstinence, piety, fish and foods without fat, water in place of wine, everything that was pious, serious, and austere. Of course, the full expression of this rich allegorical language only appeared in cities where elaborate costumes and allegorical floats were feasible, often organized by elite societies of misrule. A small village would not have all these trappings. But even the smallest community could have music, dancing, and drinking, and, as we have seen, even in small places like Sennely the inhabitants could experience personally the dramatic contrast between a joyous Carnival and a somber forty days of Lent.

Similar festivities were reproduced on a lesser scale on many other holidays. They were inherited, if not from the Roman Saturnalia, at least from medieval practices such as the Feast of Fools when the priests were mocked, profane acts were committed in the church, and a choir boy was named bishop. Carnivalesque activities encompassed both an element of letting off steam, and a lifting of restraints that opened the door, temporarily, for criticism of the existing order. They evoked an imaginary world – "the world turned upside down," in which children became priests, beggars became emperors, men dressed as women, and women ruled men. On other occasions such as All Saints' Day, the Feast of Saint John the Baptist, and the Feast of the Assumption (August 15), the same celebratory motifs reappeared, often carried out, but on a smaller scale, by youth groups. They were also manifested in the practice of "charivari" or "rough music" in which a person viewed as violating community norms was serenaded with the banging of pots and pans or other noisemaking outside his window until he paid the demonstrators a tribute. Sometimes he (or a surrogate) was ridden backwards on an ass through town amidst catcalls and mockery. The participants often wore masks and costumes, and the tone was similar to the mockery at Carnival.

This custom apparently originated in the late middle ages as a protest by the unmarried youths of the town against widows who remarried during the year when they were supposed to be in mourning.[13] It was gradually extended to older men who married young wives, women who beat their husbands, or men who were dominated by their wives, until ultimately the objective might entail any number of grievances against a local individual. The charivari was part playful entertainment, part social ostracism. It operated, like so many local customs, according to unwritten rules. If the victim responded in the correct, conciliatory way, the matter was supposed to be settled and a conflict put to rest. This noisy demonstration was a settling of scores and a form of community negotiation. But the confrontation was crude and could easily lead to hot tempers and violent conflicts that ended badly.

In 1786, in the Périgord, a certain Antoine Larfeuil, returning from hunting with a friend, was accosted by a group of harvesters who apparently had a grudge against Larfeuil, who was a "bourgeois." They challenged him to compete with a very large woman in a test of strength, and she easily threw him to the ground, amidst much mirth. This tale became the subject of ridicule in town. The next Sunday a group of some fifty villagers, principally young men, accosted Larfeuil when he was coming out of the church and followed him home, making a racket with horns, drums, and pots and pans. His friends advised him to "give this troop of people an *écu* and a pail of wine to make them stop the charivari." But he adamantly refused, and the noise continued outside his house until midnight. Finally he agreed to provide them all with food and drink at the local tavern. This should have ended the conflict, but the group was apparently angry at this long resistance because the next Sunday after church a group of hecklers "formed the plan to seize him, dress him in a ridiculous manner, mount him on a donkey and promenade him through three or four neighboring parishes." This whole episode must have been the expression of some longer-term antagonism between the ordinary residents and a prosperous neighbor.[14]

Popular honor and popular violence

In their relations with one another, the French people behaved in ways that might seem surprising to modern observers. On the one hand, they were extremely defensive of personal honor, and their attitudes toward physical and verbal violence were significantly different from ours. On the other hand, they had a common language of ritual behavior which made possible a real collective solidarity. Their annual cycle of festive celebrations tied them closely to the rhythms of nature and connected them to a part-magical, part-Christian worldview that gave meaning to their lives and helped explain their misfortunes. As individuals they interacted belligerently, but as participants in common rituals they experienced a bond which drew them together even while enforcing conformity at the expense of outsiders. Their sensitivity to honor, their relationship with violence, and their collective rituals all strengthened their acceptance of a world dominated by hierarchical differences. Consciousness of personal honor gave everyone a stake in society by telling even the most humble that they were more honorable than someone below them and that being deferential toward superiors earned them favor and a bit of reflected glory.

French society was deeply influenced by what has been called a Mediterranean sense of personal honor and shame.[15] Day-to-day relations involved a constant sparring over reputation. Men were expected to respond actively to any sign of disrespect. They retaliated in response to any violation of personal space by lashing out at the intruder. When they were the initiator, they made a point of demonstrating their superiority over those of lesser status by exacting signs of deference. This maintenance of "face" could only be real if affirmed by third-party onlookers. Honor was dependent on what others thought. Conflicts of honor therefore had to take place in public view, before witnesses. By contrast, women's honor was closely tied to their sexual reputation, both as unmarried virgins and as faithful wives. Their influence in maintaining the household and training the children – the boys until age seven when they were taken over by the men, and the girls until marriage – transmitted to everyone a common moral grounding that men supplemented with later experiences outside the home. Women's sense of values greatly influenced everyone else. They were outspoken in objecting to perceived injustice, but when it came to action, they usually had to let their fathers or husbands take the lead and depended on their men to defend their reputations from slanderous attacks by other men. They quarreled vigorously with other women and took sides in defending their husbands and families.

Male honor, once damaged, was not easily repaired. Initial conflicts turned into long-lasting feuds between families, and grudges were not easily forgotten. In 1674, peasant François Hughes was driving his wagon home from Dijon in a convoy of carters when Claude Courtot, another peasant, suddenly came up to him cursing and threatening: "By the death of Our Lord, here is the bugger who insulted my father and me in court!" Courtot pulled Hughes from his wagon, punched and kicked him, hit him on the head with a rock, and left him all bloody until others intervened. Hughes claimed, probably tongue in cheek, that he had no idea why he had been attacked. More likely their quarrel had a prior history. Bursts of indignant rage were common. When Dijon innkeeper Claude Jourdan was challenged by a group of city officials for illegally displaying and selling prepared meats outside his establishment, Jourdan, aided by his wife, grabbed the meats and shouted that "by Our Lord's death, there is NO WAY they are going to take these meats from me...fuck you Clemandot!

[the official] I won't be screwed by all these *échevins* and sergeants who are devouring the city."

Revenge taking was just as common among the more educated. In 1651 Barthélemy Camus, *avocat* in the Parlement of Dijon, confronted François Poussot, *échevin* of the city, in the great hall of the Parlement. "Assuming an arrogant posture, overcome with rage ...he put his hand on his hat and said to me, smirking, 'thanks so much for the nice verdict you have given me.' You and your colleagues are great *jean-foutres*. By the Death of God himself, I will avenge myself, especially against you." Camus then followed Poussot all the way home, "uttering such filthy and vile things that loyal service forbids me to reveal them," adding "that we were all false judges, that we were robbing the city, and that we were rogues and tax extortionists."[16]

These sorts of conflicts were intentionally theatrical. In Paris in 1652 the wife of a public writer encountered a pawnbroker in the street. They chatted for a while, and then she said she would like to reclaim some items she had pawned. He replied that they were long gone. She insisted that he would have to get them back, but he retorted that she should have reclaimed them sooner, and anyway "old tarts like her" could "go to hell." She rejoined that retrieval had been impossible because he had been in prison for two years. Responding in kind, he noted that she had been arrested ten times for prostitution, and he could have all the women he wanted at her place whenever he wanted (sexual insult). He thrust his fist in front of her face (invasion of private space); she pushed it away; he slapped her. A soldier finally broke them up. As David Garrioch notes,

each move in this dispute was staged for maximum effect. The voices were gradually raised, a signal for the passers-by to gather around. Their attention attracted, open insults broke out...Her moving off was both a sign of contempt and a measure of prudence, but it also provided the maximum audience possible and gave her the appearance of the innocent victim, pursued by the aggressor. Then there is the threat of violence as he shakes his fist under her nose, and pushing the fist away provides the actual physical contact which permits the escalation to the next stage, the slap.[17]

In 1695 when authorities in Agen tried to impound the furniture of a royal officer, the sieur Despallais, who had refused to pay certain official fees, Despallais replied "that one did not treat a man of his condition in this manner and that he would see this comedy brought to an end." He leaned out his window and shouted to his wife who was stationed at the door to tell the neighbors that his furniture was being seized. As the process-server later reported, "Instantly his house was filled with people armed with iron bars, clubs, and swords, and sieur Despallais grabbed our person, calling us a rascal of a puny process-server, kicking us with his feet and exclaiming 'here is the rogue who is demanding an *écu* for not selling my furniture.' "[18]

Early modern people had a tolerance of physical violence that is unsettling to us. They lived in a world much closer to nature, where the slaughter of animals was an everyday experience, where plague and misfortune descended suddenly and inexplicably, bringing death, where official executions of malefactors involved the searing of flesh, the breaking of bones, and the strangling of necks. It was a society in which assembled crowds, if angry enough, could dig up a corpse, rain it with blows, disembowel it, and drag the body face down through the streets, while proudly displaying its liver and heart. In 1767 fifty Burgundian villagers, men, women, and young girls, attacked the tax collection agents of the monks of the abbey of Citeaux, throwing rocks, brandishing farm implements, shouting "There they are, the dogs; let's kill them and disembowel them with our pitchforks." In Arras in 1688, 800 people gathered in front of the office of tax sub-farmer Cottet crying, "There he is! Knock his wind out, slit this thief's throat!" They pushed around his wife and clerks, smashed all his windows with rocks, tore down the panel displaying the royal insignia from the facade, ripped it into pieces, and paraded the pieces triumphantly through the town for hours.[19]

These incidents should not be taken at face value. Although dragging and disemboweling did occasionally occur, most of the time it was just talk, and in the cases cited above, none of the dire threats were carried out. Ordinary people were much more willing than we would be to kick and bruise, and they were unperturbed by nasty brawls, bloodshed or display of body parts. But they were not nearly as bloodthirsty and barbaric as they might have appeared. Most violent confrontations followed unwritten rules, and once the accepted level of punitive violence had been reached, things would somehow come to a halt, through the intervention of neutral third parties or by attempts at community arbitration.

In confrontational situations insult was the primary weapon. It was effective because a well-placed insult was just as humiliating to an opponent as a physical attack. The many curses and threats that were constantly uttered are not to be taken literally. Verbal attackers used language associating their victims with the beggars and criminals so detested and feared by society. Sacrilegious curses damned society's most sacred references – the crucifixion, the blood of Christ – to emphasize the depth of the curser's contempt. Males would be accused of dishonesty, fraud, insolvency, cuckoldry, larceny, and servile status, and denounced with terms like beggar, rogue, vagabond, and bastard. Females would be charged with sexual promiscuity, prostitution, or uncleanliness, and called whores, witches, and jailbirds. All these categories associated the enemy with conditions that everyone feared – poverty, insecurity, homelessness, cuckoldry, unfaithfulness, or disease. Insults could also be delivered through physical gestures. The slap, the refusal to take off one's hat, knocking someone's hat to the ground, the thumb to the nose, the baring of the bottom, the displaying of horns, were classic rejoinders.[20]

Local people evaluated conflicts from the perspective of their own reputations or their ties of loyalty to others, little swayed by abstract higher principles such as civic duty or the letter of the law. When a severely beaten stranger begged for assistance, men passing by might not feel at all obligated to help him unless for some reason they owed him support. Women, on the other hand, were more likely to express some sympathy by making the victim a little more comfortable, wiping off his face, or giving him a drink. As women, they could do this without becoming implicated in the affair, whereas a man would have had to take sides.[21]

Similarly, personal feuds often led to brawls, especially after bouts of drinking. Such disputes were judged by onlookers according to the community's opinion of who was in the right. Unlike a barroom brawl today, when the antagonists are asked to "step outside" with the presumption that a fair fight will ensue, an offended party, even if physically weaker, would throw down the gauntlet by issuing a verbal curse: "From this moment on be assured that I will harm you, and those close to you, and your property, and your honor." After delivering such a warning, the offended party felt justified in gathering his friends and relatives, attacking the enemy with superior force, even ambushing him in the dark.[22]

Although the royal courts were gradually gaining greater acceptance among the population, common wisdom still maintained that the community knew best. Local observers made their own judgments about the merits of a case and paid little attention to the official rules. An appeal to royal courts allowed outsiders to resolve local issues according to arbitrary rules that were not endorsed by the local people. Disputes were best solved by community arbitration, they thought, and private vengeance, even violent retribution, was justified if the victim deserved it. To appeal to the courts was considered expensive and unneighborly. It was a step taken as a last resort, or as a tactic in the process of bargaining.

Culture of the traditional nobility

Although the nobility was considered the "second estate" and enjoyed distinctive legal advantages, what it meant to be a noble depended on your point of view. To some it meant an ancient, distinguished pedigree, to others a certain elegant style of life. It was also a legal status entailing certain privileges. But nobles all shared at least a general belief in their superior birth, military courage, and a right to command, and much of the rest of society accepted this view. As the sycophantic historiographer of Toulouse put it around 1540, "the nobles are the butter and the cream of the milk of the Republic. Take them away and what remains would be dry like bad cheese, bad smelling from rusticity, arid for lack of the civility that is cultivated among nobles."[23]

Traditional nobles thought of themselves as honorable men who stemmed from distinguished lineages, men noted for their courage and their natural capacity to command others. Eventually, the more distinguished noble families also came to see themselves as pace-setters in fashion and monitors of taste in the arts. But for the general population a distinct respect for the high-born was accompanied by the conviction that the nobles encountered in everyday life could be lawless, violent, and oppressive.

It is possible to imagine ordinary gentlemen favorably as genial rural citizens. In their heyday during the period 1450–1600, a typical local noble was likely to spend most of his time thinking about maintaining his family's reputation, marrying his sons and daughters, and managing his properties. He was probably, though not necessarily, literate, but he did little reading. He would greet his tenants by name as he rode around inspecting his crops, and he would be a visible presence in the village, intervening in meetings of the village house-holders and drinking in the local tavern. He might well participate in local athletic contests and appear at markets and religious ceremonies. He would give refuge to the villagers in time of insecurity, aid the needy, and stand as godparent to babies born in the village.[24]

Such gentlemen were avid hunters and jovial companions. They would enjoy hearty meals with friends that might include "a large platter of beef, mutton, lamb, and bacon and an armful of herbs cooked together, making a life-giving stew." This emphasis on consuming meat would have separated the noble host from his peasant neighbors. Table manners would be primitive. Hosts used a common bowl into which everyone dipped their knives and fingers, and eating utensils like forks and spoons had not yet become fashionable. Pierre de Vaissière describes a meal around 1541 in which,

the cousin of the seigneur de Fontenay, arriving for a visit and finding the whole household at table about to devour a large cod "since it was a day of abstinence," without further ceremony grabbed "a chunk of the cod with his fist" and squeezed it so hard that "the butter came through his fingers and ran down his chin" then, without even wiping his still-greasy mouth, he picked up his host's glass and took a drink.[25]

For many, however, the local lord was not this amiable partner but rather a detested tyrant. Like any landlord, such country squires were in a position to be cruel. They collected rents and dues from their tenants. They claimed jurisdictional rights over property transfers, markets, road maintenance, and planting dates. Through their seigneurial court they had the last word on many local disputes concerning property and injuries. They had an exclusive right to hunt in the local forest, and they claimed special recognition of their superiority in church. Theirs was the right to sit in the front pew, to be greeted by the curate at the door of the church, to receive the holy water in a goblet instead of by sprinkling, to be buried inside the church. These were all reasons for the villagers to dislike their lord, and innumerable riots and lawsuits prove that they often did.

Nobles at all levels identified with military traditions and proudly passed down stories of the valiant wartime deeds of their ancestors. Behind the chivalric glow, however, was much ugly behavior, especially during the civil wars that erupted periodically between 1562 and 1653. Independent commanders carried out private retribution

Figure 26 Another Callot engraving, *The Duel*, portrays two noble combatants fighting for their honor with an elegance and grace that probably reflects more the combatants' idea of a duel than the real event, which would have been messier.

against enemies by demolishing their castles, pulling up their vines and burning their fields. The band of a captain Merle terrorized the Auvergne and Gévaudan and sacked four cities. In 1579 a Protestant nobleman named Laprade occupied the fortress of Chateaudouble in Dauphiné and massacred the women and children of several villages when the Protestants refused to accept his leadership.[26] There were instances of vindictive mutilation. At the battle of Jarnac in 1569, the prince de Condé surrendered to the forces of the duc d'Anjou, who was his arch enemy. He was promptly shot in the head by one of Anjou's aides. Then, in a gesture similar to a popular charivari, Anjou paraded his body around on the back of an ass to celebrate his triumph and Condé's humiliation.[27]

It is well known that early modern nobles were noted for dueling. François Billaçois has shown that duels were a growing plague that culminated in the deaths of thousands of noblemen. The custom originated in Italy and appeared in France around the 1520s, multiplying rapidly after 1560 and peaking in the first half of the seventeenth century. Duels were essentially contests between two individual nobles. One man challenged the other because of a perceived attack on his honor. The offender then accepted the challenge of the offended. The terms of combat would be agreed upon by all parties, including the seconds of the combatants. In theory, a duel was a reasonable way of resolving a conflict over honor. It was relatively inexpensive in that no special equipment was required, and the odds of victory were determined more by skill than by the status of the combatants. Rules were followed, exchanges were courteous, and the source of conflict was resolved, satisfactorily for at least one of the parties.

In Italy, duels were normally fought only until the first spilling of blood. But French duels were habitually fought to the death, and were noted for their brutality. Sometimes the seconds fought as well. Around 1598 duels on horseback appeared, and in the reign of Louis XIII firearms began to be used instead of swords. Dueling originated among common soldiers and provincial nobles. It only gradually percolated up to the high aristocracy. As the custom spread it became a scourge. Rough estimates suggest that, at the rate of 175 deaths per 100,000 noble men, the death rate from dueling was higher than the murder rate in any modern society.[28] Victorious duelists faced a moral conflict. Christian charity suggested that once you had your opponent down, having preserved your honor, you should pardon him and show mercy. Pride and the intoxication of victory, however, tempted you to humiliate him further, force him to beg for mercy, inflict further pain, or finish him off in some brutal fashion.

When it comes to violence, as Stuart Carroll has demonstrated, duels were only the tip of the iceberg. For many nobles, violence was an accepted way of life and revenge a natural counterpart to their concern for honor. Life among the nobility was a constant dialogue in which one's place and reputation were tested by encounters of all sorts. Resentments over perceived slights or insults were remembered for generations, and whole lineages could be drawn into lasting feuds. Often duels were not the one-on-one combat of the ideal, but underhanded ways of exacting vengeance on one's enemies. Similarly, political factions, even the confessional rivalries of the religious wars, often concealed long-standing clan rivalries.

"An unshakeable belief in the right to violence lay at the heart of noble egotism."[29] Quarrels arose frequently over marriage arrangements, inheritances, insults and defense of honor, the placement of symbols of authority, jurisdictions, and control of territory. If questions of honor or family interest were at stake, nobles expected even distant cousins to join in seeking satisfaction or revenge. It was especially important for the retribution to take place before witnesses so that the threatened reputation would be corrected in the eyes of the public. Family counsels were often held to decide what steps to take in defending their members' honor against an enemy clan. When drastic action such as the murder of a rival was deemed necessary, families drew for support on relatives, servants, sometimes even hired assassins. In 1553, six years after he had been attacked by Quentin de Bethencourt, Louis de Poux gathered his brother, his brother-in-law, and his cousins in a church in the Beauvaisis and, "fired up and remembering the wrong done to him by Quentin," he gave a rousing pep talk: "My friends, over there is the knave who did me wrong. I beseech you that I may have my revenge."[30]

In Touraine in 1556, two du Reynier brothers, Gabriel and François, carried out a lengthy dispute over the inheritance of a certain property. Gabriel and sixty to eighty followers "armed with arbaletes, pistols, pikes and arquebuses" occupied a strategically placed mill. François responded by assaulting the mill with a force of fifty "gentlemen and laborers" wearing coats of mail, and carrying javelins, swords, daggers and pistols, all shouting "Flesh of God!, Blood of God! Bastards, you are all dead, kill them all! Kill them all!"[31]

Family rivalries could be passed down through decades or generations. In 1611, Balthazar de Gadagne, seigneur of Champroux, a powerful man in the Lyonnais, along with his two brothers and a troop of fourteen, attacked Jean-Louis de Lévis, comte de Charlus, a major figure in the Auvergne. Gadagne ambushed Charlus's hunting party and killed Charlus, his fifteen-year-old son, and a twelve-year-old page. This was no impulsive act of violence. The Gadagne and Charlus families had been feuding for a century. In an often-repeated pattern, their hatred intensified during the religious wars. Both were Catholic, but Charlus became a fierce commander for the Catholic League who terrorized his neighbors, while the Gadagnes supported the royalist position. In 1605, the two parties had been involved in a violent property dispute which was serious enough for Henry IV himself to intervene and arrange a settlement. In 1611, a legal dispute erupted once again between them over tithe rights and other issues. This time the duc de Nevers arbitrated a settlement, and the two exchanged the kiss of peace. But in the process Charlus insulted the Gadagne clan by insinuating that they were "descended from an Italian banker" (in fact, this was true). The settlement had not resolved this particular slight. Afterwards, Charlus continued to issue further insults. Considering this the last straw, the Gadagnes summoned their followers to a secret rendezvous in Paris where they planned the assassination. They gathered the fourteen men, along with Gadagne and his two brothers, and the whole troop traveled to the Bourbonnais and lay in wait until they could carry out the murders.

Operations like this put friends, especially young male clients, in a very difficult position. One of Gadagne's conspirators, Marc de Grivel, put considerable pressure on his client, nicknamed Cadet, taking him aside and urging him, "By God's death, Cadet, if you wish to do a good turn for your friends you can do it this hour" and promising that if he cooperated, "he would never lack for means ... and that he would give him whichever horse he wished from his stable, and gold and silver." In a situation like this, the client had to choose between engaging in a dangerous, potentially prosecutable murder operation or abandoning his patron. Cadet begged off and was sworn to secrecy.[32]

In this masculine world of blood and honor, women were sometimes victims, sometimes participants. They were, of course, subjected to all the patriarchal attitudes of the time, used as pawns in marriage alliances, shunted off to nunneries, forced to tolerate their husbands' affairs, and expected to maintain their own reputation for chastity and loyalty in marriage. A minor exception was that noble women in courtly settings were allowed to be seduced by men, provided the partner was of equal or greater status, and the matter was not made public in a way that would injure the husband's reputation.

There were many instances of daughters kidnapped and raped or held captive by fellow nobles. Sometimes kidnapping was a tactic used by relatives to save a woman from a worse fate. Often it was a ploy used by the kidnapper to acquire a socially desirable partner. If the suitor was of proper status, the family would often accept the fait accompli on condition of marriage. If he was not, it became a major insult to the family, requiring revenge. Women could not participate in the military exploits of the males, but they were known to be fiercely loyal to their lineage and could be as fierce as any man in calling for revenge. There were many dynastic matrons who played leading roles in determining family strategies, and of course women frequently stood in for their absent or dead husbands in defending castles, striking deals, and managing family affairs.

Parish churches were frequent scenes of violence because they were neutral ground, where feuding families had to sit in the same space during services, and because they were perfect places to catch your enemy by surprise. Churches were filled with signs of the preeminence of the local lord, such as a private pew, a family tomb, a private chapel, or a stained-glass window displaying the donor's coat of arms. In 1580, Guillaume Auber smashed the stained-glass window containing his rival's coat of arms in an apparent attempt to protect his rights of precedence. In 1610 two cousins embroiled in a precedence quarrel over seating arrangements in the chapel of Charné fought on the steps of the chapel. The first was killed, and the second was chased into the cemetery and run through with a sword, after which his body was dumped down the steps leading to the road.[33] In February 1619, four Bridier brothers and their followers ambushed their enemies from the la Philippières family by attacking them from behind the church vestry. After a gunfight, seven men lay dead, including members of both families and the church's prior.[34]

Tales like these come down to us either because they were prosecuted in court or because they were described in applications to the crown for letters of pardon. These sources inevitably emphasize the most dramatic cases. There is no way of measuring the typicality of such episodes. It is important to understand that while noble violence was unquestionably widespread, and clan rivalries lay behind many political struggles, this was not uncontrolled violence. While the worst cases led to murders, many others were resolved through the payment of reparations or through mediation by third parties. Contemporaries had a keen sense of the relative weight of different kinds of offenses and the corresponding gesture that would suffice for reparations. Although many of the most heinous crimes by nobles were actively prosecuted by royal authority, the guilty parties, if they were important enough, were often exempted or sentenced to mere exile for a reasonably short period, during which they lived happily in Brussels or Rome. After a suitable length of time had elapsed, it was possible to obtain letters of pardon from the king, provided a case could be made for self-defense or extenuating circumstances. And even when nobles were condemned to death, they usually disappeared into the back country, only to be reintegrated into society at a later date.

According to Carroll, this underlying culture of violence reached its heights during the religious wars and the royal minorities of the seventeenth century. There is no question that after 1660 violence was brought under control to some extent. However, it would be incorrect to believe that it was eliminated by the strong hand of Louis XIV. The depth of the problem is illustrated by the Grands Jours in Auvergne in 1665. A special delegation of judges from the Parlement of Paris was sent to the remote mountains of the Massif Central to bring law and order to a turbulent area. The judges found innumerable crimes to prosecute and issued many sentences, including the conviction of eighty-seven nobles for serious crimes. Among them was the marquis de Canillac who imposed extra taxes on his tenants and terrorized them with a band of twelve mercenaries who lived in his chateau. The comte du Palais sent his thugs to terrorize five process-servers who traveled a long distance to serve him with legal documents at his chateau. The baron de Senegas had committed two or three assassinations, exacted ransoms from his tenants, and imprisoned a hapless opponent in a wardrobe where the man could hardly stand, for several months. The marquis de Salers and his band of followers besieged an opponent in the upper room of a house, then broke through the roof and stabbed the man to death, gouging out his eyes.

Such atrocities seem anomalous in the more orderly world of Cartesian logic and the court at Versailles. And in a sense they were. There is no doubt that after 1660 the countryside was better policed, royal intendants in the provinces were more skillful at defusing potential feuds, and the king was able to convey effectively the message that blood should not be shed, especially not near the presence of the king. The higher nobility, especially those at court and in Paris, were becoming more sophisticated and better educated. Many of them were touched by the moralism of the Catholic reformers. But there were allegedly 600 duels fought during the personal reign of Louis XIV, and the old nobility's intense focus on honor, along with their casual view of violent means, died very slowly. Being courteous was perfectly compatible with being violent. We should not confuse civility and courtly manners with the extinction of violent mores.[35]

The political culture of the grandees

France's highest noble families shared the same violent tendencies as their lesser counterparts, but they had a somewhat different outlook derived from their distinctive upbringing and broader perspective. Their personal relations were tied to a broader political consciousness as they wielded the tools of power in competition with the king's administrators and the people's protests. These grandees had grown up as pages in the households of other great nobles. From an early age they had learned not only how to compete in the arts of war but also how to manipulate the subtle language of differential esteem. Noble parents were becoming aware of the need to prepare their sons for life in the world of the court and the courtier. As pages, their sons learned how to address superiors, how to keep their emotions in check, and how to eat at the great table where etiquette was rigid. They developed an acute sense of where they stood in the hierarchy of loyalties and what this meant in terms of relations at court. They also established lifelong friendships with their peers and acquired permanent animosities.

The political arena was dominated by these noble leaders and their many followers. The world, as they saw it, was populated not with institutions and processes, but with struggles between themselves and their rivals. The appointments, army commissions, or marriage alliances that everyone needed for advancement were all achieved through direct personal contacts. Bonds between patrons and clients were sealed by face-to-face declarations of loyalty. They were confirmed by positive supportive actions and lubricated with ongoing exchanges of courtesies. Unlike the feudal ties of an earlier period, these were not necessarily life-long arrangements. The network of loyalties was always in flux. Clients bargained for better patrons, and patrons strove to enhance their influence by increasing the number of followers they could summon up. Underlings who needed favors had to demonstrate their loyalty to their patrons periodically, and patrons who wanted to keep their followers had to earn their support with continuing favors.

When a follower became disillusioned with the support he was receiving from a patron, he might issue a *défi* or denunciation, which had the effect of diminishing the standing of the patron and raising the stature of the protester. Here is how the vicomte de Turenne threatened to break with the duc d'Anjou in 1575:

He went "to find Monsieur in his quarters accompanied by three hundred gentlemen or captains." Anjou had just gotten up from eating. "I made a reverential gesture," recounts Turenne, "and asked him to be so kind as to recall how, during the times when I had served him, there had been nothing that I owed to my king, my life, or my worldly goods that I would not have sacrificed to serve him... that if I had ever done him the slightest injury I would have preferred complaining of my own misfortune at being ignored by him; that I had come to take leave of him and withdraw to Guyenne with all the men he could see before him, all of whom would affirm that they considered my unhappiness to be completely justified and that their expectations for the service they had rendered had proved to be totally ill founded." The gentlemen accompanying him then followed him out, and one of them, François de Beaulieu, added, "this is what you are losing when you lose Monsieur de Turenne."[36]

Thus the great nobles had a culture built upon personal rather than institutional relations. However, viewed another way, the grandees were very much involved in the politics of governing. They considered themselves part of the state, and they expected to wield important influence and to enjoy considerable behavioral latitude. Ideally, they thought, the leading nobles should sit in the royal council, or they might be consulted through an Estates-General or an Assembly of Notables. When grandees rebelled it was usually because they were not receiving the respect they expected. Grandees took up arms over factional splits within the government, opposition to royal religious policies, lack of participation in royal decision-making, and the apparent tyranny of cardinals Richelieu and Mazarin. The classic strategy was to leave court with much fanfare and retire to one's lands, implying that rebellion might follow. Faced with this prospect, rulers flattered the nobles and worked hard to bolster their grandeur without allowing them to threaten the power of the state. As Henry III put it in 1577: "inasmuch as the nobility is my right arm and the foundation on which I must rest the preservation of my authority, I want to devote all my power to maintaining them in their rights and preeminences."[37]

But if the king was vulnerable with regard to the regional grandees, they in turn felt threatened by two parallel developments. One was the growing necessity of cultivating relations with powerful people in the royal entourage in order to obtain the appointments that were increasingly obtainable only from the king, such as military commissions, governorships of provinces and fortresses, judicial titles such as *bailli* or *sénéschal*, and appointments to high positions in the church. Success required cultivating the manners of the court, a process which required a certain retooling to turn medieval warriors into elegant suitors. A second threat came from the robe nobility and the emerging nexus of financial and professional families who were moving into royal officialdom. These people were well educated and highly skilled in the arts of governance. They had classical educations, they were great orators, and they understood legal conceptions and ways of conceiving of political power and governmental institutions. Their professional skills made the traditional nobility look ignorant and backward.

The response of the more successful sword families to these challenges was to adjust their sights and modify their behavior, largely through the education of the next generation. In changing course, they followed a distinctive path that adopted some of the practices of the professional classes without sacrificing their noble distinctiveness. At about age seven, noble males were given a tutor who trained them in basic literary skills. After a certain amount of Latin and grammar, emphasis was placed on "a curriculum based on useful knowledge and a pedagogy consistent with social grace, producing not pedants but aristocrats able to use knowledge in conversation to develop and maintain a variety of important personal relationships, and to apply their learning in military and political life."[38] After being socialized in a noble environment and learning the basic skills, they were sent to a *collège* where they could learn to hold their own against better-educated commoners. Instead of completing the full curriculum, they would be withdrawn after a year or so and placed in one of the noble academies that were proliferating in the late sixteenth and early seventeenth centuries. Younger sons who were destined for the church continued with Latin at the *collège* and went on to university. Daughters never had these opportunities. They were educated at home by tutors and rarely got very far with Latin, a prerequisite for any kind of public service.

Noble academies were private schools that taught horsemanship, along with dancing and fencing to develop grace and poise. At the academy, young nobles acquired a social veneer that was not available to sons of the middle classes. Body language, such as gait, posture, and gesture, was increasingly important in making a good impression at court, as was proper dress. In 1636 the future prince de Condé attended a Parisian academy accompanied by a servant, a squire, two pages, an accountant, four footmen, two valets, a coachman, a post-man, six riding horses and an administrative staff, all of whom lodged with him.[39] The academies also taught the math and engineering skills needed by military officers who dealt with fortifications. Adolescent pupils entertained themselves by gambling, fighting duels, disrupting theater performances, and frequenting prostitutes. In the course of the seventeenth century, Paris had at least seven such academies, the most famous of which was founded by Antoine de Pluvinel in 1594. There were some twenty more in the provinces. After a year or more at college and a similar period in an academy the young noble was ready to be presented to the king and to undertake a military apprenticeship.

By 1715 the lifestyles of the top layers of noble society had been considerably transformed. They had preserved their fortunes by managing their estates more effectively, by tapping into royal pensions and court offices, and by learning the fine art of courtly manners. They had taught their bodies to speak the courtly language of hierarchy and deference. All these activities had made them more dependent on the king and reduced their degree of individual initiative. Yet, paradox-ically, as Jonathan Dewald argues, the stifling distinctions of rank and intense competition for patronage with which they were forced to live may have caused some of the most sensitive to withdraw into a private world of individual expression, producing private memoirs and journals that were introspective and honest. A byproduct of this rising sophistication was that the high nobles began to believe even more in their own superiority and the inferiority of the common people. In Charles Sorel's novel *Francion* a discussion about sex illustrates this sense of superiority:

"Don't we do it just like the peasants? Why should we have other words than they do?" "You're wrong, Raymond," replied Francion, "we do it in quite a different manner, we use many more caresses than they, who have no other desire than to sate their brutal appetites, in no way different from that of the animals; they only do it bodily, while we do it with body and soul together."[40]

The court nobles also began to feel superior to their country cousins, the rural nobles. These poor gentlemen became the brunt of jokes, as seen in this published tale, written around 1711, which describes the arrival of three travelers at the "chateau d'Argiville" on their way to Falaise, where they met Monsieur and Madame d'Argiville, the lord and lady of this run-down farm:

He was of mediocre height, a great talker, excessively devout, sleazy, dressed half for the city, half for the country. His wife, fat and redheaded, was proud like a village dame who has never encountered anyone more distinguished than her exalted accountant... The compliments from our hosts were endless, since [words are] the one thing they have a plentiful supply of in the provinces. "I don't know, said monsieur d'Argiville, what I can offer you in the way of soup. Eight days ago I had the best partridges in the world and six bottles of priceless wine; you have caught us in a bad moment but we will do what we can... Quick, wife! Have some chickens killed."[41]

Clearly the socialization described by Elias was taking place, and the higher nobility were turning away even from the culture of their country cousins.

Conclusion

The most important noble figures were broadening their horizons to encompass more education, an appreciation of art and literature, adherence to strict rules of etiquette and subtle nuances of taste in dress and behavior. But they never completely abandoned their violent streak, and they continued to share a fundamental belief in their distinctive lifestyle and superior blood. Was, in fact, noble culture really so different from popular culture? Both believed in arranged marriage as an alliance between families and frowned on elopements and unions based only on mutual affection. Both placed primary emphasis on family and looked to even distant relatives to intervene in matters of inheritance, the guardianship of children, and marriage alliances. Both accepted the same gendered assumptions that wives and daughters should be controlled by husbands and fathers. Peasants and nobles were equally defensive of their honor and ready to resort to violence against the smallest slight, albeit not in the same manner. The vindication had to be before an audience of their peers in either case. Both were unfazed, up to a point, by physical brutality. Both were prone to bursts of defensive anger when insulted and skillful at verbal retaliation. In fact, the values of the nobility were remarkably parallel to those of the peasantry. Both translated their attitudes and beliefs into action in different ways which were modulated through vastly different levels of available resources and modified by different degrees of social pretension. Their fields of operation were also different. The angry peasant had his revenge in his fields or on the road, with the help of his son or cousin, in the presence of his neighbors. The angry noble laid siege to chateaux, fought duels, invoked a whole lineage. But both shared the same culture of honor defended, retribution exacted, and dependence on networks of loyal allies and family alliances.

Most interesting is the fact that both nobles and commoners shared a common attitude toward violence and retribution. They thought in terms of humiliating the enemy, and the form of humiliation could be either physical or symbolic, or both. Sometimes it took the verbal form of insults in which you declared exactly how you intended to treat the opponent. This approach was effective because it threatened honor just as much as did physical abuse. Sometimes it took a physical form in which the threats were literally carried out. In either case the rituals, spoken or acted out, were echoes of procedures understood through official forms of punishment or actual religious practices.

Angry individuals insulted their enemies by threatening to cut them open, dump their bodies, and feed them to dogs. Usually the outcome was a far more basic beating. In their most heated moments, enraged popular crowds actually chased, stoned, beat, dragged, or mutilated the bodies of victims. More often they limited themselves to dire threats. Nobles exacting revenge also displayed and dragged their opponents, dumped them in garbage heaps, fed them to dogs, denied them Christian burial. The main difference between popular and noble retribution may have been that popular crowds only reached this stage on rare occasions and resorted more often to verbal threats, simple blows, and damage to property, whereas military nobles had more opportunities to inflict physical punishment, and they were better equipped and armed. In both cases the object was humiliation of the enemy. In both cases a common acceptance of revenge and a complacency toward physical violence sets them apart from our sensibility. But we must remember also that in both cases brutality was not the norm and many stages of accommodation and mediation were also in play.

A final distinction might be that a humiliated noble had more to lose than a humiliated commoner, because although both suffered damaged reputations, the noble had more at stake. His honor involved not just defending his personal autonomy, but also maintaining his noble power to command and his capacity to enhance his family reputation by dying a glorious and courageous death. Whereas the angry crowd mutilating the tax collector was simply insulting his corpse as an added expression of their contempt for his behavior, the noble executioner was depriving his enemy of his heroic autonomy. He was killing the essence of the man's nobility and not just his body.[42]

Suggestions for further reading: traditional culture

Popular culture – general

Burke, Peter, *Popular Culture in Early Modern Europe* (New York, 1978).

Davis, Natalie Zemon, *"The Reasons of Misrule" in Society and Culture in Early Modern France* (Stanford, CA, 1975), 97–123.

Galpern, A. N., *The Religions of the People in Sixteenth-Century Champagne* (Cambridge, MA, 1976).

Muchembled, Robert, *Cultures et société en France du début du XVIe siècle au milieu du XVIIe siècle* (Paris, 1995).

Reinhardt, Steven G., *Justice in the Sarladais 1770–1790* (Baton Rouge, LA, 1991).

Honor and violence

Carroll, Stuart, *Blood and Violence in Early Modern France* (Oxford, 2006).

Castan, Yves, *Honnêteté et relations sociales en Languedoc (1715–1780)* (Paris, 1974).

Greenshields, Malcolm, "Women, Violence and Criminal Justice Records in Early Modern Haute Auvergne (1587–1664)," *Canadian Journal of History* 22 (1987), 175–94.

  An Economy of Violence in Early Modern France: Crime and Justice in the Haute Auvergne, 1587–1664 (University Park, PA, 1994).

Traditional aristocratic values

Billaçois, François, *The Duel: Its Rise and Fall in Early Modern France* (New Haven, CT, 1990).

Dewald, Jonathan, *Aristocratic Experience and the Origins of Modern Culture: France, 1570–1715* (Berkeley, CA, 1993).

Elias, Norbert, *The Civilizing Process: The History of Manners*, trans. Edmund Jephcott (New York, 1978).

Motley, Mark, *Becoming a French Aristocrat: The Education of the Court Nobility 1580–1715* (Princeton, NJ, 1990).

Neuschel, Kristin, *Word of Honor: Interpreting Noble Culture in Sixteenth-Century France* (Ithaca, NJ, 1989).

10 | Emerging identities – education and the new elite

A dynamic element in the slowly evolving traditional culture of everyday rituals and noble domination was the impact of education. As literacy spread, France was gradually moving from a society where most important experiences were perceived orally and visually, to a society where written texts were of vital importance. In the fifteenth century most people learned through their ears and eyes and through the ongoing verbal communication of parents and neighbors. Their conception of saints and Bible stories was drawn from carvings on church facades and medallions in stained-glass windows. For them, the Catholic Mass was a mystery unfolding in the front of the church, to the sound of bells and the smell of incense. They learned about social hierarchy from differences in clothing fashions and from the order of dignitaries in public processions.

Contrast this situation with the profusion of written texts in the seventeenth and eighteenth centuries. Printed edicts posted on walls in great numbers announced new taxes and official regulations. Notarial documents which seemed mysteriously powerful to those who could not read them were essential tools in property settlements and legal quarrels, as were the signatures of the affected parties. Tax farmers arrived in town with sheafs of documents duly notarized and sealed, bearing dreadful news about sums owed. Royal officials wielded archives full of written information concerning forests, values of offices, grain supplies, and the loyalties of every important person. Clearly the ability to sign, to read, even to write, was becoming ever more important.

Lacking a better method, we fall back on measuring literacy by counting the percentage of people who did or could not sign a given set of sources. This is tricky because a man who could sign could not necessarily read, much less write. Many just left their "mark." Using this definition it appears that a significant minority of the French – something like a third – were literate, and this included a number of

Figure 27 As we have noted (see Figures 6, 19, 24), Jean Burel was a tanner from Le Puy-en-Velay whose family kept a chronicle of the events of the day. Modest artisans could be literate. This sample page shows their handwriting. The drawings depict two Protestant captains who besieged the city.

artisans and ordinary laborers. But the disparities were striking. North of a line drawn from Saint-Malo to Geneva, men had 44 percent literacy in 1690, while south of that line the figure was only 17 percent. In earlier centuries the numbers would of course have been lower. Women always had much lower rates, usually half or less than half those of men. There was a considerable improvement by the eighteenth century. By 1790, 71 percent of the men in the northern half of France were literate, but only 44 percent of the women. In the southern half, men were 27 percent literate and women 12 percent. Towns were always significantly more literate than the countryside, and within a town there was a dramatic contrast between rich and poor neighborhoods. In Provence the large towns had over 50 percent masculine literacy and the small towns, 15–30 percent.[1]

How did these people learn to read? Well-to-do families hired a tutor who taught the rudiments of Latin and grammar to the children, or at least the boys, at home. More modest families had to rely on primary schools created when communities hired a schoolmaster, usually a local priest or a young university graduate, to teach basic reading and arithmetic to children aged seven to fourteen. The remuneration was usually minimal, and the personnel changed frequently, so these "petites écoles" were ephemeral. There was no wider system of schools, but there was at least a realization, in the age of the French Renaissance, that reading and arithmetic were necessary practical skills. Girls were not always included, but some schools allowed both sexes, so that girls could also acquire some basic skills. Schooling was far from universal. Where we have surveys of whole districts, it appears that something like half the communities had primary schools. Once again, coverage was denser in the north than in the south.[2]

France had fourteen universities in the sixteenth century,[3] each of which consisted of a faculty of arts and one or more of the higher faculties of theology, law, or medicine. Some were known for specialties, such as Montpellier for medicine, Toulouse for Roman law, and Paris for theology. Unlike their modern counterparts, these universities had no campuses. They consisted of a collection of eminent doctors, "nations" of students, teachers of lesser skills, and residential *collèges*. All these elements were protected by an overarching charter granting special exemptions and privileges to a given university. Diplomas were becoming necessary for important positions. The

Pragmatic Sanction of 1438 stipulated that one-third of the church benefices of the kingdom should go to university graduates, and the Concordat of 1516 required bishops to have a degree in either theology or law. Louis XI added that his judicial officers also had to have law degrees. The universities were traditionally under the jurisdiction of the church, but the king and the Parlements were increasingly issuing directives which intervened in their functioning. By the sixteenth century, many faculties were becoming little more than diploma mills for sons of the upper classes on their way to professional positions. Discipline and scholarship were in decline, and the curriculum was dependent on tired scholastic methods and old-fashioned ideas.

Each university had an arts faculty that provided basic training in Latin grammar, mathematics, and philosophy. Students started at around age fourteen. The majority of them were housed in endowed foundations called *collèges*, which provided lodging and offered basic instruction in the liberal arts, each with its own rules and procedures. Paris had fifty of them. Rich students often brought along tutors who looked out for them. Fees were charged for instruction and for the issuing of degrees. Getting educated was a rather unstructured process, and the quality depended on who one studied with and how diligent one was. Some degrees were more or less purchasable without much actual study.

The problem for many ambitious parents was that they had to send their sons to a distant city at age thirteen or fourteen where they would be on their own. Awareness of the rising importance of legal expertise and humanistic learning for careers led many towns to set up their own municipal grammar schools, so that this basic training could be acquired closer to home. They acquired space in old hospitals or monasteries and hired instructors to teach Latin and grammar. Meanwhile in Paris a few *collèges* were adopting a new rigorous style of curriculum that was initiated by the Brothers of the Common Life in the Netherlands. As this method spread to other cities, a revolutionary new institution was created – the municipal *collège*.

Students were divided into classes according to levels of skills. The curriculum was organized into sequential units and taught in discrete, digestible portions. The whole program was conducted in purified classical Latin. Discipline was strict. Students followed a tight daily schedule, going from classroom to classroom, and sitting on orderly rows of benches. At the end of each year there were final exams and ceremonies promoting the class to the next level. Students learned to reason, to speak eloquently, and to persuade. This was an ideal preparation for men who were going to reform the church, organize the state, and preside over the royal system of courts. It gave them a common frame of reference that separated them from their less-educated peers. As one graduate described it, "I learned to study, debate, and speak publicly, made the acquaintance of well-bred classmates, many of whom are still alive today, learned how to live frugally and how to manage my time."[4]

From the start, control of the *collèges* was controversial. The municipal decision to offer secular humanistic training was a progressive step·because it challenged the usual role of the cathedral chapter or the bishop. Conflicts over jurisdiction were frequent, and mixed clerical–lay boards of directors often had to be established. The issue became even more heated when the Huguenot challenge cast suspicion on humanist teachers suspected of heresy. Indeed, many of the instructors were influenced by the logic and humanistic bent of Calvinist teaching, compared to the backward methods of the clerical establishment, and there was a risk that they might influence their pupils. During the religious wars, the *collèges* became a major source of confessional conflict. Huguenots took them over in cities where they had the power, and set up their own Calvinist *collèges* in many other places.

Once the Catholics were back in control, many city councils, unwilling to deal further with the funding problems and doctrinal complexities of running *collèges*, happily turned their schools over to the Jesuits, who were eager to gain control over such strategically placed institutions. In 1572 there were twelve Jesuit *collèges* in French territory, and by 1640 there were seventy. Although rival Catholic authorities in the universities and other religious orders tried to block the Jesuit fathers, the Jesuits' educational program was very popular with parents. Since their instruction was free, an immense problem of financing and monitoring was solved for the cities. The Jesuits' teaching program stressed the classical heritage and the humanist skills needed for professional advancement, but joined to a rigid Catholic orthodoxy that had been lacking in earlier *collèges*. This combination served the needs of ambitious families excellently.[5]

Women were excluded from *collèges* and universities. Common opinion was that they should be taught household skills, or at best learn how to complement their husbands in polite society. Certain humanists such as Vives and Erasmus thought that aristocratic women should learn Latin so that they could be truly cultivated. Certain learned women, such as Marguerite de Navarre, the sister of Francis I, and Madame de Sévigné at the time of Louis XIV, did learn to read Latin, but the opinion was virtually universal that Latin was not for them. Women learned privately at home, or as residents in convents, until the Catholic revival of the seventeenth century. At that time the Ursuline order of nuns established houses all over France which took in girls as *pensionnaires* and gave them educational training. They also set up outposts which taught the rudiments to girls free of charge. Several other religious orders of nuns also took up teaching functions. But these were small improvements. There was nothing comparable to the *collège* for women.

The culture of civic leaders

Those who mastered humanist education in the *collèges* or went on to professional studies in the university lived in a different mental universe from either the traditional nobles or the artisans and peasants. Some were priests who wanted to reform the church; others turned Calvinist. Many pupils of the Jesuits came from ambitious merchant families, and the majority were engaged in furthering themselves through state offices and state finance. The most accomplished derived a new consciousness from their classical training. They collected and read books, studied politics and statecraft, and savored contemplation and learning.

Education became the new strategy for social advancement. The most successful avenue was royal office, and the most important officers were the judges and presidents of the sovereign courts. These men combined great prestige and political influence with the eventual acquisition of nobility and the prospect of promotion into a powerful position in the government. The lesser corps of royal officers – *bailliages, sénéchaussées, trésoriers de France* – had similar influence in their own districts. Town elites now had two avenues of social progress: the lesser, more local route through municipal office; and the greater, more national route through royal officeholding.

The "lesser" group was made up of proud citizens who took on the responsibility of governing their own community. From 1400 to sometime in the later sixteenth century, the *échevinages*, *jurades*, or *consulats* were dominated by wealthy merchant families. Later on, the cities were increasingly taken over by legal-minded, humanist-educated individuals who held middling royal offices, provided legal services, or were simply independently wealthy. For example, Guy Saupin's study of Nantes shows that between 1598 and 1719, of the 249 nominees for mayor, 78.7 percent were royal judicial or financial officers and only 16.5 percent were merchants, and this in a commercial Atlantic port![6] Similar figures from Dijon show that of the 1,398 *échevins* who served from 1596 to 1667, 13.2 percent were royal officers and 48.4 percent were lawyers or legal aides, while only 8.3 percent were merchants.[7] In Paris, 61 percent of the ninety city councilors who served between 1535 and 1575 were high- and middle-level officers and royal officials.[8]

These hometown city fathers had a perspective that was very different from that of old nobles and royal officers. Their posts were elective and temporary, and they bore heavy responsibilities for actually making things happen. They were preoccupied with making budgets balance, carrying out public works, taxing the inhabitants, maintaining law and order, dealing with plagues and enemy invasions – all of which might be called "no-win" situations. It was in some ways a thankless job. Only temporarily in office, unpaid, and faced with weighty, unpopular decisions, they had few coercive tools at their disposal and no effective police force. If a disturbance broke out or an arrest was necessary, they had to rely on respect for the symbolic power of their insignia, or their personal prestige to enlist the cooperation of the perpetrators. If funds were short, they would probably be asked to open their private coffers and lend money to the city.

Échevins took on this risky role because the *corps de ville* was the highest civic position attainable and because they relished the influence it conferred on them. They proudly wore their ceremonial robes and never hesitated to dramatize their importance using every means possible. For example, in Lyon, the city consuls decorated their *hôtel de ville* with grandiose paintings representing the supposed foundation of Lyon by the Romans, and many other scenes from its long history. In their council room was a vast mural representing "the consular grandeur of Lyon," in which a woman representing the city and holding a cornucopia of plenty was surrounded by personifications of Justice, Currency Exchange, Industry, Force, Eloquence, the Nobility of the

Consuls, Charity, and Piety – an interesting mix of chivalric and mercantile values. In the foreground was the figure of "Magnificence" holding a map of the city.[9] Every year in Toulouse the eight capitouls who ran the municipal government commissioned a group portrait of themselves in full regalia and hung it in the Capitole, their pompous name for the city hall. In 1673 they added a wing called the "Hall of the Illustrious" which displayed busts of famous men from history along with the coats of arms of the eight capitouls of that year, all positioned opposite a colossal bust of Louis XIV.[10]

Such pomposity was understandable because the city fathers based their power more on reputation than on real coercive force. Their success depended on being held in respect by the citizens. They were consequently jealous of every bit of their symbolic authority, since any humiliation could undermine it. In public orations they emphasized the ancient origins of their power, and in their archives they carefully guarded the city's ancient charters, sealed with wax, and the weights and measures used to define local market standards. Large folio registers of council deliberations were bound in gilded leather like sacred relics.

Sooner or later most city councils had to confront some very difficult issues: which side to take when Protestant and Catholic forces were vying for control and how to keep the lid on disputes over toleration policies that no one liked; what to do when an epidemic of plague struck; how to raise the funds demanded by the king; how to defend a city besieged by an army. Perhaps the hardest question of all was which side to take when grandees began a rebellion and royal troops set out to quash it. Picking the wrong side might lead to dramatic retaliations against the city and death for its leaders. Most cities faced this choice in the 1590s and again during the Fronde. Given the fact that their posts were voluntary, and that the weight of legal business they handled was heavy, the city fathers had reason to be proud of their courage and resolution.

A central problem in towns was the constant bickering between rival agencies, all run by legal and professional men of similar background. From 1624 to 1627, the city of Dijon was engaged in more than thirty lawsuits against various other corporate bodies. Take, for example, an ongoing quarrel with the *bailliage* officers over who should present the incoming mayor with the symbols of office at his inauguration ceremony. Traditionally it was the city's *garde des évangiles* who did this, but the lieutenant-general of the *bailliage* was now claiming the right. The issue was who – the city government or the local royal court – had the higher claim to authority. As the city's lawyer argued, "if this were permitted it would destroy the *mairie*" because then the lieutenant-general "could claim that by virtue of confirming the election he would have jurisdiction over the [city] magistrature, which would cease to exist outside of his person."[11] In such quarrels both sides employed the thinking of legally trained citizens. It was people like this, trained in the *collèges*, who organized the city's affairs, fought its lawsuits, and planned most of the business of the city council.

Ideologically city leaders faced a contradiction of sorts. While they prided themselves on their defense of tradition and freedom of action, they also saw themselves as loyal subjects of the king, and much of their influence was dependent on royal favor. They were dependent on the monarchy to ratify their charters, finalize their election results, grant them concessions on taxes, authorize their projects, legitimize their guilds, protect their exemptions from trade restrictions and excise taxes, and lend them grandeur by association. Their proudest moments were the ceremonial greetings of kings and other dignitaries and their celebrations of national events like the birth of a Dauphin or a victory in battle.

The discourse by which they defined these relationships was a subtle way of influencing community opinion. During the crisis of the late religious wars, the city of Lyon had given its support to the Catholic League and its leader, the duc de Mayenne. But in 1594, when League fortunes were waning, a municipal uprising had overthrown the local supporters of Mayenne and swung the city over to Henry IV. As Yann Lignereux demonstrates, the city's leaders were presented with a dilemma. How could a city that had always claimed loyalty to the crown, and prided itself on its unity, justify to the king and to its own citizens such switches in allegiance? Pamphleteers quickly developed a language of otherness. The newly triumphant royalist rebels were recast as having courageously continued Lyon's long tradition of loyalty by being the first major city to declare for Henry of Navarre, while the Leaguers were portrayed as evil sorcerers who had enchanted the city and needed to be exorcised. What had been an abrupt about-face was turned into long-standing loyalty triumphing over malevolent forces.

On the day of the royalist coup, an enormous portrait of the king was hung from a window of the city hall, showing a recognizable Henry IV wearing full armor, in a triumphal pose, holding the symbols of majesty. This visual message had the effect of declaring the city's loyalty to the king while at the same time introducing him to local citizens who had not seen a portrait of him since 1589. He was presented as a recognizable individual to make clear to even the illiterate *which* king was being supported, and he was presented in a formal pose to show that he was *King* in the abstract and not just a usurper. The message was brought home with free banquets laid out in the streets to win support and to create an atmosphere of fête. Crowds were committed to the new loyalty by being encouraged to shout "Vive le Roi!" in front of the portrait. In a parallel message, city banners of white, the royal color, were displayed all over the city, while red and black scarves, the colors of Spain, were burned on public bonfires. These messages to the people were reinforced subsequently by publishing engravings depicting these same events, along with floods of portraits of the new king, showing him in victorious poses, but also portraying his aging face realistically to give personality to an otherwise abstract image.[12]

The bond was consolidated in 1695 when Henry IV actually entered the city. Royal entries required extensive planning. Long before, an *avocat* from the city was assigned to draw up a program, in collaboration with Pomponne de Bellièvre, who was serving as what we might call the king's "road manager." Experts were chosen to build the triumphal arches and other machinery needed for the entry, and a published narrative explaining how to interpret them was planned, along with engravings of scenes from the event. In the first phase, all the corps of the town would line up in rank outside the gates and there would be welcoming speeches. Cannons would fire, or fireworks would be set off. The head city official would deliver a harangue to the king and offer him the symbolic keys to the city. The people would shout "Vive le Roi." In the second phase, the king and his entourage would enter along a planned itinerary, stopping at a series of painted panels and passing through temporarily erected victory arches decorated with elaborate portrayals of mythical scenes and references to the king's life and accomplishments. In Henry IV's case, the first stop was a portrait of the king in a rustic setting, designed to convey his simplicity and closeness to the people. Then came seven stops each depicting one of the particular virtues of the prince: his clemency, his glory and valor, his trophies of war, his force, his generosity and constancy, his victories, and his distinguished ancestors. The message was hammered home again in 1598 when the city celebrated the peace with Spain, and in 1600 when another entry celebrated the marriage of Henry IV to Marie de' Medici. All these events were designed by the same municipal team led by *avocat* Pierre Matthieu. They conveyed a three-part message about the new king: that he brought reconciliation, that he was the legitimate heir, and that he was a true Catholic, exonerated by the pope.

Ceremonies of this kind served a dual purpose. On the one hand, they established a personal relationship between the king and the community. But, on the other, they were locally planned, with a program designed to solidify the allegiance of the crowds in the streets. In Dijon, as Michael Breen tells us, the entry of Louis XIII in 1629 was explicitly planned by two *avocat-échevins* to take political advantage of the king's presence. Louis XIII had recently defeated the Protestants in the long siege of La Rochelle. The parade's creators deliberately highlighted his severity toward a rebellious community because Dijon was itself faced with simmering popular unrest. Fears of insurrection were only too justified, as the serious Lanturelu uprising would show in 1630. One victory arch depicted the king as Apollo turning Niobe into a boulder because of her excessive pride, while noting that she stood for "rebel cities, both those that have been subdued and those which are yet to be subdued." Another arch represented Louis XIII as Augustus leading a rebel in chains and La Rochelle as Cleopatra being bitten by a snake, illustrating "divine vengeance and punishment for those who threaten the sanctity of kings."

In Dijon the designers intended that their message reach the populace. A week after Louis XIII's entry, the Mère Folle festive society put on a popular performance written partly in the local patois by the one of the designers of the royal ceremony. In it a pompous erudite who is scornful of the ignorance of two simple vinegrowers tries to explain to them the importance of the victory of La Rochelle. They have trouble understanding his fancy words, but eventually it turns out that they themselves participated in the royal entry procession and they had understood the message about the dangers of rebellion. The play ends with the two sides appreciating each other better and jointly singing the praises of the king. Thus the same message was transmitted in various "media." It was designed by local lawyers specifically for Dijon. A few days earlier, when the king had entered Troyes, the theme had been the city's love for the king, with no emphasis on the defeat of La Rochelle or the dangers of rebellion.[13]

Ceremonies were high points in the life of the civic authorities. They were organized not only for the rare visits of royalty, but also for a great many arrivals of other dignitaries requiring respect, such as bishops, governors, or military commanders. Each would receive a ceremonial welcome appropriate to the level of respect he deserved. In cities such as Dijon, Montpellier, or Rennes, where provincial Estates were held, the arrival of the deputies would require a flood of visits, compliments, and greetings. Then there were the annual religious festivities that also took place in the streets, plus special processions displaying holy relics, events that were organized in time of famine, drought, or plague to implore the Lord's mercy. On festive occasions the order would go out for citizens to decorate the facades of their houses or to illuminate their windows.

In eighteenth-century Toulouse, a chronicle of events kept by a resident, Pierre Barthès, between 1738 and 1780, gives us an idea of the impact of public events. The capitouls had to deal with the lodging of royal troops twenty-two times, often for ten months or more. There was significant flooding damage on twenty occasions, six prison breaks, two serious riots, and five hundred public punishments of criminals, mostly hangings. Most interesting are the seventy-two Te Deums celebrated, mostly for military victories or events in the life of the royal family, such as the recovery from an illness. These were command performances ordered by the king. They took place on two levels: for the people in the streets with fireworks and fountains flowing with wine; and for the capitouls and dignitaries behind closed church doors at the Te Deum Mass. Robert Schneider notes that, starting with Louis XIV, the length and magnificence of these public displays increased dramatically. There was a growing separation between the elite dignitaries meeting in the church and the people in the streets. The latter were increasingly treated to distractions, such as public dancing and boat races, that did not enlist their active participation, and that did not allow the crowd to experience the social hierarchy as they did when the city lined up by rank in traditional processions. The commoners were being turned into spectators, and the city magistrates were becoming agents in the transmission of royalist propaganda.

The culture of high officeholders

The officers in the sovereign courts were residents of this same city world. But their universe was broader, and they had different interests as a result of their relations to the king and their superior fortunes. In speaking of the robe, we will concentrate on the Parlements and specifically the leaders in the Parlement of Paris, although similar points could be made about the other sovereign courts. These judges had a dual identity. On the one hand, they were doctors of law who knew jurisprudence backwards and whose legal decisions enforced social norms and made crucial decisions about property, inheritance, and wardship. On the other hand, they had an opportunity to act politically when they monitored the king's legislation and when they issued directives concerning the "police" of their city and region.

The *parlementaires*, most of whom were wealthy and well connected, were men of great dignity. They appeared in imposing robes and delivered important rulings. They were scholars of the law who had the capability to handle abstract principles and apply them to specific situations. They were collectors of books, compilers of legal handbooks, and lovers of ideas. They were accustomed to delivering lengthy oral summations of the facts and principles involved in a particular case, without benefit of notes. Handbooks proclaimed that a good judge should be prudent at all times, weigh his words, never get angry or act wildly, shun luxury and vain pleasures, never accept gifts. He must wear his robes at all times in public and stick to dark clothing the rest of the time. Avoid idleness, added Nicolas Pasquier: "Let him pass from one exercise to the next, let one task succeed another in precise rotation, work coming after work." This somber advice, so reflective of the discipline learned in the new *collèges*, suggests a new definition of the virtuous man that is strikingly different from the military bravado and man-to-man loyalties that characterized the traditional noble ethic.[14]

The *parlementaires* perceived themselves as responsible caretakers of the public good. This role set them potentially in conflict with the grandees who also claimed to be working for the general interest but with very different goals in mind. *Parlementaires* were staunchly royalist. They believed fully in the authority of the monarch, but they saw themselves as participating with the king by giving edicts a critical reading and monitoring enforcement.[15] In a remonstrance in 1489 they even claimed that they shared "the sovereign justice of the realm, the true throne, authority, magnificence and majesty of the king himself."[16] This sort of pretension would not hold up. But *parlementaires* continued to scrutinize and remonstrate. The court was firm in its defense of the so-called Gallican church. As Nancy Roelker put it, "the Parlement of Paris was the chief embodiment of the nation's corporatist character and the sole reliable defender of all other *corps*. By the same token, the administrative autonomy of the French church – the Gallican liberties – was to be Parlement's special charge, to defend even, or perhaps especially, against the king."[17]

Most *parlementaires* lived in well-to-do neighborhoods not far from their *palais*. Traditionally they did not flaunt their wealth, and they lived modestly. Many walked to work in their robes. They had large libraries. We know from a study of some two hundred book collections left in wills between 1490 and 1560 that most of the books belonged to lawyers and judges and that some of these collectors owned three to five hundred books, mostly legal treatises. Among the non-legal books in private collections, the most common were the Bible, devotional manuals, and the works of Cicero, Vergil, Seneca, Plutarch, Aristotle, Thucydides, and Xenophon. Bolstered by material success, robe families carried out an immense land grab that transferred most of the best fields surrounding Paris and other *parlementaire* capitals to new urban owners. Meanwhile the judges responded to the growing magnificence of the royal court by expanding their demands for honorific privileges and extending their claims of precedence over other governmental bodies. The somber, conscientious judge of the sixteenth century was giving way to the elegant judge of the seventeenth.

As they contemplated their society, these influential jurists were increasingly conscious of the need for stronger measures to restore social order. During the religious wars and their aftermath, religious splits, factional feuding, wartime devastation, and conflicting loyalties had shaken everyone's allegiances. It seemed imperative to shore up hierarchy, make authority respected, and induce individuals to control their bodies and restrain their sexual impulses. There was a general move toward stricter rules and greater punishments. A chief cause of the problem for the judges, or at least a reflection of their own anxieties, was the unruliness of women, perceived as hot-tempered and unable to control their sexuality. If the Parlement of Dijon studied by

James Farr is any indication, these men's assumptions about gender can be read in their sentences. They began cracking down on morals even before the revived Catholic church took up the same cause. Episcopal officials began viewing sin no longer as alienation from the community requiring reconciliation, as in the medieval church, but as disobedience requiring punishment in order to save souls. The result was the criminalization of sin. If sins were crimes, then it was the duty of the courts to prosecute them. This impulse fitted nicely with the tendency to assert royal judicial control over matters traditionally judged in ecclesiastical courts. The Parlements began evoking to themselves cases concerning priests who lived with concubines or slept with parishioners. They stressed the necessity for daughters to be under the control of fathers or husbands. They prosecuted abortion, infanticide, and prostitution more vigorously.

La Roche-Flavin, whose description of *parlementaire* life was published in 1617, moaned that the sale and heredity of offices (the venality discussed in Chapter 5) was ruining the morals of the court. "These are young men without experience who are all too often the sons of important families or of councilors and the court settles for mediocre responses [in their entrance exam]." The reputations of the courts were also damaged by the crisis of the Catholic League when the judges in each court, like the town magistrates, faced the stark necessity of choosing sides between the League and Henry of Navarre. The Parisian *parlementaires* had to either support the seizure of power by the rebel Sixteen or flee the city and join a Parlement in exile that was loyal to Navarre. Provincial judges had similar problems, and deep animosities developed. In Dijon in 1595 when two such factions were reunited, the *procureur-général*, using strikingly gendered language, made a triumphant speech declaring that the royalists who had withdrawn were "the males" who had "rigorously" and "boldly" supported Henry IV, while the leaguers, "those who remained at home while the men were at war, who hatched, bred, gave birth to the surrender of the town, they are the females."[18]

Compared to the militaristic nobles, these *parlementaire* judges seem at first glance quite "modern." A closer look shows that they were often obsessed with honor and could be fanatical about issues of precedence. To read their deliberations is to move back and forth from the most solemn consultations to the most extravagant quibbling, and they seemed to see no contradiction in this behavior. Their personal loyalties sometimes overcame their sense of impartial justice. Their feuds reached the very chambers of the court. In 1641 Bernard de Segla, a senior councilor in the Parlement of Toulouse, was outraged when a clerk attached to *procureur-général* Saint-Félix refused to turn over some documents. Segla threw the clerk in jail. Deeply insulted, Saint-Felix rushed to the prison and forced the jailer to release his employee. Then he retaliated by coldly observing, in front of the entire *grande chambre*, that he had been looking the other way for years during Segla's bouts of gambling and excessive drinking.

Public ceremonies always led to personal quarrels over precedence. In 1663 during a religious service attended by the entire Parlement of Dijon, Madame Baillet, wife of a president in the court, demanded that Madame Jacob, wife of another president, be ousted from a seat which both claimed belonged to them by precedence. There was a scuffle in which Madame Jacob's valet, who was apparently helping his mistress grab the seat, struck Madame Baillet on the arm. In retaliation for this humiliation of a servant to a wife, President Baillet rallied five of his wife's brothers and brothers-in-law, all of them officers in the Parlement, and rushed in two carriages to Jacob's residence, where they stormed in and tried to grab the guilty valet, shouting threats and insults at Jacob. Jacob, who was protecting his valet by holding onto him, claimed he was struck by several blows and that his collar had been torn.

Parlementaires could be violent and lawless. In 1643 the Parlement of Toulouse was shocked to learn that Councilors Puymisson and Trelon, along with Puymisson's two younger brothers and the son of President Puget, had been part of a gang of young men from "the best families" attempting to rescue a young nobleman from city officials who had caught him in the act of raping a woman in broad daylight. The city protested that not only had officers from the Parlement caused a scuffle in which several persons had been injured, but Puget had taunted the capitouls that "they were only in power for one year, whereas his post was for life." A feud over jurisdictions followed.[19] In Aix-en-Provence, the Parlement engaged in serious resistance to the fiscally motivated creation of new "semester" chambers in the mid seventeenth century. In 1639 a tax farmer who was in Aix to purchase one of the controversial offices was murdered by six masked men. The grapevine attributed the deed to Louis de Saint-Marc and Louis Decormis, both officers in the Parlement of Aix who belonged to the party opposing the new offices. In 1648 similar masked men murdered another man who had come to the city to purchase an office. Again the suspects included several *parlementaires* and the son of the first president of the Cour des Comptes. In 1649 the same faction of *parlementaires* led a popular revolt in which some of them appeared in public armed, building barricades along with the people, and inciting the crowd to take over the city. They were still wearing their red robes.[20] In 1638 Philippe Giroux, a president in the Parlement of Dijon murdered Pierre Baillet, president in the Chambre des Comptes of Dijon, along with the servant who was accompanying him. Giroux was the lover of Baillet's wife, Marie Fyot, who was the daughter of the dean of the Dijon Parlement and who may have known about the plot to murder her husband.

These are extreme cases, but they reflect a *parlementaire* mentality that was decidedly different from the life of careful jurisprudence and sober judgment. Like kings who were capable of ordering the assassination of favorites or rivals with impunity, the royal judges operated in a mental universe laced with pride of station, loyalty to friends, and justifiable revenge against enemies. Some of them transcended; many did not.

The culture of the Jansenist opposition

One important expression of the political and religious mentality of *parlementaires* and the kinds of people they associated with was the emergence of Jansenism. This particularly austere strain of revived Catholicism grew into an important source of *parlementaire* opposition in the eighteenth century. The original theology was the product of the soul-searching of two theologians. Jean Duvergier de Hauranne, abbé of Saint-Cyran, was a student of theology from a prominent family in Bayonne. He had undergone a mystical experience in the 1620s, and for several years he had shared his country home with his long-time friend, Cornelius Jansen, who later became bishop of Ypres and a professor at the University of Louvain in the Spanish Netherlands. Both men were deeply influenced by the ideas of Saint Augustine. As Augustinians, their focus was on man's helplessness before an all-powerful God whose grace was necessary for salvation. Individuals did not have the free will to achieve salvation on their own. Like the Calvinists they had a deep sense of repulsion at the sinfulness of mankind and the decadence of worldly things. Like the other *dévots* of their generation, they advocated intense religious reform with a spiritual or mystical emphasis. But they were morally appalled by some of the practices of the Catholic revival. They continued to believe in the mystery of the sacrament and the authority of the pope, but much of the baroque triumphalism of the revived Catholic church left them cold. The issue at stake was to what degree a Christian could influence his own salvation. François de Sales and most of the church establishment endorsed the "optimistic" view that, for salvation, it was sufficient to confess one's sins and take communion while immersing oneself in the reassurances provided by a whole range of ceremonies and prayers. This pragmatic approach was advocated by the Jesuits, who were now ensconced in power positions in the *collèges* and the royal court. But to the Jansenists much Catholic pomp was pure vanity. In their "pessimism" they rejected the practice of frequent communion. Communion, they thought, was a solemn ritual that should be accompanied by a long period of purification through prayer and not trivialized by over-frequent use.

These ideas might have remained in obscurity if they had not become tied to influential families and political issues. The Arnaulds and the Marions were two rising officer-financier families, joined together by the marriage of Antoine Arnauld (1560–1619) with Catherine Marion, daughter of the powerful Solicitor-General of the Parlement of Paris. The two families had enough influence to arrange to have their eleven-year-old daughter Angélique (1593–1661) named abbess of Port-Royal, an unreformed convent in the Chevreuse Valley near Paris. It is hard to imagine this child running a convent. But Angélique did more than that. Experiencing a religious conversion when she was fifteen, she grew up to become the saintly Mère Angélique who inspired a complete reformation of the convent. The nuns were cloistered, and in 1625 the convent was transferred to Paris, where it would be more visible to fashionable benefactors. In 1633 Saint-Cyran became her spiritual advisor, giving a Jansenist flavor to the institution. He ended up in prison for criticizing Cardinal Richelieu's alliance with German Protestants in the Thirty Years War and died shortly after his release in 1640, but the cause of Jansenist reform was then taken up by theologian Antoine Arnaud, the brother of Mère Angélique. Antoine began to publish attacks on the laxity of Jesuits in *De la Fréquente Communion* in 1643. "It is horrible that we have never seen so many confessions and communions and there has never been more disorder and corruption," he exclaimed.[21]

This was the beginning of a war of polemics against the Jesuits and the Catholic hierarchy led by the Arnauld family from their retreat at Port-Royal, where they were living austere, saintly lives. Followers included the playwright Racine and the philosopher Pascal, who wrote the *Provincial Letters* attacking the Jesuits, and the writer–philosopher Pierre Nicole. So far this was a spiritual movement, but its critical tone had political implications, especially coming from families with persons in positions of real importance. In the Parisian atmosphere of spiritual activism, their austere example and elite connections won adherents in high Parisian circles. They displayed a principled moral superiority that led them to refuse compromises with the church hierarchy, and they continued to criticize the Jesuits.

A complicated history of shifting religious and political connections followed. During the Fronde many Jansenist sympathizers were in the parties opposing Cardinal Mazarin, and the Parisian parish clergy took advantage of the confusion to organize an independent council to represent their interests as opposed to the church hierarchy.[22] There was no direct connection between Jansenist beliefs and political resistance. But there was a considerable overlap between those with Jansenist convictions and those critical of the procedures of the church or the management of the royal government, and Jansenism acquired the reputation of a dissident movement of important people who thought critically from a high moral position.

When Louis XIV took personal power, he was having none of this. He closed down the Port-Royal convent in Paris in 1668, but the original convent, Port-Royal-des-Champs, continued to exemplify a certain moral purity that implicity criticized the mundane society of court and capital. Influential *parlementaires* and certain bishops continued to harbor Jansenist sympathies. In 1679 two southern bishops, Étienne-François Caulet, bishop of Pamiers, and Nicolas Pavillon, bishop of Alet, resisted the king's attempt to extend his right to appropriate the revenues and patronage rights of a bishopric while the office was vacant (the *régale*), asserting that the king was violating the rights of the church. On April 4, 1680, Caulet mounted the pulpit in his cathedral wearing his pontifical robes and issued an ordinance excommunicating anyone who accepted a position in his diocese based on the *régale* and anyone who obeyed the orders of the king. This sort of principled passive resistance continued to annoy the Sun King.

Louis XIV saw himself as God's direct representative on earth. As Bishop Bossuet, the tutor of the Dauphin, argued in *Politics Drawn from the Very Words of Holy Scripture* (1679), the royal power was unlimited, and no individual or institution had a legitimate right to question or modify the king's commands. Another round of polemics arguing the case for the king' authority over the church appeared. The king had the support of the Jesuits and his bishop appointees. But Jansenist dissidents sided with the pope. They were joined by members of the Paris Parlement who favored a more autonomous church and who saw a connection between the rights of the church and the rights of the Parlement as a corporate body to play an independent role in the state.

This current of religious–corporate independence was strengthened by a second wave of Jansenist theology spurred on by the publication of a new theological work, *Moral Reflections on the New Testament*, by Pasquier Quesnel in 1693. The king and his Jesuit confessors saw their authority challenged, while their episcopal allies feared a revival of Richerism among the lower clergy. To get the book condemned Louis XIV made a deal with the pope, who collaborated by condemning Quesnel's propositions, first in a papal bull of 1705, and definitively in 1713 in the papal bull *Unigenitus*.

This attempt to squelch the movement, ironically, revived it. Growing numbers of officers and churchmen now saw the king and the pope as wrongly condemning a genuine and legitimate spiritual movement, while at the same time stomping on the rights of powerful corporate interests. This impression was only reinforced when the old king ordered the dissolution of Port-Royal-des-Champs in 1711. Royal troops forcibly expelled the nuns, most of whom were elderly relations of important Parisian figures, and burned all their books. This outlawing of pious, well-connected Jansenists by papal order enforced by the king was a direct attack on Gallican liberties. The Parlement stalled registration of the bull and the laws enforcing it for years. In 1714 *Unigenitus* evoked an unprecedented public debate. At least 180 pamphlets were published, more than half of them attacking the bull. Quesnel's call for people to read the New Testament for themselves drew ordinary citizens into the discussion, and Richerist priests began to agitate once again for more rights within the church.

Noailles, archbishop of Paris, and eight bishops opposed the pope's condemnation.

This was the beginning of a different, more political, Jansenism among the politically aware. An indirect effect of the broadened discussion was that popular crowds began to view Jansenist clerics as saints. While the united forces of government and church were enforcing adherence to the pope's declaration, a minority of bishops were demanding a general council of the church to discuss the matter, and between 1727 and 1730 word began to spread of miracles associated with humble Jansenist clerics. Hoping to be cured, large hysterical Parisian crowds gathered at the cemetery of Saint-Médard where the body of one such saint was buried. In 1730 a royal declaration made *Unigenitus* the law of the land. In 1746 the new archbishop of Paris ordered all priests to refuse the sacraments to anyone who did not have a *billet de confession* certifying adherence to the orders of the church. Predictably, this created a group of dissident martyrs who refused to comply. Meanwhile the Parlement was vigorously refusing to register the king's repressive laws. And a Jansenist newspaper, *Nouvelles Ecclésiastiques*, was regaling a broad leadership with ideas about the rights of the common priesthood and the tyranny of the king and the orthodox bishops.

Since many *parlementaires* were Jansenist-leaning and defenders of the rights of the Gallican church, their remonstrances, now published and addressed to a broader public, increasingly called for checks on the crown, freedom of public discourse, and their special obligation to speak for the people. Whereas in the seventeenth century the robe nobility had advocated strong absolute rule in which they would participate as collaborative watchdogs, in the eighteenth century they were claiming to be the voice of a broader public opinion that would moderate the power of the king.

Conclusion

The existence of the writers, dramatists, philosophers, and inquisitive scientific amateurs – the people that we usually think of when we speak of early modern French culture – reminds us that there was much more to that culture than village rituals, cycles of festivals, competitions over honor, or displays of corporate vanity. Figures like Rabelais or Montaigne, Pascal or Voltaire, not only captured the spirit of their times but reached beyond to new insights and novel viewpoints. Their genius built upon traditional culture but was made possible by changes that were gradually transforming society. The slow advances of literacy and the dramatic spread of collèges whose graduates were taking over most of the command posts in trade and government; the tremendous influence of legal thinking in towns, law courts, and governmental bureaux; the transformation of the upper nobility from landed warriors into cultivated collaborators in the royal enterprise; the increase in civilized manners, if only among the aristocracy; the reinforcement of repressive measures and a more effective crackdown on morals – all these developments raised new types of people into positions of influence and produced new situations which stimulated new ideas and approaches.

There is no question that the "triumph of Lent" was a significant change if, by that, we mean that church and state were becoming more serious about enforcing rules, and that France was experiencing a wave of Augustinian austerity imposed with only partial success by persons of power on the rest of the population. There were certainly ways too in which the elite were withdrawing mentally and physically from close identification with both the common people and the local nobility: witness the shift from participatory urban processions to programmed entertainments for the populace and the adoption by aristocratic society of styles of behavior that separated them from their peasants and workers.

But to think of elite culture as distinct from popular culture is to miss the many things they had in common. While the people in different walks of life had distinctive forms of behavior derived from their particular traditions and socioeconomic circumstances, they had many things in common. Throughout French society men and women were sensitive to questions of personal honor and prone to be combative when it was challenged. Nobles defended their honor in duels; women in the street used insults to humiliate their adversaries. Everyone tolerated a high level of crude violence, especially when defending personal status or attacking injustice on the part of rulers. When the duc d'Anjou paraded the body of Condé on an ass he was using the same language as the crowd that threatened Larfeuil with a similar humiliation.[23] Everyone believed universally in the king's rule, though they might condemn ministers, agents, and tax collectors. Except for the Protestants, they all believed in the same Catholic approach to salvation, attended the same Mass, worshiped the same saints. To one degree or another, they all believed in signs and portents, magic and witchcraft. They all accepted that they were part of a hierarchical society in which they themselves occupied only a certain stratum and believed it right to bow down before their betters and to expect deference from their inferiors. They all fought bitterly over precedence in formal settings. They agreed that women had a different role to play than men and that while women were capable of stepping in to run a regency or train apprentices, their rightful place was to complement the men by socializing small children and running households. All classes relied on personal contacts to gain advancement and counted on long-lasting loyalties established through marriage alliance, client–patron relations, godparenthood, or lord–tenant relations to protect them from adverse forces. They shared the same legends and stories, although ideas drawn from classical authors and medieval romances trickled down from aristocratic elites to peasants in simplified form, with a considerable delay, while folk tales and superstitions percolated up from rural villages to writers like Rabelais and La Fontaine, to be passed on to a literate public.

It was by grounding themselves in these traditional foundations and then transcending them that the great observers of the human condition broke new ground. French society was still traditional through and through, but forces within it were moving forward toward something new.

Suggestions for further reading: culture of the new elite

Education and civic humanism

Breen, Michael P., *Law, City, and King: Legal Culture, Municipal Politics, and State Formation in Early Modern Dijon* (Rochester NY, 2007).

Chartier, Roger, Dominique Julia, and Marie-Madeleine Compère, *L' Éducation en France du XVIe au XVIIIe siècle* (Paris, 1976).

Heller, Henry, *Labor, Science and Technology in France, 1500–1620* (Cambridge, 1996).

Huppert, George, *Public Schools in Renaissance France* (Urbana, IL, 1984).

Lignereux, Yann, *Lyon et le roi: de la bonne ville à l'absolutisme municipal, 1594–1654* (Seyssel, 2003).

Lougee, Carolyn, *Le Paradis des femmes: Women, Salons, and Social Stratification in Seventeenth-Century France* (Princeton, NJ, 1976).
Wolfe, Michael, ed., *Changing Identities in Early Modern France* (Chapel Hill, NC, 1997).

Jansenism

Abercrombie, Nigel, *The Origins of Jansenism* (Oxford, 1936).
Doyle, William, *Jansenism: Catholic Resistance to Authority from the Reformation to the French Revolution* (New York, 2000).
Sedgwick, Alexander, *Jansenism in Seventeenth-Century France: Voices from the Wilderness* (Charlottesville, VA, 1977).
    The Travails of Conscience: The Arnauld Family and the Ancien Régime (Cambridge, MA, 1998).
Van Kley, Dale K., *The Religious Origins of the French Revolution: From Calvin to the Civil Constitution, 1560–1791* (New Haven, CT, 1996).

11 | Monarchs and courtly society

The royal court was the focal point of French society. Despite the continuing existence of other seats of magnate power and the concentration of regional influence in the various provincial capitals, the entourage around the king was clearly the place to be, and its importance over other power centers increased through time.[1] But the court was mobile. Well into the seventeenth century the whole court spent much of its time on the road, dragging all the paraphernalia of government from chateau to chateau while magnates and petitioners came and went according to the dictates of personal business and patronage obligations. The attendance of local nobles increased when the king was nearby. When the king was at war, usually in spring and summer, the able-bodied men would accompany him on campaign, leaving the women and the elderly behind. Festivities were grandest in the winter when attendance was most complete.

The royal household

This loosely defined "court" was simply the collection of persons surrounding the king. They performed essentially four functions. The royal household consisted of important nobles who held posts as great officers of the crown. The household also included ceremonial positions whose importance was limited to overseeing protocol concerning the throng of resident courtiers. These important household officers, along with their subordinates and the many servants who actually did the work, technically speaking constituted the household. The "court" also included a second group of ecclesiastical or noble dignitaries who were temporarily or permanently living and traveling with the king. It was this growing body of courtiers, plus the officers of the household who together made up the court proper. A third function was the governance of the realm, which was largely handled by professionals from the robe tradition who did not belong to the throng of courtiers. These included the king's ministers, his councilors and secretaries, and, as time went on, whole offices full of subordinate clerks and employees. There was no formal line between political functionaries and courtiers, since great nobles and members of the royal family might also hold governmental positions. But as a rule these government officials did not participate in the life of the court, and the courtiers were not directly involved in the process of governing. The fourth function of the royal entourage was not formally defined. It was the role played by king and courtiers in patronizing and promoting drama, the plastic arts, literature, and scholarly erudition: in short, their cultural leadership.

Thus, broadly speaking, the court consisted of the king, his family, a body of courtiers, many of whom held official titles in the king's household, the subordinates and servants of these people, and the king's ministers and agents who administered the realm. The court gradually grew in size and complexity. Medieval kings were attended only by a small circle of vassals and prelates, who might serve as either household officers or political councilors. The rest of the nobility stayed on their lands or visited the king briefly in their capacity as vassals giving counsel or fulfilling military obligations. The elaborate ceremonial life of the court only began to emerge toward the end of the fifteenth century, very much under the influence, first of the rival court of the dukes of Burgundy who were known for their banquets and ceremonies, and then of the ducal courts encountered in Italy during the Italian wars.

The persons with titles granting the privileges of the court were called *commensaux*, a word for which there is no good English equivalent. They enjoyed extensive privileges including free room and board, exemption from many taxes, plus allowances of food, candles and fodder. When the household was fully developed around 1600, its hierarchy included nine Great Officers of the Crown, all of whom were powerful nobles appointed and dismissable by the king.[2] Below them were the first level of *commensaux*: high officials, all of them nobles, who headed agencies of the court including the Grand Prévot de France, in charge of policing the roads, and the Grand Veneur, in charge of hunting. Second-level *commensaux* included household positions that were subordinate to the highest positions, such as *maîtres de l'hôtel* commanded by the Grand Maître de l'Hôtel. They could also be non-noble specialists attached to the court such as doctors, surgeons, and jewelers. Third-level *commensaux* were non-noble craftsmen with less distinguished skills.

Functionally speaking, the household was organized into three main divisions, the chapel (for the king's spiritual needs), the chamber (for activities involving the king's person), and the *hôtel* (for provisioning). Under these rubrics were many departments such as chaplains, barbers, carvers, grooms, musicians, purchasers of furniture, stables, bread supply, fruit supply, transportation of furniture, messengers, and lodging directors. In addition there were military forces attached to the court, including the Scottish guard (bodyguards), the hundred Swiss, and the two hundred *gentilshommes de l'hôtel*. All these posts were constantly being created, abolished, or redefined. Many of the ones held by great nobles were largely ceremonial, although some of them involved formal duties or the management of important activities. They were honors bestowed by the king or by one of his household officers who had the authority to name subordinates. The appointments did provide modest stipends, but their main attraction was being able to live at court and having influence close to the monarch. The real work was done by servant underlings.

How big was the household? These positions can be roughly grouped into an "inner household" and a "wider court," to borrow the terminology suggested by Jeroen Duindam. At the time of Louis XII (around 1500) some one hundred persons enjoyed the legal privileges of the court. About that time Anne of Brittany, the very influential wife of Louis XII, created her own household, a feminine entourage of twelve matrons-of-honor and forty ladies-in-waiting. Francis I extended this practice by adding households for each resident queen and princess. He also designated gentlemen of the bedchamber who served the king in rotation. By the mid sixteenth century the inner household had grown to about 1,000 persons, and the wider household, including the hunt, the stables, the military guards, and the households of the queen and the queen-mother, numbered about 2,500. In the 1580s these figures were respectively 1,100 and 3,000. The presence of adult family members with their own households always increased the size of the court. In 1578 Henry III's troublesome younger brother the duc d'Anjou had a household of 1,123.[3] Louis XIII's brother Gaston had a household of 542 in 1628.

We can observe the system at its height in the figures for 1699, when the inner household had 1,077 persons and the outer household contained an additional 4,125.[4] Around that time a hypothetical breakdown of the entire entourage at Versailles might include about 1,000 persons with household posts close to the king, fifty priests making up the royal chapel, another 700 persons connected to the hunt, the stables, and the basic security services, 1,590 constituting the households of other royal family members, and 1,660 in the various military corps attached to the court, making a total of 5,000. Of these, the majority, possibly as many as 80 percent, would be noble. In addition there were 5,000 auxiliary troops not considered part of the royal household, making a grand total of 10,000. These positions ranged from highly prestigious and extremely influential posts close to the king, to servants and common soldiers. In all there were perhaps 5,000 nobles at the court, or 10,000 considering that many honorific posts had two alternating incumbents. But the king would have had personal relations with a much smaller number, perhaps several hundred, who constituted the real aristocracy at Versailles. They were the ones he allegedly knew by name and sight.

Court culture

By the time of Francis I (1515–47), the royal court had become so socially desirable, so rich in honorific positions and potential pensions, and so useful as the center of political decision-making that it gradually began to outshine other venues as a center of patronage and influence. The children of nobles could be placed there as pages or ladies-in-waiting in order to learn manners and make influential contacts. Hoping for favors, nobles attended. Artists hoped for patronage. The prevailing atmosphere of the court was entirely dependent on the personality of the reigning monarch. When a king was young and sociable, like the young Francis I, it could be a jovial company of ladies and gentlemen throwing themselves into hunting parties, masquerades, and amorous intrigues. If the king was awkward or insecure like Louis XIII, the ceremonies would be kept to a minimum and socialites might seek their entertainment elsewhere. If the king was elderly or pious like the older Louis XIV, protocol could become strict and formal. During a minority or a period of serious ideological conflict, the court might split into factions. Rivalries could form around competing court figures, often tied to issues of royal succession. For example, the allies of the duchesse d'Étampes, the mistress of Francis I, lined up against the allies of Diane de Poitiers, mistress of the king's son and heir, in the 1540s. Obviously the mistresses were stand-ins for the king and his adult son. In similar fashion the persons loyal to Cardinal Richelieu's pragmatic policies in the 1620s and 1630s were vehemently opposed by the queen-mother Marie de' Medici, the king's brother Gaston d'Orléans, and other grandees, who plotted repeatedly against the cardinal.

The sixteenth-century court traveled a great deal. Solnon estimates that Charles IX moved thirty times per year or an average of once every twelve days. Shifting the court was an immense operation. Contemporary observers claimed that such expeditions could involve as many as 12,000 horses. A safer estimate would be 6,000 to 8,000 men and horses. This army of horseback riders, carriages, hordes of individuals on foot, and wagons pulled by mules conscripted from the region, and loaded with state papers, furniture, utensils, and supplies of food and wine, would clog the roads, halting local traffic for hours. Often the company had to split up and take several parallel routes because the main road was too small. This immense caravan would drain the region of fodder and supplies. Upon arrival at a destination, the important people would begin a scramble for lodging. The royal party might settle into a designated chateau or the mansion of a prominent local family, and the rest would stay in private homes, at inns, or out in the open. It was not uncommon for everyone to pitch tents and sleep in the open air. Royal chateaux were cold and empty much of the time. When the royal party was coming, furnishings and tapestries had to be brought and installed, along with kitchen utensils, and a vast amount of food had to be acquired from local sources. After the royal party left, the halls and chambers would need to be cleaned of garbage and human waste.

Most kings stayed in Paris only intermittently. The Valois kings favored the chateaux in the Loire Valley. Francis I tried to develop a closer relationship with the capital, especially after the city was induced to guarantee his loans, but he usually stayed on the outskirts in residences such as the chateau de Madrid. In the heart of the city, he tore down the medieval fortress called the Louvre and began the first section of the palace that is there today. Catherine de' Medici added the Tuileries Palace, which was a free-standing chateau at the far western end of the Louvre complex. Her sons added more sections of the new Louvre's elegant courtyard, the Cour Carrée. Henry IV stayed often at the Louvre, but he preferred Fontainebleau. His widow, Marie de' Medici, built her own Italianate Luxembourg Palace on the Parisian left bank. Their son, Louis XIII, spent no more than nine years in Paris during his twenty-five year personal reign. When in Paris, he stayed mostly in the Louvre, but the rest of the time he was away on military campaigns. The young Louis XIV and his mother, Anne of Austria, used Richelieu's nearby Palais Cardinal (today the Palais Royal), which was more secure. This did not keep them from having to flee in the night in January 1649 for fear of attacks by angry crowds during the Fronde. When Louis XIV assumed power he tended to avoid the capital, adopting instead a circuit of cha-teaux on the outskirts, from Saint-Germain-en-Laye, to Fontaine-bleau, sometimes stopping at the small but elegant hunting lodge that his father had built at Versailles. He only settled the court permanently into the much expanded chateau of Versailles in 1682. Construction of the newer wings and the gardens continued for the rest of his reign.

The cultural level of the persons around the king was mixed at best. Francis I introduced an appreciation for humanist learning and refined conversation to the court, on the lines of the model presented in Castiglione's *Courtier*, along with the many other influences from Italy. There were always persons at court who appreciated poetry, collected paintings, and kept journals or wrote works of their own. On the other hand, the court was a violent place where assassinations went unpunished, cruel humor was common, and the ethics of the battlefield were more influential with dagger-carrying nobles than the refinement of the new learning. Men flaunted their mistresses and engaged one another in ambushes and duels. Henry II made an effort to promote etiquette at court by organizing rituals centered on the king. Henry III went much farther in this direction, but court for-malities could not eliminate the rising level of violence during the religious wars. Henry IV's gallantry with mistresses and the crude manners of his entourage did little to counteract this trend. After the tense period (1624–61) when First Ministers Richelieu and Mazarin had to deal with the insecure Louis XIII and the minority of Louis XIV, Louis XIV resumed the structuring of court life that Henry III had begun. Etiquette became more formal, and courtesy and restraint were the order of the day. But this improved civility did not rule out ignorance and crudity on the part of some of the courtiers.

Figure 28 Recreation at the Renaissance court. The courtiers are engaged in a game of quintain, a tilting exercise in which the mounted combatant charged a post and tried to spear a ring or emblem hanging from it. Note the audience and the musicians. By Antoine Caron (1521–99).

The most spectacular aspect of life at court was the profusion of extravagant festivities. By the sixteenth century, these ceremonies had become too elaborate to be affordable by anyone but the crown. They focused attention on the royal court, both to entertain the nobility and to impress the public with the magnificence of the monarchy. In addition, they created bonds among the courtiers themselves by directly enlisting their participation. These entertainments suited the predilections of the nobles by allowing them to display their military prowess and, for a magical moment, to see themselves as heroes from the fantastic world of chivalric romances. At the same time the festivities engaged the interest of scholars and writers attached to the court by including elements from classical mythology, literature, and poetry, and even citations in Latin or Greek. The festivities also borrowed some of the boisterous spirit of Carnival, along with the use of festive floats representing allegorical scenes.

Royal festivals evolved with time. The court had inherited tournaments and jousting matches from medieval predecessors. In the past these exercises had been genuine physical combats, but by the time of Francis I they had become mere pageants with little physical danger. Open combat on horseback had been replaced by jousting on opposite sides of a barrier, which kept the combatants far enough apart to avoid the most penetrating blows. As these contests lost some of their glamour, elements were added such as ceremonial challenges, parades, costumes, and fancy horsemanship. Eventually the competitive element was abandoned altogether in favor of programmed entertainments used to celebrate and publicize special events. Jousting gave way to planned scenarios in which costumed companies of knights carried out an allegorical program replete with decorated floats and poetic recitations. These entertainments had originated at the ducal courts of Italy. Their introduction was another aspect of an Italianization which was further extended by the two Medici queens and their imported entourages. As time went on, the French introduced their own distinctive elements. Gradually themes and styles of aristocratic entertainment evolved, from tournaments to masked balls, to formal horse shows called carrousels, and finally in the seventeenth century to the theater and the opera.

For example, in 1518, a festival was held to celebrate the wedding of Madeleine de la Tour d'Auvergne, an important French heiress, and the duke of Urbino, who was the nephew of the Medici pope Leo X.

The proceedings began with a nocturnal open-air banquet under a vast tent illuminated by torches and lanterns, followed by a ballet danced by seventy-two costumed ladies. A week of jousting matches and tournaments followed, capped by a grandiose mock battle in which all the knights assaulted a mock fortress built of wood, complete with wooden cannons shooting fake cannonballs.[5]

These occasions had an impact well beyond the participants because detailed descriptions of them were published, often with texts and detailed engravings, sometimes long after the event. They were discussed by learned connoisseurs and copied by local scholars who used similar themes in designing royal entries to their cities. A wider public must have learned about the magnificence of the event in printed accounts or from common spectators who sometimes attended in large numbers.

A sense of the importance attributed to these ceremonies can be gained from a set of extremely elegant tapestries called the "Valois tapestries," which portray in precise detail the principal festivals organized by Catherine de' Medici. This set was apparently commissioned by the government of the Netherlands to flatter Catherine de' Medici into allowing her younger son, the duc d'Alençon, to assume the leadership of the Netherlands. They commemorate some of Catherine's best moments. The meeting of the French and Spanish courts at Bayonne in 1565 provided the occasion for chariots celebrating "virtue and love" and a special banquet held on an island in the Ladour River, on the way to which the guests were treated to a water show involving musical swans, Neptune in his chariot drawn by sea horses, and Arion riding on a dolphin, all to singing and instrumental "water music." On the island they encountered shepherds and shepherdesses dancing to bagpipes.[6] The tradition continued under Henry IV. In 1605 a carrousel held in Paris grouped the horsemen for the first time into quadrilles, in imitation of the festivals in Florence and Turin. The defenders' challenge was presented to the king by "Turks" and "Moors," part of a contingent of "paladins of Thrace." The attackers who accepted the challenge were "French paladins" including the "knights of the sun."

The culmination of this tradition was the carrousel held in 1612 in the Place Royale (today Place des Vosges) to celebrate the dual marriages of the young Louis XIII with Anne of Austria, daughter of Philip III of Spain, and her brother, the future Philip IV of Spain, with

Figure 29 *The Water Festival at Bayonne* by Antoine Caron (1521–99). This is a representation of the actual festival that took place on June 24, 1565.

Figure 30 This is an unusual view of the famous carrousel of June 5, 1662 which shows the spectators and not just the royal entourage in their costumes. These horse ballets were a spectator sport. After Henri de Gissey (1621–73).

Elizabeth of France. This event was transmitted to posterity by an often reproduced engraving and a much admired descriptive account, *The Romance of the Knights of Glory*, published by François de Rosset in 1613. At the center of the ceremonies was the "Palace of Felicity," a mock castle with four angular towers and a central dungeon decorated with all sorts of allegorical symbols. Seven quadrilles paraded into the square. First came the defenders of the castle, the "Knights of Glory," with names typical of chivalric romances – Almidor, Léontide, Alphée, Lysandre and Argante. They were accompanied by a float pulled by lions, then five giants, and a large rock covered with nymphs. Then came the float of "Triumph" holding twelve sybils reciting the poetry of Malherbe, then five pages bearing the coats of arms of the five defenders. Other quadrilles followed, including Amadis of Gaul, Perseus accompanied by Polish and Chinese slaves, the nymphs of Diana, and the Nine Illustrious Romans. The festivities lasted for three days and culminated in the final assault on the castle, which was devoured by flames. This carrousel ended the series until 1656, when Mazarin organized a smaller carrousel in which eighteen-year-old Louis XIV carried the emblem of the sun. The young king consciously revived the tradition with the well-known carrousel of 1662, held next to the Louvre in the square still called the Place du Carrousel.[7]

The personal taste of the monarch also set the tone for the arts. Francis I had been intrigued by Italian art even before he had ever seen the country, and he made the acquisition of paintings and sculpture a major aspect of his diplomacy, sending agents to acquire works in Rome and Florence and enticing artists to come to France. His fabulous gallery of paintings at Fontainebleau became the core of the Louvre collection of today, including the *Mona Lisa*, four other works by Leonardo da Vinci, and works by Fra Bartolomeo, Perugino, Pontormo, Raphael, Titian, and Michelangelo. He induced Leonardo da Vinci, Andrea del Sarto, and Benvenuto Cellini to come to France. Francis also acquired 213 tapestries and a vast collection of valuable manuscripts. Humanists and poets found a welcome place at the Renaissance courts of Francis I and Henry II, although under the latter the persecution of heretics and the beginning of the censorship of books put a damper on creativity. With Henry II's support, French painting enjoyed a revival under the "School of Fontainebleau" and the Pleiade circle of poets, most of whom were well supported by aristocratic patrons, flourished.[8] In the later sixteenth century, cultural patronage was reduced by civil war, and the best painters moved to Rome.

In the early seventeenth century, Henry IV and Louis XIII were not as enamored of paintings, but other court figures understood their importance for enhancing reputations. Marie de' Medici in exile commissioned a series of massive canvasses by Rubens to celebrate key moments in her life – her arrival in France, her marriage to Henry IV, her assumption of the regency – in each of which she is the focus of attention, surrounded by gods and goddesses of the ancient world in a dramatic, legitimizing, baroque allegory.

Cardinals Richelieu and Mazarin also understood the importance of artistic expression. It was Richelieu who laid the groundwork for the so-called "classical" flowering of French painting and literature. During his ascendancy, he acquired at least five chateaux, including Reuil near Paris with its spectacular gardens. He built the Palais Cardinal in the heart of Paris, near the Louvre, and installed a theater for the performance of the dramas produced by playwrights he patronized such as Pierre Corneille. He organized the Académie Française in 1634 to improve the stature of the French language and literature. He commissioned paintings by a whole stable of new talented French painters such as Champaigne and Vouet, and set up galleries of portraits in all his residences. An inventory of his collections lists 262 paintings and a library of 6,000 titles. Richelieu was a solitary figure, who depended on Louis XIII's constant support in order to maintain his authority. For this reason he needed to keep rival grandees out of sight and away from the king. Therefore he supported art that glorified himself and the state rather than the elegance of the court. He commissioned at least twenty-five self-portraits by Philippe de Champaigne. Richelieu's successor, Mazarin, continued the same activities. The two cardinals might have dangerously outshone the shy Louis XIII and the juvenile Louis XIV in a time when court life was in decline. Fortunately for the monarchy, both cardinal-ministers left their libraries, galleries, and collections to the king, laying a firm foundation for Louis XIV, who could continue the artistic patronage while transferring attention to himself and refocusing attention on the court as a reflection of the grandeur of the king.

Both cardinals also made effective use of patronage by cultivating a stable of publicists who defended governmental policies in popular tracts and learned treatises. They took advantage of the profusion of widely disseminated engravings that, like modern-day political cartoons, were beginning to influence public opinion. This phenomenon began in earnest during the religious wars, when both Calvinist and Catholic Leaguers accused each other of apostasy, unspeakable cruelty, and allegiance with the Devil. Pamphlets flourished again during the regency of Marie de' Medici, and they began to be used by the government as ways to manipulate public opinion. The scatological sarcasm of attacks on the policies of the First Minister only increased during the Fronde rebellion (1648–53), along with the virulence of the royalist responses. This flood of pamphlets for and against came appropriately to be called Mazarinades.

The court of Louis XIV

The ultimate destination of any discussion of the royal court is inevitably Versailles. Louis XIV's court has traditionally been described as a "gilded cage" designed to entrap and bedazzle the nobility while removing them from their provincial power bases and turning them into obsequious courtiers grubbing for favors. This picture is so ingrained that it is difficult to escape its influence, yet it needs serious modification. The mystification is easily understood. From his first assumption of personal power in 1661, every move Louis XIV made was reinterpreted for posterity and broadcast in what could only be called a grand artistic plan for royalist self-promotion. In 1662 Jean-Baptiste Colbert, one of the king's loyal ministers, was already planning what we might today call "image-making" or "spin control" on behalf of the king. Colbert was envisaging the raising of "triumphal arches, obelisks, pyramids, and mausoleums" to the glory of the king, along with "feasts, masquerades, carrousels and other similar diversions." Colbert organized a "little academy" of selected writers and humanist scholars whose assignment was to promote the royal reputation by designing medals commemorating the king's deeds and commissioning poems and orations praising his successes. The king's own memoirs, intended for the instruction of his son and written some ten years later with the help of an outline by Colbert and contributions from other writers, conceptualized the reign in terms of how "disorder had reigned everywhere" when he acceded to the throne and how his assumption of personal power had coaxed everyone back into obedience. The same scenario was invoked when Le Brun painted murals on the ceiling of the Hall of Mirrors at Versailles, including Louis in a toga sitting on his throne over a banner that read "the king assumes personal power," followed by scenes dramatizing his military successes.

Versailles represented the culmination of a century of artistic flattery. Catherine de' Medici had enjoyed tapestries portraying her festivities. Marie de' Medici had commissioned Rubens' series of colossal canvases glorifying her regency. Now Louis XIV was decorating the grandest hall in Europe with the official story of his regime. He surrounded himself with tapestries in which he was portrayed as Alexander the Great, and statuary showing him as Apollo, the god of the sun. The overpowering elegance of the chateau and park at Versailles, where every statue and fountain was part of a symbolic program glorifying the king, add weight, even today, to the legend. By the end of his reign Colbert's vision of victory arches and laudatory statues in every major city had become a reality, along with monumental building projects in Paris – the massive Invalides to house disabled war veterans, the new boulevards replacing fortifications, the classical eastern facade of the Louvre, Roman-style victory arches, and the astronomical Observatory. All these overpowering messages induce us to accept the Louisquatorzian legend at face value.

Louis XIV really did rule more firmly and effectively than any king since Francis I. With his innate sense of dignity, his belief in his superiority of birth and station, and his masculine infatuation with hunting, warfare, and feminine company, he satisfied perfectly the expectations of the traditional male nobility, and in a broader sense the general population. But we need to nuance the usual stereotype. First, the ceremonial court was not Louis XIV's creation. Displays of equine prowess and pageants filled with magical enchantment had been common at the courts of the Valois kings. The carrousel of 1662 was modeled after those forty years earlier, and when Louis organized his spectacular three-day entertainment called the "Pleasures of the Enchanted Island" in 1664 in the gardens of Versailles, it recapitulated much of the imagery from 1612. The Valois monarchs had also created much of the protocol and ritual that we associate with Versailles, including the king's *lever* and *coucher*. Louis's regime was in fact completely traditional. It saw an intensification of long-established traditions, led by a king who was at last capable of bringing them back to life.

A second corrective is that we should not associate Louis's court exclusively with residence at Versailles, since the ritual surrounding the king was fully developed during the youthful years from 1661 to 1682 when the court was still moving about. From 1662 to 1665 king and court were lodged mainly in Paris; in 1666–73, 1676 and 1678–82 they were at Saint-Germain; in 1674, 1675, and 1677 they were at Versailles. But even these extended stays included short-term moves. In 1671, when they were nominally residing in Paris, king and court celebrated Carnival at Vincennes, spent time at Versailles, Saint-Germain, Chantilly, Fontainebleau, and Compiègne, visited Amiens and Boulogne, inspected the frontier towns of Flanders and the fortifications at Dunkirk, and spent fifteen days in Tournai.[9]

A third corrective concerns the way we interpret the quality of life at court. It had glamour and charm, but it could also be degrading and intensely boring. On the bright side, lodging was free for favored courtiers. There were ballets and plays every few evenings, along with balls, parties, and banquets. Hunting was an almost daily activity.

Louis threw himself into it with great pleasure, accompanied by a large group of favored courtiers on horseback, while the ladies followed, riding or in carriages. In a single day in August 1685 at Versailles, 5,000 partridges and 2,000 pheasants were released for their hunting pleasure. Every fall the whole court moved to Fontainebleau because of its excellent hunting in the nearby forest. Louis also enjoyed escorting favored guests on foot around the extensive grounds of Versailles, whose groves and fountains were something like a theme park devoted to royal magnificence.

In 1676 Madame de Sévigné, who was not a regular at court, gushed about a stay at the not-yet-completed Versailles.

at three o'clock we are in the king's beautiful apartment... Everything is divinely furnished; everything is magnificent; you move from one place to another without any crowding... The courier arrives around six o'clock and the king retires to read his letters, then he returns. There is always some music that he listens to which creates a pleasant effect. He chats with those who are accustomed to having that honor. Finally everyone stops gambling ... they climb into coaches... they ride on the canal in gondolas where they find music playing; we come back about ten and discover a comedy being performed; midnight rings... so there, that is how we spend our Saturdays.[10]

As the king and his generation of courtiers grew older, the atmosphere grew more subdued. The festivities in the gardens became less frequent, and activities moved indoors. Many attributed the new sobriety to the influence of Madame de Maintenon, the king's former mistress, whom he married secretly in 1684 after the death of the queen. In 1682 Louis invented a new social gathering called the *soirées d'appartements*. These events took place three times a week on Monday, Wednesday, and Thursday evenings in the king's suite of apartments. The principal ladies and gentlemen of the court were expected to attend. The guests would socialize or play gambling games in the beautifully decorated, candle-lit rooms. In one room there was music and dancing. In another, billiard tables were surrounded by carpeted benches for observers. A third featured tables filled with elegant pastries, pyramids of fruits, and warm drinks. Protocol was relaxed so that the king could stroll from room to room, chatting with the guests, graciously telling them not to bother to rise in his presence.[11]

But all this gracious living had its down-side, and the life of the courtiers could also be extremely unpleasant. Life was stressful and competitive. Traveling from chateau to chateau was tedious enough, but even after everyone had settled at Versailles, the charm of sharing the royal presence must have been severely undermined by the physical discomfort that it entailed. For much of the reign of Louis XIV, Versailles was a perpetual construction site. The trees in the grand alleys were just saplings, and the palace was constantly being modified. In 1680 Visconti reported that the massive displacement of soil was producing bad air and smelly swamps and that the water in the fountains was putrid. That August the air made everyone sick.[12] There were about 364 apartments in the chateau and the outlying adjacent buildings. Two-thirds of them went to members of the royal family, the princes of the blood, the officers of the royal household, and other courtiers – 256 in all. Most of the apartments, consisting of a small sitting room with an antechamber for the servants, were cramped. Many without fireplaces were drafty and cold in the winter, stiflingly hot in the summer. Few had any cooking facilities. Most people ate at one of the king's many tables or at the tables of royal family members. Louis himself gave out the lodging assignments, and being granted a room in the actual palace was considered a great favor. Courtiers were always trying to maneuver their way into one of the more desirable wings, especially the rooms closest to the king.

The scramble for accommodation was only one aspect of the constant struggle for position. Another was the battle for the king's attention. The day was built around the royal schedule. Everyone rose and dressed at dawn in order to appear in the royal apartments by 7.30 when the king would rise. Attendance was strictly regulated according to status, with three levels of privilege. A few household officers and dignitaries with a special right of *grande entrée* were allowed to stand at the king's side while he was awakened and given his robe. Those with *seconde entrée* would come rushing into the room when the door was opened a little while he was sitting in an armchair having his hair combed. Finally the doors would be opened all the way and the majority of courtiers holding *entrées de la chambre* would pour in, vying for position. Hoping for a moment to catch the king's ear or present a petition, the whole crowd would follow him to his morning chapel service. Then when he went off to his council meetings, they could all relax and pay one another visits, exchanging compliments and gossip. The king ate his main midday meal alone. Afterwards the crowd would gather in the courtyard hoping to accompany him on his afternoon promenade or hunt. He ate dinner in public, attended the *appartement*, and retired to his chambers. The ritual of the *coucher*, when the king went to bed, was the inverse of the ritual of the *lever*.

Life among several hundred permanent residents who had nothing to do but attend entertainments and maneuver for position could also be humiliating. The king was a master of manipulation. He knew the leading nobles by sight, and he made sure that positions in the church, the army, and the provincial administrations went only to those who paid him court and served loyally. He invented a whole science of petty distinctions that kept the courtiers competing among themselves and turning to him as arbiter. Strict rules were established concerning sitting and standing. Courtiers were expected to remain standing in the presence of the king, but certain princesses had the right to sit on a *tabouret*, or stool.

Title and rank were viewed as a force field radiating out from each individual, and transforming the status of those around him. One day when the Dauphin was returning to Versailles in the company of two subordinates, their carriage broke down on the road, leaving them stranded. As it happened, the prince de Condé and two of *his* subordinates passed by and stopped to help. The Dauphin and his followers climbed into Condé's coach, but not before the Dauphin had apologetically expelled Condé's two followers from the carriage. They were left standing by the roadside even though there was room for them in the carriage because, according to the rules of precedence, "the servants of the princes of the blood do not enter the carriages of the king." Louis XIV later told the Dauphin that he had acted appropriately because "any carriage you are riding in becomes *your* carriage and from that moment on the servants of a prince of the blood are not permitted to enter it."[13]

These fine distinctions led to endless quarrels. The marquis de Saint-Maurice describes a case in 1669:

Monday evening while the queen was gambling, Madame la comtesse de Soissons who was seated next to her, left the room, and the comtesse de Gramont, who was croupier, sat down on the stool next to her. When Madame la comtesse returned, she said to [Gramont] that "that was her seat." The other replied proudly, "We will see about that," without getting up. Madame la comtesse replied to this with scornful laughter. (The queen said nothing.) The comte de Gramont then spoke up and said, "Madame, the chairs are not nailed down here; my wife will stay put. We are from just as good a family as you are." When the king heard about this he criticized the conduct of the comte and comtesse de Gramont, calling them extravagant and ordering them to ask Madame la comtesse's pardon. Gramont opposed this and appealed to the marshals of France. They sentenced his brother and sister-in-law to do whatever the king had ordered. So Gramont had to say to Madame la comtesse that he greatly regretted having failed in showing respect, that he did not believe he could have said that his family was as good as hers, but that since she claimed to have heard this, he asked for her pardon.[14]

Such seemingly trivial quarrels were part of a social milieu in which the king maintained total control in doling out honors and everyone had to be on guard for changes which might affect them adversely. He demanded loyalty and obedience, and within the circle of obedient courtiers, he distinguished very carefully between those of ancient pedigree and those of recent vintage, and he rewarded them accordingly. Those of ancient family who had served well would be given their due, sometimes to the extent of bailing them out of financial ruin or forgiving gambling debts. Those who did not pay court or who fell into ill repute might be exiled or denied favors. Louis appointed only men of high status to ambassadorial posts, provincial governorships, and military commands. At the same time, he kept the grandees out of his political councils, which were dominated by robe–administrative families such as the Le Telliers and the Colberts.

If the male courtiers were left with little to do but pursue their ambitions, the women were even more at a loose end. The men at least had a significant role to play in the army, for warfare was one of Louis XIV's primary activities. They also could hold ceremonial court offices that sometimes entailed real duties of presiding, organizing, and screening. The women had a more ambiguous role. They were often influential in handling family inheritances and training younger children, and they were capable of defending themselves fiercely in matters of status, as the conflict between Soissons and Gramont demonstrates.

The most important court women were attached to the households of the various queens and duchesses. These feminine subgroups became a focal point for all sorts of intrigues and affairs. The king set a bad example by undertaking an endless series of barely concealed affairs with ladies-in-waiting, three of whom became virtually institutionalized as resident official mistresses, greatly humiliating the queen, who had to pretend not to notice. A brood of illegitimate royal children was produced, all of whom became major figures at court. This behavior was a throwback to the lifestyles of Henry IV and Francis I, and Louis made it all seem quite official and proper. In 1674 Primi Visconti noted that "the king treats [the queen] with all the honor befitting her status. He eats and sleeps with her, fulfills all his family duties, makes conversation with her as if he had no mistresses. As for her, she spends most of her time at devotions." In 1678 he wrote that:

> the king treated his favorites like members of his family, each in a separate category. The queen received their visits along with those of the [king's] natural children as if it were a duty she had to fulfill, since everything functioned according to each person's rank and the wishes of the king. When they attended mass at Saint Germain, they [all] positioned themselves in plain view of the king: Madame de Montespan with her children at the platform on the left facing everyone, and the "other one" on the right . . . There they prayed, rosary or missal in their hands, raising their eyes in ecstasy like saints.[15]

Plunging into religious activities was one of the few forms of escape available to court women. It was in fact the recourse taken by Louis's rejected mistresses who usually retired to convents.

Certainly the nobles at the court of Louis XIV had much to contend with. But were they relegated to the position of servants? Did Louis XIV keep them neutralized by a delicate balance-of-power game in which only the king came out ahead? We must remember the social and economic position of these figures. Although the king removed them from day-to-day governmental decision-making, their authority and influence were enhanced by the king's reinforcement of rank and his support of noble traditions. While they might scramble for rooms or fight over footstools at Versailles, out in the larger world they were persons of enormous prestige with positions that their proximity to the monarch could only enhance. The prince de Condé had his own magnificent establishment at Chantilly and hundreds of servants in his Parisian household. The duc d'Orleans supported a large household in the Palais Royal in Paris and amassed a fortune with the help of the king. Other great nobles were building mansions in the town of Versailles, outside the palace. Most of them also had accommodation in Paris, where much of the business

Figure 31 The marriage of the duc de Bourgogne to Marie-Adelaide de Savoie on December 7, 1697. Although this is hardly a normal day, the picture gives us a fair idea of how the king and his courtiers would have looked at Versailles fairly late in the reign. By Antoine Dieu (1662–1727).

activity took place. These nobles had clerks keeping account books and managing estates. They, or their managers, paid close attention to their fortunes.

Furthermore, the courtiers were only the cream of the nobility –1–5 percent of the entire group. They were kept out of the royal councils, but they were given positions befitting their rank, such as governorships, ambassadorships, ecclesiastical titles, and military commands. In addition, there was another nobility – the robe dynasties that we saw in Chapter 5 – who by the later reign were achieving a status that was arguably comparable, although not equal, to that of court grandees. They wielded considerable political power in their own right and increasingly integrated themselves with courtly families by marriage or common financial interests.

We should not imagine Louis XIV as a ruler sitting on top of a vast pyramid of subjugated and impoverished nobles; but rather as the ally of a class of wealthy and powerful families enjoying revenues from their vast estates, ties to regional *parlementaire* elites, and relatives or clients holding most of the leadership positions in the state administration. To be sure, Louis XIV made them give up any remaining dreams of independent glory. But at the same time he helped them regain their social and cultural leadership, even as they became more dependent on the royal state for their subsistence.

It would be misleading to think of the court as a set of monitored, disciplined ranks ranged in neat circles around the king for another reason. There was always politics at court, if only because the king would one day die and everyone had to plan for the future. In a system where there was no possible political opposition, cabals or factions were likely to form. Le Roy Ladurie has offered a very complicated analysis of the cabals at Versailles around 1709, based on the detailed memoirs of the duc de Saint-Simon. Far from being automatons, people at court formed complex networks of relationships built around multiple factors. Le Roy Ladurie identifies three main groups, each of which was tied to the royal succession. One followed the lead of Madame de Maintenon, the wife of the king. It included remains of the Louvois lobby. A second was led by Monseigneur, heir to the throne. These two were friendly rivals who together formed the "dominant party" at Versailles. Through various kinds of influence, they controlled the robe "technocrats" who ran the government and formed "a sort of protean holding company under the aegis, real or mythical," of Maintenon. It included a group of leading nobles, some principal military leaders, experienced government ministers and their provincial agents, and the king's two legitimized bastards, the comte de Toulouse and the duc de Maine. The third cabal was grouped around the duc de Bourgogne, second in line to the throne, and a group of influential ministers, several of whom were from the Colbert family. Each group was based, not on a political program, but on the personal relationships of its members. These consisted of a combination of personal rivalries, family ties, religious leanings, social status, professional connections, and even personal friendships. Thus, although Louis XIV was in control of the whole government, the real power structure involved networks of relationships that joined together court figures, family dynasties, and official governmental positions, with ties to officers and nobles in the provinces.

For some forty years, the court society of Louis XIV set the tone for the French and European aristocracy. But its in-grown pettiness and stifling ritual were just extreme expressions of more widely felt noble prejudices, and the Louisquatorzian court was the intensely

Figure 32 Louis's entourage in 1688 – this time dwarfed by the magnificent gardens of Versailles, which Louis loved to show off to guests. By Étienne Allegrain (1644–1736).

concentrated expression of a much broader aristocratic consolidation. During his long reign, Louis XIV had skillfully managed a complex operation in which he had personally protected the reputation of the monarchy, arbitrated relationships among his courtiers, intervened to preserve lineages threatened with extinction, and mitigated the impact of his love life on public affairs. But the skill to handle this finely tuned balancing act could not be passed on.

The eighteenth-century court

Under Louis XV and Louis XVI, the system lost its flexibility and became a straitjacket that the participants could not escape. After Louis's death in 1715, the court moved back to the Tuileries in Paris, where the young Louis XV lived until he was thirteen years old. In 1722 they returned to Versailles, but the great tradition had been broken by seven years of absence. Rituals had to be artificially revived in consultation with old-timers who remembered them. Louis XV was a timid man who withdrew whenever possible to a more intimate private life. Unlike Louis XIV, he did not live twenty-four hours a day in public view. He scrupulously observed the *lever*, the *coucher*, and other ceremonies, but the life had gone out of them. When the courtiers had completed the *coucher* and retired for the night from the royal bedroom, Louis XV would get up again and trot off to his private apartment, where he really slept, often with one of his mistresses. The courtiers at Versailles were left following a routine that no longer had any meaning without the king's heartfelt involvement. They felt bored and isolated. As the comte de Tessin wrote to his wife, "I have nothing very amusing to report from here. It's always the same routine: visits in the morning, then to the royal *lever*, then to the main meal, then the cavagnole [a gambling game] which lasts until you are dropping to sleep... What to report? Hunt, meal, gambling; gambling, meal, hunt; meal, hunt and gambling – there you have it."[16] Attendance at Versailles remained an obligation, but the aristocracy now preferred to live in Paris where elegant townhouses were all the rage. Louis XV became known for his scandalous personal life and for being dominated, unlike Louis XIV, by his mistresses, especially the marquise de Pompadour, for whom he built the Petit Trianon in the park of Versailles, to which they retired for elegant, private dinner parties. Pompadour actively manipulated court politics between 1745 and 1764. Although plays and operas continued to be performed at court, the new productions now opened in Paris and came to Versailles only after they had been well received by the public, reversing the earlier practice.

Enchanted by the Parisian social scene, the aristocrats still had to put in time at court for form's sake, but everyone tried to avoid staying there any longer than necessary. In 1759 Louis XV established rules dictating that only those who could produce documentation showing nobility going back at least to 1400 could be "presented at court." This presentation became the badge of high society. Being chosen was a special honor. Women had to undergo a formal ceremony at which they were introduced to the queen, and men had to go hunting with the king and wait for an invitation to ride back in the royal carriage.

When Louis XVI came to the throne in 1774, he proved even less capable of playing the part of Louis XIV. Confronted with the thunderous sound of all the courtiers racing from the death scene of Louis XV to salute the new twenty-year-old king, Louis is supposed to have cried out, "Oh what a burden! They have taught me nothing! I feel as if the whole universe were falling on me!"[17] Constantly overweight and obsessed with hunting, the king was timid and hated ceremonies. He often appeared sloppy or inept. One official complained that at his *coucher*, when "they took off his jacket, vest, and shirt leaving him naked down to his belt, he would be scratching and rubbing himself in the presence of the whole court and sometimes very distinguished foreigners, as if he were alone."[18] He kept no mistresses, but court life and the king's reputation were greatly influenced by Marie Antoinette, his intelligent but frivolous queen. They spent much time at the Petite Trianon, and Marie Antoinette extended it by adding gardens, a Greek "temple of love," and her picturesque imitation farm.

Conclusion

Looking back over three centuries, was the royal court extravagant and exploitative with respect to the rest of society? This lavish expenditure did, after all, serve a purpose. In addition to providing lodging and entertainment for jaded aristocrats, the court also served as the center of a government that made no sharp distinction between aristocratic living and official governing. It gathered around the king the ministers and secretaries who actually ran the government and the powerful families whose influence could not be ignored. The court's final settlement at Versailles made possible the development of ministerial departments with permanent archives close to the king.

Whether he wanted to discuss military strategy, tax collection, the marriage arrangements of a prince, negotiations with foreign leaders, or legal reform, Louis XIV's experts were close at hand. He could discuss affairs of state without leaving his apartments. He could keep an eye on potential rebels and he could in a sense civilize them by subjecting them to daily rituals and proper manners. Meanwhile, living at court taught some of them to appreciate literature, art, and theater, thanks to the regular presentation of operas, plays, ballets, and concerts at court, and the necessity of talking about them. This acculturation process was enhanced by the creation of a series of royal academies whose members debated and then imposed elegant rules about form and content. Between the sixteenth and the eighteenth centuries, the courtiers began to develop an exquisite taste for luxury which spread to the high nobility, to rich Parisians, and then to provincial centers. It was the beginning of a preoccupation with fashion that would run rampant in the eighteenth century. The court's expenditure on furniture, clothes and construction created jobs for skilled artisans and promoted French production of luxury goods that would greatly influence the eighteenth-century economy, though perhaps not in the most "modern" direction.

In the end, despite all these advantages, the court was wasteful, extravagant, and socially reactionary. From top to bottom, every function increased the gap between the favored few on the top and those less favored. From Francis I to Louis XIV, the scramble intensified for positions at court that would entitle nobles to live at the king's expense and enjoy exemptions from taxes and fees. Household officers received modest salaries, but they also expected many kinds of customary tips and gifts. The great officers received modest *gages* in the neighborhood of 1,200 livres per year in the early sixteenth century, rising to 3,000 livres in 1600 and 3,500 to 10,000 in the period 1660–1740. On the other hand, important officers received supplementary income from performing their functions and enormous gifts from the king in the form of brevets ranging from 14,000 to 30,000 livres. The monarch gave incredible gifts to favored grandees who lived at court, with figures ranging under Louis XIV from 150,000 to 800,000 livres. His officers were then in a position to collect fees from petitioners who needed audiences with the king or his ministers, and to make deals with financiers proposing tax farms. Of course living at court was also very expensive. Acquiring the proper wardrobe, carriage, and servants was essential, as was entertaining one's peers. Most household offices, like judicial posts, had to be purchased, and they therefore represented a sizeable investment. In the eighteenth century the post of Lord Chamberlain cost 600,000 livres; the Master of the Horse, 600,000; the Captains of the Guard, 400,000. The household offices taken together added up to a capital investment of 33,761,000 livres. Those assuming such an office generally borrowed the money from other nobles, who then shared in the proceeds. Thus the court was like a company jointly owned by its shareholders.[19] It was easy to live beyond one's means, and more than one family had to be bailed out of debts by favorable royal edicts.

Still, kings intervened actively to protect families of ancient lineage from bankruptcy. This aristocratic payoff was greatest in the first half of the seventeenth century when the government was threatened by dissention and the grandees had to be persuaded to stay at court. Louis XIV cut back on this extravagance by reducing the number of recipients of pensions and moderating their stipends, but always without jeopardizing their claims of superiority in terms of status and privileges. Although no exact measurements are possible, estimates suggest that the total cost of the court, including the royal household, the households of other royal family members, pensions to courtiers, the soldiers on duty at court, and royal building projects, comprised 13 to 30 percent of the total royal budget throughout the seventeenth and eighteenth centuries. The proportion varied from year to year, largely in inverse relation to the size of the military budget. In 1663 the court made up 35 percent of the total. In 1675, during the Dutch War, it cost 15 percent. In 1688 it was 21 percent. All these figures represent a sizeable share of the royal budget, especially given the fact that most of the money went for courtly extravagance and the upkeep of those attached to the court.

If we break down this total cost of the court during the personal reign of Louis XIV into its component parts, we find that roughly 27 percent of it went for the household proper, 15 percent for other royal family households, 25 percent for the pensions of notable persons, 25 percent for building projects, and 8 percent for military forces at court. If these average percentages of the total cost of the court are applied to the total royal budget for a known year, say 1688, the cost of pensions and royal family households would make a grand total of 14 percent of the whole royal expenditure on maintenance of the king, his family members, and pensions paid to prominent individuals – 19 percent if we add construction costs, mostly used for Versailles. While the bulk of the king's revenue was spent on warfare, and in the eighteenth century increasingly on interest on the royal debt, these figures represent a substantial burden laid on the taxpayers for the support of a courtly aristocracy that was exempt from most taxes.[20]

Thus the cost of the court was not the main fiscal problem facing the monarchy. Nevertheless, the obvious extravagance of the later years of Louis XV and the reign of Louis XVI was a contributing factor to the bankruptcy of the state, and in public relations terms it was a prime factor in the alienation of the citizenry. In 1774 Louis XVI gave Marie Antoinette 300,000 livres of jewelry, and in 1775 the queen herself purchased a set of diamonds worth a further 460,000 livres.[21]

Through the centuries the royal court had developed as a hybrid combination of aristocratic support and governmental rule, merging the frivolity and wastefulness of noble privilege with the central direction of the king. It seemed impossible to have one without the other. The kings were there because they served a necessary function, but who became king was purely a matter of tradition, and as for their talent and personality, the country was subjected to the luck of the draw. When powerful leaders such as Francis I, Henry II, Henry IV, and Louis XIV were in control, the court became the playground of the favored ladies and gentlemen. They were kept in their place by entertainments and a satisfying atmosphere which enhanced the value of gradated rank by giving them the respect they felt they deserved. When kings were weaker because of their young age, their timidity, or the existence of serious ideological disagreements within ruling circles, the court was split by factions and characterized by the withdrawal of grandees and their followers to provincial strongholds. This situation prevailed during the religious wars and the Fronde. The reign of Louis XIII was similarly challenged, but the genius of Cardinal Richelieu held things together – barely. Under Louis XV and Louis XVI the withdrawal was more to urban salons and progressive ideas, but the court was equally weakened. Thus the civilized, elegant court was the corrective for the factionalized, disruptive courtiers who turned rebellious. It represented an acknowledgment of the continuing importance of the major noble families and a reinforcement of their social advantages. The actual courtiers were stand-ins for the broader aristocracy. The king needed their support. The aristocrats needed his validation of their titles and social positions. They both wanted the society of privilege to continue, at the expense of the general population, who were footing the bill for their pleasurable existence.

Suggestions for further reading: the royal household and court life

Household and court before Louis XIV

Cohen, Sarah R., *Art, Dance and the Body in the French Court of the Ancien Régime* (Cambridge, 2000).

Crawford, Katherine, *Perilous Performances: Gender and Regency in Early Modern France* (Cambridge, MA, 2004).

Knecht, R. J., *Renaissance Warrior and Patron: The Reign of Francis I* (Cambridge, 1994).

"Popular Theatre and the Court in Sixteenth-Century France," *Renaissance Studies* 9 (1995), 364–75.

Solnon, Jean-François, *La Cour de France* (Paris, 1987).

Yates, Frances A., *The Valois Tapestries*, 2nd edn (London, 1975), 53–68.

Household and court at Versailles

Barker, Nancy Nichols, *Brother to the Sun King, Philippe, Duke of Orléans* (Baltimore, MD, 1989).

Berger, Robert W., *Versailles: The Chateau of Louis XIV* (College Park, PA, 1985).

Duindam, Jeroen, *Vienna and Versailles: The Courts of Europe's Dynastic Rivals, 1550–1780* (Cambridge, 2003).

Forster, Elborg, ed. and trans., *A Woman's Life in the Court of the Sun King: Letters of Liselotte von der Pfalz, 1652–1722* (Baltimore, MD, 1984).

Kettering, Sharon, "Brokerage at the Court of Louis XIV," *Historical Journal* 36 (1993), 69–87.

Le Roy Ladurie, Emmanuel, with Jean-François Fitou, *Saint Simon and the Court of Louis XIV*, trans. Arthur Goldhammer (Chicago, 2001).

Levron, Jacques, *Daily Life at Versailles in the Seventeenth and Eighteenth Centuries*, trans. Claire Eliane Engel (New York, 1968).

Pitts, Vincent J., *La Grande Mademoiselle at the Court of France 1627–1693* (Baltimore, MD, 2000).

Walton, Guy, *Louis XIV's Versailles* (Chicago, 1986).

12 | *Aristocracy's last bloom and the forces of change*

The eighteenth century saw the culmination of the society that had been evolving since the fourteenth century. It was a society guided by powerful royal direction, buttressed by aristocratic–ecclesiastical supports, and built upon seigneurial–agrarian foundations. For the most fortunate groups, the last seventy years before the Revolution saw an age of prosperity, optimism, elegance, and prettiness. Louis XV and Louis XVI did their best to perpetuate the traditions of ritualized grandeur established by their magnificent predecessor, but they were not up to the task, and as a result the social center of gravity shifted away from king and court toward a broader-based aristocratic society. The prelates of the Catholic church, overwhelmingly aristocratic in their origins, continued to wield great influence.

For the majority of French people the picture was not so rosy. Rural populations suffered the loss of additional farmland to urban accumulators. Seigneurial lords, many of them recently minted social climbers, manipulated traditional seigneurial authority to grab valuable forests from village communities. Consolidating their holdings at the expense of poorer villagers, they continued shifting their revenues from seigneurial dues to land rents. Some well-connected *coqs de village* got rich and rose socially, but the majority of the peasantry lost ground. Certain ports and manufacturing centers generated trade and created jobs, but these were only favored pockets. Taxes were still burdensome and badly distributed. Grain shortages became more frequent after the 1760s, owing to inadequate yields and poor distribution. Large numbers of people took to the roads as beggars, or flocked to cities to become servants and menial laborers. Mothers abandoned children at the doors of charitable organizations in increasing numbers. Poor relief became a vexing problem. In short, powerful currents of change were enhancing the traditional advantages of the already privileged and the wealthy, creating a golden age of cultivation and creativity for some, but at the same time producing hard times for the majority. The system was straining without bringing about needed transformations.

This chapter, unlike the others, will not explore a particular aspect of society. Instead, we will approach the period from 1715 to 1789 as the climax of a long evolution. It is time to focus on aristocratic style-setters, rising consumerism, and the city of Paris as a cultural center. We will resist the temptation to view everything in terms of the coming Revolution. Instead, we will look at society as it would have appeared to prosperous contemporaries, as a vibrant, comfortable existence far removed from social strife. We will first survey the changes that were straining the old system. Then we will focus on the last splendid flowering of the old regime's aristocratic society.

Forces of change

After the desperate last years of the War of Spanish Succession, when the country had to bear the cost of holding off a vast European coalition by supporting the largest army Europe had seen since ancient times, things began to look up. Estimates of total population in 1710 suggest 22.5 million. From that point there was a gradual rise to some 23.8 million in 1730 and 24.5 million in 1750, followed by a rapid increase to 26.6 million in 1770 and 28.1 million in 1790. The increase in the first half of the century was 11 percent, in the second half 18 percent. These were modest gains compared to some parts of Europe, but they provide an indicator that growth was under way. The expansion was the product of fewer devastating wars, better weather, more abundant crops, better communications, more effective quarantining of the sick, and the disappearance of the plague, last experienced in Provence in 1720. This prosperity continued until the 1770s when there was a slump. Population increase was beginning to press against resources that had not expanded at the same rate, and the incidence of hunger, begging, and social unrest increased.

The first new factor was the economy's impressive development. The eighteenth century saw a boom in trade that put new wealth into new hands and stimulated consumption of luxury goods. The manufacture of tapestries, mirrors, porcelain, and numerous other items produced by skilled artisans increased, as did the export of wines and textiles. Agricultural production also increased moderately, with considerable disparity between regions where land was being consolidated into larger farms and regions of tiny plots with large numbers of marginal peasants. Following the lead of the rich farmers who supplied the Parisian market, certain regions became better integrated into regional market systems, but it is probably fair to say that the rise in productivity was modest and mostly achieved without major technological innovation.

Following plans issued by Controller-General Orry in 1738, the monarchy undertook a major program of constructing well-engineered highways linking regions and towns. By 1782 there were 30,000 kilometers of new roads. They reduced transport time, made travel by carriage more palatable, speeded the spread of news, and helped alleviate regional grain shortages.[1]

These shortages continued, although agriculture made considerable progress in a few favored locations where good conditions combined with close urban markets. Around Paris Jean-Marc Moriceau found that the "great farmers" had successfully constructed vast collections of properties which were partially consolidated, and that they were beginning to use them to try new crops and superior systems of rotation. Thus there was a great enthusiasm among cultivated elites for progressive methods, some of which improved crop yields, while the majority of cultivated fields in most places were still fragmented into small parcels encumbered by traditional restrictions. As Moriceau reminds us, "one can never underline enough the disparity that often existed between assembling of properties and restructuring of properties. The first was just as swift and massive as the second was slow, progressive, and marginal."[2]

The most striking economic development was in foreign trade, especially the Atlantic trade. We have noted the booming port cities in Chapter 4. The total value of foreign trade rose from 215 million livres in 1716 to 1,062 million in 1784, while the value of French exports rose from 50 million livres in 1715 to 200 million in 1745. The bulk of this trade was still with traditional European destinations: 91 percent of it in 1716. By 1787, the balance was shifting, with colonial trade up from 9 to 17.2 percent. Growth rates tell a bigger story. Trade with Europe increased 300 percent, while colonial trade rose 1,000 percent.

A large share was with the Antilles islands of Martinique, Guadaloupe, and Saint-Domingue (later known as Haiti). Imports of sugar and indigo from the Antilles climbed from 4.4 million livres in 1716 to

77 million livres in 1754 and continued to increase after the interruption of the Seven Years War. French merchants processed these commodities and reexported them throughout Europe. A new class of plantation owners made fortunes in the Caribbean and retired to lavish households in Bordeaux or Nantes. Several thousand artisans and laborers migrated to the Antilles where they served as plantation managers and taskmasters to their slave labor force. Saint-Domingue alone had 427,000 African slaves, most of them brought in by French slavers. A few Africans even began to appear in French cities. They acted as servants of repatriated planters or claimed to have been freed by their masters. They were small in number, but their presence was the cause of judicial controversies about the legal existence of slavery within metropolitan France.

By the 1760s some industrial concentration, usually in the form of protoindustry, was beginning to appear. Tasks like spinning and weaving were farmed out to peasants working in their homes for low wages, using materials delivered on behalf of the merchant, who then collected the finished product and marketed it. Certain industries took on international importance, such as the production of fine silks in Lyon, linens in Brittany, Indian printed cottons in Rouen, and a wide variety of other fabrics in Valenciennes, Amiens, Sedan, and many other places. Still, industrial production remained a small portion of the economy. During the eighteenth century, industry's share of total production rose from 26 percent to 43 percent, but only 19 percent of the labor force were engaged in industrial work.[3]

Historians continue to debate how advanced the French economy was compared to Great Britain's well-known example of the development of capitalism. Once considered backward, stifled by feudal anachronisms and excessive government intervention, the French economy is now recognized as having made impressive progress in many areas, but having done so using largely traditional means rather than revolutionary innovations. As Paul Butel put it, "there is consensus for excluding a technological revolution but also for rejecting immobilism and for discerning a rise in production through a multitude of 'small steps' undertaken by dispersed local efforts, with strong regional differences."[4]

These impressive developments have to be set against the reality of growing poverty and vagabondage. This failure of the growing economy to alleviate the plight of the masses was the second new factor that we need to examine. Growth in certain sectors did not make up for the fact that the population was growing faster than the production of necessities, especially food. The great famines and waves of plague that had disrupted previous centuries were gone, as were devastating wars on French soil. But these disasters were replaced by a more generalized impoverishment that kept people living at an unhealthy subsistence level. As Olwen Hufton so eloquently put it:

It was fully possible for relative emancipation from famine and plague to produce a greater number of poor than ever before. A starving population, generally speaking, cannot reproduce itself; an undernourished one has no difficulty in so doing. In the hierarchy of wretchedness there is a world of difference between the man who is literally starving, even for a short period, and the one who is merely undernourished all the year round . . . Indeed, the most striking consequence of population movement was the broadening of the base of the social pyramid perhaps more than ever before, a proliferation of people who experienced increasing difficulties in providing themselves with the bare necessities of existence.[5]

Increasing numbers of people were living on the edge of subsistence, tied to inadequate plots of land that were too small or too burdened with obligations to support a family. Wage labor on the larger farms or cottage labor remunerated by urban capitalists could sometimes fill the gap, but wages were low and failed to keep up with the cost of grain, which was being pushed upward by demand. Such work was seasonal and subject to market slumps that led to an immediate cessation of employment. The supply of grain, which provided the main source of food for most of the population, was limited by low yields which were in turn caused by the extreme subdivision of plots and archaic methods. Urban wages were sometimes better, but they too failed to keep up with inflation. Beyond these problems of employment were the structural problems of age and disability. Widows, unmarried girls, men who were victims of accidents or who were too old to perform heavy labor, people who succumbed to the many diseases that were still devastating despite the absence of the plague, were in great danger of falling into homelessness and vagabondage. These were not new problems, but they were intensified by the pressure of population, the decline in the number of viable family farms, and the failure of grain production to increase as fast as the population.

Hufton estimates that as many as 30 to 40 percent of the population could be considered poor, and one-third of them would be forced at some time in their lives to depend on charity to survive. In towns one-fifth to two-thirds of the population were indigent.[6] Girls streamed out of country villages to the nearest town where they found menial employment as servants, sometimes doing industrial spinning or lace-making. Boys became farmhands or went to the city to be servants or to do menial jobs in the linen, cotton, or silk industries, where they worked in damp cellars. Whole communities migrated seasonally to other regions to harvest crops or pick grapes.

Attitudes toward itinerants hardened. It was not easy to distinguish between a vagabond and a migrant worker. Those who haunted the highways looking for work inevitably begged along the way. For example, a young girl from Savoy left home at age twelve in 1767. She worked briefly in Bourg-en-Bresse, then found temporary refuge with nuns. Soon she left for Grenoble, where she failed to find work. She went to Fontainebleau, then to Amplepuis, a town near Villefranche, where she spun cotton for a short time. At age fifteen she headed for Villefranche-sur-Saône to find work and was arrested for vagabondage. Another young girl, arrested in 1733, came from Franche-Comté. She had worked as a servant for a miller's wife in Châlons-sur-Saône, then for a innkeeper's wife in Tournus. She was fired when it became evident that she was three months pregnant. She begged on the highways and gradually made her way to Lyon, where she gave birth in the Hôtel Dieu.[7]

Within villages one-half to two-thirds of the beggars were children. France was plagued with banditry, and beggars proliferated in public places. Peasants became increasingly concerned about bands of vagabonds who damaged the crops and stole the produce. Everyone could see that the problem was getting worse, and there was a tendency to blur together the jobless, the helpless, and the criminal element. The roads were filled with

ragged urchins, desperate mothers with small children, paupers stooped by age, young men with weathered faces, female servants on the move – some pregnant, some merely between jobs – men with scars and furtive looks, peddlers without merchandise, shipwrecked sailors, soldiers traveling without certificates of leave, camp followers, insolent beggars, pickpockets, vagabonds, rogues, and thieves.[8]

Of course there were success stories. Some of these men and women learned trades, saved dowries, made successful marriages, and moved up in the world. But the collective picture was bleak because the new wealth that was coursing through the veins of French society was not breaking down the conditions standing in the way of progress, and good times were only reaching certain segments of the population. These problems slowly grew in intensity until around 1760. They became more serious from then until the Revolution, as grain prices fluctuated more severely, grain riots became more frequent, and crime took its toll on the well-being of respectable citizens.

This brings us to the third new factor to consider: the increasing reach of the royal government. Under Louis XIV's controller-general Colbert, the inner circle of royal ministers had begun to think strategically about how France could be better coordinated, economically and socially. Talented administrators, if not the kings themselves, began to think in terms of positive legislation that could unify the country and facilitate trade and public order. By this time the royal council members had offices staffed with subordinate agents and clerks who maintained detailed statistics on trade, population, and every aspect of provincial affairs. Colbert had commissioned a few ambitious surveys that required beleaguered intendants in the provinces to scramble, virtually alone, to collect an immense variety of local information. Now such surveys were commonplace. Between 1724 and 1728 there were at least seven of them. Now intendants were backed up by numerous subdelegates who reported to them from the major towns of their districts, and by expanding government agencies in Paris or at Versailles. Major projects were undertaken for a geographical survey and map of the kingdom. Efforts were made to improve medical treatment and to develop schools of medicine and surgery. New sources of expertise were created such as the École des Ponts et Chaussées to train the engineers who designed the new system of national highways. The government also continued Richelieu's and Louis XIV's tradition of setting standards for the arts and letters by supporting academies for the arts and sciences.[9] A good symbol of this preoccupation with rational, systematic approaches to governmental knowledge was the use of Henry IV's grand gallery of the Louvre which connected the old Louvre with the Tuileries Palace in Paris. Intricate large-scale models showing every building in key cities on the borders of France were displayed there so that officials could study how to defend or assault them. Later, the remodeling of the same space was begun for a planned display of the royal collection of paintings. Later, under the revolutionary government, it would become the Louvre Museum.

Another extension of government was the transformation of the *maréchaussée*, which had always been a small force of mounted military policemen, into a rural police force to patrol the highways. In the 1760s it consisted of 3,265 men organized into brigades of four or five and distributed throughout the countryside. Their purpose was to police rural areas and, more particularly, to arrest beggars. Although the force was too small to provide real security, it was a vast improvement on the past.[10]

While there were serious flaws in the leadership of both Louis XV and Louis XVI, the government as an institution was filled with intelligent, well-connected administrators, many of whom were aware of social problems and had developed a variety of ambitious programs to resolve them. Men like Orry, Turgot, Necker, Maupeou, and Argenson tried a number of ambitious plans, some with partial success. The real problem in the government was the revolving door of ministers chosen, then abandoned; the nefarious influence of factional politics at court; and the indecision or constant shifting of policy on the part of the two eighteenth-century kings. In an age when enlightened thought was stimulating ideas of reform and progress even among the king's closest associates, the problem was not a lack of initiative, but rather the inability of the government to carry any particular policy to fruition.

One of the most serious problems was poor relief, the fourth new aspect of eighteenth-century society. Clearly something had to be done about the beggars and bandits described above. The original solution, invented by towns like Lyon in the sixteenth century and adopted for Paris in 1656 by Louis XIV, was the general hospital. This was not a medical facility, but a poor house where those caught begging were locked up and made to work while learning a useful trade. Those considered able-bodied (and viewed as lazy) were forced to work. Those considered the "worthy poor" because they had an infirmity or were crippled or sick, were fed and housed. Children, the elderly, and the sick were included.

In 1662 the king issued an edict requiring every town in France to set up such a hospital. The directors were granted the power to hire guards with the authority to arrest beggars on the street and drag them to the hospital. They were authorized to use flogging, shackling in irons, and being locked in a cell as disciplinary methods. No funding was offered to the cities, and few hospitals were actually established until a revival of interest in the 1690s. When these measures failed to reduce the population of beggars, an important new declaration in 1724 established more rigorous rules requiring all able-bodied men to work. It set up levels of punishment to recognize the difference between able-bodied, legitimate beggars, and true vagabonds, and for the first time to provide royal funding for local hospitals and the police. The intention was to clear the country of beggars and make everyone join the work force. This move brought about a wholesale locking-up of beggars in 156 designated hospitals. These facilities had to be reorganized to serve more like prisons and less like charitable institutions. Between 1724 and 1733 large numbers of beggars were imprisoned, but the program did not succeed in eradicating beggars. The hospitals were too small and the funding too limited. But the fact that the government was allocating funds at least meant that the hospitals were being taken on as a responsibility by the crown.

In the 1770s, another form of relief, the *atelier de travail*, was tried. This was essentially a public works program financially underwritten by the government. Local people nominated by the curé would be employed to build roads or to do repair work for local seigneurs. Women, children, and unskilled men would do the rough work, while the more skilled men would do the paving and stone work. The workers were paid a wage on a scale adjusted to their supposed needs. Some donations came from the government. Private parties were solicited, and the traditional work services owed by some peasants to their lords (*corvées*) were sometimes commuted into road work. This program was successful in a few places. But there was not always appropriate work to be done, and the *ateliers* did nothing for those who could not work.

In the late 1760s, a more stringent repression was instituted in response to general outrage among officials about the extent of the problem. The intendant of Burgundy in 1759 lamented that "the number of beggars in the kingdom had increased so much, their insolence and excesses carried to such a point that it is absolutely necessary to provide a remedy...Beggars have neither religion nor morals, thus one must not be surprised that they commit all sorts of crimes and wanton acts."[11] In 1764–7 new repressive declarations were issued which further criminalized the landless poor. *Dépôts de mendicité*, which were in effect prisons, were to be established in every district under the direction of the intendant. Vagrants found on the roads were to be arrested by the *maréchaussée*. Proof of guilt was either being caught in the act of begging, or being denounced by someone who had been solicited by the beggar, especially if the solicitation had been threatening. One could also be arrested on suspicion. Guilt could then be established if a search of the beggar's sack revealed pieces of stale bread or possession of the sort of worthless coins that were usually given to beggars. Those guilty of having exercised no trade for six months and owning no property were either sent to the galleys or locked up in a *dépôt*.

By 1773, 72,056 persons had been arrested. Of those, 50,009 had been locked up in thirty *dépôts*, and 968 sent to the galleys.[12] The depots were hastily equipped sections of old buildings or fortresses. They were crowded, damp, and airless. The water provided was sometimes foul. Beggars were often sickly anyway, and most received short sentence, so that there was a rapid turnover of prisoners who quickly fell ill as disease swept through the crowded population. Hufton reports that overall 13,899, or almost 20 percent of the 72,056 persons arrested by 1773, died in the *dépôts*. At Vannes 28 percent of the inmates died in little over two years. The prisoners were supposed to be trained to work, but they were often too weak, and many facilities had no room for this training.[13]

The fifth new factor in the eighteenth century was the rising importance of public opinion and the explosion of the means by which the educated public received and exchanged ideas about politics and society. This phenomenon is often called, after Habermas, the "rise of the public sphere." It entailed the new ideas and attitudes that we associate with the "Enlightenment," and the acceleration of the transmission of those ideas and attitudes by new modes of communication, and their reception by a broader public. Political discussion was increasingly infused into this discourse. All this was fueled by the general prosperity of the upper crust of wealthy nobles, royal administrators, merchants, lawyers, and other middle-class professionals. The extension of literacy to a broader segment of urban society was a contributing factor. The long tradition of humanistic learning, reinforced by the scientific and philosophical ideas of major seventeenth-century thinkers such as Descartes, Galileo, Locke, or Newton, was now being repackaged into witty, accessible essays and disseminated to a broader public. The flood of texts radiated fashionable, secular attitudes, promoting a spirit of optimism about human progress and directing considerable sarcasm toward the church, the government, and all kinds of intolerance.

These tendencies were amplified by a major increase in the volume of published books, from under one thousand in 1715 to four thousand in 1789, and a rise in the number of newspapers from four to eighty.[14] Reading societies and lending libraries sprang up in every major town, and learned academies were established in every major city, growing from fifteen to thirty in the course of the century.[15] Cafés where people could meet and read newspapers or engage in polite conversation about books or political affairs proliferated.

This explosion of exchanges among those with education and leisure time can make it seem as if the whole society was on the move. In fact, the new ideas coexisted with the continuing influence of a massive Catholic establishment and a vast governmental apparatus, both of which had powerful vested interests. As Colin Jones put it, "the public sphere on which the *lumière* of the *philosophes* was projected was not easily accommodated within the purview of the royal court. Intellectual exchange – *le commerce des esprits* – worked best among the literate and urbane social elite and in the kind of commercial society which France was fast becoming."[16] Both the state and the church had leaders who were receptive to many of the new ideas, but as institutions they were deeply conservative.

Already in the later years of Louis XIV, social and intellectual life had migrated from the court at Versailles to the aristocratic salons of Paris. Elegant ladies, most of them from families with new wealth, held weekly salons where literary and scientific figures mingled with aristocrats and commoners. Socialites frequented the opera and the theater, where new productions were now premiered rather than at court. Essays, some of them quite subversive, circulated by hand. Even the royal censors were sometimes indulgent. Projects spreading enlightenment, such as the multi-volume encyclopedia of Diderot and d'Alembert, were widely distributed, and a new reading public swooned over the emotional excesses of Jean-Jacques Rousseau.

Spoken and unspoken critiques generated dissatisfaction with the system and loss of confidence in the monarchy. Jansenists, who were antagonized by crackdowns on their religious practices by the king and his episcopal allies, joined with constitutionalist opponents of royal absolutism in the Paris Parlement to rally public opinion against royal "despotism." Prominent attorneys published legal briefs arguing the merits of notorious cases. Designed to impress a wider audience, they defined their terms in generalized contrasts such as constitutional liberty versus royal despotism, or masculine virtue versus feminine corruption. Louis XV was discredited by a whole new popular literature, some of it pornographic, portraying him as dominated by women and sexual excess. Louis XVI was similarly discredited by exaggerated reports about the reputation of his queen, Marie Antoinette.

The new ideas reached a refined audience in Parisian salons and in regional capitals. Meanwhile, the broadest critiques reached a wider segment of the literate and semi-literate population. As we have noted, the majority of the population were immersed in local life and more concerned with bread prices or local quarrels.

Paris and the beginnings of a consumer society

All these changes were accompanied by the flowering of an elegant, comfortable style of life for aristocratic society and some increase in material wealth for middle-class groups below them. When Louis XIV was breathing his last, the charismatic force of his stately regime was already being seriously eroded by the growing attraction of the Parisian social world. The court at Versailles had dominated the social landscape for a generation. Now, at the end of the reign, the elegant, attractive world of Parisian salons, with exchanges of courtesy visits, trips to opera and theater, promenades in carriages and strolls in the Tuileries gardens, was already under way. Court aristocrats were devoting more time to applying their individual good taste to remodeling their Parisian townhouses, in competition with trend-setters from the robe and finance. After 1760 this dynamic interaction of money, taste, ideas, and public criticism began to take on a life of its own, making Paris the cultural capital of Europe.

Ironically, it was Louis XIV, reputed to shun the city, who had begun the reconstruction of the city. He had built the classical facade at the eastern end of the Louvre Palace. He demolished the ramparts at the northeastern edge of the old city and replaced the walls with

Figure 33 A classic view of Paris in 1680. We see the Louvre Palace on the left, the domed Collège des Quatre Nations, created by Mazarin, on the right, and the Pont Neuf in the background, in front of the towers of Notre-Dame cathedral. The Seine is crowded with barges and merchandise. By Adam Perelle (1640–95).

inner boulevards which were soon teeming with theaters and cafés. He raised victory arches celebrating his own glory at main entrances to the city, created the esplanade leading up to the Invalides military hospital, established the parade ground at the Champ-de-Mars where the Eiffel Tower would one day stand, and began the extension westward of the grand axis that would become the Champs-Elysées. The Sun King also created the post of lieutenant-general of police, a sort of intendant of the capital city, along with a team of lieutenants who became keepers of the peace, and spied for the government on the mood of the population. Dens of thieves were removed. Street lights began to appear. Louis XV added the Place Louis XV, which is today the massive Place de la Concorde, to the west of the Tuileries gardens.

Behind this developing urban facade was a vibrant cultural life taking place in salons hosted by elegant ladies. An active press spread critical thinking; the medical school carried out interesting experiments; the royal academies promoted the arts and sciences. There was a profusion of cafés, libraries, and bookstores. When Englishman Arthur Young visited Paris in 1787, he found a city both squalid and culturally invigorating. He went to theater or opera performances every evening and met with a whole network of cultivated persons connected to important artistic or scientific institutions: the secretary of the Royal Society of Agriculture, the chemist Lavoisier, and the Astronomer Royal. He also visited the Military Academy founded by Louis XV, saw an exhibit of paintings at the Louvre, and admired the new Place Louis XV and the Champs-Elysées. At the same time he found it "incredible, to a person used to London, how dirty the streets of Paris are, and how horribly inconvenient and dangerous walking is." He went on,

Walking, which in London is so pleasant and so clean, that ladies do it every day, is here a toil and a fatigue to a man, and an impossibility to a well dressed woman. The coaches are numerous and, what is much worse, there is an infinity of one-horse cabriolets, which are driven by young men of fashion and their imitators, alike fools, with such rapidity as to be real nuisances and render the streets exceeding dangerous, without an incessant caution.[17]

Young sampled the night life as well: "At night [went] to *l'Ambigu Comique*, a pretty little theater, with plenty of rubbish on it. Coffeehouses on the boulevards, music, noise, and *filles* without end, everything but scavengers and lamps. The mud is a foot deep and there are parts of the boulevards without a single light."

This elegant culture, which nostalgic conservatives looked back on so longingly after the Revolution, resulted from both the expenditure of aristocrats and the infusion of middle-class wealth. France was experiencing elements of a "consumer revolution" led by the rich. Wealthy style-setters were interacting with the producers of luxury goods in a race to display the latest fashions, and in the process producing a rise in fashion-consciousness and the beginnings of the manipulation of taste through advertising. People began to define their individuality in terms of material possessions. In Paris at least, specialized shops began to appear, along with the practice of shopping as a pastime.

The chief trend-setters were the cream of the aristocracy, both traditional sword families and wealthy parvenus from the high robe or finance, sometimes tied by marriage to new colonial fortunes. The nobility as an officially defined legal order was considerably renewed by new blood. Chaussinand-Nogaret figures that a fourth of the nobles were newcomers in the eighteenth century, even two-thirds if we include those ennobled during the seventeenth century.[18] These rising families introduced an element of financial worth and earned merit into an order that thought of itself as a hereditary military class. Almost half of the new nobles derived their position by purchasing offices of *secrétaire du roi* that conferred full nobility after twenty years. The rest rose through purchase of royal office or by serving in a municipal office conferring nobility. The new contingent of the elite thus came from the high reaches of the bourgeoisie – the families with money and talent.

In the last decades of the *ancien régime*, the fashion leaders were the royal favorites. Those who lived at court had vast fortunes drawn from land rents, ecclesiastical positions, pensions from the king, and salaries attached to provincial governorships, ministries, and ambassadorships. Under Louis XVI, eighty-six dignitaries enjoyed pensions and salaries totaling three million livres. Another 483 courtiers shared second-rank pensions of 5,608,268 livres. Holding a post in the royal household required the recipient to purchase the office. These offices together produced a total capital investment of 33,761,000 livres, from which the incumbents received substantial *gages*.

These grandees collected substantial revenues and spent prodigiously. The princesse de Lamballe, favorite of Marie Antoinette, whose head was later paraded on a pike by revolutionaries in 1792 at the time of the September massacres, received 950,000 livres a year for her various court assignments, while her brother received 54,000. Ten members of the Polignac family collectively received 2,500,000 livres in cash plus pensions totaling 437,900 livres.[19] To cite one example of sources of income, the prince de Robecq had an annual income of 214,233 livres, 61 percent of which he derived from his estates in Flanders, his principality of Robecq, his lordships in Touraine, Burgundy, Brie, and Holland, and his wife's dowry. Another 38 percent came from various military governorships accorded by the crown, and 1 percent from his membership of the Order of the Holy Spirit, an honorific title also bestowed by the crown. His annual expenses were 208,684 livres, including 58,000 for food, 3,450 for his wardrobe, 17,406 paid to servants and employees, 2,054 for theater tickets, concerts, books, and newspaper subscriptions, 12,627 for maintenance of his town house in Paris, and another 1,438 for his townhouse in Lille, capital of his principal governorship. At least his accounts were balanced, unlike those of many others.[20]

Money poured into an ever-widening list of useless extravagances to the point of generating negative public opinion. Madame Elisabeth, Louis XVI's sister, was reported to have spent 30,000 livres on fish and 70,000 livres on meat in one year. Madame de Guéménée owed 60,000 livres for shoes; Madame de Matignon paid her hairdresser 24,000 livres to create a different hair style for each day of the year. Of course focusing on such sensationalist reports exaggerates the importance of exceptional examples. In fact, the 42 million livres spent on the court in 1788 constituted only 6.63 percent of the state's expenses, which were composed of debts incurred during the American war against Great Britain.[21] It became increasingly clear, however, that for whatever reason the government was virtually bankrupt, and frivolous expenditure was blamed.

Even worse, anti-royal sentiment was fueled by pornographic novels depicting Louis XV's mistresses or Marie Antoinette in compromising positions, and innumerable tracts and news sheets spread the public notion that the king was under the spell of corrupt women. Scandalous stories of this sort had a large role in changing public opinion.

In the bustling streets of Paris, where financiers and aristocrats riding in carriages shared the streets with craftsmen of all sorts and thousands of lackeys, porters, and laborers, class differences were there for everyone to see. While the common citizens worried over the price of bread and other foods, the aristocratic trend-setters were vying with one another to see who could construct the most elegant townhouse filled with the most exquisite furnishings. It seemed as if style was king, and luxury, accompanied by quite a bit of good taste and intellectual refinement, was the only desirable way of life.

Important families divided their time between a Parisian *hôtel*, a house or apartment at Versailles, and various country properties. In Paris their family seats migrated westward, as the old family *hôtels* in the eastern Marais district near the Bastille and the Hôtel de Ville were gradually rebuilt closer to the Louvre. High society then pushed farther westward along the rue du Faubourg Saint-Honoré on the right bank and the rue Saint-Dominique on the left bank, reaching toward the road to Versailles. These newer, eighteenth-century townhouses took advantage of the larger plots on the edge of the city to build larger and more imposing villas, with tall entrance gates leading to spacious courtyards and extensive stables.

In the days of Louis XIV, fashions had been set by the king, who shrewdly understood that by setting and then modifying the dress standards, his example would be taken up by people at the court, followed by the Parisian middle classes, and this would promote French luxury industries. But even Louis could not control every aspect of fashion, and the impetus gradually shifted to leading court ladies and Parisian socialites. In the eighteenth century principal figures at court and in the city engaged in an ongoing competition to distinguish themselves by appearing first with the latest fashions. The duchess of Fitz-James bought fifty pairs of shoes and forty dresses in one year, and eighty-five pairs of stockings in another.[22] Last month's clothes were passed on to the servants or to the booming second-hand market, where they spread the styles more widely among the middle and lower classes. Provincial high society watched closely and adopted Parisian fashions, with a short delay. As the baronne d'Oberkirch noted, "although we lived in the provinces, we were completely up to date with the fashions and news from Paris. Several of our friends sent bulletins and veritable newsletters." When she was at court, she reported, "in the morning I went to visit Madame the Duchess of Bourbon, who wanted to show me a new style. She had invented a sort of hat...that she wanted to make fashionable."[23]

A new relationship that was developing between aristocratic consumers and artisanal producers had wide repercussions. As style became ever more visible, important people began to patronize particular tailors, and the tailors began to create exclusive styles for them. Competition among trend-setters drove fashion forward, while the craftsmen began to understand that novelty was advantageous to them. Leading merchants worked to establish reputations as court-appointed suppliers. Shops began to appear where clothing was attractively displayed. Emblems on store signs or business cards and the use of the names of notable patrons provided a primitive kind of advertising. An immense diversity of fabrics, colors, and accessories entered the discourse. Newspapers began to offer columns on the latest styles at court, and the first journals devoted exclusively to discussions of fashion began to be published around 1768. The *Galerie des modes* published 400 engravings of fashions between 1778 and 1787.[24] The provincial press followed suit and offered its eager readers updates on the latest Parisian fashions.

In the 1770s and 1780s Marie Antoinette herself became the nation's leading fashion plate, under the influence of her dressmaker, Rose Bertin, who met with her weekly to keep her wardrobe up to date. Bertin opened a shop in Paris and started a business designing and peddling frivolous new styles to aristocratic ladies and prominent actresses. She was jokingly known as the "first minister of fashion," and people at court were scandalized by the fact that she was allowed to have frequent private audiences alone with the queen.[25]

This luxury industry was driven by aristocratic demand. It extended to a whole range of items, not just clothing. The great spent fortunes on renovations to townhouses and rural chateaux, filling them with the furniture, tapestries, paintings, clocks, porcelain, and jewelry that we see today in museums. Letters begin to describe the gourmet dishes served at formal dinners, as chefs competed to produce new sauces and exotic recipes. Carriages of all sizes and capacities were proliferating, along with the necessary horses. The duc de la Tremouille purchased fifteen carriages in many different styles, worth at least 3,000 livres apiece, between 1777 and 1787. The larger models required four to eight horses to pull them. The result was the need for colossal stables. The king's brother, the comte d'Artois, had 242 horses. In 1779, the duc de Ponthièvre had sixty-six horses to pull carriages, thirty-two for hunting, fifteen heavy carts, and ten others.[26]

In the 1770s English gardens were all the rage for country estates, but they were dreadfully expensive. Instead of the formal plantings and extended vistas of Versailles, the idea was to create an artificial, imaginary landscape: "the garden is tastefully laid out in the English manner and has some very pretty features, ponds, islands, walks among rocks, bridges, all mixed in with sarcophaguses, obelisks."[27] Marie Antoinette had her own English garden at Versailles near the Petit Trianon.

These luxuries were only for the very rich. However, the new wealth was trickling through the economy and influencing the middle class as well, at least in Paris. Beyond the growth of luxury industries, a broader segment of society was experiencing an increase in the level of material possessed by average people. Having more meant developing new habits and different attitudes. Evidence collected by Daniel Roche shows that Parisians in general were spending more on more diverse kinds of clothing. They were eating better, with access to a much wider range of fruits, vegetables, and meats. Stoves that heated better were replacing fireplaces for some. Indoor running water was still nearly non-existent, but small continuously running fountains were established in some neighborhoods, in addition to the ornamental fountains in aristocratic gardens that had always been a privilege of important people. Nocturnal street lighting was improved. There was much more reading of books and newspapers. Stimulants like coffee and tobacco were much more prevalent. In short, a sizeable number of people were focusing more on consumption, while enjoying a greater diversity of products to consume.

These commodities and their uses brought about something of a modernization of consumer behavior. A consequence was increased individualism. People began to think in terms of earning money to purchase desired things instead of focusing on subsistence. One bought things for oneself or others instead of identifying totally with the collective interests of family or confraternity. From scorning the things of this world and looking to salvation in the next, many people began to think of their identity in terms of the acquisition of goods which would demonstrate their individual good taste. It was now possible to think positively about granting oneself small pleasures ("I've worked hard; I deserve a night at the theater.") Whereas traditionally the government tried to impose dress standards that reflected status, such as distinguishing noble from commoner, now fashion was serving to delineate class, which was increasingly tied to wealth and gender.

In fact, Jennifer Jones argues that in the eighteenth century we can see the emergence of different attitudes toward gender and identity. In the Parisian labor force, male and female guilds were beginning to differentiate themselves in gendered terms. Earlier relations had been largely determined by power struggles between the males in the guilds which monopolized most of clothing production, and the females, who were relegated to limited areas such as linen weaving and the production of certain kinds of clothing for women and children. In the eighteenth century both sides began relying on gendered reasoning to make their cases for extending their reach. The male tailors argued that it was in the public interest for them to control production because they had greater skill. The female guilds argued that modesty required that women being fitted for clothing should deal with other women, and that the female seamstresses should be shielded from the advances of men. Using this argument, the women eventually won a larger share of women's and children's clothing.

Fashion created new trades. Hairdressing grew rapidly and over-came challenges from the old wigmakers' guild. Hairdressers were predominantly men. Women, however, emerged in the new trade of *marchandes de modes*, which we might translate as fashion designers. According to the *Encyclopédie*:

Their art is not to make anything; it consists in ingeniously furnishing a new look with all the varied and gracious ornaments of other arts, particularly that of braid and trimmings. Women's hairstyles, except for the arrange-ment of the hair, is the realm of the *marchande des modes*, and that which they practice the most, just as much as the adornment of the neck, arms, and the trimmings of clothing and all that can be considered embellishment and properly brings out the beauty and elegance of the dress. But the decoration of the head, and finally the bust, is their talent *par excellence* and the triumph of their art.[28]

In 1776 they were officially incorporated as a guild, along with the feather-makers and artificial flower-makers. They opened shops all over Paris and made a specialty of hats and bonnets. Other women, mostly young girls, appeared as *grisettes*, or shop girls. They waited on customers and were paid a wage. It was unusual for young women to be so much in the public gaze, and there was talk, probably by men, about their immorality and vulnerability. The landscape now included successful businesswomen and young female employees. Larger shops began to offer fixed prices rather than haggling as in the traditional marketplace, and prosperous ladies and gentlemen began to frequent shops rather than expecting the merchant to wait on them at home.

Women were getting a new image. They had always been thought of (by men) as licentious, sexually threatening, disorderly, and sinful. Now femininity was associated not only with domesticity but also with taste, consumption, and fashion. With these came extravagance and excessive spending. At the court of Louis XIV, women's and men's styles had been rather similar, since clothing signaled status more than gender. Now women's fashion had became an essential part of the concept of femininity and fostered a whole industry. Men adopted the basic suits that, with minor variations, have prevailed ever since. Meanwhile, Paris was becoming the fashion capital of Europe, and France was learning to develop its reputation for discriminating taste and luxury industries. As Jones concludes:

By the late 1780s, the empire of fashion was no longer depicted as a despotism, and *la mode* was no longer portrayed as a corrupt, tyrannical queen to dethrone. Now *la mode* had been transformed into a being so gentle, so sweet, and so naturally feminine that women would gladly submit to her caprices.[29]

Conclusion

France, or at least Paris, would have appeared to an intelligent observer in 1788 as the center of the civilized world. Things looked good. France had won the War of American Independence in 1783 and was busy adulating such American *philosophes* as Benjamin Franklin and Thomas Jefferson. High society was achieving new heights of extravagant taste and conspicuous consumption, and provincial capitals were following suit. Despite some censorship, new ideas were being freely exchanged; fine plays and novels were widely distributed and appreciated; governmental reforms, such as the creation of representative assemblies in the provinces, were under way; colonial trade was producing new wealth; many people lived more comfortably and had more possessions than their grandparents. There were, of course, problems, but there was no reason to believe that they could not somehow be resolved as they had been in the past. Nobody had the slightest idea that a full-fledged revolution with striking world consequences was about to unfold.

But, to echo Charles Dickens, "It was the best of times, it was the worst of times." The early modern society that we have been examining was becoming rusty and bloated and unable to change. Progress on the surface was accompanied by underlying poverty and considerable resentment, even as old and new aristocrats enjoyed their finest – and last – flowering. This is not the place to discuss the origins of the Revolution. We have approached it blindly, as contemporaries did. But looking with hindsight over the previous four hundred years, we can see basic characteristics of the society that were causing new problems and generating resentment.

The nobility had survived and prospered by reeducating itself, by cultivating royal support and by co-opting new wealth from the robe and finance. Its secret weapon was *privilege* – the many kinds of special treatment and legal advantage that even poor nobles enjoyed. Kings had been successful in building increased control over the budding nation, but only with the support of the high nobility and at the expense of creating a semi-independent class of robe officers who both supported and challenged them. The monarchs' co-dependent financial relationship with robe officers and financial cartels made it hard to compete with nations like Great Britain that had better credit mechanisms. The degree to which the church hierarchy and the nobility sucked resources away from the land made agricultural advance problematical. Many seigneurial controls and the serious fragmentation of ownership of the fields left too many peasants with low yields and inadequate resources for improvement. There were also cultural warning signals. A tradition of collective violence prepared local communities to invoke direct action if government became unacceptable. The religiously devout, whether Protestant or Catholic, were unhappy with the king's authoritarian interventions in the nature of their beliefs. The judges of the Parlements were similarly annoyed at high-handed attempts to stomp on their participation in governmental decision-making. The church's attempt to reform popular superstitions made new enemies in the countryside. The last two eighteenth-century kings suffered from moral lapses, poor decision-making, and an incredibly bad press, which saddled them with failings seen through gendered prejudices, to the effect that they were dominated by dangerous women. A growing middle class, which was increasingly flirting with material comforts, suffered from rising expectations and from jealousy of the conspicuous high society above them. Ideas were stimulating demand for progress in every area of life.

In 1788 an assembly of notables called for the Estates-General to be convoked; Louis XVI gave in and agreed; political debates proliferated right down to the villages. The society that had evolved since 1400 was about to be irrevocably changed.

Suggestions for further reading: eighteenth-century France

General surveys

Chaussinand-Nogaret, Guy, *The French Nobility in the Eighteenth Century: From Feudalism to Enlightenment*, trans. William Doyle (Cambridge, 1985).

Lewis, Gwynne, *France 1715–1804: Power and the People* (London, 2004).

Jones, Colin, *The Great Nation: France from Louis XV to Napoleon* (London, 2002).

Society from various perspectives

Adams, Christine, *A Taste for Comfort and Status: A Bourgeois Family in Eighteenth-Century France* (College Park, PA, 2000).

Forster, Robert, *Merchants, Landlords, Magistrates; The Depont Family in 18th Century France* (Baltimore, MD, 1980).

Hufton, Olwen H., *Bayeux in the Late Eighteenth Century: A Social Study* (Oxford, 1967).

The Poor of Eighteenth-Century France 1750–1789 (Oxford, 1974).

Jones, Colin, *Charity and Bienfaisance: The Treatment of the Poor in the Montpellier Region 1740–1815* (Cambridge, 1982).

Schwartz, Robert, *Policing the Poor in Eighteenth-Century France* (Chapel Hill, NC, 1988).

Smith, Jay M., *Nobility Reimagined: The Patriotic Nation in Eighteenth-Century France* (Ithaca, NY, 2005).

Sonenscher, Michael, *The Hatters of Eighteenth-Century France* (Berkeley, CA, 1987).

Work and Wages: Natural Law, Politics and the Eighteenth-Century French Trades (Cambridge, 1989).

Economic development and consumerism

Brennan, Thomas, *Burgundy to Champagne: The Wine Trade in Early Modern France* (Baltimore, MD, 1997).

Gullickson, Gay L., *Spinners and Weavers of Auffay: Rural Industry and the Sexual Division of Labor in a French Village, 1750–1850* (Cambridge, 1986).

Fox, Robert and Anthony Turner, eds., *Luxury Trades and Consumerism in Ancien Régime Paris: Studies in the History of the Skilled Workforce* (Aldershot, 1998).

Jones, Jennifer, *Sexing La Mode: Gender, Fashion and Commercial Culture in Old Regime France* (Oxford, 2004).

Moriceau, Jean-Marc, *Les Fermiers de l'Île de France, XVe–XVIIIe siècle* (Paris, 1994).

Roche, Daniel, *A History of Everyday Things: The Birth of Consumption in France, 1600–1800*, trans. Brian Pearce (Cambridge, 2000).

Rosenband, Leonard N., *Papermaking in Eighteenth-Century France: Management, Labor, and Revolution at the Montgolfier Mill, 1761–1805* (Baltimore, MD, 2000).

Thomson, J. K. J., *Clermont-de-Lodève 1633–1789: Fluctuations in the Prosperity of a Languedocian Cloth-Making Town* (Cambridge, 1982).

Vardi, Liana, *The Land and the Loom: Peasants and Profit in Northern France 1680–1800* (Durham, NC, 1993).

Life in the capital

Farge, Arlette, *Fragile Lives: Violence, Power and Solidarity in Eighteenth-Century Paris* (Cambridge, MA, 1993).

Garrioch, David, *Neighbourhood and Community in Paris 1740–1790* (Cambridge, 1986).

The Making of Revolutionary Paris (Berkeley, CA, 2002).

Ranum, Orest, *Paris in the Age of Absolutism: An Essay* (University Park, PA, 2002).

France overseas

Ames, Glenn J. and Ronald S. Love, eds., *Distant Lands and Diverse Cultures: The French Experience in Asia, 1600–1700* (Westport, CT, 2003).

Bamford, Paul, *Privilege and Profit: A Business Family in Eighteenth-Century France* (Philadelphia, PA, 1988).

Boulle, Pierre, *Race et esclavage dans la France de l'Ancien Régime* (Paris, 2007).

Crouse, N. M., *The French Struggles for the West Indies, 1665–1713* (New York, 1943).

Louder, Dean R. and Eric Waddell, *French America: Mobility, Identity, and Minority Experience across the Continent* (Baton Rouge, LA, 1993).

Manning, Catherine, *Fortunes à faire: The French in Asian Trade 1719–48* (Aldershot, 1996).

Peabody, Sue, *"There Are No Slaves in France:" The Political Culture of Race and Slavery in the Ancien Régime* (Oxford, 1996).

Pritchard, James, *In Search of Empire: The French in the Americas, 1670–1730* (Cambridge, 2004).

Stein, Robert Lewis, *The French Slave Trade in the 18th Century: An Old Regime Business* (Madison, WI, 1979).

　The French Sugar Business in the Eighteenth Century (Baton Rouge, LA, 1988).

Appendix 1: A brief synopsis of early modern French history

This summary may help orient readers unfamiliar with the political evolution of the French monarchy by sketching the narrative which is not covered in this book.

I. Period of late medieval crises (1320–1483)

The outbreak of the plague, or Black Death, in 1348 resulted in a serious drop in population which shifted the balance of power between lords and their peasants in favor of the latter. The episodic Hundred Years War between England and France (1338–1450) periodically devastated key provinces and undermined royal power. By the early fifteenth century France had been partitioned into English, Burgundian, and royal zones. The monarchy's nadir was reached in 1420 when Charles VII was induced to sign the Treaty of Troyes which ceded the succession to the French crown to Henry V of England. In the 1420s and 1430s, inspired by Joan of Arc, Charles began to rally his forces. He gradually recaptured most of the kingdom, which he pieced back together by confirming the privileges of each reintegrated area. In 1438 he issued the Pragmatic Sanction of Bourges, which claimed extensive authority to regulate the national "Gallican" church. He and his son, Louis XI, established the practice of collecting the annual *taille* and other taxes without consent.

II. The French Renaissance (1483–1559)

The reconstituted monarchy soon began a series of wars in Italy to assert dynastic claims to rule certain areas. This adventure eventually culminated in a confrontation with the Habsburg emperor Charles V, who inherited not only the Holy Roman Empire, but also Spain, most of Italy, and the recently discovered New World. Italian influences spread among the aristocracy, at court, and within the church.

Humanistic learning and the artistic styles of the Renaissance offered
new ways for monarch, courtiers, and educated townsmen to redefine
themselves. In 1516 Francis I signed the Concordat of Bologna with
the pope which made official the king's right to name most of the
kingdom's prelates. One offshoot of humanism, Calvinism, began to
spread among urban artisans and professionals. The Treaty of Cateau-
Cambrésis in 1559 ended the Habsburg–Valois wars, but Henry II
died unexpectedly at a critical moment, just as the demobilized army
was dumping unemployed soldiers onto the roads and Protestant
militants (Huguenots) were coming out into the open with their
challenges to the traditional Catholic culture.

III. The era of religious wars (1559–1629)

Three sons of Henry II ruled in succession, dominated by their Italian
mother, Catherine de' Medici. Their regime was weakened by the
looming Protestant threat and the unilateral taking up of arms by
leading magnates. The result was a series of eight "religious" wars in
which Catholics battled Protestants over a combination of confessional conflicts and political rivalries. The grandees at court took
sides, and the rival factions mobilized their regional client networks.
Towns developed splits between Protestant and Catholic factions.

The monarchy tried to find a middle ground by issuing edicts of
pacification after each war, but violence always broke out anew. In
the ultimate phase in the 1590s, the militant Catholic League, led by
the Guise family, turned against King Henry III himself, who was
trying to defend royal power even if it meant tolerating Protestants. In
1588 Henry III had Henry of Guise, the league's leader, assassinated.
In 1589 Henry III himself was assassinated. This left Henry of
Navarre, a Calvinist and leader of the Protestant faction, as legitimate
heir to the throne. He raised an army to fight the Guises.

A radical Catholic party, the "Sixteen," seized the city government
in Paris in 1588 and the Catholic League called in Spanish troops to
oppose Henry of Navarre, now King Henry IV. The king converted to
Catholicism (1593) and gradually pacified the country. In 1595 he
issued the controversial Edict of Nantes which granted certain rights
of worship to Protestants, while favoring Catholic orthodoxy. Religious rivalries continued to simmer in local communities, and the
armed Huguenot church raised several more limited armed rebellions

to defend their rights (1619–22, 1625, 1627–8). Conspiratorial noble rebellions also broke out periodically against Henry IV and Louis XIII, with limited success.

IV. Era of Richelieu and Mazarin (1624–1661)

Despite these difficulties, King Louis XIII worked diligently to strengthen the state, in close collaboration with his brilliant, reclusive First Minister, Cardinal Richelieu. The Cardinal was intensely unpopular because he favored strengthening royal influence at the expense of nobles' independent authority and the autonomy of the more independent provinces. He built a team of loyal agents, drawn mostly from the robe nobility or from financial circles. He placed them in central administrative offices and sent them out into the provinces as royal intendants, to gather information and see that the king's will was done.

This ambitious program of internal reform was undermined by Richelieu's international ambitions to make France dominant in Europe at the expense of the Habsburg control of Spain, Italy, and the Empire. In 1635 he intervened militarily in the Thirty Years War (1618–48), which was already raging in Germany, on the side of the Protestant princes. This raised alarm among devout Catholics. France was drawn into a disastrous Europe-wide war that was tremendously expensive. Taxes on peasants and towns were raised to unknown heights. Officers in the royal courts were threatened with surcharges, a reduction of stipends, and the creation of superfluous offices. Even as Richelieu and Louis XIII tried to build what has been called royal absolutism, they had to deal with this episodic social disorder. Royal policies antagonized many different groups simultaneously. Towns saw waves of brief but violent uprisings directed by angry crowds. There were extended uprisings by peasant armies in the southwest. The Parlements, feeling that their authority was threatened and fearing that their fortunes invested in offices were in jeopardy, employed every form of legal obstruction to fend off royal initiatives. Nobles at court raised periodic armed conspiracies.

Richelieu died in 1642 and Louis XIII in 1643. The heir, Louis XIV, was only five years old, so the government was run by the regent, Louis's mother Anne of Austria, and her First Minister, Cardinal Mazarin. Both were very unpopular. In 1648 the civil war known as the Fronde broke out in response to their reputation as foreigners who were robbing king and country, the continuing burden of special taxes, and the seeming endlessness of the war, which continued between France and Spain until 1659. Mazarin was forced to flee the country twice, but the coming of age of the king in 1651 and the incompatibility of the various rebel forces ultimately brought about the success of the royal army and the reconciliation of at least the most powerful rebels with the king. Mazarin continued to run the government while grooming the young king for office, and in 1661 when Mazarin died, Louis XIV assumed personal power.

V. The age of Louis XIV (1661–1715)

Louis consolidated the various governing initiatives that had been started by his predecessors. He revived the monarchy by providing a strong, consistent leadership and an unprecedented degree of pomp and ceremony. While lavishing favors on those among the nobility who collaborated according to his wishes, and scorning those who did not, he developed a larger, better organized central administration and regularized the system of intendants in the provinces. His court, ultimately installed at Versailles, became a glamorous playground for the high aristocracy. In the first twenty years of his reign, he supported the program of his Finance Minister Colbert to lower taxes and encourage production and trade. But the king was determined to dominate the international scene.

A series of increasingly ruinous wars, the War of Devolution (1665–6), the Dutch War (1672–8), the Nine Years War (1688–97) and the War of Spanish Succession (1701–14) pitted France against large coalitions of the other European powers. The administration expanded to meet the challenge. The colossal expansion of the army brought about a much better organized force and stimulated development of its support systems within the government. But both army and administration continued to be shaped by the play of client ties and the influence of noble privileges. Disasters multiplied. The countryside was badly overtaxed; Colbert's reforms were abandoned; the general public was subjected to bad harvests and years of famine in 1694 and 1709. The ravages of troops and the conscription of peasants into coerced militia brigades increased the dissatisfaction. The forced conversion of the Protestants by the Edict of Nantes in 1685 generated a potentially subversive underground of insincerely converted Protestants. Communities of Protestant merchants in exile appeared all over Europe, denouncing the excesses of the king. Louis's quarrels with the pope and his dogmatic opposition to the views of pious Jansenists within the church created a potential backlash for the future.

VI. The aristocratic last flowering (1715–89)

Louis XIV left the monarchy in a weakened state, with massive debts, an administration bloated with superfluous officers, and an outlook still focused on continental grandeur at the expense of naval might and colonial trade. Aristocratic fashion was shifting from the royal court to the fashionable salon life of Paris. The last two kings, Louis XV and Louis XVI, were unable to maintain the quality of leadership of their predecessor. Both were vulnerable to negative images transmitted by a growing public opinion – Louis XV for his domination by mistresses, and Louis XVI for the bad reputation of his wife, Marie Antoinette. France remained fully engaged in European affairs, fighting the War of Polish Succession (1733–5), the War of Austrian Succession (1740–8), the Seven Years War (1756–63), and the War of American Independence (1778–83). There were some successes, including the incorporation of Lorraine into the kingdom in 1766, and the defeat of Great Britain in 1783, but it became increasingly clear that France's preoccupation with continental land wars and the country's archaic system of overtaxing the countryside and undertaxing privileged groups was diverting resources from the capitalist and colonialist enterprises of its chief competitors.

Meanwhile new wealth was being generated for colonial traders and planters from the booming Atlantic ports who were poorly integrated into the royal system. Jansenist indignation was merging with constitutional resistance to absolutism in the Parlements. The ideas of the Enlightenment and a growing literate public were spreading awareness of the backwardness of French traditions, compared with those in England and Holland. As king and court became increasingly out of touch, the rest of society was moving on, and the groundwork was being laid for opposition to the system.

Appendix 2: Genealogy of the French Monarchy

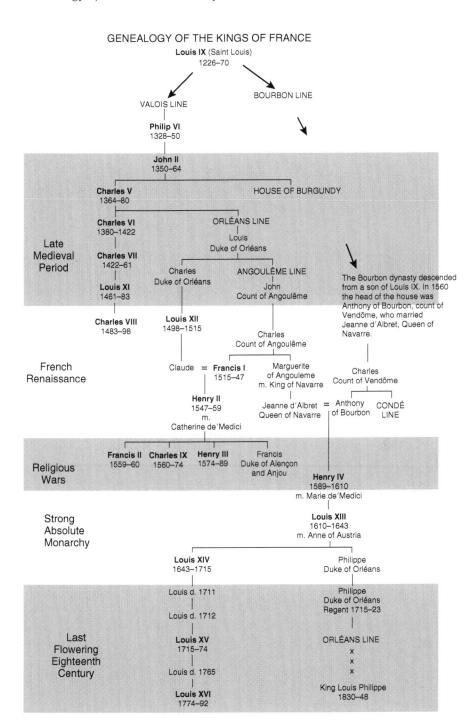

GENEALOGY OF THE KINGS OF FRANCE

Louis IX (Saint Louis)
1226–70

VALOIS LINE

BOURBON LINE

Philip VI
1328–50

John II
1350–64

Charles V
1364–80

HOUSE OF BURGUNDY

Late Medieval Period

Charles VI
1380–1422

ORLÉANS LINE

Louis
Duke of Orléans

Charles VII
1422–61

Charles
Duke of Orléans

ANGOULÊME LINE

Louis XI
1461–83

John
Count of Angoulême

The Bourbon dynasty descended from a son of Louis IX. In 1560 the head of the house was Anthony of Bourbon, count of Vendôme, who married Jeanne d'Albret, Queen of Navarre.

Charles VIII
1483–98

Louis XII
1498–1515

Charles
Count of Angoulême

French Renaissance

Claude = Francis I
              1515–47

Marguerite
of Angouleme
m. King of Navarre

Charles
Count of Vendôme

Henry II
1547–59
m.
Catherine de'Medici

Jeanne d'Albret = Anthony
Queen of Navarre | of Bourbon

CONDÉ
LINE

Religious Wars

Francis II   Charles IX   Henry III
1559–60   1560–74   1574–89

Francis
Duke of Alençon
and Anjou

Henry IV
1589–1610
m. Marie de'Medici

Strong Absolute Monarchy

Louis XIII
1610–1643
m. Anne of Austria

Louis XIV
1643–1715

Philippe
Duke of Orléans

Louis d. 1711

Philippe
Duke of Orléans
Regent 1715–23

Louis d. 1712

Last Flowering Eighteenth Century

Louis XV
1715–74

ORLÉANS LINE
x
x
x

Louis d. 1765

King Louis Philippe
1830–48

Louis XVI
1774–92

Notes

Introduction

1 The dates indicate when the province was definitively annexed. Other provinces within the medieval kingdom, such as Brittany and Bourbonnais, remained semi-independent during part of the early modern period.

2 These are rough figures drawn from various historians' estimates. For consistency they refer to the territory of modern France. The earlier figures would be smaller by several million if they referred only to the actual kingdom at that date. Jacques Dupâquier, *La Population française aux XVIIe et XVIIIe siècles* (Paris, 1979), 34–7; Emmanuel Le Roy Ladurie, *The French Peasantry 1450–1660*, trans. Alan Sheridan (Aldershot, 1987), 8–20.

3 The importance of the local *pays* is stressed in Yves Durand, *Vivre au pays au XVIIIe siècle: essai sur la notion de pays dans l'ouest de la France* (Paris, 1984).

4 Fernand Braudel, *The Identity of France*, trans. Siân Reynolds, 2 vols. (New York, 1988), I, 129–30.

5 Ibid., I, 54.

6 Ibid., II, 170–78.

7 Françoise Bayard, *Vivre à Lyon sous l'Ancien Régime* (Paris, 1997), 199.

8 Pierre Chaunu, *La Civilisation de l'Europe classique* (Paris, 1966), 204–5; François Lebrun, *La Vie conjugale sous l'Ancien Régime* (Paris, 1975), 139.

9 Conditions such as the unequal distribution of resources between lords and peasants, the nature of exactions extracted from the production of peasant farmers by lords, churchmen, and king, and the state of agricultural technology will be discussed later.

10 Guy Bois, *The Crisis of Feudalism: Economy and Society in Eastern Normandy (c. 1300–1550)* (Cambridge, 1984), 50–77.

11 Le Roy Ladurie, *The French Peasantry*, 28.

12 Emmanuel Le Roy Ladurie, *Les Paysans de Languedoc*, 2 vols. (Paris, 1966), I, 142–3.

13 Le Roy Ladurie, *French Peasantry*, 29.
14 Bernard Guenée, *Tribunaux et gens de justice dans le bailliage de Senlis à la fin du moyen âge (vers 1380–vers 1550)* (Paris, 1963), 54.

1 Rural communities and seigneurial power

 1 Jean Gallet, *La Seigneurie bretonne (1450–1680): l'exemple du Vannetais* (Paris, 1983), 169.
 2 Emmanuel Le Roy Ladurie, *Les Paysans de Languedoc*, 2 vols. (Paris, 1966), 455–6.
 3 Guy Bois, *The Crisis of Feudalism: Economy and Society in Eastern Normandy c. 1300–1550* (Cambridge, 1984), 149–51.
 4 Pierre Goubert, *Beauvais et le Beauvaisis de 1600 à 1730: contribution à l'histoire sociale de la France du XVIIe siècle* (Paris, 1960), 158.
 5 Fernand Braudel, *The Identity of France*, trans. Siân Reynolds, 3 vols. (New York, 1990), I, 156–60.
 6 Jean Jacquart, *La Crise rurale en Île-de-France 1550–1670* (Paris, 1974), 135–64.
 7 Gérard Aubin, *La Seigneurie en Bordelais d'après la pratique notariale (1715–1789)*, Publications de l'Université de Rouen no. 149 (Rouen, n.d.), 85.
 8 The information on Brittany is drawn from Gallet, *La Seigneurie bretonne*; the information on the Bordelais is drawn from Aubin, *La Seigneurie en Bordelais*.
 9 Tenures granted to nobles were juridically different from tenures granted to commoners, but their place in the *mouvance* of the seigneurie was similar. They usually did not owe degrading *cens* and *corvées*. Instead, they owed feudal homage to the lord and tribute payments at designated moments such as the marriage of the eldest son.
10 Gallet, *La Seigneurie bretonne*, 238.
11 Ibid., 541–4; Jonathan Dewald, *Pont-St-Pierre 1398–1789: Lordship, Community, and Capitalism in Early Modern France* (Berkeley, CA, 1987), 251–6.
12 More on this in the next chapter.
13 Bois, *The Crisis of Feudalism*, 242–50.
14 James Lowth Goldsmith, *Les Salers et les d'Escorailles, seigneurs de Haute Auvergne, 1500–1789* (Clermont-Ferrand, 1984), 81–7.
15 *Banalités* can be counted either way: they were seigneurial in that they depended in part on the lord's coercive monopoly, but they can be considered *réserve* if they are thought of as a return on an investment.
16 Most of the figures are quoted in Aubin, *La Seigneurie en Bordelais*, 289–96.

17 Dewald, *Pont-St-Pierre*, 263–6.
18 Jacquart, *La Crise rurale en Île-de-France*, 409–30.
19 Goubert, *Beauvais et le Beauvaisis*, 17–19 and maps 3–5.
20 Aubin, *La Seigneurie en Bordelais*,182–3.
21 Ibid., 92.
22 Ibid., 240.
23 Ibid., 309.
24 Ibid., 248.
25 Ibid., 345.
26 Ibid., 375.

2 Peasant life, agriculture, and social distribution

1 Jean Gallet, *La Seigneurie bretonne (1450–1680): L'example du Van-netais* (Paris, 1983), 203.
2 This simple explanation ignores many other subtleties of the tax system such as *taille réelle* and *taille personnelle*, but this is not the place to discuss them.
3 In the provinces with Estates, about one-third of the country, the king did have to bargain periodically with an assembly for his money, but there was little possibility of his being refused, the discussion being mostly about the precise level of the grant and the ways it would be collected.
4 The royal tax officials were supposed to take ability to pay into consideration, but they often followed out-of-date lists or favored certain communities.
5 Pierre Goubert, *Beauvais et le Beauvaisis de 1600 à 1730: contribution à l'histoire sociale de la France du XVIIe siècle* (Paris, 1960), 178–82.
6 Summary of *prélèvement* by Jean Jacquart, *La Crise rurale en Île-de-France, 1550–1670* (Paris, 1974), 368–89; he summarizes these figures in *Histoire de la France rurale*, ed. Georges Duby and Armand Wallon, 4 vols. (Paris, 1975) II, 241–3.
7 Jean-Marc Moriceau, *Les Fermiers de l'Île-de-France: l'ascension d'un patronat agricole (XVe–XVIIIe siècle)* rev. edn (Paris, 1994).
8 Examples from the Lyonnais in Jean-Pierre Gutton, *Villages du Lyonnais sous la monarchie (XVIe–XVIIIe siècles)* (Lyon, 1978), 151–3, 121–2.
9 Natalie Zemon Davis, *The Return of Martin Guerre* (Cambridge, MA, 1983).
10 See Introduction.
11 François Lebrun, *La Vie conjugale sous l'Ancien Régime* (Paris, 1975), 49–52.

12 Abel Hugo, *La France pittoresque*, 3 vols. (Paris, 1835), I, 237–8, quoted in Lebrun, *La Vie conjugale*, 107.
13 Quoted in ibid., 25.
14 Quoted in Jean-Louis Flandrin, *Families in Former Times: Kinship, Household and Sexuality*, trans. Richard Southern (Cambridge, 1979), 123.
15 Lebrun, *La Vie conjugale*, 83–4.
16 Flandrin, *Families in Former Times*, 122.

3 Domination by the nobility

1 Philippe Contamine, *La Noblesse au royaume de France de Philippe le Bel à Louis XII* (Paris, 1997), 13.
2 Ibid., 65–9; Ellery Schalk, "Ennoblement in France from 1350 to 1660," *Journal of Social History* 16 (Winter 1982), 101–10.
3 James B. Wood, *The Nobility of the Election of Bayeux, 1463–1666* (Princeton, NJ, 1980, 22–5.
4 Jean-Marie Constant, "L'Enquête de noblesse de 1667 et les seigneurs de Beauce," *Revue d'histoire moderne et contemporaine* 21 (1974), 555.
5 Wood, *The Nobility of the Élection of Bayeux*, 38–9.
6 Contamine, *La Noblesse*, 10–11.
7 Constant, "L'Enquête," 548–66.
8 Guy Rowlands, *The Dynastic State and the Army under Louis XIV: Royal Service and Private Interest, 1661–1701* (Cambridge, 2002), 154.
9 For example, Jean Meyer, *La Noblesse bretonne au XVIIIe siècle* (Paris, 1972), 57–9. See also James B. Collins, *The State in Early Modern France* (Cambridge, 1995), 133–6.
10 Madeleine Foisil, *Le Sire de Gouberville: un gentilhomme norman au XVIe siècle* (Paris, 1981); and Emmanuel Le Roy Ladurie, "La Verdeur du bocage," in *Le Territoire de l'historien* (Paris, 1973), 187–221.
11 Serge Dontenwill, *Une seigneurie sous l'ancien régime: l'Étoile en Brionnais du XVIe au XVIIIe siècle (1575–1778)* (Roanne, 1973), 79–81.
12 Jonathan Dewald, *Pont-St-Pierre 1398–1789: Lordship, Community and Capitalism in Early Modern France* (Berkeley, CA, 1987), 90–126.
13 Ibid., 97.
14 Jean-Marie Constant, *La Noblesse française aux XVIIe et XVIIIe siècles* (Paris, 1994), 224–6.
15 Kristen Neuschel, "Noble Households in the Sixteenth Century: Material Settings and Human Communities," *French Historical Studies* 15 (1988), 595–622.

16 Laurent Bourquin, *Noblesse seconde et pouvoir en Champagne aux XVIe et XVIIe siècles* (Paris, 1994), 47, 93–101.

17 Jean-Pierre Labatut, *Les Ducs et pairs de France au XVIIe siècle* (Paris, 1972), 248.

18 Details from Stuart Carroll, *Noble Power during the French Wars of Religion: The Guise Affinity and the Catholic Cause in Normandy* (Cambridge, 1998).

19 In 1646 40 percent of Condé's income derived from landed estates, 26 percent from royal pensions and offices, 25 percent from church benefices (he controlled fourteen abbeys and priories) 6 percent from loans worth a million livres, mostly to the crown, and 1 percent in pensions from the *gabelle* farmers of Berry. Katia Béguin, *Les Princes de Condé: rebelles, courtisans et mécènes dans la France du Grand Siècle* (Paris, 1999), 34–54.

20 Ibid., 136–8.

21 Nancy Nichols Barker, *Brother to the Sun King: Philippe, Duke of Orléans* (Baltimore, MD, 1989), 166–98.

22 Robert Forster, *The House of Saulx-Tavanes: Versailles and Burgundy, 1700–1830* (Baltimore, MD, 1971).

4 City life and city people

1 Philip Benedict, "French Cities from the Sixteenth Century to the Revolution: An Overview," in Philip Benedict, ed., *Cities and Social Change in Early Modern France* (London, 1989), 7–8; Fernand Braudel, *The Identity of France* trans. Siân Reynolds, 2 vols. (New York, 1988–90), II, 415–18.

2 These figures are taken from Benedict, "French Cities," 24–5. They are only approximations, and others could be cited. See, for example, Roger Chartier *et al.*, *La Ville classique*, vol. III of *Histoire de la France urbaine*, ed. Georges Duby (Paris, 1981), 47–8.

3 Others were Rouen, Orléans, Bordeaux, Marseille, Lille, and Rennes.

4 This and other quotations are taken from the interrogation of Pierre de Gaillard in André Mateu, "Les Révoltes populaires de la juridiction d'Agen dans leur contexte socio-économique," Thèse de doctorat de 3e cycle, University of Toulouse, 1980, 1610–19.

5 Jean-Pierre Leguay, *La Rue au moyen age* (Rennes, 1984), 12–15.

6 Louis-Sébastien Mercier, *Panorama of Paris: Selections from Le tableau de Paris*, ed. Jeremy D. Popkin (University Park, PA, 1999), 220.

7 Françoise Bayard, "L'Émergence de nouvelles élites socio-politiques à Lyon dans la première moitié du XVIIe siècle: mythes et réalités," in

Sociétés et idéologies des temps modernes, ed. J. Fouilleron, G. Le Thiec, and H. Michel, 2 vols. (Montpellier, 1996), I, 3–13.

8 Frederick M. Irvine, "From Renaissance City to Ancien Régime Capital: Montpellier, c. 1500–c.1600," in Benedict, *Cities and Social Change*, 125–7.

9 Although it is of little importance, Pocquelin was probably the great-grandfather of the playwright Molière. Pierre Goubert, "Une fortune bourgeoise au 16e siècle," in *Clio parmi les hommes* (The Hague, 1976), 82–96.

10 Pierre Goubert, "Types de marchands amiénois au début du 17e siècle," in *Clio parmi les hommes*, 97–111.

11 David A. Bell, *Lawyers and Citizens: The Making of a Political Elite in Old Regime France* (Oxford, 1994), 21–58.

12 Joanna Virginia Hamilton, "The Merchants of Vannes, 1670–1730," doctoral dissertation, Georgetown University, 2001, 123–80.

13 Sara Beam, "The 'Basoche' and the 'Bourgeoisie Seconde': Careerists at the Parlement of Paris during the League," *French History* 17 (2004), 367–87.

14 James R. Farr, "Consumers, Commerce, and the Craftsmen of Dijon: The Changing Social and Economic Structure of a Provincial Capital, 1450–1750," in Benedict, *Cities and Social Change*, 169–73; Michael Sonenscher, *Work and Wages: Natural Law, Politics and the Eighteenth-Century French Trades* (Cambridge, 1989), 7; Gayle Brunelle, *The New World Merchants of Rouen, 1559–1630* (Kirksville, MO, 1991), 10; René Toujas, "Un Recensement des métiers jurés ou inorganisés de Toulouse en 1673," *Actes du 102e Congrès National des Sociétés Savantes, Section d'histoire moderne et contemporaine*, vol. II (Paris, 1978), 225–35.

15 F. Dumas, "Les Corporations de métiers de la ville de Toulouse au XVIIIe siècle," *Annales du Midi* 12 (1900), 479.

16 Alain Lottin, *Chavatte, ouvrier Lillois: un contemporain de Louis XIV* (Paris, 1979), 79–80.

17 Richard Gascon, *Grand commerce et vie urbaine au XVIe siècle: Lyon et ses marchands*, 2 vols. (Paris, 1971), I, 391.

18 Archives Municipales (AM) de Lyon, BB171, 32r–44r.

19 Sonenscher, *Work and Wages*, 68.

20 Julie Hardwick, *The Practice of Patriarchy: Gender and the Politics of Household Authority in Early Modern France* (University Park, PA, 1998), 1–4.

21 William Beik, *Urban Protest in Seventeenth-Century France: The Culture of Retribution* (Cambridge, 1997), 36. From Archives municipales de Dijon B81, May 4, 1644.

22 Figures refer to female clothing merchants in Nantes in 1749.
23 Nancy Locklin, "Women in Early Modern Brittany: Rethinking Work and Identity in a Traditional Economy," Ph.D. dissertation, Emory University, 2000, 57. Much more information is provided in Nancy Locklin, *Women's Work and Identity in Eighteenth-Century Brittany* (Aldershot, 2007).
24 Carol L. Loats, "Gender, Guilds, and Work Identity: Perspectives from Sixteenth-Century Paris," *French Historical Studies* 20 (1997), 15–30.
25 Daryl M. Hafter, "Female Masters in the Ribbonmaking Guild of Eighteenth-Century Rouen," *French Historical Studies* 20 (1997), 1–14.
26 Clare Crowston, "Engendering the Guilds: Seamstresses, Tailors, and the Clash of Corporate Identities in Old Regime France," *French Historical Studies* 23 (2000), 339–71.
27 Olwen Hufton, *Bayeux in the Late Eighteenth Century: A Social Study* (Oxford, 1967), 82–3.
28 Ibid., 81–9.
29 Pierre Deyon, *Amiens, capitale provinciale: étude sur la société urbaine au 17e siècle* (Paris, 1967), 350, quoting municipal deliberations of 1717.
30 Gascon, *Grand commerce*, I, 400–4.
31 André Lespagnol, ed., *Histoire de Saint-Malo et du pays Malouin* (Toulouse, 1984), 127.
32 Charles Higounet, ed., *Histoire de Bordeaux* (Toulouse, 1980),
33 Paul Butel, *Les Négociants bordelais, l'Europe, et les îles au XVIIIe siècle* (Paris, 1974), 167.

5 The monarchy and the new nobility

1 In the south the *bailliages* were called *sénéchausées* and the *bailli* was called a *senéchal*.
2 Françoise Autrand, *Naissance d'un grand corps de l'état: les gens du Parlement de Paris 1345–1454* (Paris, 1981), 133–4.
3 Quoted in Jonathan Dewald, *The Formation of a Provincial Nobility: The Magistrates of the Parlement of Rouen, 1499–1610* (Princeton, NJ, 1980), 18.
4 Roland Mousnier, *La Vénalité des offices sous Henri IV et Louis XIII* (Paris, 1971), 41, 43; Dewald, *Formation of a Provincial Nobility*, 5.
5 That is, if the grandfather and the father each served for at least twenty years or died at their post, then the third generation, the son, acquired hereditary nobility for all his posterity.
6 Sharon Kettering, *Judicial Politics and Urban Revolt in Seventeenth-Century France: The Parlement of Aix, 1629–1659* (Princeton, NJ, 1978), 221–5.

7 David D. Bien, "Offices, Corps, and a System of State Credit: The Uses of Privilege under the Ancien Régime," in Keith Michael Baker, ed., *The Political Culture of the Old Regime* (Oxford, 1987), 89–114.

8 Françoise Bayard, *Le Monde des financiers au XVIIe siècle* (Paris, 1988), 25–67.

9 Ibid., 122.

10 Ibid., 102.

11 Ibid., 297–301.

12 Ibid., 390–420. These last percentages are drawn from a short list of eleven cases and cannot be taken as typical of the hundreds of financiers.

13 Ibid. 390–413.

14 Madeleine Foisil, *Mémoires du Président Alexandre Bigot de Monville: le Parlement de Rouen: 1640–1643* (Paris, 1976), 11–22.

15 Ibid., 26.

16 These figures accounted for about 40 percent of the taxes paid. The rest came from other groups in the city. Frederick M. Levine, "From Renaissance City to Ancien Régime Capital: Montpellier, c.1500–c.1600," in Philip Benedict, ed., *Cities and Social Change in Early Modern France* (London, 1989), 115.

17 Ibid., 117.

18 James R. Farr, "Consumers, Commerce, and the Craftsmen of Dijon: The Changing Social and Economic Structure of a Provincial Capital, 1450–1750," in Benedict, *Cities and Social Change*, 134–73.

19 Ibid., 43.

20 Robert J. Kalas, "The Selve Family of Limousin: Members of a New Elite in Early Modern France," *Sixteenth Century Journal* 18 (1987), 147–72.

21 Denis Richet, *De la Réforme à la Révolution: études sur la France moderne* (Paris, 1991), 22–78.

22 Ibid., 14.

6 Ecclesiastical power and religious faith

1 Esther Benvassa, *The Jews of France; A History from Antiquity to the Present*, trans. M. B. DeBevoise (Princeton, NJ, 1999).

2 Thirty-five bishops had revenues of between 8,000 and 15,000; forty-one had revenues above 15,000 and below 30,000. Joseph Bergin, *The Making of the French Episcopate 1589–1661* (New Haven, CT, 1996), 110–12.

3 Bergin, *The Making of the French Episcopate*, 144–5.

4 Ibid., 183–201; Joseph Bergin, *Crown, Church and Episcopate under Louis XIV* (New Haven, CT, 2004), 58–70.

5 Ronald Hubscher, ed., *Histoire d'Amiens* (Toulouse, 1986), 182.

6 Gabriel Audisio, *Les Français d'hier: des croyants, XV–XIX siècle*, 2 vols. (Paris, 1996), II, 112.

7 Quoted in Roger Doucet, *Les Institutions de la France au XVIe siecle*, 2 vols. (Paris, 1948), II, 753.

8 Claire Dolan, *Entre tours et clochers: les gens d'église à Aix-en-Provence au XVIe siècle* (Aix, 1981), 196–206.

9 Louis Perouas, *Le Diocèse de La Rochelle: sociologie et pastorale* (Paris, 1964), 195–6.

10 Bernard Hours, *L'Église et la vie religieuse moderne XVIe–XVIIIe siècles* (Paris, 2000), 6.

11 Philip T. Hoffman, *Church and Community in the Diocese of Lyon 1599–1789* (New Haven, CT, 1984), 50–1.

12 Louis Châtellier, *La Religion des pauvres: les missions rurales en Europe et la formation du catholicisme moderne XVIe–XIXe siècle* (Paris, 1993), 38–9.

13 Audisio, *Les Français d'hier*, 123–5.

14 Ibid., 44–5.

15 Jean-Marie Le Gall, *Les Moines au temps des réformes: France (1480–1560)* (Paris, 2001), 32–4.

16 Yves Durand, *Un couvent dans la ville: les Grands Carmes de Nantes 1318–1790* (Rome, 1997), 73–116.

17 Laura Mellinger, "Politics in the Convent: The Election of a Fifteenth-Century Abbess," *Church History* 63 (1994), 130.

18 Louis Desgraves, *Évocation du vieux Bordeaux* (Paris, 1960), 93.

19 Dolan, *Entre tours et clochers*, 189–94.

20 Bergin, *Making of the French Episcopate*, 211.

21 Ibid., 247, 293–332.

22 René Pillorget, "Réforme monastique et conflits de rupture dans quelques localités de la France méridionale au XVIIe siècle," *Revue historique* 253 (1975), 85–8.

23 Quoted ibid., 103.

24 Ibid., 80–5.

25 Théodore Beza, quoted in Megan C. Armstrong, *The Politics of Piety: Franciscan Preachers during the Wars of Religion, 1500–1600* (Rochester, NY, 2004), 25.

26 Ibid., 27, 149–50.

27 Père Berthod, *Mémoires du Père Berthod*, in M. Petitot, ed., *Collection des mémoires relatifs à l'histoire de la France*, vol. XLVI (Paris, n.d.), 374; and Sal Alexander Westrich, *The Ormée of Bordeaux: A Revolution in the Fronde* (Baltimore, MD, 1972), 87–91.

28 Robert M. Kingdon, *Geneva and the Coming of the Wars of Religion in France 1555–1563* (Geneva, 1956), 60.

29 Ibid., 58.

30 Quoted in Janine Garrisson, *Les Protestants au XVIe siècle* (Paris, 1988), 184. She is quoting Lucien Romier, *Les Origines politiques des guerres de religion*, vol. II (Paris, 1914), 273.

31 Quoted in Garrisson, *Protestants au XVI siècle*, 185.

32 Denis Crouzet, *Les Guerriers de Dieu: la violence au temps des troubles de religion (vers 1525–vers 1610*, 2 vols. (Seyssel, 1990), I, 77, 83–5, 86.

33 Penny Roberts, *A City in Conflict: Troyes during the French Wars of Religion* (Manchester, 1996), 123–62.

34 Allan A. Tulchin, "The Michelade of Nimes, 1567," *French Historical Studies* 29 (2006), 1–35.

35 Philip Benedict, Lawrence M. Bryant, and Kristen B. Neuschel, "Graphic History: What Readers Knew and Were Taught in the *Quarante Tableaux* of Perrissin and Tortorel," *French Historical Studies* 28 (2005), 175–229.

36 Raymond A. Mentzer, "Ecclesiastical Discipline and Communal Reorganization among the Protestants of Southern France," *European History Quarterly* 21 (1991), 163–83.

37 Gregory Hanlon, *Confession and Community in Seventeenth-Century France: Catholic and Protestant Coexistence in Aquitaine* (Philadelphia, PA, 1993), 127–32.

38 Ibid., 91–116.

39 Nîmes, Archives Départementales du Gard G 450.

40 Paul Gachon, *Quelques préliminaires de la révocation de l'édit de Nantes en Languedoc (1661–1685)* (Toulouse, 1899), cxxiii–cxlv.

41 Bergin, *Making of the French Episcopate*, 145–55.

42 Bergin, *Crown, Church and Episcopate under Louis XIV*, 50–80.

43 Louis Noguier, "Palais épiscopal de Beziers: mobilier des évêques," *Bulletin de la Société Archéologique de Béziers*, 3rd series 1 (1895), 5–36.

44 Jean Burel, *Mémoires de Jean Burel; journal d'un bourgeois du Puy à l'époque des guerres de religion*, ed. Augustin Chassaing, 2 vols. (Saint-Vidal, 1983), II, 252, 304, 367.

45 J.-M. Vidal, *Henri de Sponde (1568–1643)* (Castillon, 1929), 9.

46 Quoted in Victor L. Tapié, *France in the Age of Louis XIII and Richelieu*, trans. D. McN. Lockie (Cambridge, 1984), 285.

47 Audisio, *Les Français d'hier*, 380.

48 Françoise Bayard, *Vivre à Lyon sous l'Ancien Régime* (Paris, 1997), 133. Michel Taillefer, *Vivre à Toulouse sous l'Ancien Régime* (Paris, 1997), 324–5.

49 Barbara Diefendorf, *From Penitence to Charity: Pious Women and the Catholic Reformation in Paris* (Oxford, 2004). 37–8. This whole section is based on Diefendorf's extended discussion.

50 Ibid., 41–2.

51 Hours, *L'église et la vie religieuse moderne*, 41.

52 Audisio, *Les Français d'hier*, 382.

53 James Collins reports that a document concerning Marie de Luxembourg's financial management, BNF nouv. acq. fr. 21,878 (for 1586), shows that the Mercoeur household consumed 42,000 litres of wine and sent a servant to Rennes to bring back butter (personal communication).

54 Quoted in Jacques LeGoff and René Rémond, eds., *Histoire de la France religieuse*, 4 vols. (Paris, 1988), II, 421.

55 Elizabeth Rapley, paraphrasing Archbishop Denis de Marquemont of Lyon, in *The Dévotes: Women and Church in Seventeenth-Century France*. (Montreal, 1993), 115.

56 Emmanuel Le Roy Ladurie, *Les Paysans de Languedoc*. 2 vols. (Paris, 1966) I, 453–63.

7 Warfare and society

1 John A. Lynn, *Giant of the Grand Siècle: The French Army, 1610–1715* (Cambridge, 1997), 55.

2 James B. Wood, *The King's Army: Warfare, Soldiers, and Society during the Wars of Religion in France, 1562–1576* (Cambridge, 1996), 67–85.

3 Ibid., 70.

4 David Parrott, *Richelieu's Army: War, Government and Society in France, 1624–1642* (Cambridge, 2001), 164–222.

5 Ibid., 331–48.

6 Lynn, *Giant of the Grand Siècle*, 223.

7 Quoted ibid., 237.

8 Parrott, *Richelieu's Army*, 313–30.

9 Guy Rowlands, *The Dynastic State and the Army under Louis XIV: Royal Service and Private Interest, 1661–1701* (Cambridge, 2002), 161–86.

10 Lynn, *Giant of the Grand Siècle*, 233.

11 Rowlands, *The Dynastic State*, 73–149.

12 Corvisier, *L'Armée française de la fin du XVIIe siècle au ministère de Choiseul*, 2 vols. (Paris, 1964), I, 119–21.

13 Quoted in Lynn, *Giant of the Grand Siècle*, 360.

14 Ibid., 347–96.

15 Ibid., 380–93.

16 Jean Nicolas, *La Rébellion française: mouvements populaires et conscience sociale (1661–1789)* (Paris, 2002), 392–400.

17 Lynn, *Giant of the Grand Siècle*, 321–7; Corvisier, *L'Armée française*, I, 373–565.
18 Lynn, *Giant of the Grand Siècle*, 377–9, 442.
19 A. Navereau, Le Logement des gens de guerre (Poitiers, 1924), 7–33.
20 Lynn, *Giant of the Grand Siècle*, 184.
21 M. Rossignol, *Le Bailliage de Dijon après la bataille de Rocroy (1643): procès-verbaux de la visite des feux* (Dijon, 1857), 40–2. I am indebted to Jeffrey Houghtby for this quotation.
22 Gaston Roupnel, *La Ville et la campagne au XVIIe siècle: étude sur les populations du pays dijonnais* (Paris, 1955), 21.
23 Corvisier, *L'Armée française*, I, 74–5.
24 Lynn, *Giant of the Grand Siècle*, 186–7.
25 Toulouse, Archives Départementales de La Haute-Garonne C 2131, 1640 bundle.
26 Ibid., 1650 bundle.

8 Social bonds and social protest

1 Christian Desplat, *La Vie, l'amour, la mort: rites et coutumes XVIe–XVIIIe siècles* (Biarritz, 1995), 165.
2 Roderick Phillips, "Women, Neighborhood, and Family in the Late Eighteenth Century," *French Historical Studies* 18 (1993), 11.
3 David Garrioch, *Neighbourhood and Community in Paris, 1740–1790* (Cambridge, 1986), 72–87.
4 Yves Castan, *Honnêteté et relations sociales en Languedoc (1715–1780)* (Paris, 1974), 171–2.
5 Georg'ann Cattelona, "Control and Collaboration: The Role of Women in Regulating Female Sexual Behavior in Early Modern Marseille," *French Historical Studies* 18 (1993) 18, 20–2, 27–8; Archives Municipales de Dijon, I 143, January 31, 1700.
6 This section is based on Natalie Zemon Davis, "The Reasons of Misrule," in *Society and Culture in Early Modern France* (Stanford, CA, 1975), 97–123.
7 William Beik, *Urban Protest in Seventeenth-Century France: The Culture of Retribution* (Cambridge, 1997), 79–84.
8 "Journal d'un bourgeois de Rennes au XVIIe siècle," manuscript in Rennes, Archives Départementales de L' Île-et-Vilaine 1F 306, pp. 143, 157–8, 165, 199.
9 Albert Babeau, Le Guet et la milice bourgeoise de Troyes," *Mémoires de la Société Académique d'Agriculture, des Sciences, Arts et Belles-lettres du Département de l'Aube*, 3rd series, 15 (1878), 334.
10 Robert Descimon, "Paris on the Eve of Saint Bartholomew: Taxation, Privilege, and Social Geography," in Philip Benedict, ed., *Cities and*

Social Change in Early Modern France (London, 1989), 69–133; Robert Descimon, "Milice bourgeoise et identité citadine à Paris au temps de la Ligue," *Annales ESC* 48 (1993), 885–906.

11 Paul Butel, *Vivre à Bordeaux sous l'Ancien Régime* (Paris, 1999), 132–5.

12 Robert A. Schneider, *Public Life in Toulouse, 1463–1789: From Municipal Republic to Cosmopolitan City* (Ithaca, NY, 1989), 107–10; Michael Sonenscher, *Work and Wages: Natural Law, Politics and the Eighteenth-Century French Trades* (Cambridge, 1989), 207–8.

13 Sonenscher, *Work and Wages*, 206.

14 Ibid., 295–6.

15 Cynthia Truant, *The Rites of Labor: Brotherhoods of Compagnonnage in Old and New Regime France* (Ithaca, NY, 1994), 96.

16 Ibid., 68–90.

17 Ultimately there were three associations, the Enfants de maître Jacques (*devoirs*), the Enfants de maître Soubise, and the Enfants de Salomon (*gavots*).

18 Jacques-Louis Menetra, *Journal of My Life*, ed. Daniel Roche, trans. Arthur Goldhammer (New York, 1986), 40–2.

19 Schneider, *Public Life in Toulouse*, 205, 216.

20 Ibid., table 4, p. 231.

21 Jean Nicolas, *La Rébellion française: mouvements populaires et conscience sociale (1661–1789)* (Paris, 2002), 530.

22 Aix-en-Provence, Bibliothèque Méjanes 939 (RA 25), "Mémoires d'Antoine de Félix," 23–5.

23 William Beik, *Louis XIV and Absolutism: A Brief Study with Documents* (Boston, 2000), 164.

24 Emmanuel Le Roy Ladurie, *Carnival in Romans*, trans. Mary Feeney (New York, 1979).

25 Yves-Marie Bercé, *Histoire des Croquants: étude des soulèvements populaires au XVIIe siècle dans le sud-ouest de la France*, 2 vols. (Paris, 1974.), I, 369.

26 Ibid., I, 364–402.

27 Ibid., I, 426–7.

9 Traditional attitudes and identities

1 Peter Burke, *Popular Culture in Early Modern Europe* (New York, 1978); Norbert Elias, *The Civilizing Process: The History of Manners*, trans. Edmund Jephcott (New York, 1978).

2 Michel Foucault, *Discipline and Punish: The Birth of the Prison*, trans. Alan Sheridan (New York, 1977).

3 A. N. Galpern, *The Religions of the People in Sixteenth-Century Champagne* (Cambridge, MA, 1976), 47–8.

4 Gérard Bouchard, *Le Village immobile: Sennely-en-Sologne au XVIIIe siècle* (Paris, 1972), 288–90.

5 Ibid., 298.

6 Ibid., 302–6, 316–23.

7 Galpern, *Religions*, 184–7.

8 Quoted in Robin Briggs, *Communities of Belief: Cultural and Social Tension in Early Modern France* (Oxford, 1989), 325.

9 Christian Desplat, *La Vie, l'amour, la mort: rites et coutumes XVIe–XVIIIe siècles* (Biarritz, 1995), 34, 58.

10 Steven G. Reinhardt, *Justice in the Sarladais 1770–1790* (Baton Rouge, LA, 1991), 190–1; François Lebrun, *La Vie conjugale sous l'Ancien Régime* (Paris, 1975), 41–8.

11 Penny Roberts, "Contesting Sacred Space: Burial Disputes in Sixteenth-Century France," in Bruce Gordon and Peter Marshall, eds., *The Place of the Dead: Death and Remembrance in Late Medieval and Early Modern Europe* (Cambridge, 2000), 131–48.

12 Robert Muchembled, *Cultures et société en France du début du XVIe siècle au milieu du XVIIe siècle* (Paris, 1995), 319–21.

13 Henri Lalou, "Des charivaris et de leur répression dans le midi de la France," *Revue des Pyrénées* 16 (1904), 493–514; Claude Gauvard and Altan Gokalp, "Les Conduits de bruit et leur signification à la fin du Moyen Age: le Charivari," *Annales ESC* 29 (1974), 693–704.

14 Reinhardt, *Justice in the Sarladais*, 199–201.

15 J. G. Peristiany, ed., *Honor and Shame: The Values of Mediterranean Society* (London, 1965).

16 Archives Municipales de Dijon (AM), I 110: August 24, 1674; AM Dijon G6: July 16, 1642; AM Dijon B81: June 6, 1651.

17 David Garrioch, *Neighbourhood and Community in Paris, 1740–1790* (Cambridge, 1986), 41–2.

18 William Beik, *Urban Protest in Seventeenth-Century France: The Culture of Retribution* (Cambridge, 1997), 34–5.

19 Jean Nicolas, *La Rébellion française: mouvements populaires et conscience sociale (1661–1789)* (Paris, 2002), 178, 70, respectively.

20 Garrioch, *Neighbourhood and Community in Paris*, 38–44.

21 Yves Castan, *Honnêteté et relations sociales en Languedoc (1715–1780)* (Paris, 1974), 190–4.

22 Ibid., 182–4.

23 Quoted in Arlette Jouanna, *Le Devoir de révolte: la noblesse française et la gestation de l'état moderne* (Paris, 1989), 15.

24 Pierre de Vaissière, *Gentilshommes campagnards de l'ancienne France* (Paris, 1925), 104–18.
25 Ibid., 123, quoting *lettres de remission* and du Fail.
26 J. H. M. Salmon, *Society in Crisis: France in the Sixteenth Century* (New York, 1975), 208–10.
27 Jouanna, *Le Devoir de révolte*, 55.
28 Stuart Carroll, *Blood and Violence in Early Modern France* (Oxford, 2006), 258.
29 Ibid., 263.
30 Ibid., 113.
31 Vaissière, *Gentilshommes campagnards*, 156.
32 Carroll, *Blood and Violence in Early Modern France*, 113–14, 286.
33 Ibid., 71–3.
34 Ibid., 69–70.
35 Ibid., 308–29; quotes, 310.
36 Description and quotation from Jouanna, *Le Devoir de révolte*, 105.
37 Ibid., 111.
38 Mark Motley, *Becoming a French Aristocrat: The Education of the Court Nobility 1580–1715* (Princeton, NJ, 1990), 97.
39 Ibid., 155.
40 Quoted in Jonathan Dewald, *Aristocratic Experience and the Origins of Modern Culture: France, 1570–1715* (Berkeley, CA, 1993), 192.
41 Eustache Lenoble, *Voyage à Falaise*, quoted in Pierre de Vaissière, *Gentilshommes campagnards*, 425–6, and abridged by William Beik.
42 Carroll, *Blood and Violence in Early Modern France*, 165–79.

10 Emerging identities – education and the new elite

1 Roger Chartier, Dominique Julia, and Marie-Madeleine Compère, *L'Éducation en France du XVIe au XVIIIe siècle* (Paris, 1976), 87–107.
2 François Lebrun, Marc Venard, and Jean Quénart, *Histoire générale de l'enseignement en France*, vol. II: *De Gutenberg aux Lumières (1480–1789)* (Paris, 1981), 265–8.
3 The universities were in Paris, Toulouse, Montpellier, Orléans, Cahors, Angers, Aix, Poitiers, Valence, Caen, Nantes, Bourges, Bordeaux, and Dôle.
4 Henri de Mesmes in 1542, quoted in Lebrun *et al.*, *Histoire de l'enseignement*, 325.
5 Ibid., 317–88.
6 Guy Saupin, *Nantes au XVIIe siècle: vie politique et société urbaine* (Rennes, 1996), 153–6.

7   Michael P. Breen, *Law, City, and King: Legal Culture, Municipal Politics, and State Formation in Early Modern Dijon* (Rochester, NY, 2007), 62.

8   Barbara Diefendorf, *From Penitence to Charity: Pious women and the Catholic Reformation in Paris* (Oxford, 2004), 43–4.

9   Françoise Bayard, *Vivre à Lyon sous l'Ancien Régime* (Paris, 1997), 42–4.

10 Robert Mesuret, *Évocation du vieux Toulouse* (Toulouse, 1960), 299–303.

11 Michael P. Breen, "Representing the City: Avocats and the Negotiation of Municipal Authority in Seventeenth-Century France," in *Entre justice et justiciables: les auxiliaries de justice du moyen-age au XXe siècle*, ed. Claire Dolan (Quebec City, 2005), 347–64.

12 Yann Lignereux, *Lyon et le roi: de la bonne ville à l'absolutisme municipal, 1594–1654* (Seyssel, 2003), 50–6.

13 Michael P. Breen, "Addressing *La Ville des Dieux*: Entry Ceremonies and Urban Audiences in Early Modern Dijon," *Journal of Social History* 38 (2004), 341–64.

14 Carole Duprat, "Magistrat idéal, magistrat ordinaire selon La Roche-Flavin: les écarts entre un idéal et des attitudes," in Jacques Poumarède and Jack Thomas, eds., *Les Parlements de province: pouvoirs, justice et société du XVe au XVIIIe siècle* (Toulouse, 1996), 707–19. Quote by Nicolas Pasquier, cited in George Huppert, *Public Schools in Renaissance France* (Urbana, IL, 1984), 44–5.

15 Nancy Lyman Roelker, *One King, One Faith: The Parlement of Paris and the Religious Reformations of the Sixteenth Century* (Berkeley, CA, 1996), 68–78.

16 Ibid., 76.

17 Ibid., 67.

18 Farr, *Authority and Sexuality in Early Modern Burgundy (1550–1730)* (Oxford, 1995), 4.

19 Archives Municipales de Toulouse BB 33, April 14 – May 13, 1643.

20 Sharon Kettering, *Judicial Politics and Urban Revolt in Seventeenth-Century France: The Parlement of Aix, 1629–1659* (Princeton, NJ, 1978), 183–5, 251–6.

21 Quoted in Jacques Le Goff and René Rémond, eds., *Histoire de la France religieuse*, 4 vols. (Paris, 1988), II, 366.

22 This so-called Richerism was derived from the ideas of theologian Edmund Richer, who had argued in 1611 that all levels of the church, including the parish clergy, should have a say in governance. Richard M. Golden, *The Godly Rebellion: Parisian Curés and the Religious Fronde, 1652–1662* (Chapel Hill, NC, 1981).

23 See Chapter 9, pp. 267, 275.

11 Monarchs and courtly society

1 This chapter relies heavily on the excellent description of the court by Jean-François Solnon, *La Cour de France* (Paris, 1987).

2 These were the Chancellor (held for life, judicial affairs), the Constable (held for life, military affairs), the Marshals of France (military commanders), the Grand Maître de l'Hôtel (provisioning), the Chamberlain (royal household), the Admiral (navy), the Grand Master of the Horse (Grand Écuyer, in charge of horses, messengers, riding school for nobles) and the Grand Master of Artillery (1601). The Grand Almoner, the head of the ecclesiastical staff, had similar status. Jeroen Duindam, *Vienna and Versailles: The Courts of Europe's Dynastic Rivals, 1550–1780* (Cambridge, 2003), 90–8; R. J. Knecht, *Renaissance Warrior and Patron: The Reign of Francis I* (Cambridge, 1994), 117–20.

3 Solnon, *La Cour de France*, 47.

4 Duindam, *Vienna and Versailles*, 56–63.

5 Solnon, *La Cour de France*, 111–12.

6 Frances A. Yates, *The Valois Tapestries*, 2nd edn (London, 1975), 53–68.

7 Jacques Venuxem, "Le Carrousel de 1612 sur la Place Royale et ses devises," in Jean Jaquot, ed., *Les Fêtes de la Renaissance* (Paris, 1956), 191–203.

8 Knecht, *Renaissance Warrior and Patron*, 425–61.

9 Solnon, *La Cour de France*, 263–4.

10 Quoted Ibid., 297.

11 Ibid., 298.

12 Primi Visconti, *Mémoires sur la cour de Louis XIV, 1673–1681*, ed. Jean-François Solnon (Paris, 1988), 152.

13 Solnon, *La Cour de France*, 327.

14 Marquis de Saint-Maurice, *Lettres sur la cour de Louis XIV*, ed. Jean Lemoine (Paris, 1910), 274–5. The countesse de Gramont was English. Courtiers perceived her as putting on airs because she claimed blood relations with the English monarchy.

15 Visconti, *Mémoires*, 34, 121.

16 Quoted in Solnon, *La Cour de France*, 431.

17 Quoted in Ernest Lavisse, *Histoire de France depuis les origines jusqu'à la Révolution*, 9 vols. (Paris, 1903–10), IX, pt. 1, 1–2.

18 Solnon, *La Cour de France*, 433

19 Guy Chaussinand-Nogaret, *The French Nobility in the Eighteenth Century: From Feudalism to Enlightenment*, trans. William Doyle (Cambridge, 1985), 54.

20 Figures derived from Duindam, *Vienna and Versailles*, 65–8, and William Beik, *Louis XIV and Absolutism: A Brief Study with Documents* (Boston, 2000), 103–7.

21 Solnon, *La Cour de France*, 516; Chaussinand-Nogaret, *The French Nobility*, 55; Duindam, *Vienna and Versailles*, 64.

12 Aristocracy's last bloom and the forces of change

1 Emmanuel Le Roy Ladurie, *L'ancien Régime: l'absolutisme bien temporé (1715–1770)*, 2 vols. (Paris, 1991), II, 115–18.

2 Jean-Marc Moriceau, *Les Fermiers de l'Île de France, XVe–XVIIIe siècle* (Paris, 1994), 245.

3 Paul Butel, *L'Économie française au XVIIIe siècle* (Paris, 1993), 202.

4 Ibid., 64.

5 Olwen Hufton, *The Poor of Eighteenth-Century France 1750–1789* (Oxford, 1974), 15.

6 Ibid., 23–4, 126.

7 Jean-Pierre Gutton, *La Société et les pauvres: l'exemple de la généralité de Lyon 1534–1789* (Paris, 1971), 144.

8 Robert Schwartz, *Policing the Poor in Eighteenth-Century France* (Chapel Hill, NC, 1988).

9 Michel Antoine, *Louis XV* (Paris, 1989), 320–51.

10 Colin Jones, *Charity and Bienfaisance: The Treatment of the Poor in the Montpellier Region 1740–1815* (Cambridge, 1982), 140–3.

11 Schwartz, *Policing the Poor*, 157.

12 Ibid., 162.

13 Hufton, *The Poor of Eighteenth-Century France*, 232.

14 David A. Bell, *Lawyers and Citizens: The Making of a Political Elite in Old Regime France* (Oxford, 1993), 84.

15 Jones, *Charity and Bienfaisance*, 178.

16 Ibid., 178.

17 Arthur Young, *Travels in France during the Years 1787–1788–1789*, ed. Jeffrey Kaplow (Garden City, NY, 1969), 69, 77.

18 These conclusions are based on a very low estimate of 26,000 noble families; thus the proportion of newcomers might be lower. Guy Chaussinand-Nogaret, *The French Nobility in the Eighteenth Century: From Feudalism to Enlightenment*, trans. William Doyle (Cambridge, 1985), 30.

19 Ibid., 53–6.

20 Ibid., 57–8.

21 Jean-François Solnon, *La Cour de France* (Paris, 1987), 508, 518.

22 Jennifer Jones, *Sexing La Mode: Gender, Fashion and Commercial Culture in Old Regime France* (Oxford, 2004), 130.
23 Natacha Coquery, *L'Hôtel aristocratique: le marché du luxe à Paris au XVIIIe siècle* (Paris, 1998), 128.
24 Jones, *Sexing La Mode*, 181–4.
25 Ibid., 96.
26 Coquery, *L'Hôtel aristocratique*, 36–7.
27 Baronne d'Oberkirch quoted in Coquery, *L'Hôtel aristocratique*,111.
28 Quoted in Jones, *Sexing La Mode*, 92.
29 Ibid., 198.

Index

18074395R00232

Printed in Great Britain
by Amazon